Grounded at Kai Tak

Royal Asiatic Society Hong Kong Studies Series

Royal Asiatic Society Hong Kong Studies Series is designed to make widely available important contributions on the local history, culture and society of Hong Kong and the surrounding region. Generous support from the Sir Lindsay and Lady May Ride Memorial Fund makes it possible to publish high-quality works that will be of lasting appeal and value to all, both scholars and informed general readers, who share a deeper interest in and enthusiasm for the area.

Recent titles in the series:

A Pattern of Life: Essays on Rural Hong Kong by James Hayes, edited by Hugh D. R. Baker (2020) (City University of Hong Kong Press)

A Stormy Petrel: The Life and Times of John Pope Hennessy by P. Kevin MacKeown (2020) (City University of Hong Kong Press)

More than 1001 Days and Nights of Hong Kong Internment: A Personal Narrative by Chaloner Grenville Alabaster, edited by David St Maur Sheil, Kwong Chi Man, and Tony Banham (2022) (Hong Kong University Press)

My Dearest Martha: The Life and Letters of Eliza Hillier, edited by Andrew Hillier (2021) (City University of Hong Kong Press)

Settlement, Life, and Politics—Understanding the Traditional New Territories by Patrick H. Hase (2020) (City University of Hong Kong Press)

War and Revolution in South China: The Story of a Transnational Biracial Family, 1936–1951 by Edward J. M. Rhoads (2021) (Hong Kong University Press)

Grounded at Kai Tak

Chinese Aircraft Impounded in Hong Kong, 1949–1952

Malcolm Merry

HKU PRESS
香港大學出版社

Hong Kong University Press
The University of Hong Kong
Pokfulam Road
Hong Kong
https://hkupress.hku.hk

ISBN 978-988-8754-15-1 (*Hardback*)

British Library Cataloguing-in-Publication Data
A catalogue record for this book is available from the British Library.

10 9 8 7 6 5 4 3 2 1

Printed and bound by Hang Tai Printing Co., Ltd. in Hong Kong, China

Contents

1
The Saga of the Chinese Aircraft

This is the story of the struggle for possession of 71 aeroplanes belonging to the two main Chinese airlines which were stranded at Kai Tak airfield in Hong Kong at the end of the Chinese civil war. They remained there for three years whilst a contest for ownership of them took place in the courts and among politicians and diplomats on three continents. In the process the struggle became entangled with the anti-communist policies of the United States in the emerging 'Cold War', British hopes for restoration of her pre-war commercial position in China, disagreements between nations about recognition of the new government in Peking, and the delicate balance that the government of Hong Kong had to keep to preserve that colony's interests. The fate of the planes strained relations between London and Washington, London and Hong Kong, and Washington and Hong Kong, and prevented the establishment of formal relations between any of them and the new government in Peking.

The tale involves: five governments; two American war heroes; businessmen adventurers; secret intelligence services; the British Prime Minister Clement Attlee, his Foreign Secretary Ernest Bevin and other policy-makers at the UK Foreign and Colonial Offices; the US President Harry Truman, his Secretary of State Dean Acheson and principal officers of the Department of State; the Premier of the People's Republic of China Chou En-lai; the President of the Republic of China Chiang Kai-shek; the Governor, Attorney-General, two Chief Justices and three other Supreme Court judges of Hong Kong; leading advocates at the English and Hong Kong bars and a former Lord Chancellor of England. The saga incited the ire of the government of the People's Republic of China and raised anxiety about the future of Hong Kong.

The end of the civil war

During the spring and summer of 1949 the civil war in China between the Nationalist Kuomintang government of the Republic of China under Chiang

Kai-shek and the insurgent Communists led by Mao Tse-tung was approaching resolution. As Communist forces progressively took control of mainland China, the two principal domestic airlines moved most of their passenger and cargo aircraft, together with maintenance workshops, machinery, spare parts and other valuable equipment, to safety at Kai Tak airfield in Kowloon, part of the then British Crown colony of Hong Kong. They also transferred their main offices from Shanghai to the central district on Hong Kong Island.

Both airlines were then controlled by the Nationalist government which hoped to keep the aircraft beyond the reach of the insurgents. The aeroplanes, 82 in all, were parked upon the airport perimeter and decommissioned by the suspension of their certificates of registration.

Troubled Hong Kong

At first the Hong Kong authorities welcomed the aircraft but their attitude soon changed when they realized that the planes might become the subject of a factional squabble which would place Hong Kong in an invidious position between the warring sides and threaten to destabilize the colony. Hong Kong was already in a troubled condition: devastated by Japanese occupation during the Second World War and now inundated with people many of whom were fleeing the chaos in China, the city suffered from over-crowding and an acute shortage of housing. Availability of food was dependent upon uncertain supplies from the mainland. Unemployment and poverty were widespread. Social tensions were exacerbated by factionalism with supporters of one or other side in the civil war vying for support from and control of trade unions, schools and newspapers. The economy, which had been recovering quite well from the Japanese occupation, had been set back by disruptions, restrictions and blockades arising from the civil war.

The authorities were also concerned that the Chinese aircraft would impede expansion of the military facilities of the Royal Air Force base at the airfield. That expansion was part of the build-up of British forces in Hong Kong designed to deter aggression from the mainland. In 1949 a number of temporary army barracks were opened to accommodate a doubling of the garrison, roads capable of taking tanks and other heavy vehicles were constructed in border areas, and work began on another airfield in the rural New Territories. In the meantime the colony had to make do with modest Kai Tak which had been regarded as inadequate for future needs more than a decade earlier.

The small airfield was becoming packed with aircraft. However, the directors and managers of the Chinese airlines refused to move their aeroplanes. They saw advantages in keeping the planes in a jurisdiction under foreign control yet close to China. The American airline Pan Am had invested both money and personnel in one of the airlines in anticipation of a boom in air carriage within and to the mainland once the civil war was over and saw no point in decamping to Formosa, as Taiwan was then commonly called in English, which was likely to be under Nationalist control whilst the rest of China became a communist state. The directors thought the Communists might look more favourably upon readmitting the planes if they were based in neutral Hong Kong. Approaches by the Governor to the US Consul-General and to local directors of Pan Am asking that the planes be removed proved fruitless.

Uprising

The airlines' directors, now based in Taipei, were in for a shock, however. A few weeks after the declaration on 1 October 1949 of the formation by the Communists of the Central People's Government of the People's Republic of China, the new Premier, Chou En-lai, declared the planes the property of his government. The general managers and most of the staff of the airlines switched allegiance to that government. In mid-November they and members of a trade union sympathetic to the Communists seized control of the planes, claiming to act on behalf of the new government. Defectionist aircrew flew a dozen of the planes back to China. The Nationalists responded by dismissing the defectors, appointing new managers and asking the Hong Kong authorities for help. But the authorities maintained determined neutrality and refused to intervene, except to announce that the aircraft would not be permitted to fly pending clarification of whether the Communist government accepted the existing Anglo-Chinese air agreement.

To the discomfort of the Hong Kong and the British governments, which hoped to foster good relations with the new masters in Peking and were considering early recognition of the change in government, the dispute escalated with both sides resorting to the courts and to self-help measures. Court injunctions were granted but the communist sympathizers remained in possession of the aircraft. Political rhetoric raised the temperature.

Two American aviation entrepreneurs who operated a small third airline in China, Lee Chennault, a retired US air commander and founder of the Flying Tigers, and his business partner the unconventional Whiting Willauer, then stepped in. They obtained permission from Chiang Kai-shek to represent the Nationalist government in efforts to wrest back the aircraft. They surreptitiously let down the tyres of some of the aircraft and circulated rumours designed to discourage removal of further planes. They posted guards around the planes but the Governor of the colony, Sir Alexander Grantham, fearing that fighting and political trouble would break out, ordered the police to remove the guards. Communist sympathizers then resumed control of the planes.

Sale and resale

The plot thickened in mid-December when the Nationalists, now in Taiwan but still recognized by most countries as the government of China, agreed to sell the aircraft and equipment on complicated terms to Chennault and Willauer. They in turn swiftly resold the planes to an American company in which they and a group of shadowy investors held interests. The scheme was devised and the investors led by a political fixer and Washington insider, Thomas 'Tommy the Cork' Corcoran.

The company engaged the colourful William 'Wild Bill' Donovan, soldier, politician and lawyer-turned-spymaster, to direct a campaign in Hong Kong, London and Washington for the release of the planes to the company.

American pressure

The extensive influence of Donovan and the investors became apparent when the US State Department lent its support to the campaign. During the final weeks of 1949 and the early weeks of 1950, as an application was being prepared to Hong Kong's Chief Justice for the planes to be put under the custody of court-appointed receivers pending a decision upon their ownership, American interests in London and Hong Kong exerted unrelenting diplomatic and political pressure. Their concerns were to prevent the aircraft being used to invade Formosa and to ensure that American property rights be respected.

Urgency was given to their efforts by Britain's impending formal recognition of the new regime in Peking. Official recognition had been debated between Western governments for months. Now that the Central People's Government (CPG) of the People's Republic of China (PRC) was in charge of nearly all of mainland China, Britain's Labour government wanted to accept reality and extend formal recognition soon in the hope of striking up good relations with Peking and assisting British investment in China. But they also wished to move in step with their allies in the Commonwealth, Europe and, if possible, America. The US administration, however, had different priorities. Guided by the 'Truman doctrine' of defending freedom by resisting totalitarian expansion, constrained by an emerging anti-communist mood at home, and encumbered by a history of support for the failed Nationalists coupled with antagonism towards the Chinese Communists, the administration was in no hurry to accord recognition. Although both were reluctant to admit it, the UK and the US each adopted their own policy towards Communist China.

The Americans feared that recognition by Britain, and thus Hong Kong, would retrospectively bestow title to the aircraft on the new government which now controlled the airlines. They wanted Governor Grantham to take immediate executive action to release the aircraft into US control. Donovan confronted both Grantham and the colony's attorney-general, suggesting dire consequences for Britain and themselves if this was not done. The pair refused, saying that such action would amount to deciding title to the planes, a legal matter for the courts.

The Foreign Office in London was so concerned that it convened a meeting of its most senior policy and legal advisers to discuss their options and to suggest to ministers the course to take. Their meeting concluded that ownership was for the courts to decide and that the British government could not interfere with the process of justice. This became a mantra for both British and Hong Kong officials throughout the saga. But at the same time the Foreign Office was reassuring the State Department that the outcome would be acceptable.

In the first week of January 1950 the American company began legal proceedings claiming possession of the planes and other assets of the Chinese airlines. Later the same day the UK government extended formal recognition to the CPG of the PRC as the government of all China and confidently offered to establish diplomatic relations with them. The reply was: only if you give us our planes back and vote for us to join the United Nations.

Rival claimants

The CPG having demanded the return of its 'sacred property' and intimated that future relations with Britain would be affected by the attitude of the authorities in London and Hong Kong to the return of the aircraft, the fate of British investments on the mainland seemed to hinge on the outcome of the dispute.

The US Civil Aviation Authority meanwhile cut corners to enable the airliners to be registered speedily as American. Registration was a pre-requisite to their being allowed to fly. The Nationalist government in Taipei certified the genuineness of the sale to the US investors. The authorities in Peking likewise registered the planes as belonging to the PRC. Hong Kong and Britain, caught in the middle, played for time and searched for excuses to impound the planes.

In anticipation of the court hearing, the Chief Justice asked the Foreign Office in London a series of questions about which regime was recognized by Britain as the government of China, and as of what dates. The reply, which took more than two weeks to prepare, was complex and revealing, yet turned out to be economical with the truth.

Consternation

Pressed by all sides and concerned to offend none, Hong Kong and UK officials consistently maintained that ownership of the planes was a legal matter solely for the courts whose processes could not be interfered with. But this tactic was thwarted when first the Chief Justice and then the appeal court, no doubt wary of offending the new government of China, refused to decide the merits of the case, saying that to do so would contravene the CPG's immunity as a sovereign state from legal action in domestic courts. The communist sympathizers were left in charge of the aircraft.

This was widely misinterpreted as the judges' awarding the aircraft to the communists. It caused consternation in Washington DC and alarm in London, though relief in Hong Kong. The US Secretary of State, Dean Acheson, issued a vigorous protest. The British Ambassador to Washington warned of anger in the US Congress. Internal differences emerged within Whitehall, with the Colonial Office and the Governor adhering to the agreed line that the fate of the planes was a matter for the courts, and the Foreign Office and ministers issuing private assurances to the US State Department that the communists would not get the planes whatever the legal result whilst maintaining the outward pose of neutrality.

Although the aircraft were not allowed to fly out, this did not prevent hundreds of tons of spare parts and other equipment, worth millions of dollars, from the airlines' stores being sent on commercial ships to northern China. This raised security concerns among British military authorities and led to arguments between Washington and London about whether the parts were covered by an embargo on export of military equipment to the PRC. The equipment was said to have been carried on British-registered vessels and guided through the Nationalist blockade of the China coast by British warships. Chennault and Donovan used their Congressional contacts to stoke anger against the perfidious British and question the continuation of American economic and military aid to them.

When workers began painting red insignia on the fuselages and preparing the planes for flight, the Governor was instructed to hold the aircraft at all costs. He was told by the Colonial Office to refuse to accept registration of the aircraft from either side, employing a creative interpretation of air regulations suggested by Foreign Office lawyers and initially half-heartedly approved by the English Attorney-General, Sir Hartley Shawcross. The Governor, wanting to be rid of the planes and believing that letting the Communists have them was the quickest, and for the colony the best, way out, pushed back. He insisted on maintaining strict neutrality and that irreparable harm would be done to Hong Kong and British prestige if they failed to follow the legal rules. Time bombs were set by desperate Nationalist sympathizers, damaging seven of the planes. Chou En-lai blamed the Hong Kong government for failing to protect them.

Sir Hartley then had second thoughts and recommended that the British government use powers under the Royal Prerogative to ensure a judicial adjudication of the question of title. Accordingly an extraordinary Order-in-Council was made imposing changes in the law, so overriding the immunity, laying down special and precise procedures for trial of the question, and giving directions for the detention of the aircraft pending the outcome. This was done despite the Governor's reservations, the reluctance of the judges and the evident breach of international law. It provoked a strong reaction from Peking.

The Chinese airlines, now under communist control, disdained to take part in the ensuing litigation. Forced to rule on ownership of the planes and somewhat out of their depth, the Hong Kong judges' eventual reasons for decision were implicitly political, sometimes emotional and legally far from sound, symptomatic of the fears and pressures under which they laboured. Diplomatic and political manoeuvring took place in the background, with continuing tensions between London and Hong Kong as well as between them and Washington where politicians used their imperfect and almost hysterical understanding of the dispute to burnish their anti-communist credentials. The Governor and the Colonial Office feared trouble between Communist and Nationalist supporters in Hong Kong.

Negotiations between Britain and the CPG for the establishment of diplomatic relations made no progress. The Communists insisted that the UK clarify who owned the aircraft as a precondition to any discussion. The Foreign Office said the question was sub judice and could not be a subject for negotiation.

Changes in attitude

As the nature of the Communist regime became more apparent during the first half of 1950, attitudes towards it gradually hardened. The international scene and political considerations were transformed by the outbreak of the Korean War in the summer of 1950, followed by Chinese intervention in that war during the autumn. The PRC now seemed an aggressive, totalitarian, Marxist-Leninist state with a formidable military capacity rather than a group of traditional Chinese agrarian reformers.

The US feared that Formosa would shortly be invaded and sent warships to patrol the Taiwan Strait, ostensibly to keep the two Chinese sides apart. Resultant embargoes on trade with China damaged Hong Kong's economy.

Leading case

As the legal case made its way slowly through the Hong Kong courts, authorities there and in London, fearing that the American company might abandon its appeal or that the communists might dismantle the aircraft and ship them out, continued to debate how best to prevent the planes' removal.

The legal issues were eventually resolved in mid-1952 by Hong Kong's then highest court, the Judicial Committee of the Privy Council sitting in London. There, removed by distance and time from the original realities surrounding the dispute, a more forensic analysis took place. The judgment, delivered by Britain's most experienced lawyer-politician, became one of the leading public international law cases on the recognition of governments.

By the time of the final adjudication, the planes had spent more than three years deteriorating in heat, humidity and storms on the apron at Kai Tak. For the winner it was to prove a costly, pyrrhic victory.

2

Hong Kong in 1949

What sort of place was the city into which the Chinese aeroplanes flew, the Hong Kong of 1949? Constitutionally it was a British Crown Colony, that is to say it had an administration staffed principally by expatriate Britons and headed by a Governor, the representative of the King of England (then George VI) and appointed by the government of the United Kingdom. It was not a settled colony or dominion with its own representative parliament and government drawn from the parliament's members. It did have a small Legislative Council, a sort of junior legislature, but its members were appointed by the Governor and were mainly government officials.

The Governor was answerable to the Secretary of State for the Colonies, a British government minister, who was the politician in charge of the Colonial Office, a department of the government of the United Kingdom. That minister and his deputies were members of the British parliament (either the House of Commons or, occasionally, the House of Lords) so there was an ultimate though remote politician answerable for Hong Kong affairs to an elected legislature. In practice though both the policies and the day-to-day administration of the colony were in the hands of a Governor assisted by colonial civil servants in Hong Kong.

Sir Alexander Grantham

In 1949 that Governor was Sir Alexander William George Herder Grantham. He was an experienced colonial civil servant, having served as Colonial Secretary (chief of administration and deputy to the governor) for a dozen years in, successively, Bermuda, Jamaica and Nigeria, before appointment to the governorship of Fiji and then Hong Kong. Dapper and formal but, aside from a penchant for polka-dot bow-ties, unassuming in appearance, his receding hair above a long face revealed a domed skull which, along with sharp eyes, were suggestive of the intelligence that he brought to a difficult job.[1] Unlike many of his predecessors, Grantham had been familiar with Hong Kong when he was appointed. He spoke Cantonese, since between 1922 and 1934 he had been a 'cadet', a member of the high-flying administrative grade recruited at a young age into the Hong Kong government. Before that he had studied at Wellington College, a private school west of London noted for its military connections, and then at the Royal Military College, Sandhurst. He had fought as a teenage officer in the First World War before more study, this time at Pembroke, one of the oldest colleges at Cambridge University. He had also attended the Imperial Defence College, as well as reading for the Bar, in his late 30s after his first spell in Hong Kong. So he had substantial military, as well as administrative, experience and solid academic credentials. He was also somewhat familiar with China having been brought up partly in Tientsin (Tianjin) where his father had practiced as a barrister and in Peking (Beijing) where his mother and step-father had lived, in addition to his earlier dozen years in Hong Kong.

Given that background, it is hardly surprising that Grantham was conventional and conservative and made steady progress through the higher ranks of the Colonial service. His earlier career in Hong Kong provided him with deeper local knowledge of the colony than most Governors. It also gave him genuine concern for Hong Kong's well-being. As his conduct during the dispute about the Chinese aeroplanes was to show, Grantham was quite prepared to resist the British government view if in his opinion that view was not in the best interests of the colony. The judgment of one prominent historian is that Grantham, 'handsome, charming and intelligent' as well as being well-liked in the colony, was a great Governor.[2] That of another author is more reserved: that Grantham was honest, hardworking, efficient and fond of colonial regalia.[3] The view of one who knew Grantham, his first Colonial Secretary, Sir David MacDougall, is that he was slow and cautious, 'always listened to power' and 'didn't take a single step without consulting everybody'.[4] But MacDougall's opinion is not necessarily inconsistent with the first two and would not be thought a point of criticism by many.

---

1. In the entry for Grantham in *Dictionary of Hong Kong Biography* (see note 2) the historian Steve Tsang describes Grantham as tall, but that may have been an illusion given by Grantham's appearance next to his diminutive first wife, Lady Maurine, an American. Grantham was of medium height, certainly shorter than his physically imposing successors Sir David Trench and Sir Murray MacLehose.
2. Steve Y. S. Tsang, 'Grantham, Sir Alexander William George Herder', in *Dictionary of Hong Kong Biography*, ed. May Holdsworth and Christopher Munn (Hong Kong: Hong Kong University Press, 2012), 162–164.
3. Philip Snow, 'MacDougall, David Mercer', in *Dictionary of Hong Kong Biography*, 297–299, and *The Fall of Hong Kong: Britain, China and the Japanese Occupation* (New Haven: Yale University Press, 2003), 320.
4. Snow, *The Fall of Hong Kong*, 320, and *Dictionary of Hong Kong Biography*, 299.

Grantham had been appointed in 1947 to succeed Sir Mark Young, a far-sighted Governor of refined tastes from a family of colonial administrators whose tenure had been abruptly interrupted by Japanese invasion and occupation in December 1941. Young had been interned in mainland China, Formosa and Japan, during which time his health had suffered and he had visibly aged. After several months of rest and rehabilitation, Young returned to take charge of Hong Kong for a year from May 1946. His restoration was more than symbolic, however, for with the support of the Colonial Office and the Labour government in Britain he championed reform, part of which was the introduction of a measure of democratic representation through an elected municipal council.

The proposal met with opposition from vested interests within the Hong Kong establishment, including wealthy Cantonese businessmen. It also met with scepticism from Young's successor. Grantham's view was that most of the Chinese population in Hong Kong had moved there temporarily for economic reasons and that they owed no loyalty to the place, still less to the British Crown. He feared that mainland politics would permeate any democratic body, that there would be agitation for the end of colonial rule, and that the mercantile essence of the colony would suffer. Despite reservations from London about Grantham's view, Young's proposals were amended in 1949 then later (after a change of government in Britain) abandoned. Instead, Grantham created an extra position on the Legislative Council for a non-official Chinese member, taking the number of members who were not also government officers to four, two expatriate and two Chinese.[5]

Despite the fate of the democratic reforms, Grantham's government was generally more open than its pre-war predecessors. This was partly the influence of MacDougall, who had been a cadet officer at the time of the Japanese invasion and had escaped to England from where he helped to plan the restoration of British government in 1945. He had been in charge of civil affairs in the temporary military administration that ran the colony for eight months immediately after the Japanese surrender, as well as being Hong Kong's first post-war Colonial Secretary. MacDougall espoused 'the 1946 outlook', that is to say the attitude that Hong Kong's governance must modernize and democratize with a view to decolonization. But MacDougall found Grantham less sympathetic to that outlook than Young and abruptly left the government two years after Grantham had taken over, being replaced by John Fearns Nicoll, a colonial servant of less-assertive personality who was destined to be Governor of Singapore.[6]

5. A detailed account of the fate of the reforms is given by Steve Y. S. Tsang in *Democracy Shelved: Great Britain, China and Attempts at Constitutional Reform in Hong Kong, 1945–1952* (Oxford: Oxford University Press, 1988).
6. MacDougall, a married man, had been in a liaison with a young Chinese woman, conduct frowned upon by Grantham.

Grantham was not totally opposed to the new outlook, but he was a pragmatist who realized that the priority for most people in the Hong Kong of 1949 was to have security so that they could earn a living and provide for their family. He perceived them as apolitical. 'We are but simple traders,' he explained with studied exaggeration, who 'want to get on with our daily round and common task. This may not be very noble, but at any rate it does not disturb others.'[7] To that end, he sought to establish a stable, enlightened, responsive and responsible government, efficient yet limited in scope, and maintain order and the rule of law. A minimal amount of welfare would be provided, mainly medical, social and agricultural, and later, under force of circumstances, housing. People would have a fair degree of freedom, especially of the economic sort. There would be consultation but no elections and no party politics. Grantham called this a partnership between government and community. At times he even referred to it as a 'democracy' that could be held up as an example to others. By this he presumably meant that his government was ultimately answerable to elected politicians at Westminster and that residents of Hong Kong enjoyed more individual freedom than those elsewhere in the region.

Grantham's clear-eyed view was that Hong Kong existed as a British colony only by the indulgence of China and that the indulgence depended upon the colony's being useful to China. Consequently, his government must do nothing to antagonize those in charge in the mainland, nor must it do anything to jeopardize that usefulness. Accordingly, his attitude was conciliatory yet firm towards each of the Nationalist and Communist regimes in turn. He would not provoke, nor would he appease, them. In the civil war, his government would be unrelentingly neutral. This attitude underlaid Grantham's handling of the crisis concerning the Chinese aircraft which unfolded in late 1949.

Return to China?

Hong Kong's survival after the Second World War as a British imperial enclave on the south China coast was something of an anomaly. Britain had returned most of its concessions to China during the 1920s and 1930s.[8] All the remaining foreign possessions extracted from the weak Imperial Chinese government during the nineteenth century had been returned pursuant to an agreement between the allies made in 1943. One of those allies, the United States of America led by Franklin Roosevelt, had wanted Hong Kong to be retroceded to China. Chiang Kai-shek's Nationalist government, also one of those allies, had expected to take over Hong Kong once hostilities ceased.

7. Jan Morris, *Hong Kong: Epilogue to an Empire* (London: Penguin, 1989), 72.
8. Hankow and Kukiang in 1927; Chinkiang in 1929; Amoy and Wei-Hai-Wai in 1930.

But the death of Roosevelt and the weakness of the Nationalists had enabled decisive action by Britain in August and September 1945 to reassert its authority over the territory. A force of Royal Navy ships commanded by Admiral Sir Cecil Harcourt was sent to take over from the Colonial Secretary, Franklin Gimson who, newly released from internment, had been sworn in as Acting Governor by the ailing Chief Justice and set up a skeletal administration at the old French Mission Building in the Central district on Hong Kong Island almost as soon as Japan's capitulation was announced. The formal Japanese surrender to Harcourt two weeks later was arranged despite allied agreement that Chiang's government had primary responsibility for the China theatre containing Hong Kong. Roosevelt's successor, Harry Truman, was more concerned about communism than colonialism. The allied Supreme Commander in the Pacific, General Douglas MacArthur, was sympathetic to the British position. Lingering solidarity between allies and the reigniting of the civil war on the mainland disinclined Chiang to press the issue.

In the immediate post-war period the Nationalist government had strengthened its influence within the colony. Several of its ministries had established representative offices there. The KMT had attempted to gain control of trade unions, teachers' organizations and newspapers. A Special Commissioner for Hong Kong had been appointed and took up residence in the city.[9] The Nationalists confidently expected that the colony would return to China within a few years.

The 1943 allied agreement had mentioned the New Territories, the large extension of the Crown colony agreed by the Second Convention of Peking 1898. Under the 1943 agreement the government of China was entitled to raise the question of terminating the 99-year cession (or 'lease') of the extension. After the Japanese surrender the Nationalist authorities were looking for the right moment to start these discussions. But the New Territories constituted nine-tenths of the land in the colony, including the northern portion of Kowloon, and essential public facilities for the whole of Hong Kong had been built there in the intervening decades. These included reservoirs, the railway to Canton, army barracks and the airfield at Kai Tak. Any retrocession would render the city unviable.

There had been some desultory efforts by the Nationalists to assert their claims in the immediate post-war period. Initial steps towards building a new civil and military airport at Ping Shan, a flat area in the northwest of the territory near the border with China, met with objections from the mainland. Pro-Nationalist newspapers and student demonstrators pressed for the return of the 'leased area of Kowloon'.[10] However, the main efforts centred upon the status of the Kowloon Walled City which had been a small fort and magistrate's

9. Snow, *The Fall of Hong Kong*, 276.
10. Snow, *The Fall of Hong Kong*, 269–278.

compound under imperial China. The 1898 convention was short and in places ambiguous but seemed to reserve the walled city from the lease. The convention provided that within the city 'Chinese officials now stationed there shall continue to exercise jurisdiction except insofar as may be inconsistent with the military requirements for the defence of Hong Kong'. Britain soon seized it nonetheless, citing spurious military requirements. But it remained a bone of contention and any attempt to enforce building regulations or restrictions on land use was strongly resisted.

Unauthorized and unsafe buildings proliferated in the walled city as the population swelled after the Second World War. In 1946 an unsuccessful attempt was made by the magistrate for Pao On County (from which the New Territories had been carved out in 1898) to establish civil administration in the walled city. In 1947 a residents' association was set up to run the city, ostensibly as part of Pao On. By 1948 the area had become a 'cesspool of iniquity' in Grantham's phrase, a teeming slum inhabited mainly by Hakka and Hoklo, rather than Cantonese, people, a haven for gangsters, drug dealers, prostitutes and gamblers.[11] Prosecutions were impossible because of the dispute over jurisdiction. The police feared to enter the city, despite the removal of its wall by the Japanese to provide landfill for extensions to Kai Tak airfield. This was not just because of physical danger but also because any incursion spurred the inhabitants to protest to the Special Commissioner and to authorities in Canton and Nanking that Chinese sovereignty was being violated and in turn led to complaints from local Nationalist organizations.

When clearance of the walled city had been attempted in January 1948 there had been angry resistance from a crowd of residents and their supporters. Armed police opened fire and one resident was killed. In reaction, a mob burned down the British Consulate-General and staff quarters in Canton and British women and children had to be evacuated. Offices of Hong Kong-based companies were attacked. There was a student protest in Shanghai.[12] The Communist authorities were as assertive as the Nationalists had been in claiming jurisdiction. In 1949 they declared that Britain had no right to evict squatters in the walled city. When in December 1949 Hong Kong's Chief Fire Officer proposed to take fire prevention measures there which would have entailed demolition to create fire breaks and lanes, no action was taken.[13] Grantham had decided that it was better to leave the walled city well alone, anachronism though it had become. The numbers living inside the city swelled further as refugees looked for space there.

11. Alan Smart, *The Shek Kip Mei Myth: Squatters, Fires and Colonial Rule in Hong Kong, 1950–1963* (Hong Kong: Hong Kong University Press, 2006), 59.
12. Luard, *Britain and China*, 183.
13. Smart, *The Shek Kip Mei Myth*, 65.

Since they had become focused upon domestic issues and bogged down in fighting the Communists, the KMT's attitude towards retrocession of Hong Kong became even more relaxed. The Governor of Guangdong Province, Chiang Kai-shek's brother-in-law T. V. Soong, talked in 1947 about getting Hong Kong back in 25 years' time.[14] There was no desire for Sino-British friendship to sour over the issue. The Foreign and Colonial Offices advised the British government that it should retain the colony but consider handing it over to a friendly and stable Chinese government. In mid-1949 there was no prospect of that. Britain's possession of Hong Kong remained precarious, as Sir Alexander Grantham was well aware. That was why he was anxious not to disturb anybody. But that desire became impossible to fulfil in the matter of the stranded Chinese aeroplanes.

External security

By January 1949 it was apparent that the Communists were likely to triumph in the Chinese civil war. What would their attitude be to a colonial enclave on China's southern rim? On the surface they were implacably denunciatory of colonialism. However, Mao Tse-tung had been reassuring when asked about Hong Kong by a reporter in late 1946. Perhaps we may ask for a discussion in 20 or 30 years' time, he had said, but as long as Chinese subjects were not treated as inferior he was not interested in Hong Kong and would not allow it to become a bone of contention between the two countries. Two years later, similar reassurances were forthcoming from the local head of the Xinhua (New China) news agency, the de facto representative of the Chinese Communist Party in the colony: it was not CCP policy to take Hong Kong by force or agitate for its return, he said.[15]

There were indeed good reasons for any Chinese government to wish to preserve the status quo. Hong Kong under British rule was of economic value to mainland China as a stable and free trading port and as a source of foreign exchange. To the Communists, the colony was also a route by which to circumvent trade blockades and embargoes, a potential means of dividing Britain from America, a window on the world, and a base for its subversive activities in southeast Asia. For both sides in the civil war, the colony was a place from which to launch secret operations against the other.

Despite these considerations and the discreet indications of Communist goodwill, the British government deemed it sensible to exhibit its resolution

14. Alexander Grantham, *Via Ports: From Hong Kong to Hong Kong* (Hong Kong: Hong Kong University Press, 1965), 138. Paul Soong Tse-ven was the brother of the Soong sisters and thus Chiang Kai-shek's brother-in-law. He had held various high positions (including minister of finance, premier, and foreign minister) in the Nationalist government.
15. Snow, *The Fall of Hong Kong*, 312; Tsang, *Dictionary of Hong Kong Biography*, 153.

to retain the colony. Should Hong Kong be lost, that would shatter morale in other British colonies, especially in southeast Asia. Consequently, in late 1948 a Gurka battalion was restored to Hong Kong, taking the garrison back to its former strength. In April and May 1949 the build-up of land, sea and air forces was intensified. The numbers of soldiers were increased to 30,000, consisting of two brigade groups each of three battalions, a step made easier by the retention of compulsory national military service in Britain. Buildings and land were commandeered and turned into barracks. Food was stockpiled for an emergency. New roads were built, and existing ones improved, to accommodate tanks and other armour in the northern New Territories close to the border with China. In the summer the garrison was reinforced with tanks, artillery and anti-aircraft guns. Two cruisers, a destroyer and two frigates joined the naval squadron, with an aircraft carrier on call. Additional fighter aircraft were sent, too, an RAF station opened at Shatin, and construction of an RAF airfield at Sek Kong began. A commander for all British forces, initially Lieutenant-General Francis Festing, was appointed. A defence council was set up composed of representatives of all three services and local political figures.[16]

The Minister of Defence, Mr Albert (A. V.) Alexander, declared in the House of Commons that 'Hong Kong is the Gibraltar of the East. It must be held.' He added: 'His Majesty's Government have constantly in mind the necessity of ensuring the defence of Hong Kong.'[17] A commoner and closer analogy, used by the Foreign Secretary Ernest Bevin, was with Berlin. Later in the year Alexander arrived to inspect the forces. Britain's attitude was conciliatory but it was determined to defend the colony, he explained. A newsreel was put together showing military exercises being carried out over a strong, confident commentary. The message was that there would be no repeat of 1941. The purpose was to discourage any attack by Communist troops as they neared the colony and to ensure that support was available to the civil authorities should guerrilla attacks occur or disorder break out. Once that had been achieved, the additional forces would be quietly withdrawn.

As it happened, Communist troops steered clear of the border. They were under instructions to avoid any incidents there, but British leaders were not to know this. An episode that occurred in the spring and summer of 1949 had increased distrust of Communist intentions. In April there was a pause in the civil war with Communist forces to the north of the Yangtze and the Nationalists to the south. Most governments maintained their legations at the capital Nanking even though the city was in imminent danger and even

16. Luard, *Britain and China*, 185.

17. Debate, House of Commons, February 1949. An account of the build-up of forces and its context appears in W. R. Louis, 'Hong Kong: The Critical Phase, 1945–1949', *American Historical Review* 102, no. 4 (Oct 1997): 1052–1084.

though the Nationalists had decamped to Canton. For some time, with the consent of Nationalist authorities, Britain had kept a Royal Navy boat on rotation duty on the river at Nanking from its base downstream at Shanghai, to evacuate diplomats and other of its nationals if that should become necessary. On 19 April 1949 the frigate, or fighting sloop, *Amethyst* departed up the river routinely to relieve the destroyer *Consort*. Next day the frigate was attacked by PLA artillery on the north bank as she proceeded towards Nanking. This may have been a mistake by a local commander. *Amethyst* fired back but was badly damaged; 19 officers and ratings were killed, including the captain. The helmsman was critically wounded and the boat ran aground. Many of the crew were then evacuated and an Assistant Naval Attaché from the embassy in Nanking, Lieutenant Commander Kerans, was sent to assume command. *Consort* was sent from Shanghai and, under heavy fire, tried twice to take *Amethyst* in tow, unsuccessfully. Two other Royal Navy warships fared no better.

Britain protested that its boats had been on peaceful missions of mercy. Communist commanders were unmoved, initially ignoring British messages then insisting that permission to proceed past their positions should first have been sought and pointing out that they too had lost men and equipment to shells from the warships. A young junior diplomat who was fluent in Mandarin, Edward Youde, a future Governor of Hong Kong, was sent behind Communist lines to try to negotiate. All he could obtain was a promise to let *Amethyst* go if she first helped People's Liberation Army troops to cross the river. This was obviously unacceptable since it would have involved Britain directly in the civil war. Communist radio poured out tendentious and provocative attacks on British imperialism, describing events as the foiling of a joint naval attack with the Kuomintang aimed at preventing the Red Army from crossing the Yangtze. The crew managed to refloat *Amethyst* and move her upstream to relative safety where temporary repairs were carried out. There the ship remained trapped during three months of stalemate.

The incident received blanket press coverage. On 5 May there was a debate in Parliament in London. The Opposition spokesman, Harold Macmillan, asked why it was necessary to keep a warship at Nanking. The city remained accessible by road and rail. The 'gunboat mentality' was rather out-of-date, he suggested, pointing out that the USA had withdrawn all their craft from the capital. He also pointed out that there had been no trouble at Peking and Tientsin during the recent Communist takeover of those cities. After the Communists' imminent advance into Nanking, a destroyer could only become an embarrassment, he claimed. The policy that Britain had followed of avoidance of involvement in the civil war and in Chinese internal affairs had been gravely jeopardized by the serious lack of judgment of His Majesty's Government, Macmillan asserted. As it was, 'British prestige had suffered a grievous wound: we have lost face where face matters most of all.' Of course much of this was political rhetoric but the points made beneath the rhetoric were telling.

These points were, however, to be lost in subsequent developments. The PLA crossed the river and the civil war moved on. Commander Kerans and the naval hierarchy considered whether to scuttle *Amethyst.* Instead, in late July Kerans risked a dash back to Shanghai under cover of darkness. *Amethyst* survived the perilous journey with much less damage than in April. 'Have rejoined the fleet,' she signalled nonchalantly. On her homeward voyage, the ship's crew and ship's cat Simon were received with full publicity as heroes at Shanghai, Hong Kong and, in November, at their home port, Plymouth in southwest England.[18] A civic reception was arranged by the mayor. The First Sea Lord (operational commander of the Royal Navy) and Lord Hall, the First Lord of the Admiralty (political head of the navy), spoke proudly and patriotically. Kerans was interviewed, dutifully praised his men and thanked God.[19] Medals were awarded. The British talent for portraying endurance as triumph was much in evidence. The Western press vilified the Communists and glorified Kerans and his crew, without pausing to ask what British gunboats were doing in the heart of China and the midst of a civil war, or why the British Ambassador remained in Nanking if it was so dangerous as to require evacuation by naval vessels. There was more than a hint of imperialism involved: until 1943 Britain had maintained Victorian-era treaty rights enabling it to patrol the Yangtze and Pearl rivers. Furthermore, the conduct seemed at odds with the neutrality between the warring sides in the civil war which Britain had earnestly pursued until then.[20]

When *Amethyst* had stopped in Hong Kong on its way back to England she had been greeted with firecrackers and cheers. In suit, bow-tie, coat and hat, the smiling Governor Grantham went on board to convey his congratulations. He must have privately been concerned that the whole episode would jeopardize Britain's, and therefore Hong Kong's, stance of neutrality and wondered whether Communist assurances of benign intentions towards his colony were to be trusted. But the episode must also have sharpened his resolution to keep Hong Kong out of Chinese politics and Chinese politics out of Hong Kong.

Interviewed on American television five years later Grantham maintained that, despite the Japanese conquest of 1941, Hong Kong was defensible because, unlike then, the free world now had command of the air and sea.

18. 'Able Seacat Simon' had been adopted from the dockside in Hong Kong. She proved excellent at catching rats, was injured during the fighting, and became something of a cult figure but died of an infection during quarantine in Britain.
19. Ten years later, after a career in naval intelligence in the Far East, Kerans became member of parliament for the northeastern English seaport of Hartlepool, its last Conservative MP until 2021. He advocated recognition of the PRC at the UN.
20. The *Amethyst* incident is dealt with by Malcolm H. Murfett in *Hostage on the Yangtze: Britain, China and the Amethyst Crisis of 1949* (Annapolis, MD: Naval Institute Press, 1991).

He cited the advice of unnamed 'highest military authorities' in support and hinted that the USA would intervene if the PLA did decide to attack.[21] In 1949 the US had little military or strategic or commercial motivation to help defend Hong Kong, but that was to change. No doubt Grantham had in mind the view of Admiral Arthur Radford, the US regional commander and later chairman of the Joint Chiefs of Staff, who had told Grantham in late 1952 that Hong Kong could be held. Other commanders, British and American, were not so optimistic. In mid-1949 it must have seemed likely that even the strengthened garrison would have been overwhelmed by the PLA's force of numbers, as Radford's predecessors then felt and as was to be demonstrated in Korea less than eighteen months later.[22] But that was not the point, for the purpose of the strengthening and its accompanying publicity was to deter a would-be aggressor by showing that Hong Kong would be more stoutly defended than it had been against the Japanese. It was also to emphasize that the taking of Hong Kong would require a definite act of aggression which would cost the perpetrator militarily and politically.

The arrival of more fighter aircraft at RAF Kai Tak had ramifications for the Chinese transports parked at the airfield. The space that they took up was needed by the military. One airline, CNAC, had a substantial repair and maintenance shop in a building on the waterfront of the aerodrome. Several planes were habitually stationed around the building awaiting attention. The RAF needed the space. The airport authorities gave CNAC notice to quit in June.[23]

Internal security

The battle between the Nationalists and Communists was always threatening to spill over into Hong Kong. Nationalist government organs operated openly in the city. The Bank of China was firmly established and was erecting a new local headquarters which promised to be the tallest building in the Central business district. The Nationalists appointed a special commissioner for Hong Kong.[24] Both parties attempted to gain influence over unions, schools, organizations, bookshops and newspapers. The Federation of Trade Unions, which

21. CBS Television, *Longines Chronoscope*, September 1954, available on YouTube.
22. Chi-kwan Mark, *Hong Kong and the Cold War: Anglo-American Relations, 1949–1957* (Oxford: Clarendon Press, 2004), 31–33, 43–48, 56–57. In May 1952 the British Chiefs of Staff concluded that Hong Kong could hold out for two weeks, enough for evacuation only, because Chinese air power had increased. So either Grantham had not been told this or his replies were part of the continuing deception.
23. Hugh Farmer, 'The Aircraft Maintenance Industry in Hong Kong – post WW2', The Industrial History of Hong Kong Group, 3 October 2020, https://industrialhistoryhk.org/aircraft-maintenance-industry-hong-kong-post-ww2/.
24. Luard, *Britain and China*, 182; Snow, *The Fall of Hong Kong*, 276–277. Internal security is examined by Steve Y. S. Tsang in *Democracy Shelved: Great Britain, China and Attempts at Constitutional Reform in Hong Kong, 1945–1952* (Hong Kong: Oxford University Press, 1988).

was controlled by communists, had strong membership among those working in the utilities, shipyards and textile mills. Nationalist supporters were more prevalent in skilled trades.

The Communists had maintained offices in Hong Kong in the 1930s and their followers had sought refuge in the colony from the KMT and the Japanese. The guerrillas of the communist East River Column had been active in resisting the Japanese and had co-operated with the British both during and immediately after the Second World War. In 1947 the Central Committee of the CCP had established a bureau in Hong Kong and the Xinhua news agency had opened a Hong Kong branch. The branch's first head was Qiao Mu (Chiao Mu), later the CPG's foreign minister, and its Work Committee was headed by Zhang Hanfu who went on to become the deputy foreign minister. One of the East River Column's leaders, Huang Zuomei, who had received an award from the British for his wartime assistance to them, became head of Xinhua's Hong Kong branch in 1949. In 1948 Qiao Mu had made reassuring noises about not changing the status quo in Hong Kong. The communists were tolerated by the authorities so long as they did not cause trouble. After the declaration of the People's Republic in October 1949, communist activists were told by Peking not to challenge British authority.[25]

The Hong Kong government was, however, concerned enough about developments that in the summer of 1949 they introduced legislation requiring organizations to be registered if they were to operate legally. This Societies Ordinance enabled a society's registration or exemption to be refused or cancelled, and it thereby to become unlawful, if affiliated with political movements outside Hong Kong. The legislation also gave the police powers of entry, search, seizure and arrest.[26] The police raided the homes of known communist leaders. The fruits of one of these raids provided revealing information about the true nature of Chinese communism: ruthless, fervent, efficient and cynical.[27] This convinced the British and Hong Kong authorities that they were dealing with hardline, orthodox Marxist-Leninists. In August 1949 the Hong Kong government took powers to expel non-British subjects suspected of promoting sedition or disturbing public order.[28] Carriage of arms, ammunition and explosives was made punishable with life imprisonment. Schools could be closed if they became centres of propaganda and agitation. These powers were

25. James T. H. Tang, 'World War to Cold War: Hong Kong's Future and Anglo-Chinese Interactions, 1941–55', in *Precarious Balance: Hong Kong between China and Britain, 1842–1992*, ed. Ming K. Chan (Hong Kong: Hong Kong University Press, 1994).
26. Societies Ordinance 1949 (later Cap 151).
27. Qiang Zhai, *The Dragon, the Lion, and the Eagle: Chinese-British-American Relations, 1949–1958* (Kent, OH: Kent State University Press, 1994), 31.
28. Expulsion of Undesirables Ordinance 1949.

used, though with moderation, to suspend a left-wing union, deport trade union activists and shut down a school.[29]

Despite being used sparingly, the measures nevertheless came under attack from China. They reflected the emphasis that Grantham placed upon maintenance of order that, along with minimal interference with commerce, low taxation and fair justice, he hoped would convince the population to accept British rule and concentrate upon family and livelihood.

Also, in early November, a few weeks after the establishment of the People's Republic of China, the government took steps to guard against foreign agents operating in the colony by enacting the Representation of Foreign Powers (Control) Ordinance. The nub of this legislation was that no one should function on behalf of any foreign power without the consent of the Governor.[30]

The police force, expanded by recruits from Africa, Palestine, Shanghai and other places departing from British control, was kept on alert. By 1949 the force's numbers were much higher than at the beginning of the decade. Its officers were largely European, the ranks mainly Chinese and Indian. At least Hong Kong was spared the racial conflict evident in other British colonies.

Law and judiciary

As a Crown colony, Hong Kong's law in 1949 was essentially English law, though adapted to local circumstances where necessary. Chinese customary law applied in certain traditional family and personal matters such as marriage, inheritance and adoption and also to land matters in the rural parts of the New Territories. Otherwise the system was one of common law, that is to say case law overlaid by local legislation, called Ordinances. The Ordinances were often copied, with adaptations, from England. The Colonial Office in London supplied British colonies with standard versions of the statutes most commonly required for effective government.

Applying this law was a small body of judges, headed by a Chief Justice. At the lower level were the magistrates, dealing predominantly with criminal cases and licensing matters. There was as yet no intermediate court.[31] In the New Territories, the administration's District Officers doubled as magistrates, hearing minor disputes, both criminal and civil.

29. Luard, *Britain and China*, 185; Francis Yi-hua Kan, *The Position of Hong Kong in Britain's Policy towards the Two Rival Chinese Regimes during the Early Years of the Cold War*, in Civil Wars Vol 2:4 (London: Routledge/Frank Cass), 131-132; James T. H. Tang, *Britain's Encounter with Revolutionary China, 1949–54* (New York: St. Martin's Press, 1992), 185–186; Francis Yi-hua Kan, 'The Position of Hong Kong in Britain's Policy towards the Two Rival Chinese Regimes during the Early Years of the Cold War', *Civil Wars*, no. 2 (1999): 106–137.
30. Representation of Foreign Powers (Control) Ordinance 1949, s 3.
31. The District Court was established by statute in 1953.

More serious cases, both criminal and civil, were dealt with in the High Court, part of the Supreme Court, by the Chief Justice and a handful of associates, known as puisne (pronounced pew-ny) judges. These judges were all expatriate: English, Irish and Scottish, with the occasional New Zealander or Australian. They were all male, middle class (in British terms) and, since they retired at the age of 55 years with a generous pension, middle aged. Some had begun their judicial careers in Hong Kong in the magistracies and been promoted to the High Court bench. Occasionally a judge had been an administrative officer in government and had converted to law by study and passing the Bar examinations in England whilst on long leave. But the main source for High Court judges was the judicial branch of the Colonial Legal Service which supplied senior law personnel to dependencies throughout the British Empire. So a Hong Kong judge often had experience of other colonial jurisdictions.

The judiciary of 1949 was small, befitting a minor jurisdiction with a land area of only a few hundred square miles and a population of less than two million who were culturally inclined to avoid going to court. The judges conducted hearings, and wrote judgments, solely in English, relying upon interpreters to translate the oral evidence of witnesses where necessary.

In 1949, in common with many small colonial jurisdictions, Hong Kong had no Court of Appeal. There was, however, a route of appeal provided by the Full Court and the Privy Council. The Full Court consisted of a panel of three judges drawn from the High Court bench. There were so few judges available at any one time (because of leave, illness, other responsibilities and so on) that it was not unusual for the panel to include the judge who had conducted the trial which was being appealed, in effect reviewing his earlier decision. The Judicial Committee of His Majesty's Privy Council heard further appeals from colonial jurisdictions, theoretically in exercise of the monarch's power to dispense justice throughout Crown dominions.[32] The judges, normally five in number, advised the monarch as to their opinion on the outcome of a case in a written, usually unanimous, report. The outcome was incorporated into an Order in Council and a final decree. The judges there were predominantly those who sat in the ultimate court for the United Kingdom, the Appellate Committee of the House of Lords, although the committee could also draw on senior commonwealth judges and retired members of the Lords. In the late 1940s with the British Empire and Commonwealth still extensive, it was a busy court.

In charge of the Hong Kong judiciary in 1949 was Sir Leslie Gibson, who had come up through the colonial administrative arm. Born in 1896, after

32. The Judicial Committee had been placed on a statutory basis by four Acts of Parliament from the late Victorian era. It also heard appeals from other Crown dependencies such as the Channel Islands and the Isle of Man.

school in his native Coventry, Leslie Bertram Gibson had joined the Malayan civil service. Some years later he decided to change to the service's legal arm by obtaining a law degree from the University of London and being called to the Bar. He then transferred to the colonial legal service and spent several years as Crown counsel in Malaya. In 1940 he was promoted to be Attorney General of Trinidad; then Attorney General of Palestine in 1944. This was a fairly typical career path for a would-be judge, except that Gibson lacked experience of private practice. Colonies usually recruited Chief Justices (and their police chiefs) from overseas to ensure they were free of malign local influences. So when Sir Henry Blackhall stepped down as CJ of Hong Kong in 1948, Gibson was a natural choice to succeed him. Only his age told against him: at 52 years old, he was less than three years from the compulsory retirement age.

Another important figure in the local legal establishment was the Attorney General. In 1949 the holder of that office was another longstanding colonial servant, John Bowes Griffin. He had held various legal positions in Uganda (where his father had been Chief Justice), the Bahamas and Palestine before appointment to Hong Kong in 1946. In 1952 he was to return to Uganda as Chief Justice.[33] As with Gibson, Griffin's experience was entirely in colonial government service.

Overcrowding

Daily life for residents of Hong Kong was difficult in the post-war years. Although the economy was doing well and taxes were low, the cost of living was high. A particular problem was that accommodation was expensive and inadequate. In the four years after the end of the Second World War, approximately 1,285,000 people were thought by the United Nations to have settled or resettled in Hong Kong. This was quite possibly an under-estimate for the flow of refugees from China had shown a marked increase since late 1948. Anyway, by the middle of 1949 urban Hong Kong was bursting at the seams. In June that year the population of the colony was estimated to be 1,857,027. This was an increase of only about 220,000 on the estimate for 1941, just before the Japanese takeover. But the latter figure had been inflated by refugees from the Japanese after 1937, when the estimated population had been little more than a million.[34] In the meantime there had been much devastation and deterioration of the housing stock.

The lack of housing affected all ranks. When he and his wife first arrived in Hong Kong in August 1949, stopping over en route to an abortive attempt

33. In 1958 he became Speaker of the Uganda legislature. His sister, Alice Mary Boase, was prominent in the public life of Uganda in the 1950s and in retirement wrote a memoir of colonial life, *When the Sun Never Set: A Family's Life in the British Empire* (London: Radcliffe Press, 2005).
34. Smart, *The Shek Kip Mei Myth*, 43; Tsang, *Dictionary of Hong Kong Biography*, 109 and 114.

to take up the post of US Consul-General in Shanghai, Karl Rankin found Hong Kong jammed with people fleeing the mainland. Hotels were full and accommodation of any kind was difficult to get. On their return in September following the US decision to close its consulates in China, the couple initially had to stay aboard a US warship anchored in the harbour. Eventually they found a room in the quarters of a colleague. When a dozen US congressmen arrived on a fact-finding mission at the end of the year, they were put up in the homes of consular staff. Office space and transport were problematic as well.[35]

There had been some new building since the end of the war, but not nearly enough to accommodate the demand for housing. The residential towers and massive estates of modern Hong Kong were then unknown. Most of the population lived in three- or four-storey commercial-residential tenement blocks in crowded areas. Typically a landlord owned a whole block or floor and let each floor to a principal tenant who in turn sublet spaces within the floor to numerous others. By 1950 there was an average of 18 residents for each domestic floor. This compared with 16 per floor in 1939, itself a time at which the population had been bloated by immigration.[36]

Resourceful landowners provided a solution of sorts. Much of the colony's vacant land close to the urban areas was hillside and unsuitable for large buildings. But huts and shacks might be erected there, if precariously. Erstwhile farmers in villages north of Kowloon were only too willing to let portions of their uncultivated land to incomers: not only their land but adjoining pieces belonging to no one except the Crown. The result was the formation of 'squatter' encampments, packed slum areas with little or no sanitation and attendant risks of disease, fire and crime. 'Squatter townships spread in an unsightly rash around the permanent buildings . . . filling the valley floors and mounting the steep hillsides.'[37]

The majority of the occupants were not truly squatters for their patches of ground had been let (or licensed) to them by the owner, the Crown lessee. Their structures, however, were unauthorized and breached the Crown lease of the land. Those who built on government land were truly squatters since they had no permission to occupy in addition to no permission to put up their structures. The government however was in no mood to object to either type of occupation. Any attempt to enforce the law would have been futile and would have caused unrest. Leniency was expedient. By referring to the occupiers indiscriminately as squatters, the administration was emphasizing the illegal aspects of their presence.[38]

---

35. Karl Lott Rankin, *China Assignment* (Seattle: University of Washington Press, 1964), 11–21.
36. Smart, *The Shek Kip Mei Myth*, 54.
37. Hong Kong Annual Report, 1957, 14, quoted by Mark, *Hong Kong and the Cold War*, 16.
38. The realities as well as the legal position were explained by the Full Court in *In re A Compensation Board Ex Parte the Attorney General* [1971] HKLR 338, 345, 357, 367–368.

The position was to become worse as 1949 progressed. As the Communists advanced through China, refugees advanced across the open border into the British colony. Hundreds of thousands more people arrived in the latter half of the year, mainly from Guangdong and Fujian. Not all of them were really refugees seeking shelter from trouble to the north. A portion was poor economic migrants hoping for a better life in a prosperous city. Yet the description 'refugee', like 'squatter', suited both the government and the press for it suggested that the presence of these incomers was temporary and that in due course they would return whence they had come. By the close of 1949 the number of squatters was estimated to be around 300,000, more than six times that in June.[39]

The population increase was not entirely due to immigration. As in other places, there was a post-war baby boom in Hong Kong.[40] This must have been due in part to the relatively young age of the migrants. It must also have been due in part to the colony's booming economy.

In any event, the administration had on its hands a housing crisis. Rent controls, imposed on pre-war buildings as a temporary measure in 1945 but made permanent in 1947, created a protected class of tenants but made the crisis worse for the mass of people by removing premises from the open market.[41] The only realistic way of tackling the crisis was for the government to provide subsidized basic accommodation. The Housing Society, a philanthropic organization established by well-known community figures to improve living conditions for the poor, had shown the way, building a modest amount of low-rental housing, starting in 1948.[42] Support would soon be available from the United Kingdom's Colonial Development and Welfare Fund. Grantham was persuaded that more had to be done but he encountered resistance from conservative business interests.[43] The swollen population led also to social problems, not least unemployment and under-employment. The Hong Kong government reacted quickly, setting up temporary hospitals and a Social Welfare Department. The problem of the planes stranded at Kai Tak was a distraction that Grantham could have done without.

Trade and industry

What work was there for the immigrants to do? The answer is: plenty. Hong Kong was swiftly back on its feet economically after the war. Entrepreneurship

39. Smart, *The Shek Kip Mei Myth*, 54.
40. In 1952 the birth rate was 32 per 1000: Smart, *The Shek Kip Mei Myth*, 43.
41. Smart, *The Shek Kip Mei Myth*, 14.
42. Rebecca Lai-har Chiu, *Professional Building Management Practices in Hong Kong* (Hong Kong: Hong Kong University Press, 2006).
43. Smart, *The Shek Kip Mei Myth*, 106.

thrived. Commerce, dominated by long-established British firms (hongs), prospered again. Unemployment was to become a temporary problem.

The lifeblood of Hong Kong had traditionally been trade, particularly the China trade. The colony's long-established role as an entrepôt quickly regained vigour once hostilities ceased in August 1945. The civil war on the mainland boosted that role. By 1949 the colony was in the middle of an import-export boom. Selling and buying took place even with communist areas in northern China. In and between 1949 and 1950 there was a 66 per cent increase in trade.[44] A frisson of concern swept through in May 1949 after Communist forces crossed the Yangtse and took Nanjing and Shanghai, with the Hong Kong dollar temporarily affected, but the concern was soon shrugged off. The Nationalists instituted a blockade of Shanghai after its fall and of the Pearl River delta later in the year. These resulted in the redirection of traffic to the safety of Hong Kong's port.[45]

The colony remained reliant on the mainland for food and raw materials which formed the bulk of its imports. The rural areas of the New Territories however continued to grow much of the rice consumed and immigrant farmers there expanded the production of vegetables for the city. Both agriculture and fishing were the subject of early post-war governmental co-operative and education schemes aimed at increasing efficiency and maintaining prices. These were supported by British government funds made available under the Colonial Development Act of 1945.

A much larger change overtook the manufacturing sector. This was almost entirely the product of private industry and was directly the result of the civil war engulfing the mainland. The turmoil of war and uncertainty over the future of private enterprise in China resulted in the relocation of factories and offices to Hong Kong. The shipbuilding industry had existed in the colony for decades before the Second World War. Similarly, there had been factories, mostly small scale. There had been considerable textile production by knitting and weaving workshops. More than a fifth of the workforce had been engaged in manufacturing, according to the 1931 census.[46] New industries had been developed between the World Wars, especially after the outbreak of hostilities between Japan and China in 1937 triggered demand for equipment by the Chiang Kai-shek's National Revolutionary Army.

However, after 1945 growth in manufacturing had been exponential. Most notably, and notoriously, this was the consequence of the relocation of heavy industry from central China, especially Shanghai, to Hong Kong. Since

44. Smart, *The Shek Kip Mei Myth*, 44; Leo Goodstadt, *Profits, Politics and Panics: Hong Kong's Banks and the Making of a Miracle Economy* (Hong Kong: Hong Kong University Press, 2007), 86.
45. Steve Y. S. Tsang, *A Modern History of Hong Kong* (Hong Kong: Hong Kong University Press, 2004), 146.
46. Smart, *The Shek Kip Mei Myth*, 45; Tsang, *A Modern History of Hong Kong*, 107–108, 114; Goodstadt, *Profits, Politics and Panics*, 103–104.

much of the machinery for this industry ordered from America and elsewhere passed through Hong Kong anyway, it was relatively easy for mainland purchasers who feared the communist advance to direct the machinery to remain in the colony. During 1948 no fewer than eight large cotton spinning mills were erected in Hong Kong by Shanghai industrialists.[47] These supplied yarn to hundreds of smaller, mainly locally owned, knitting and weaving workshops. Whole districts, especially those already developing such as Tsuen Wan, were turned into factory areas. Workers, often women, were drawn in from elsewhere, from farms in the New Territories as well as from recent immigrants.

But it was not only in those districts that the transformation took place. Small factories opened in residential buildings and in squatter camps, so-called cottage industries, often family-based.[48] Seemingly the whole community joined in, seizing the opportunity and intent upon making a success of their livelihood.

The post-war invasion by Shanghai billionaires and business adventurers was thought to add a touch of colour to the colony. They brought flair and glamour as well as cutting-edge factories and jobs. Their plants were partly financed by capital fleeing the mainland and partly by diverted Nationalist government money which had been allocated to subsidize mainland enterprises. Other, smaller industrial enterprises depended upon self-financing and loans from local banks which were flush with deposits, many from mainland and overseas Chinese.[49] The turmoil on the mainland and uncertainty about communist intentions towards Hong Kong had not dented its role as a safe financial haven.

47. Goodstadt, *Profits, Politics and Panics*, 57 and fn 90.
48. By the end of the 1950s, 63 per cent of Hong Kong's factories were in residential buildings: Goodstadt, *Profits, Politics and Panics*, 138.
49. Goodstadt, *Profits, Politics and Panics*, 103–105.

3

China in 1949

A new China

In late September 1949, as the last of the Chinese aeroplanes were arriving at Kai Tak, the Chinese Communist Party convened a conference of all political parties interested in forming a new China under Communist leadership. This Chinese People's Political Consultative Conference was chaired by Mao Tsetung. It framed a new Constitution, the 'organic law', for the country which was to be called the People's Republic of China, adopted a programme of policies for the new government which was to be known as the Central People's Government, and made provision for elections.

It fell to Mao, as chairman, to declare the foundation of the People's Republic. This he famously did on 1 October 1949 to a mass crowd from the walls of the Forbidden City overlooking Tiananmen Square in old Peking. At the time, the declaration might have seemed a little premature. Although Communist forces had been in control of Peking since the end of January that year and they had made striking advances since then, at least five provinces had yet to fall to them. However, at the beginning of the year a series of battles in the valley of the River Hwai and along the eastern section of the Lunghai railway, located on a broad plain between Peking and Shanghai (known collectively as Hwai-Hai), in effect decided the issue in favour of the Communists.[1]

Unlikely victory

Yet the Communist victory would have seemed highly unlikely in the immediate aftermath of the Second World War or at any time during the following two years. During the Japanese occupation of the most valuable parts of China from 1937 to 1945, the Communists and their small army had been confined to poor, remote rural areas, mainly in the north. The forces of

1. The account in this chapter owes much to Lucien Bianco's *Origins of the Chinese Revolution, 1915–1949,* (Stanford, CA: Stanford University Press, 1971), Ch. 4, 5, 6, and 7, and to Witold Rodzinski's *The Walled Kingdom: A History of China from 200 BC to the Present* (London: Fontana, 1984), Ch. 16.

the internationally recognized government of the Republic of China, the Nationalists (or Kuomintang) under the leadership of 'Generalissimo' Chiang Kai-shek, retreated to the southwest of the country and set up their administration at Chungking.[2] The Japanese held all the important cities in the north, centre and south, including most of the coastal areas. As they withdrew in 1945, Chiang's troops moved in. Only in Manchuria and the northeast had the Communists been able to take some territory: those areas had been liberated from the Japanese by the Soviet Union which had declared war on Japan and invaded Manchuria only a few days before the explosion of the atomic bombs at Hiroshima and Nagasaki which led to Japan's capitulation in mid-August. After stripping the region of its Japanese-built industrial plant, the Soviets had been content to leave it to their fellow communists but they delayed their departure by several months at the request of the Generalissimo. This enabled him to organize the airlifting of his troops to the main cities in the region by his ardent supporters the American military which still had large forces in China. Consequently, Communist influence in the region was confined to the countryside: the major centres had become government garrison towns.

The Nationalist army had been trained first by the Russians, then by the Germans and had been supplied by the United States of America during the struggle with Japan. The army commanded more men, better equipment and greater funding than that of the Communists. It had suffered little depletion in the Pacific War, for Chiang had been careful to conserve his resources. Chiang's reluctance to attack the enemy had driven to distraction his 'adviser', the commander of American forces in China, the Mandarin-speaking General Joseph Stilwell. Chiang knew that he could leave the Japanese to the Americans and concentrate on the resumption of the civil war with the Communists that had been interrupted by the Japanese aggression. Likewise the Communists had conserved their energies for the internal struggle ahead. Little wonder then that the only part of the Pacific theatre in which the Japanese had gained ground during the final stages of the Second World War had been China.

On the resumption of domestic hostilities it had been the Nationalists who appeared to be in the better position. They were the internationally recognized government of the country. They had been in charge, nominally at least, since 1927. They commanded the power of the state, a state which had been one of the triumphant allies and which had a permanent seat on the Security Council of the newly created United Nations organization. They held the coast and the ports; they controlled the industry and commerce of the great cities of eastern China with their modern facilities, including airports. Ostensibly they governed a far larger portion of China and the Chinese than the Communists. They had financial and material support from the United

2. A breakaway KMT faction ran a regime that collaborated with the Japanese invaders from Nanking.

States of America. Their forces were almost four times the size of those of the opposition and they alone had tanks, aeroplanes and heavy artillery. The Communist forces seemed capable of little more than guerrilla tactics.

Kuomintang weaknesses

The Nationalists, however, had a fundamental weakness in that their support was concentrated in cities and among the minority with an interest in the maintenance of the status quo. Originally, when founded (or, more precisely, re-founded) by the father of the republic Sun Yat-sen in 1919, the Chinese National People's Party or Kuomintang (KMT) had enjoyed wide approval from those who had supported the replacement of imperial rule with a parliamentary republic. As its name implied, the KMT was then a nation-wide movement for republicans of all classes. It sought modernization of China along Western lines guided by Sun's principles of democracy, nationalism and livelihood, which translated into opposition to warlords, resistance to imperialism and concern for the welfare of ordinary people. During the 1920s, modernizers such as merchants, students, overseas Chinese and young army officers who had promoted the 1911 overthrow of the Ching Emperor had been joined in the KMT by traditional classes and interest groups, landowners, scholars, gentry, bureaucrats and senior military officers, including warlords who wielded power in the regions into which the country had come in effect to be divided.

The KMT had obtained funds and advice from abroad, especially from Japan and the Soviet Union. The party had a socialist wing and sought support from peasants and workers. Many communists, especially amongst the young, had joined both the KMT and the Communist Party which had been founded in Shanghai during 1921 by a group of students and intellectuals including Mao Tse-tung. The KMT had been re-organized to reflect a centralized, soviet style. Sun's deputy, Chiang Kai-shek, had been sent to Moscow to study military tactics. Russians had helped to train officers for a new revolutionary army at an academy headed by Chiang at Whampoa near Canton, a KMT stronghold. This army would support the KMT and free it from reliance upon warlords. Chou En-lai was among a number of young communists on the academy's staff. Sun's policies, set out in 1923, included an alliance with the Soviet Union, co-operation with the communists, and assistance to workers' movements. The party had a Labour and Peasant Department which assisted workers to establish trade unions.

The KMT therefore had begun as a broad movement containing a diversity of opinion, rhetorically bound together by allegiance to Sun and intent to improve China. This did not last for long after Sun's death in 1925. The party soon openly split into factions, all declaring themselves Sun's true heirs, and led by personalities or cadres seeking power. The factionalism had been stimulated by labour unrest in Shanghai and Canton and exacerbated by shootings and strikes. The appearance of unity had been maintained by repeated declarations of devotion to Sun's principles and by devolving leadership of the KMT upon a committee of three, reflecting various shades of opinion within the party. Only one of the three, Chiang Kai-shek, commanded an army however. The other committee members faded into the background. Chiang required the recall of the academy's Russian advisers and dismissed its communist employees. Then he arranged for the replacement of key members of the KMT organization, including communists, with his own supporters.

Chiang as commander-in-chief used the new National Revolutionary Army to oust communists from the wider party. This was done in a most brutal way at Shanghai, which contained the headquarters not only of (foreign dominated) finance, commerce and capital but also of the Communist Party. The communists and their small army retreated to the periphery, mainly in remote Shensi and mountainous Kiangsi. Chiang then turned the army on regional power brokers, the warlords. He led a successful expedition to force them into submission. The KMT directly or through allies achieved control of the most important areas of China except Manchuria. Although there remained a parliament (yuan) and a prime minister, Chiang as President and head of the NRA had become China's 'strongman' and was undoubtedly in charge of what was in effect a conservative, bourgeois, nationalist regime. It was also militarist and authoritarian and run by an oligarchy with little active support from the mass of China's population of between 400 and 500 million. By the late 1920s Chiang's government was recognized by other states. As if to emphasize his domination, he designated Nanking as the new capital in place of Peking. Nanking was more central and closer to the south of the country to which both the KMT and Chiang had strong links.

So, for a time, China enjoyed relative stability and peace. The KMT seemed to have unified most of the country. The communists appeared to have been marginalized. The invasion and installation of a puppet government in Manchuria by Japan in 1931 did not greatly threaten that. The KMT government achieved some infrastructural and agricultural modernization. It also made mild attempts at social reform but they were largely ineffectual. Disparities in wealth were great. The economy remained dominated by favoured supporters of the government and foreign interests. Incompetence, corruption, speculation and extortion were as commonplace as they had been during the Ch'ing empire. Chiang Kai-shek was more interested in political intrigue and military matters. He promoted Confucianism and self-improvement. His KMT had become the party of the establishment, enjoying the toleration if not support of finance, commerce, business large and small, landlords, the police and the army.

Japanese invasion

It was only in 1937 when Japan intruded and declared war upon China proper that the Generalissimo's rule was disturbed. The following eight years were consumed by a struggle by both Nationalists and Communists for the survival of China. They agreed an uneasy truce so that common cause could be made against the invader. In reality each side operated separately. The Communists concentrated upon pervading the countryside and improving the condition of the rural population, most of whom lived in extreme poverty, within the areas that they controlled. Chiang retreated across the mountains of Szechwan to Chungking, then a large, remote market town surrounded by hills on the upper reaches of the Yangtze, and avoided confrontation with the invaders.

Almost without resistance, the Japanese occupied coastal areas and major cities. They then attempted to subdue the rest of the vast land and its huge population by terrorism: murder, rape, torture, looting and burning. The harder they tried, the more frustrated and the crueler they became, for China was too large and too populous to be subdued in this way. The resulting enmity of Chinese towards Japanese echoes to this day.

What little contest the Japanese encountered came principally from harassing raids by Mao's guerrillas. As a result communists became identified in the mind of peasants in their areas as much with Chinese patriotism as with socialism. With the NRA almost in hiding, the communists were also able to increase their forces and the areas under their influence. They sent political cadres into Japanese-controlled territory to establish local underground organizations that would both oppose the invaders and prepare the ground for resumption of the civil conflict.

Chennault, Willauer, and the Flying Tigers

One part of the Nationalists' forces that was active in opposition to the Japanese was its modest air force. This included a group of American pilots, drawn mainly from the US Army and Navy (both of which maintained air arms), who volunteered to help China before the USA officially entered the war. The American Volunteer Group was established in early 1941 by Captain Claire Lee Chennault (pronounced Shen-awlt), a retired US Army flying officer.

Chennault, who had been born in Texas in 1890 and was originally a schoolteacher, became a US military pilot during the First World War but had been forced to retire in 1937 because of deafness. He then went to China as a freelance adviser where he became friendly with Chiang Kai-shek and his wife. Chennault was engaged by Chiang to set up an aviation school to train Chinese airmen. He also recruited pilots to assist the Chinese cause against Japan. Aided by US sympathy for that cause and exploiting his connections,

Chennault persuaded the American government to support the volunteers with P-40 airplanes and money. Chennault, with his stocky frame, jutting jaw and trenchant views, was the personification of the volunteers' defiance of the Japanese. He became well known in America for his advocacy of aid to China. He made Madame Chiang an honorary commander of the group. He organized training of new pilots in Burma. By November 1941 he had a hundred of them in three squadrons. They flew people and supplies over the mountains and into Kunming. Since China's ports were controlled by the Japanese and Russia had ceased to convey goods to China through Central Asia, this route was effectively the only way to send help to the Nationalists.

In establishing the volunteer group, Chennault was assisted by an American named Whiting Willauer. Educated at Princeton and Harvard and with a background in Naval Intelligence, the sophisticated and tall 'Whitey' Willauer was quite a contrast with Chennault, the small, self-made, blunt-speaking military man. Willauer was working in China as a member of an organization called China Defense Supplies Incorporated. He was thirteen years younger than Chennault. The three things the men had in common were that they both enjoyed flying, they both loved China and they both craved adventure.

The volunteers were written up by the Western press in romantic and heroic terms. Their nickname, the Flying Tigers, was part of the publicity. The name was inspired by the fangs painted on the long noses of their fighter planes. It had been suggested by the son of a friend of Willauer. Chennault liked the name and asked Walt Disney to design the emblem for the group. Although the publicity was exaggerated, it was grounded on fact for the pilots were undoubtedly courageous and skilful. The air route from Burma across the Himalayas, modestly belittled as 'The Hump', was notoriously dangerous. Moreover, the coverage given to their exploits provided an uplifting story during a period in which Japan seemed to be enjoying a procession of victories.

The friend whose son had suggested the nickname was Tommy Corcoran, who had played a vital role in the setting up of the group. Thomas G. Corcoran, a Harvard law graduate, had been one of a number of bright young lawyers who had been brought into government by US President Franklin Roosevelt in the early 1930s to help draft and promote his New Deal legislation. 'A strenuous and intelligent Irishman of the synthetic New England variety', the witty, charming, small and noisy Corcoran had been passionately devoted to Roosevelt and his economic policies.[3] He had cultivated his connections with the White House and developed into the President's trusted adviser, facilitator, fixer and errand boy. It was Roosevelt who first called him 'Tommy the Cork'. Corcoran's influence meant that he had been able to place a number

3. Conrad Black, *Franklin Delano Roosevelt: Champion of Freedom* (New York: PublicAffairs, 2003), 275.

of his friends and acolytes, mainly Harvard law graduates, into influential jobs in the administration.

In April 1941, however, Roosevelt suddenly suggested that Corcoran resign from government service and take up a secret project devised and named by the President himself. The project was to set up a new venture to be called China Defense Supplies Incorporated. The purpose of this private company was to send American-made military equipment to China to aid the Nationalist government. Roosevelt did not think that the US Congress would support military aid to China for fear of sparking war with Japan. The company was a way of circumventing that obstacle. Tommy Corcoran, who knew Claire Chennault and his efforts in China, persuaded the President to support Chennault's idea of allowing American servicemen to volunteer to fight even before war had broken out between Japan and the USA. Roosevelt made a secret executive order permitting the recruitment of reserve officers from the US army, navy and marines for the volunteer group.

Tommy Corcoran did not involve himself explicitly in the venture. Instead, his brother David became an executive of the company. It had two chairmen. One was Roosevelt's elderly uncle, Frederick Delano, who had done business in China. The other, nominated by Chiang Kai-shek, was T. V. Soong, a former minister in the Nationalist government who happened to be Chiang's brother-in-law. Tommy Corcoran was officially only the company's outside legal adviser. A priority for China Defense Supplies was clandestinely to assist the Flying Tigers and Chennault in supplying goods to be flown from airfields in Burma into southwest China. Whitey Willauer, who had been a roommate at school and college of Tommy Corcoran's other brother Howard, was recruited to supervise the sending of the supplies. Tommy had previously secured Whitey a job at the Federal Aviation Administration and now arranged Whitey's transfer to the Foreign Economic Administration which was quietly financing aid to China. Another of Corcoran's contacts, William S. Youngman, was the public face of China Defense Supplies in China. James J. Brennan, a close associate of Corcoran, was in charge of the finances.[4]

In early December 1941, when Japan attacked the US fleet and airfields at Pearl Harbor in Hawaii, it also attacked a number of British possessions in the Far East, including Hong Kong and Burma. The American Volunteer Group was eventually forced out of Burma but not before it had joined with the Royal Air Force in resisting Japanese aggression there. They managed to inflict losses on the Japanese air force and helped to delay the taking of Rangoon, the principal city and port in Burma, for two months. The Group then relocated to southwest China and continued operations from there until

4. spartacus-educational.com/JFKcorcoran.htm.

July 1942. After that it was absorbed into the US Army Air Force and most of the pilots chose to return to their original units.

Although the Group operated independently for only seven months and its achievements were marginal to the war effort, by July 1942 Chennault's name was known internationally. He was re-engaged as a US military commander, was 'wildly over-promoted' to General commanding the American 14th Air Force in China, and assisted the Nationalists until the end of the war.[5] After that, Chennault continued to advise and admire Chiang Kai-shek. Chennault and his wife Anna became firm friends with Corcoran.

The US Army Air Force and the Chinese Air Force continued to fly in supplies to southwest China during the war. The quantity flown over the Hump was necessarily much smaller than might have been transported by train or road. In the scheme of things, the amount was negligible. Some of it was destined for the American military, including Chennault's own men, rather than the Chinese. Most of the rest was diverted before it could reach Chiang's troops. The cost in fuel, planes and pilots was enormous.

Civil Air Transport

After the war, their experience with the Flying Tigers gave Chennault and Willauer the inspiration for setting up a commercial airline in China. They saw opportunities in China's fledgling post-war airline industry. They approached for financial help the fixer Tommy Corcoran, who was now operating a very lucrative lobbying business under the guise of a corporate lawyer, exploiting the many contacts he had in the administration and among directors of businesses which had done well from government contracts arranged by him during the New Deal and the Second World War.

Chennault and Willauer called their new airline Civil Air Transport (CAT). Through a Panamanian company named Rio Cathay that he controlled, Tommy Corcoran took a share of the equity in the airline. So did the Nationalist government. CAT did not seek to compete with the principal domestic carriers CNAC and CATC which ran routes to a timetable. Instead, CAT flew on a contract basis for private clients rather than as a regular passenger airline. It had been greatly assisted by the award of a US$4 million contract from the United Nations Relief and Rehabilitation Administration which had been arranged by Corcoran through his friendship with the director of the relief programme.

CAT delivered supplies to and evacuated Nationalist troops during the civil war as well as taking passengers between major centres. In 1949 business was brisk, particularly to Taipei, as wealthy people and businesses sought to

5. Max Hastings, *Nemesis: The Battle for Japan 1944–45* (London: William Collins, 2014), 221.

evade the oncoming Communist armies. Despite this, CAT's operations were losing money. The costs of repeated evacuations and relocations in the face of the Communist advance, bribes to local airport authorities and spiralling inflation consumed all the operating profit. But CAT was more than a business venture.[6]

Civil war again

Each side was ready to renew the civil war when the Japanese surrendered in August 1945 but were restrained from doing so immediately by the population's longing for peace and pressure from the United States of America. After an American-brokered truce and negotiations had disintegrated in mid-1946, the NRA made gains in Communist heartlands in the centre and north until the spring of the following year. This was despite the Communist armies which had fought the Japanese having been formed into an expanded new force, the People's Liberation Army. The Nationalist gains were somewhat illusory, however, for they consisted of taking and fortifying large towns rather than controlling the countryside where most of the population lived.

The Communists' military tactics during the early stages of the conflict were to remain mobile, avoid set-piece or protracted battles and disadvantageous positions, abandon towns and concentrate upon destroying isolated enemy forces in skirmishes and small operations, slowly sapping their opponents' strength. The cumulative effect was that the NRA made little headway and lost many men (to defections as well as capture, death and injury) and much equipment, most of which had been supplied from American army surplus. The Communists had thoroughly infiltrated the peasantry, so the garrisoned towns had in effect been cut off from the land around and were under informal siege.

This illustrated both a weakness of the Nationalist position and a strength of Communist tactics. By seeking to dominate through the establishment of garrisoned cities, government armies were extending their lines of communication and committing to the exercise, expensive in money and men, of supplying those garrisons. In consequence their troops were spread thinly along roads and rail tracks and in a few large cities. This was inefficient and tactically obtuse and encouraged a defensive mentality. By concentrating upon winning the hearts of the rural population, the Communists could ignore and isolate the cities, at the same time avoiding fixed positions which their forces were not yet strong enough to hold. The tactic owed much to Mao's insight that in China revolution hinged upon the support of the vast rural peasantry rather

6. William M. Leary, *Perilous Missions: Civil Air Transport and CIA Covert Operations in Asia* (Tuscaloosa: University of Alabama Press, 1984), 90, 99.

than, as in Europe, of the urban industrial proletariat. In the late 1940s daily life for three-quarters of the hundreds of millions of people who lived in the countryside remained as relentlessly harsh as it had for centuries. The French historian of the communist revolution in China, Lucien Bianco, observed that 'the living conditions that prevailed from one end of rural China to the other – poverty, abuse, early death the only prospect' were the source of the revolution and the real strength of the CCP.[7]

As a result of initiatives by the Communist general (and future vice-president) Lin Piao in Manchuria during 1947, the NRA advance was brought to a halt. Then at the end of that year came what Mao himself described as the turning point. The Communists gained control of much of Hopei and Shansi provinces. Their policy of radical agrarian reform, instituted since 1946 in the 'liberated areas', was proving popular with the masses. Confiscation of land from its owners and redistribution of it to peasants and the poor, abolition of land tax, reductions in rents, and moderation of interest rates attracted followers to the cause and volunteers to serve in the PLA. So did the replacement in communist propaganda and peasant minds of the Japanese with the Americans as the hated foreign invader and colonizer. Political education sessions and meetings at which villagers were encouraged to air grievances stimulated both class consciousness and acceptance of social change among a population which had previously been quiescent.

By contrast, during this period the KMT's conduct did much to enhance the attractions of socialism. The civil war led to debilitating falls in industrial and agricultural production and in employment, all of which had already been devastated during the struggle against the Japanese. Only half the country's rail tracks were operating. Enormous expenditure on the NRA left little money for domestic improvements. In an attempt to pay for the war, the government had resorted to creating more currency which further escalated the inflation which had already been high during the struggle against Japan.[8] The price index of 100 in 1937 had increased to 1800 by July 1945 and 60,000 by April 1947. The exchange rate of the Chinese fapi to the US dollar, 400 to 1 in 1945, deteriorated to 50,000 to 1 by June 1947. This led to a loss of support from business and the salaried middle classes. In turn, peasants (mainly from the south and centre of the country) had been alienated by being drafted into the NRA and forced to serve under brutal officers, in parts of the country which felt alien to them, on little or no pay. Administrators were frequently greedy, rapacious and corrupt. Property re-taken from the Japanese usually ended up in their hands or those of KMT functionaries rather than those of its original owners. American aid, intended for the troops and the people, went no further than Chiang and his supporters. The moderate Democratic

7. Bianco, *Origins of the Chinese Revolution*, 87.
8. Japanese tactics in China had included the issuing of large amounts of counterfeit currency.

League, which promoted a third force in Chinese politics, was outlawed. Its leaders had to resort to Hong Kong for their meeting and planning, as did certain dissidents within the KMT.

At first, these failings went unnoticed or under-reported outside China. The post-war US Ambassador to China, Major-General Patrick J. Hurley, a 'handsome, vain and reckless' former Oklahoma cowboy who sought 'simplistic answers to complicated problems', refused to forward to Washington DC dispatches by his staff which were critical of the Nationalists.[9] The Western press tended to view Chiang as a victorious hero and valuable ally from the Second World War whom they wished to see succeed against a foe that they associated with totalitarian Soviet Russia. Consequently, they built up Chiang's reputation and exaggerated his successes. Their view was encouraged by the Westernized, English-speaking elite in China. Naturally, foreigners knew little of opinion at lower levels and outside the major cities.

Accordingly, though with increasing reluctance, the US government continued to supply aid, both in money and materiel, to the KMT government. This exacerbated ill-feeling towards America among Communist supporters. Elections to the National Assembly in November 1947, duly won by the KMT, appeased the Americans and gave the illusion of democracy. But the ills of post-war China could not be cured simply by voting.

During late 1947 Communist tactics changed from the avoidance of big battles to traditional confrontation of enemy forces. Soon the PLA's territorial advances became apparent. It already controlled much of Hopeh and Shansi in north central China. In April 1948 it captured Yenan, the main town in the long-established communist stronghold of Shensi; then over the summer three cities on the Yellow River, Loyang and Kaifeng in Honan and Tsinan the capital of Shantung, followed. A large blow was struck in the autumn when Lin Piao took over Manchuria in a matter of two months, capturing 400,000 Nationalist troops and much American-supplied equipment. At the beginning of November the major fortress city Mukden (Shenyang) surrendered. Two weeks later the strategically important town Chinchow fell: the way was open to Peking for Lin Piao's army.

Meanwhile Chiang Kai-shek had been re-elected as President in April 1948, although not without opposition and he had to accept as Vice-President a rival general, Li Tsung-jen. Hyper-inflation continued to escalate: the exchange rate of the US dollar increased from 220,000 to 12 million for each Chinese fapi between January and August 1948. Repressive measures against hoarding of goods and the issuing of a replacement currency, the 'gold yuan', initially at a rate of four to the US dollar, made no difference, for by the following April

9. Dean Acheson, *Present at the Creation: My Years in the State Department* (New York: W.W. Norton, 1969), 133; Arthur Ringwalt, 'Oral History Interview with Arthur R. Ringwalt', interview by Richard D. McKinzie, 5 June 1974, trumanlibrary.gov/library/oral-histories/ringwalt.

the rate was five million to one. As the military reverses piled up, the regime became more desperate. In November 1948 Chiang asked the USA for further military assistance. In December his American-educated wife, the eloquent and elegant Soong Mei-ling, made an appeal to the US for more aid. Both requests were politely declined, for the US administration, if not US politicians, had begun to shed their delusions about Chiang and the KMT.

In the area around Tianjin and Yingkou the Communists established a Northeast People's Government. They proved efficient, not corrupt, and implemented reforms that proved popular and helped to assuage fear of the prospect of their ruling all China.

The beginning of the end

The Communists did not let off the pressure. Their campaign in the Hwai valley began in November 1948. It ended a little more than two months later in resounding success. In a series of clashes on a plain outside Soochow, between Shanghai and Nanking, KMT armies were surrounded and gradually split up and destroyed by the PLA. The scale of the battles was enormous. The PLA deployed two field armies containing 600,000 men. The surrounded troops numbered 400,000 in 51 divisions. Another army of 500,000 was sent by Chiang in an unsuccessful attempt to break through and relieve them. Hordes of peasants, estimated to number two million, assisted the PLA to dig trenches around the KMT forces and to carry supplies.

Whilst these battles were raging, Communist forces were also making advances in the north. It was clear that the government positions were disintegrating. Chiang Kai-shek offered to negotiate but it was too late for that. His former Second World War allies refused to mediate. The Communists demanded complete surrender, removal of 'the war criminal' Chiang and the dismantling of the KMT.

Chiang Kai-shek understood the message. He resigned (or 'retired') as President on 21 January 1949, formally leaving Li Tsung-jen to pick up the pieces. In fact Chiang remained active: he spent his time arranging for the transfer of troops, arms, gold and foreign currency to Formosa (Taiwan) to which he planned to retreat and developing contacts with nearby countries.

The Nationalist position continued to worsen. Stopping off at Shanghai in February 1949 before a visit to Hong Kong, Sir William Strang of the Foreign Office was struck by the 'brooding air of menace' as the mighty metropolis awaited its fate. However, in April the fighting temporarily stopped whilst peace feelers were put out and desultory discussions took place.[10]

10. Peter Lowe, *Containing the Cold War in East Asia: British Policies towards Japan, China and Korea, 1948–53* (Manchester: Manchester University Press, 1997), 95.

Formosa

Chiang chose Taiwan as the Nationalist refuge because it was an island off the coast of southeast China sufficiently far away to be difficult to attack yet large and close enough to act as a springboard for a future invasion of the mainland. Moreover, the island was firmly under Nationalist control and most of the inhabitants were not sympathetic to communists. Another possibility was Hainan, a large island off the southern coast not far from his old stronghold Guangdong, but part of Hainan was adjacent to a peninsula which jutted out from the mainland and so would be more difficult to defend.

In 1949 what is now known as Taiwan was habitually referred to in English as Formosa. This was because of its attractive coast and striking interior of mountains, hills and valleys, 'formosa' being Latin for beautiful. That made it a somewhat strange choice as a redoubt. Even stranger, the island was to a certain degree not Chinese in outlook. The population had always been somewhat independent-minded, as islanders tend to be. They were predominantly Fukinese, their forebears having crossed the strait from Fujian Province in an earlier age. There was a small indigenous population of native Taiwanese too. Over the centuries various European powers, the Spanish, Dutch, British and Portuguese, had occupied parts of the island even though it had been part of the Ch'ing Empire since 1683. Moreover, for five decades from 1895 the island had been ruled by Japan. It, together with the Pescadores, had been ceded to Japan after its victory in the Sino-Japanese War at the end of the nineteenth century. Formosa had not been in status a colony: it was regarded by the Japanese as if it were one of their home islands. Indeed, since there was as yet no peace treaty concluding the Second World War and re-ceding the island to China, legally Formosa remained part of the Japanese empire in 1949. Resources had been put into the island by the Japanese. It had enjoyed strong economic development and a relatively high standard of living. Its public facilities had been modernized. It had been largely well administered. The education system had been improved. Japanese conduct there had been in marked contrast to its conduct on the mainland.

It had been agreed and declared at the Cairo conference of allied powers in 1943 that all territories that Japan had 'stolen' from China should be restored. That had been confirmed in the Potsdam Proclamation in July 1945. In October that year, following Japan's capitulation and by arrangement with the allies, Japanese forces surrendered to Chiang Kai-shek as commander-in-chief of the Republic of China. Nationalist China took over Formosa and installed a Governor from the mainland, even though there had as yet been no Sino-Japanese peace treaty and no retro-cession of the island to China.[11]

11. James Crawford, *The Creation of States in International Law*, 2nd ed. (Oxford: Oxford University Press, 2006), 198–200.

The Nationalists found an island much altered from the late Imperial period when it had been taken from the Ch'ing. The people spoke Japanese as well as Fukinese and their local dialects, but Mandarin Chinese, the language of the new administration and the mainland immigrants who followed, was little understood. The manners of sophisticated Formosans tended towards the Japanese. The architecture of the towns was influenced by Japanese style. The streets of Taipei and the nearby ancient harbour town of Tamsui (where the British consulate occupied the old Spanish fort Santo Domingo) were cleaner and more ordered than in mainland cities.

Accordingly, the incoming Nationalists and those who accompanied them were regarded with suspicion, almost as invaders, by the established population of Taiwan. Suspicion was exacerbated when the newcomers took over jobs, bought up property and flaunted their new wealth. The new government introduced newspaper censorship and unpopular impositions such as state monopolies and brought with them corrupt habits. Land that had been confiscated by the Japanese was not returned to its original owners but given to supporters of the new regime. The Nationalists and their policies imported inflation. Services started to deteriorate and break down. The incomers also brought new diseases with them.

The resentment thereby generated spilt over into protests in 1947 following the killing by police of an elderly cigarette-seller who had been breaking the hated government monopoly. The Governor Chen Yi and his undisciplined police force reacted to the protests with shocking violence. On 28 February 1947 there was a massacre of civilians, not all of whom were protesting, thus adding a fresh day to the lexicon of memorably awful dates in modern Chinese history. Chen Yi imposed martial law and brutal repression. There was an international outcry. The US ambassador John Leighton Stuart, who had been born and brought up in China, was so alarmed that he mounted an independent investigation. Chen Yi was soon replaced by a more moderate governor.

Resentment resurfaced when Chiang Kai-shek and his cohorts moved to the island during 1949 and established a provisional capital for the Republic of China at Taipei in December that year. Hundreds of thousands of NRA troops had been air-lifted in during the summer. The air force began to relocate to Formosa in August with dozens of planes arriving every day loaded with fuel and ammunition. The navy brought over its vessels too. Gold, silver, antiques, and foreign currency reserves followed. Then over a period of about four months after 1 October there was an exodus of about two million more troops and many civilians and refugees, mainly from southern China, to the island. Chiang Kai-shek intended their stay to be temporary. He planned to consolidate resources and then invade the mainland.

Before that, however, Chiang had to face the threat of an invasion of Formosa by the PLA. The prospects of successfully resisting such an invasion were considerably improved by the NRA's performance in beating off the PLA's attempt to take Quemoy. This island, also known as Kinman, was much smaller than Taiwan and closer to the coast of Fujian. In late October 1949 the PLA attempted to establish a bridgehead there, using commandeered fishing junks and wooden boats as troop carriers and landing craft. Having underestimated KMT strength and encountering adverse weather, they failed.[12] The battle of Quemoy was a rare victory for the NRA. Quemoy, along with Matsu, another Nationalist-held offshore island further up the coast, was to suffer heavy shelling by the Communists in the future, and fewer than six months later the NRA was unsuccessful in resisting a similar PLA invasion of Hainan.

The Americans had been pessimistic about the Nationalists' chances of establishing themselves in, and resisting an invasion of, Taiwan. Their representatives had reported on the incompetence and corruption of Chiang Kai-shek's administration and army. They had no trust in Chiang and began looking for alternatives to support. The strategic value of the island had been noted by US military chiefs. In mid-1949 the State Department sent one of its diplomats, Livingston Merchant, to try to establish contacts with indigenous leaders of the independence movement in Formosa. Merchant found the indigenous groups unimpressive. Instead, Merchant was amazed at the amount and quality of men and equipment Chiang had been able to move from the mainland and the effectiveness of the NRA's organization. Unknown to Merchant, this was in part because Chiang was being surreptitiously helped by Japanese military advisers.[13]

Merchant thought that Nationalist morale was surprisingly high. The positive experience at Quemoy later in the year must have raised their spirits further. It was notable that the PLA had not been able to use air power there. That suggested that it was imperative to keep aeroplanes out of the hands of the communists if what their opponents called 'Free China' was to survive.

China in chaos

This then was the background to the fleeing of the Chinese aeroplanes to Hong Kong in 1949. China was in chaos. The government was divided and broken. The economy was in ruins. The currency was worthless. The black market was thriving. Corruption was rampant. Essentials were in short supply, their prices escalating daily. The population, worn out by twelve years of war

12. en.wikipedia.org/wiki/Battle-of-Guningtou.
13. Livingston Merchant, 'Oral History Interview with Livingston Merchant', interview by Richard D. Mckinzie, 27 July 1975, trumanlibrary.gov/library/oral-histories/merchant; Lowe, *Containing the Cold War*, 116, 151.

and privation, lived in misery. Even nature turned against them, flooding the centre of the country. The 'strongman' had proved to be weak, peevish, jealous and incompetent.

By the end of January 1949, the outcome of the civil conflict was obvious and inevitable. China would soon have a communist government.

4

Great Britain in 1949

Empire in eclipse

The 1940s had been a difficult decade for the United Kingdom of Great Britain and Northern Ireland. Six years of war against Germany and Japan had been draining for the country which had emerged from the conflict diminished in status. It had suffered a precipitous decline in power and wealth.

Financially the war had been disastrous. To pay for armaments, many of the country's overseas assets had been sold, often at discounted prices to hard-bargaining Americans. Almost half the gold and dollar reserves had been spent. The foreign debt was crippling. Britain had gone from the world's largest creditor to its largest debtor.[1]

Emotionally the war had been exhausting for British citizens. They had endured constant physical destruction and nervous strain. The centres of the United Kingdom's main cities had suffered severe bomb damage. Whilst ultimately the death and destruction may have been worse in other countries, only China had been forced to endure a longer agony. The destruction had caused a shortage of housing and run down the national infrastructure.

There had been little by way of entertainment. Food had been rationed: whilst this meant the population had avoided obesity, the diet was sparse, lacked variety and was hardly healthy. The food shortage was partly the consequence of almost a third of the nation's merchant fleet having been sunk during the war.[2]

Militarily the country's pretensions had been exposed as hollow: even with the support of its numerous colonies and former dominions, Britain had been able to do little more than hold on in Europe, waiting for the Soviet Union and the United States of America to join in and defeat Germany, whilst in the Far East it had quickly crumbled before the Japanese onslaught. Territorially it had been diminished, losing ground to aggressors, then obliged by circumstances

1. David Marquand, *Britain since 1918: The Strange Career of British Democracy* (London: Weidenfeld and Nicholson, 2008), 123.
2. Marquand, *Britain since 1918*, 143.

to begin the shedding of the world-wide empire upon which its claim to great power status had rested.

In truth, that empire had never relied upon military might. The English were not natural soldiers. Their strengths lay in commerce, industry, finance, law and administration. As the German general Erwin Rommel had observed, the English astutely recruited other people—Scots, Irish, Canadians, Australians, Africans, West Indians, Sikhs, Nepalese, and so forth from throughout the empire—to do their fighting. They maintained a powerful navy as befitted an island nation, but that was as much to protect commerce as to resist invasion. Militarily, the Germans and the Japanese had successfully called the British bluff.

Nevertheless, Great Britain's self-image was that it remained a major player on the world stage. For all its suffering, others had fared worse, so in 1949 it was still economically and militarily the most powerful country in western Europe, as well as the most densely populated. It remained at the heart of a worldwide, though shrinking and changing, empire. That empire was to play an important role in providing foreign currency for the post-war reconstruction of the United Kingdom but also for the improvement of the countries of the empire themselves.

Real austerity

At the end of the war, the system of American military aid to Britain known as lend-lease had been swiftly terminated. However in 1945 a loan had been negotiated with the Americans. The terms of the loan were stringent and its amount was less than British negotiators had hoped for. The credit was soon dissipated since post-war Britain, with an ambitious social programme, a large military, heavy overseas debts and a much reduced income from exports and foreign investments, was living beyond its means.

The solution was to rein back spending wherever possible, to concentrate on expanding exports, which had fallen to a fraction of their pre-war level, and to restrict imports. For six years the people of Britain endured genuine austerity, much severer than the mild restraint masquerading under that name 65 years later. Consumption was cut, as was investment. Food imports were reduced. All staples, even those not imported, were rationed: meat, butter, eggs, sugar, tea, cheese, jam, even children's sweets. Soap, clothes and fuel were also rationed. Wages were frozen. Taxation, already heavy, was further increased. In the harsh winter of 1947 a fuel shortage meant people struggled to keep warm. Daily life was grim. The pervading image of the era was of people drably dressed in old, unstylish clothes, patiently queueing on monochrome rain-soaked streets, with desolate bomb sites in the background. People, even manual workers, dressed formally. There was no money for luxuries such as casual wear. Domestic heating was from polluting coal fires which created smoke and smog. Occasional entertainment was provided by a limited number of BBC channels on radio and weekly visits to the cinema. One of the few readily available pleasures was to smoke cigarettes.

More than three-quarters of a million British houses had been destroyed or damaged by enemy action. Between the two world wars there had been a marked expansion of suburban housing but in towns many people lived in small, crowded, basic accommodation—pre-war slums with no hot water and no inside bathroom or lavatory.[3] With little appreciation of the virtues of rest and exercise, the poor diet, and widespread consumption of tobacco and alcohol, male life expectancy was about 65 years, which was also the retirement age.

More than a quarter of government expenditure in 1947 was on defence, so that had to be pruned too.[4] This prompted a hasty withdrawal from India that year and led to reluctance from the Labour government to expand overseas commitments.

The United Kingdom was far from alone in Europe in suffering post-war economic hardship. Realizing that austerity increased the lure of communism, in 1947 the United States Secretary of State, General George Marshall, promoted a plan for loans called the European Recovery Program to be extended to western Europe. The US Congress accepted the arguments in favour of the Marshall Plan, the loans becoming known as Marshall Aid.

The austerity had worked, however, in that exports increased, eliminating the balance of payments deficit in 1948 and increasing the amount of US dollars earned. Productivity rose too. Marshall Aid then began to flow. By early 1949 Britain's economic outlook had greatly improved. But not so its financial position: the country still had large debts and heavy expenditure. The pound sterling, convertible at 4.80 to the US dollar, was plainly overvalued. When recession struck the United States, reducing UK exports, there was a balance of payments crisis. After a spell of painful resistance to the inevitable, the British government announced a 30 per cent reduction in sterling's exchange rate to 2.80 to the dollar in July 1949.[5] Nevertheless there remained a widespread 'sterling area', based on the empire, in which the British pound was used to settle debts. At the end of the 1940s sterling was used for about half of all international transactions.

---

3. David Kynaston, *Austerity Britain, 1945–51* (London: Bloomsbury, 2007).
4. Marquand, *Britain since 1918*, 124–126.
5. Marquand, *Britain since 1918*, 141.

Welfare state

At home, after the end of the fighting, Britons had turned inward. The war had created a break with the past, a sort of watershed, which broke down barriers and inhibitions and altered if not revolutionized attitudes. In 1945 the electorate had voted decisively for a new government whose central promise was of domestic social reform. The next five years brought forth a welter of legislation aimed at improving the lives of the population.

The Labour government embarked on a mildly socialist, egalitarian programme, much of it based on wartime reconstruction plans and accepted by the opposition Conservative Party. The coal mines and the railways were taken into public ownership, as were other 'commanding heights' of the economy such as transport services and fuel and power utilities. About two million workers were thereby transferred from the private to the public sector.[6] A National Health Service was instituted to provide free and comprehensive health care. Social security was extended through a system of compulsory unemployment insurance funded by deductions from wages and contributions from employers, supplemented by taxes. Free education was extended. Central planning became the order of the day.

All this cost money, as did the determination to maintain armed forces at a level commensurate with the maintenance of great power status and a worldwide empire. That determination motivated the decision in 1949 to produce, at great expense, Britain's own nuclear bomb.

The livelihood developments found echoes in British dominions and dependencies, even in Hong Kong.

From empire to commonwealth

Despite the austerity, in the later 1940s Britain still maintained larger military forces than before the war and stationed troops around the globe for the defence of the interests of Britain and its empire. Although ostensibly opposed to imperialism, the Labour government elected in 1945 'hoisted the burdens of empire with all the enthusiasm of the converted'.[7] This was rationalized as a mission to improve the lives of those under British rule, paving the way to their independence. To that end a Colonial Development and Welfare Act was passed in 1945 (enlarging similar legislation from the 1930s) and the Colonial Development Corporation was founded in 1947.[8]

6. Marquand, *Britain since 1918*, 131–132. But, as Marquand points out, the true 'commanding heights' of the economy, financial services such as banking, were not nationalized.
7. P. J. Cain and A. G. Hopkins, *British Imperialism 1688–2000*, 2nd ed. (London: Longman, 2002), 628.
8. Cain and Hopkins, *British Imperialism*, 628, 630–631.

The Colonial Office, operating from the same building in Whitehall as the Foreign Office, undertook to supervise programmes of reform throughout what was increasingly referred to as the British Commonwealth. The minister initially in charge was a Welsh socialist and former miner named Arthur Creech-Jones. His successor in 1950 was Jim (Jeremiah) Griffiths, another Welsh socialist and former miner. Jones had long been interested in colonial matters, though his emphasis was upon Africa. Neither he nor Griffiths was a leading member of the government. Griffiths had helped set up the welfare state in the late 1940s and was becoming more prominent but had no special interest in the colonies. The Colonial Office civil servant who had most to do with Far East and Hong Kong affairs in this period was the long-serving Assistant Under-Secretary in charge of the Eastern Department, J. J. (John) Paskin, who visited Hong Kong briefly in January 1949.

The Empire in the Far East involved relations with other states so was as much a Foreign Office interest as a Colonial Office one. The man in charge of foreign policy in 1949 was at the very heart of the Labour administration. He was Ernest Bevin, the Foreign Secretary, a patriotic working-class nationalist who saw the British Empire as a force for good. Of humble, west country origins, the illegitimate son of an unmarried domestic servant who had died when he was young, Bevin had only an elementary education but by hard work, force of personality and acuteness of perception he had hauled himself up through the rough-and-tumble of the labour movement to build the largest trade union in Europe. He was then recruited to become Minister of Labour in the wartime coalition government. A large man 'built like a battle tank', he was blunt and ungrammatical yet loquacious in expression, a marked contrast to the new Prime Minister, the wiry, taciturn, middle class, Oxford-educated Clement Attlee. A barrister by training and an officer during the First World War, Attlee had acquired socialist leanings through voluntary work among the poor in London's East End. By 1949 he had a quarter-century of experience in foreign affairs as minister and leader of the Labour Party. Attlee was fond of Bevin, valuing the latter's experience and robust common sense.[9]

Bevin's leanings were more social democratic, acquired during years as a workers' representative and trade union office-holder. As a result, Bevin disliked communists, the British versions of whom he regarded as hypocritical, impractical pseudo-intellectuals who were set upon exploiting the working classes in pursuit of ideology. He viewed their sponsor, the Soviet Union, with suspicion.

By 1949 Bevin was almost 68 years old and the burdens of nine continuous years in high office, in addition to decades as a senior union official, were beginning to tell. He suffered from insomnia and a litany of physical ailments

9. Marquand, *Britain since 1918*, 119–121; Denis Healey, *The Time of My Life* (London: Penguin, 1990), 102–104; John Bew, *Citizen Clem: A Biography of Attlee* (London: Quercus, 2016).

including angina. Much of the burden was therefore borne by his deputies, younger, fitter and better-educated men who had been elected to Parliament in the great Labour victory of 1945. His Minister of State in 1949 was Hector McNeill, an engineering graduate of Glasgow University, former journalist and Clydeside Member of Parliament. In 1949 McNeill was involved in an important decision concerning the planes at Kai Tak.

McNeill was succeeded in 1950 by Kenneth Younger, an Oxford graduate and qualified barrister. Younger was from a long-established line of Scottish Tories and had attended Winchester College, one of the best and most expensive private schools in England. Despite his background, Younger was an avowed socialist. He had been an intelligence officer during the Second World War after which he sought a political career. Owing to Bevin's absence through illness, unexpected responsibility was thrust upon Younger. In effect he supervised the Foreign Office for months. He was to play a key role in the story of the Chinese aircraft.

Bevin and his deputies were supported and advised by experienced civil servants, ambassadors and diplomatists at the British Foreign Office in Whitehall. In 1949 they were led by the formidable Sir William Strang, a veteran of foreign affairs now in his mid-fifties and at the summit of his career. Since pressing problems in Europe and the Middle East dominated the attention of ministers in the late 1940s, policy regarding China and the Far East was heavily influenced by what Younger described as 'a very strong team' of senior officers. The man in overall charge of the Far Eastern policy and chairman of the consultative inter-departmental Far East Committee was a large and opinionated Australian war veteran, Sir Esler Dening. The Head of the Far East Department was Sir Peter Scarlett. The Head of FO's General Department, who was destined to chronicle the saga of the Chinese aircraft grounded at Hong Kong, was Sir William Montagu Pollock. The British Ambassador to China was Sir Ralph Stevenson who had been in post since 1946. None of these officials had particular knowledge of the Chinese Communist Party. There was a handful of journalists and former diplomats who had achieved some contact with prominent CCP members and who maintained that the party was more Chinese than Marxist but their views were regarded as eccentric and were not heeded by the Foreign Office.[10]

China was hardly a priority for Britain in the years immediately after the end of the Second World War. There were more pressing problems closer to home. The UK's interests in China were largely commercial; it was also concerned about its remaining empire in the Far East which was mainly in southeast Asia but included of course Hong Kong.

---

10. Qiang Zhai, *The Dragon, the Lion, and the Eagle: Chinese-British-American Relations, 1949–1958* (Kent, OH: Kent State University Press, 1994), 30.

The long-serving Legal Adviser to the FO was Sir Eric Beckett, a legendary hard worker and most knowledgeable expert on public international law. One of the few who could rival Beckett's grasp of the subject was the similarly long-serving legal adviser to the Colonial Office, Sir Kenneth Roberts-Wray. All the senior officials except Montagu Pollock (who was younger) had been born in the 1890s and had survived military service in the First World War.[11]

Britain's most important international relationship in 1949 was with the United States of America. The United Kingdom's ambassador to Washington in 1949 was Sir Oliver Franks. Before his appointment the previous year Franks had already enjoyed two careers, the first in academe as Professor of Moral Philosophy at one of Britain's most ancient institutions, the University of Glasgow, and as Provost of the Queen's College, Oxford, where he had been an undergraduate. During the Second World War he had taken leave to become a civil servant, displaying extraordinary organizational abilities to rise to Permanent Secretary of the vital Ministry of Supply. Tall, private, abstemious and somewhat aloof, with an extraordinarily large forehead, Franks' interlude as a diplomat coincided with the start of Marshall Aid and the foundation of NATO, and also with the difficult business of the Chinese aeroplanes.

The Labour government's principal legal adviser, its Attorney General, Hartley Shawcross, was of a younger generation. Sir Hartley, the grandson of a Lancashire mill-owner and son of a professor of English and his suffragette wife, was more of a liberal than a socialist. Born in Germany and educated in London and Geneva (where he learnt fluent French), he had been a precocious student with political ambitions who decided on a career at the Bar instead of medicine after being advised by Labour politicians visiting Geneva for a conference (for whom he volunteered to act as translator) that law would better prepare him for politics. He practiced and taught law in Liverpool, becoming King's Counsel and a part-time judge (recorder and chairman of the Enemy Aliens Tribunal) in the early part of the Second World War, then Commissioner for Northwest England in which capacity he was to administer the region in the event of loss of contact with London following a German invasion. He was elected to Parliament for a Northwestern constituency in the Labour landslide of 1945 and was immediately made Attorney General. In that post he was the chief British prosecutor at the Nuremberg trials of Nazi leaders accused of war crimes, achieving worldwide fame for his eloquent exposition of how the defendants had violated conventions and norms of international law. As Attorney General, Shawcross was also a principal British delegate to the newly established United Nations. One of his party colleagues,

11. Geoffrey Warner, ed., *In the Midst of Events: The Foreign Office Diaries and Papers of Kenneth Younger, February 1950–October 1951* (London: Routledge, 2005), entry for 9 September 1951; James T. H. Tang, *Britain's Encounter with Revolutionary China, 1949–54* (New York: St. Martin's Press, 1992), 11–13.

Hugh Dalton, described Shawcross as 'able, obstinate and self-important' and 'too keenly conscious of his good brains and his good looks'. Shawcross certainly was handsome, had the self-confident, almost haughty, bearing typical of a successful barrister of those times, and spoke in a matching, slightly nasal, semi-drawl. By 1949, Shawcross was in his late 40s and had become restless in a role that carried no seat in the Cabinet and involved him in political matters only when they called for legal advice. He was keen to become a senior minister and thought himself worthy of succeeding Bevin as Foreign Secretary. He was however to be drawn into attempts to resolve the government's dilemma concerning the Chinese planes grounded in Hong Kong. The dilemma was to test him both as a lawyer and a politician.

Still a big player

Bevin regarded his country as still a substantial player upon the world stage. He saw Britain as a kind of third force in international politics, leading a coalition of not just its extensive current and former empire but also the countries of western Europe.[12] He, and the Labour government, also regarded Britain as having a duty to improve conditions in the poorer parts of the Commonwealth. Britain's retreat from empire had begun well before the independence of India in 1947. The settled dominions had been granted self-government decades earlier, an accomplishment formalized in 1931 with the Statute of Westminster and the creation of the British Commonwealth of Nations. The Commonwealth was envisaged as a voluntary association of independent, equal, sovereign states united by background and interests. Many members of the Commonwealth retained links to the British Crown although this was not obligatory. In fact the association had no constitution or written rules or requirements in 1949.

The war and a Labour government accelerated the de-colonization process. During the late 1940s independence was granted in short order to India, Pakistan, Burma and Ceylon, which meant the empire lost its south Asian centrepiece, and there was also an abrupt, acrimonious departure from Palestine. Nevertheless, in 1949 there was still an extensive network of territories ruled from London, including much of southern, eastern and western Africa, southeast Asia and the Caribbean. In addition, Britain had close ties and influence with its former dominions, the self-governing nations of Australia, Canada (both of which spanned a continent), South Africa and New Zealand. Hong Kong was only a tiny part of that network but was growing in importance.

12. Marquand, *Britain since 1918*, 143.

The interests of the Crown colony were an important factor in Britain's policy towards China. At the end of 1948 a Foreign Office paper on developments in China anticipated a communist victory in the civil war and was apprehensive about its effects upon the colony. The paper considered that the fate of Hong Kong would depend upon whether the communists would find the presence of a well-administered British port convenient for their trade. It predicted an influx of refugees to the colony. It foresaw a risk that the 'emergency' in Malaya, the Singapore Federation and the three British territories in north Borneo, all of which had significant Chinese populations and had been suffering from a militant communist insurgency for some time, would be exacerbated by a communist victory.

Aside from the formal empire, there was a considerable unofficial empire of countries in which Britain had extensive contacts and interests. These were mainly commercial interests although they were reinforced by links, usually financial, educational and personal, with the ruling elite. So Britain was influential in the kingdoms and emirates of the Middle East, as well as in countries as diverse as The Argentine (Argentina), Brazil, Siam (Thailand), Egypt, and the Sudan. Included in this category was Shanghai.

Shanghai investments

Shanghai was the most important metropolis in China, its major port as well as its commercial capital. Until seized by the Japanese in the early 1940s it had been one of the world's great cities. In trying to summarize, for a late twentieth century audience, the difference during the interwar years between Shanghai and Hong Kong, the business magnate and philanthropist Lawrence Kadoorie (Lord Kadoorie of Kowloon), whose family had held large investments in both cities, would liken it to the difference between London and Hastings. The analogy was exaggerated and underplayed the significance of Hong Kong which was always much more than a south coast resort but it was intended to show just how extraordinary Shanghai was. During its heyday, foreign settlements had lain at the heart of Shanghai. The largest of these had been the Anglo-American International Settlement which had been run by a Municipal Council dominated by British residents.

Shanghai and its hinterland was the industrial engine of the Chinese economy. Investment there was extraordinarily profitable. Shipping and shipbuilding, port facilities and oil depots dominated its river frontage. The foreign trade that passed through its port was as voluminous as that of all other Chinese ports combined. The main industrial product was textiles: it had numerous knitting and weaving mills and silk filatures. There were many other types of factory, such as chemical works and flour mills, too.[13]

Before the Second World War, Britain had held the largest economic stake in China of any foreign power, with more than a third of all the foreign investment, most of it private. Since the 1920s the British government and banks had co-operated with the Chinese Nationalist government in providing loans. Britain had been the main overseas investor in Chinese manufacturing. More than a thousand British firms operated there. British banks, most notably the Hongkong and Shanghai Banking Corporation, had financed nine-tenths of foreign trade in Shanghai. About half of foreign-registered vessels using Chinese ports were British; they operated along the coast and on internal waterways as well as to and from the ports. The Chinese maritime customs were managed by Britain, in exchange for a generous cut of the revenue.[14]

During the 1930s British interests in Shanghai had been greater in value than those in Hong Kong. In 1939, 77 per cent of British investment in China had been in Shanghai, just 9 per cent in Hong Kong.[15] Much of Shanghai's economy was operated by British enterprises. The UK was the main source of imported manufactured goods to China and a major exporter of raw materials from China. British firms had entered into joint ventures with Chinese entrepreneurs throughout the Shanghai area. Although by 1936 Japanese, American and other nations' interests were gaining ground, British business remained pre-eminent in the country and looked forward to a prosperous future. Then Japan attacked China and the optimism was shattered. Angered by the Japanese attack, the United States, whose businesses were already one of the larger investors, increased its financial support to China. This continued throughout the war years and until disillusion with Chiang Kai-shek set in afterwards.[16]

At the end of the Second World War the areas formerly occupied by foreign settlements or concessions in no fewer than nineteen cities had been handed over to the Republic of China, but that did not affect vested property rights and most of the pre-war enterprises were restored to their previous owners. So it was that at the beginning of 1949 Britain again found itself one of the main sources of private foreign capital for China with heavy investments in the Shanghai region. These included shipbuilding, dockyards and other port facilities and utility companies, but the main strengths were in shipping,

13. F. L. Hawks Pott, *A Short History of Shanghai* (Shanghai: Kelly & Walsh, 1928), 132–136; Wenguang Shao, *China, Britain and Businessmen: Political and Commercial Relations, 1949–57* (Basingstoke: Macmillan, 1991), 3–4, 9.

14. Cain and Hopkins, *British Imperialism*, 596, 614; Shao, *China, Britain and Businessmen*, 2.

15. David Clayton, *Imperialism Revisited: Political and Economic Relations between Britain and China, 1950–54* (London: Macmillan, 1997), 8; Leo Goodstadt, *Profits, Politics and Panics: Hong Kong's Banks and the Making of a Miracle Economy* (Hong Kong: Hong Kong University Press, 2007), 42–43, 65.

16. Cain and Hopkins, *British Imperialism*, 613.

commerce and financial services (banking and insurance particularly). As well as giving Britain dominance in China trade, these businesses produced handsome 'invisible' earnings for Britain even though Shanghai's role in finance had declined with the abolition of the International Settlement. Major British enterprises operating in China, such as Imperial Chemical Industries, British American Tobacco, Lever Brothers and Shell-BP, still formed an influential business lobby.[17]

The advance of the Communist armies in 1948 and 1949 naturally created apprehension as to the continuance of these investments. Business conditions in China became difficult. Inflation and corruption were endemic; local KMT functionaries were hostile towards foreigners. In certain of the 'liberated areas' new radical leftist authorities had imposed onerous industrial and commercial taxes and confiscated property. Many Chinese-owned manufacturing concerns relocated to Hong Kong.[18]

United Kingdom government policy towards China was directed at protecting British investments if at all possible. Britain needed all the foreign income that it could get. A cabinet paper predicted that a communist takeover would cause commerce in China to ebb. It suggested, however, that expropriation of assets and expulsion of foreigners might not happen for some time. There was little that the UK, or the USA for that matter, could do, the paper concluded; the best hope lay in maintaining de facto relations, investigating the possibilities for trade, and remaining for as long as possible so as to 'keep a foot in the door'.[19]

Attitude towards communists

The consequences of the likely change in government in China had been a matter of concern to British policy-makers for some time and dominated their thinking about the Far East during 1949. Publicly at least, the official line was one of neutrality as between the factions in the civil war and cautious optimism that good relations could be established with any new regime. Many, however, shared the American tendency to view Chinese communists as little different from their fellows in the Soviet Union. Dening was under no illusions about the nature of the communists, though he thought that once they had established themselves they would be willing to trade and work with other nations.

The optimistic view was expressed in confident terms by the outspoken left-wing Labour Member of Parliament, Woodrow Wyatt, in the House of

17. Cain and Hopkins, *British Imperialism*, 609; Tang, *Britain's Encounter*, 158; Shao, *China, Britain and Businessmen*, 5–9.
18. Shao, *China, Britain and Businessmen*, 52.
19. CP (48) 299; Tang, *Britain's Encounter*, 33.

Commons in February 1949. It was obvious, he said, that the Communists were going to win the day and become the absolute masters of China:

> If we are not friendly to the Communists, we shall lose our entire trade in China, we shall lose Hong Kong and we shall lose Malaya. There is no hostility to Great Britain by the Communists. They want to continue trading with us and maintain co-operation with us.

There was an additional reason to be as friendly as possible, added Wyatt. That was the attitude of overseas Chinese. They were a strong element in southeast Asia—in Burma, Malaya, Borneo and Indonesia—and they 'always tend to go in whichever way they think the power has gone'. So Britain must be careful not to 'tip the overseas Chinese against us'.[20]

Wyatt had indeed touched upon a consideration for the British government. The UK still ruled in Malaya and Borneo (both parts of the future Malaysia) and was facing the emergency there led by communists who were predominantly from the Chinese minority. The UK also still held Burma (although not for long) where there was agitation for independence. As in Indonesia, commerce in Burma was dominated by the Chinese inhabitants. All three places were important sources of raw materials, such as rubber and timber, for export in exchange for hard currency.

20. Debate, House of Commons, February 1949. Wyatt was a polemical journalist who later became Lord Wyatt and a firm supporter of Margaret Thatcher.

5
The USA in 1949

The last of the five governments involved in the saga of the Chinese aeroplanes at Kai Tak was that of the United States of America. In 1949 that government was led by President Harry S. Truman, a Democrat. Both houses of the US Congress, however, were controlled by the rival Republican Party.

Most prosperous nation

The US had emerged from the Second World War as by far the richest and most powerful nation in the world. It had the largest naval and air forces, and its army, although not the largest in manpower, had the most advanced weapons. The US alone had the atomic bomb. As one American diplomatist and commentator of the era, the quiet, introverted conservative George Kennan, reflected: 'We have about 50 per cent of the world's wealth but only 6.3 per cent of its population . . . we cannot fail to be the object of envy and resentment'.

Before the war the USA's dominance had not been quite so clear. Economically the 1930s had been marked by the Great Depression with unemployment, poverty, industrial sluggishness, bank failures and a low stock market. Militarily the US had been a medium-sized power with a modest navy and an army that was only the seventeenth largest in the world. There had been a strong isolationist tendency in the population that opposed intervention in foreign wars. The Japanese assault and ensuing war changed all that. The need to rearm transformed industry and solved the unemployment problem. At the same time America escaped the domestic destruction caused by bombing and fighting that others had suffered.

Both people and government became used to the projection of power which a huge military capability bestowed. US forces were present in western Europe and east Asia as well as the Americas.

Civil aviation

One of the many areas of commerce in which the USA led the way was that of civil aviation. The first passenger and freight-carrying airlines were established in the 1920s and 1930s; by the end of the latter decade, aviation was an undoubted growth industry. One US carrier, Pan-Am, had even expanded into China, setting up a joint enterprise with CNAC, an airline there.

The Second World War had given a great boost to aircraft technology that enabled aircraft to fly further and faster. It was apparent that there was tremendous economic potential for expansion of air routes provided that nationalistic obstacles were not erected and that sufficient international regulation was put in place to ensure safety and efficiency. To that end, during the closing months of the war the US administration organized a conference in Chicago to discuss and set up a world civil aviation regime. Delegates from many countries convened in the cavernous halls of the massive Stevens Hotel in the city. The result was the Convention on International Civil Aviation made on 7 December 1944.[1] The Chicago Convention, as it is known in airline circles, was to feature in the story of the Chinese aircraft grounded at Kai Tak.

US and China

America's interest in China, which commercially stretched back into the mid-nineteenth century and developed to become educational and evangelical, greatly increased in the 1930s and 1940s. Sympathy was invoked in the USA by the suffering of the Chinese people and Nationalist government at the hands of the Japanese. This began in 1931 with the latter's occupation of the vast, resource-rich area in northeastern China known as Manchuria and their re-designation of it as Manchukuo with a compliant government nominally headed by the previously overthrown Chinese Emperor Pu Yi. The United States' concern was magnified when Japan created an excuse to invade the heartlands of China in 1937 and start what became known as the Pacific War. US sources gave financial and material support to Chiang Kai-shek and his armies in that struggle. The Flying Tigers formed part of that support.

Although there was sympathy for China, at that time the US had no appetite to engage in war. A large domestic pacifist movement advocated that the US stand aloof from overseas conflicts. This precluded direct engagement and overt official military aid to the KMT Nationalists in Nanjing. Aid to the Nationalists was made official and was stepped up after Japan attacked the USA itself in December 1941. The weaknesses of the KMT were not then well known. The US provided advisers as well as armaments and supplies.

1. 15 UNTS 295. The Stevens is now one of Chicago's Hilton Hotels.

Franklin Roosevelt

The US President almost throughout the eight years up to 1941 was Franklin Delano Roosevelt. He had many virtues, but also a prejudice towards republics and against colonialism which coloured his view of the Republic of China and the Nationalists in their battles with Japan and Mao Tse-tung's Communists respectively. For a long time he and his advisers were unable to see the weaknesses of Chiang Kai-shek and his army and administration. Roosevelt insisted upon the Republic of China being treated not just as an ally but also nominally as of equal importance to Britain and the USSR despite China's poverty and Chiang's unwillingness fully to commit his troops to fight the Japanese.

The United States' policy objective for China had been set in January 1945 as Roosevelt's presidency was drawing to a close. The objective was long-term and so idealistic that today it would be called a 'vision': to assist in the development of a united, democratically progressive and co-operative China capable of contributing to the security and prosperity of the Far East.[2] This would require at a minimum the pacific settlement of the Chinese civil war.

Roosevelt would have no time to aim for this goal. He had been visibly ailing for more than a year before he died in April 1945. He was succeeded by his Vice-President, Harry S. Truman.

The Truman administration

Truman was a very different character from the sophisticated, condescending, east coast patrician Roosevelt. Truman was from a farming family but had run a men's clothing shop in a small town in his native Missouri in the Mid-West. He had become a minor judge and then somewhat unexpectedly a US Senator at the age of 50 in 1934. There he served solidly for a decade, most notably in charge of a committee keeping a check on armaments expenditure, before being a safe compromise choice as Roosevelt's running-mate in the 1944 presidential election. Truman had an ordinary background, a straightforward manner, and a good deal of down-to-earth common sense. He had none of Roosevelt's politician's sinuousness. Consequently, the Washington establishment tended to under-estimate Truman, so had low expectations when he was suddenly elevated to the presidency. In fact, Truman was aware of his own limitations, was not afraid to take advice or make decisions, had a solid knowledge of history, and was a sound judge of character.

Truman had to face several difficult issues thrown up by the final months and the aftermath of the war. Should the appalling new weapon, the atomic bomb, be used against Japan? What approach should the USA take towards

2. Memorandum from John Carter Vincent, Chief of the State Department's Division of Chinese Affairs, to Joseph Grew, Acting Secretary of State, 25 January 1945.

its wartime ally but now peacetime rival Russia which seemed to be reneging on agreements made in 1944 and 1945? How fast and to what degree should the US disengage from its wartime positions? To what extent should America assist European and other countries which had been shattered by the war? What attitude should the US strike towards the contesting domestic parties in China?

Truman had inherited from his predecessor a powerful set of foreign policy advisers and military commanders. One of the wartime commanders, George Marshall, had afterwards become the President's special representative in China in which capacity he had spent a year unsuccessfully attempting to broker a settlement between Chiang Kai-shek and Mao Tse-tung, as we have seen. Then in 1947 Marshall became Secretary of State, the US foreign minister. He had no expertise or particular interest in foreign affairs and was not by nature a politician. However, the Under-Secretary of State was an experienced political and diplomatic player: the Yale and Harvard graduate and lawyer, Dean Acheson. In January 1949 Marshall, exhausted and ill, retired and Acheson succeeded him as Secretary of State. Another younger adviser who played an increasingly important part was Clark Clifford, a mid-western lawyer-turned-naval-officer who had taken advantage of a temporary wartime secondment to the White House to become close to Truman.[3]

Acheson was backed up by a large and experienced team of diplomats at the Department of State. These included three who were to play roles in the story of the Chinese aircraft. Two of them were career foreign service officers, Walton Butterworth and Livingston Merchant. Both were Princeton graduates in their late forties who were respectively Assistant Secretary and Deputy Assistant Secretary of State for Far East Affairs in 1949. Two years earlier they had been in Nanking as part of Marshall's mission. The third was Lewis Douglas, the US Ambassador to Britain. Douglas was not a career diplomat but a political appointee, a conservative Democrat from a wealthy mining family in Arizona who had been a congressman, Roosevelt's Director of Budget, and holder of numerous business appointments.

Two other Far East specialists within the department were Philip C. Jessup and Dean Rusk. By 1949, Jessup was a roving ambassador for the department although his background was as a legal academic specializing in international law. Acheson asked Jessup to head a team to produce a report on US policy towards China. The theory that the nationalism evident within the Chinese Communist Party might be exploited to separate the party from its counterpart in the USSR found expression in a paper by the US National Security

3. Clifford was designated 'special counsel' to the President. He was to spend 35 years in public life as an adviser but turned down numerous public appointments from successive Democratic presidents, preferring the better-remunerated role of a lobbyist for big business (or influence pedlar) under the description 'corporate lawyer'.

Council in February 1949. This advocated that America not intervene in the Chinese civil war but attempt to exploit differences between the two communist parties. A year later, when Rusk took charge of the China division of the department in succession to Butterworth, the theory was looking rather threadbare.[4]

The US ambassador to China in 1949, John Leighton Stuart, was a curious appointee. He had neither a diplomatic nor a political background. He had been born in China, the son of Christian missionaries. Although educated in the USA and possessed of a strong southern accent, he had spent almost all his career in China as a teacher and president of a university. He was principled and saintly, some would say innocent and naïve.

The Truman Doctrine

Well before 1949 Soviet Russia had become openly hostile towards its wartime allies the USA and Britain. Its leader, Joseph Stalin, had imposed compliant totalitarian governments on central and eastern European nations such as Poland and Czechoslovakia which had been promised representative democracy in allied agreements. An 'iron curtain' was said to have descended across the European continent and a 'cold war' had broken out between Russia and its satellites on the one side and the free democracies led by America on the other.[5]

Truman and his advisers were alarmed by the extent to which communism was spreading among war-shattered nations with the apparent encouragement of the Soviet Union. In Greece the Monarchist government had been fighting a communist insurrection since early 1946: Britain, which had been helping the government there, could no longer afford to do so. Turkey was coming under pressure from the Russians to allow their fleet to cross through the Bosphorus and the Dardanelles, the straits between the Black Sea and the Aegean Sea, thereby allowing them to operate in the Mediterranean and beyond. In southeast Asia, there was internal communist activity in Korea, Vietnam, Malaya and Borneo.

Acheson and Clifford persuaded Truman that something must be done. They and Marshall met Congressional leaders to urge them to support financial and economic intervention. The Senate majority leader Arthur Vandenburg and most of his fellow Republicans were convinced by their arguments. The fear of the communist threat was strong.

4. The main promoter, if not originator, of the theory was another 'China hand' from the State Department, John Paton Davies, who had been born to missionaries and brought up in China. By 1949, however, Davies had left the department.
5. The phrase 'iron curtain' was given wide publicity in a speech by Winston Churchill at Fulton in Harry Truman's home state, Missouri, in 1946. Truman was present at the speech. The phrase 'cold war' was first used by the American foreign policy specialist Bernard Baruch on 24 October 1948.

Truman revealed the new approach publicly in March 1947 when in a speech to a joint session of Congress he pledged American support for 'free peoples who are resisting attempted subjugation by armed minorities or by outside pressures'. He reasoned that because totalitarian regimes coerced free peoples, they represented a threat not just to international peace but also to the security of the United States. The 'armed minorities' included the communists in Greece. The 'outside pressures' covered Russia's attempts to influence Turkey. Truman also knew that Greeks and Turks were rivals and that aid extended to one without the other would sow resentment.

The speech to Congress was the foundation of what became known as the Truman Doctrine. It had been formulated by Dean Acheson. It signified that there would be no return to isolationism. The US would become the champion of freedom and democracy. But it also presaged a policy of resisting the spread of communism by all means short of military intervention, a policy that came to be known as 'containment'.[6] This policy became the basis for American foreign policy around the world and eventually the beneficiaries of it were not confined to freedom-loving governments.

Marshall Aid

The support to which the President referred would be primarily economic and financial rather than military. Both he and Marshall recognized that freedom would become more attractive and easier to sustain if accompanied by prosperity. The recovery of western Europe had been painfully slow. Accordingly, three months later in a speech at Harvard the Secretary of State offered financial aid for a programme of European economic recovery. It was logical, Marshall said,

> that the United States should do whatever it is able to do to assist the return of normal economic health in the world without which there can be no stability and no assured peace.

The purpose was the revival of a working world economy which would facilitate the emergence of political and social conditions in which free institutions could exist.[7]

So was born what the press called Marshall Aid or the Marshall Plan. Its official title was the European Recovery Programme (ERP). The plan was of course attractive to European governments, not least the British one which, as we have seen, was in acute financial straits. Ernest Bevin, the UK's Foreign

6. Containment was a phrase and approach devised by a US diplomat, George S. Kennan, who became an acknowledged American foreign policy expert.
7. John Simkin, 'Marshall Plan', Spartacus Educational, spartacus-educational.com/USAmarshallP.htm (accessed 7 November 2020).

Secretary, was an enthusiastic supporter and quickly started organizing western European governments to take advantage of the programme. At a conference in Paris in September 1947 sixteen governments agreed on the terms of a four-year plan. Only the Czechoslovak government, forbidden by its Soviet masters, declined to take part. In early April 1948 the US Congress approved the first appropriation of funds for the programme which was intended to last for four years.

The ERP was complemented by a Military Assistance Programme, or MAP. As its title implied, this was a scheme of support for the armed forces of American allies, most notably the United Kingdom, who were engaged in resisting expansion of totalitarian regimes across the world. The main threat was the USSR. The assistance took the form of loans or discounted sales of equipment of which, after the unexpectedly early end to the war in the Pacific, the USA had much surplus to its requirements.

There may then have been some concern that the second two-year stage of the programme, due to start in 1949, might fall victim to a change in government in Washington DC. That would have been allayed when in November 1948 Truman was somewhat unexpectedly re-elected as President in his own right.

Cold War

The Truman Doctrine and the policy of containment became the bases of American foreign policy during the era of enmity between the United States and its allies on the one side and the USSR and its affiliates on the other side that became known as the Cold War. A stark and audacious instance of the Cold War was the blockade of West Berlin which began in June 1948. The former German capital city lay in the eastern part of Germany. After the Second World War, the country was occupied by and divided between four powers, the United States of America, Great Britain, France and the Soviet Union, under their agreement made at Yalta in 1944. In 1949 the three western zones were merged into one, the eastern zone not participating. Instead the East became a communist dictatorship under Russian supervision. Consequently, Berlin was surrounded by hostile forces.

The city itself was, like the country, divided in zones between the four powers. Access to the city from western Germany was along specific corridors. On 1 April 1948 the Soviets suddenly refused American, British, and French supply trains passage along those corridors. Stalin thought that the three powers would simply abandon West Berlin and he would be rid of an outpost of capitalism which was demonstrably and embarrassingly more prosperous than its eastern portion. He expected that after being forced to leave Berlin, American resolve to remain in Europe would be weakened. Instead, the three other occupiers organized a massive airlift of supplies, especially food and fuel, into West Berlin's three airports. Day after day, they flew in tons of supplies, using the most modern aircraft. In all, 2.245 million tons were delivered. It was a splendid display of the potential of modern air power. After almost ten months, the blockade was lifted. The west's, especially the American, determination had passed the Soviet test. The three western zones in Germany formed the Federal Republic of Germany in May 1949. The Eastern Zone controlled by the Russians became a separate country, the German Democratic Republic, in October that year.

In January 1949 the Soviet Union had exploded its first atomic bomb. The USA was no longer the world's only nuclear power. The Cold War intensified. The desire for a common defence scheme for western Europe and America became more pressing. Bevin was at the forefront of discussions to set up such a scheme. In April 1949 those bore fruit with the formation of the North Atlantic Treaty Organisation (NATO).

These events all contributed to the building up of anti-communist feelings within the US. The feelings were heightened in July 1949 by the trial on espionage charges of a senior federal employee, Alger Hiss, who happened to have worked for a time with Dean Acheson.[8] In this atmosphere, any hint of weakness in the administration in confronting the communist threat was seized upon and exploited by opposition politicians.

Central Intelligence Agency

The Cold War and the Communist threat were powerful stimulants for what is now termed the security state. When it had entered the Second World War the United States, somewhat surprisingly, had no organization for the collection and distribution of military intelligence.[9] The importance of such a body was perceived by Colonel William Donovan, another lawyer-turned-politician who had been many times decorated for bravery during military service in the First World War. A tall, burly, handsome figure from a modest Catholic background, Donovan had been a notable athlete in his native Buffalo, New York, and a strong American footballer at college where he had acquired the nickname 'Wild Bill' for his robust style of play.[10]

Between the wars, Donovan returned to his law practice in Buffalo and married a Protestant heiress. He became the chief federal prosecutor (US

8. Hiss had never been Acheson's assistant, as alleged, although they had worked together at the State Department and Hiss' brother was Acheson's law partner: Dean Acheson, *Present at the Creation: My Years in the State Department* (New York: W.W. Norton, 1969), 250–252.
9. There had been one, the 'Black Chamber' during the First World War, but it had been disbanded thereafter because spying was regarded as ungentlemanly.
10. An alternative explanation is that he acquired it from his troops during the First World War on account of his aggression.

attorney) in the district but that was not active enough for him and eventually he transferred to a larger practice in New York City. President Hoover offered him the governorship of the Philippines, which he turned down. Instead he ran for Governor of New York state as the Republican candidate but lost, a rare setback for this high achiever. The energetic and flamboyant Donovan also travelled widely, meeting leaders and gathering information for business and investor clients about local conditions as he went. He anticipated that another world conflict was coming and that knowledge about military and political matters would play a crucial part in it.

Donovan had been deputed by his fellow New Yorker and Columbia law school graduate Franklin Roosevelt to visit Britain in July 1940 to assess its ability to withstand German aggression. Donovan returned impressed and full of suggestions, including the need for intelligence-gathering. He struck up friendship with the head of British intelligence (MI6) in New York, a slight Canadian and former air ace named William Stevenson. In official circles Colonel Stevenson was informally called 'Little Bill' and Donovan 'Big Bill'. It is not known whether Donovan preferred this sobriquet to the one acquired at college. Big Bill introduced Little Bill to leading members of the Roosevelt administration, the Secretaries of State, of Defence and of the Navy, thereby helping Britain to obtain clandestine military assistance from the US.

Donovan became Roosevelt's unofficial head of information co-ordination. After America entered the war, his position became formalized as the head of what was opaquely called the Office of Strategic Services. Now a Major-General, Donovan quickly established a wide network of spies. He was in charge of US military intelligence-gathering until the end of the war. He promoted the continuation of the office's role during peacetime but OSS was instead abolished and, stopping only to assist in evidence-gathering for the Nuremberg war-crimes prosecutions, the restless Donovan returned to law practice, this time with a New York firm. It was during this period that he was summoned to play a part in the saga of the Chinese aircraft at Kai Tak. It was a part in which he was to suffer another unfamiliar defeat.

The cessation of overseas information-gathering was soon judged a mistake. In September 1947 a new body, the Central Intelligence Agency, was formed under the National Security Act. Its Director would report directly to the President. The CIA was supposed to be concerned with external security and information-gathering. In practice it soon acquired a wider remit, unofficially delving into US internal matters (the province of the FBI) and indulging in covert operations. Donovan was not appointed the CIA's Director but he was regarded as its founding father, a status marked by a statue in the foyer of the agency's new headquarters in Langley, Virginia.

Given the Truman administration's policy of containment of communism, the CIA naturally focused upon the Soviet Union and Europe, but it was also active in Asia. The fear in the late 1940s was that communist activity in southeast Asia would jeopardize not just countries with communist insurgents but also others in the region such as Thailand (Siam). That was one reason that Donovan was appointed as US ambassador to Thailand in the mid-1950s. Furthermore, the CIA was also concerned about the deteriorating position of Chiang Kai-shek's regime in China. Its efforts there were headed by Alfred T. Cox.

An athlete in his youth but not a lawyer, Colonel Cox had experience as an intelligence officer with OSS. Having been a paratroop commander in the US Army during the Second World War, he trained Chinese commandos thereafter. With the CIA, he became an expert on Far East aviation and a special assistant to Chennault. Naturally, he took a role in the story of the Chinese aircraft at Kai Tak. He operated behind the façade of the Office of Policy Co-ordination which handled covert CIA operations in China.

China lobby

Decision-makers in the upper echelons of the US government in 1949 could not afford to ignore a considerable body of opinion within the Congress, the press, business and the military supportive of the Nationalist government of China. That support was the product of sympathy for China stemming from its treatment by the Japanese, its continued suffering from civil conflict, and personal loyalty to Chiang Kai-shek. Chiang was thought of in America as a wartime ally and a democratic leader of Christian principles with a charming and persuasive English-speaking wife. Rising anti-communist feeling in America suggested to many that they must support the Nationalists. Consequently, America's policy towards China had an emotional charge which was entirely lacking in other nations and which manifested itself in US domestic politics.

The term 'China lobby', or 'China bloc', for those who shared this strand of opinion suggests a degree of organization that did not really exist. But there was certainly a diffuse collection of sympathizers with the Nationalist (or 'ChiNat') cause amongst US opinion-formers. They embraced ex-President Hoover, conservative Senators and Representatives in Congress, military leaders, current and former CIA officials, businessmen, and owners of and writers for newspapers and magazines.[11] For Republicans, allegations of the Democratic administration's insufficient support for the Nationalists as the Communists gained ground in China were a useful political tool. The two

11. Republican Senators Styles Bridges, Harry Cain, William Knowland, Alexander Smith, Robert Taft and the young Richard Nixon were all supportive of the Nationalists, as was Democrat Senator Lyndon Johnson. In the House, the main proponent of the ChiNat cause was Walter Judd. The foremost supporters in business were the news magnate Roy Howard and the millionaire textile importer and magazine owner Alfred Kohlberg.

main news magazines, *Time* and *Life*, were enthusiastic ChiNat supporters. So was their proprietor, the businessman and philanthropist Henry Luce, and his wife, the writer and Republican politician Clare Wilkes Booth.[12] Both magazines sold millions of copies each week, television not yet being Americans' main source of news. Chiang Kai-shek appeared on the cover of *Time* on numerous occasions, sometimes with Madame Chiang.

Claire Chennault, his second wife Anna and Whiting Willauer were only too happy to exploit this sympathy, as were Tommy Corcoran and the CIA's Cox. The diminutive Anna Chennault (Chan Sheng Mai) had been brought up in Peking where her father was an editor and teacher. As a teenager Anna had left China when the Japanese invaded in 1937, had attended college in Hong Kong, and had then become a journalist with the Chinese central news agency (Xinhua). Covering both the world war and the civil war there, she was a persuasive propagandist for the Nationalist cause. She also helped her husband in his post-war airline ventures.

During 1948 and the early months of 1949 Claire Chennault raised the alarm in Washington DC about the communist advance through China. He circulated his views among members of Congress. He enjoyed enthusiastic support from a number, such as Representative Walter Judd and Senator William Knowland, as well as from General Douglas MacArthur. The general advocated an economic blockade, destruction of Chinese coastal facilities, and fighting with 500 planes under the command of 'someone like Chennault'. For his part Chennault called for a massive, immediate grant of aid to the KMT. He also made proposals to the CIA as to how to stop the communists. Its Office of Policy Co-ordination decided to use Chennault's airline CAT for covert operations in China. Chennault worked closely with Knowland, the 'Senator for Formosa', who relied upon Chennault for information and analysis.[13]

Relations with Communist Chinese

The influence of the China lobby posed a dilemma for the Democrat administration in Washington DC. The rottenness of the KMT regime had become apparent to the administration, if not to the American public, during 1948 and early 1949. Chiang Kai-shek's military position had deteriorated despite US aid. In June 1949 Roger Lapham, a former mayor of San Francisco and a Republican businessman who headed the US Economic Cooperation

12. Luce, the son of Presbyterian missionaries, had been born in Shandong.
13. Victor S. Kaufman, 'The United States, Great Britain and the CAT Controversy', *Journal of Contemporary History* 40, no. 1 (2005): 95–113; Peter Lowe, *Containing the Cold War in East Asia: British Policies towards Japan, China and Korea, 1948–53* (Manchester: Manchester University Press, 1997), 87, 91, 109.

Administration Programme in China, reported on the KMT's weaknesses and concluded that US$125 million in aid had been 'thrown down the rat hole'. He advocated recognition of the inevitable communist government. Dean Acheson was open-minded about establishing relations with any new Chinese government which might emerge from the civil war. He had commissioned the State Department's own assessment of the history and future of US policy on China from a panel of experts.[14]

There was hope that the Communists might prove a better, or at least a cleaner, government than the Nationalists. The US had sent representatives to communist areas in 1944. The Chinese Communist Party had accepted mediation with the Nationalists through General Marshall in 1946 and 1947. In March 1949 the National Security Council, advisers to the US President, resolved to maintain contacts with the Chinese Communist Party.[15] However, by then Mao was looking to Moscow for political and economic assistance. Moreover, US opposition politicians saw the administration's China policy as a weak point that could be exploited. Ambassador Stuart advised Washington that it should not make the first move to recognize the anticipated communist government, advice accepted by Acheson.[16]

Consequently, open-mindedness did not extend to support. In the spring of 1949 the United States banned the export of goods of high military significance to China. It supported a blockade by the Nationalists of ports which were under Communist control, including Shanghai. It advocated wider sanctions too. In the middle of the year in the face of the Communist advance, the US recalled Stuart from China, began to close its consulates on the mainland and advised its nationals to leave. Despite reservations by some at the State Department, the US continued to back Chiang Kai-shek after he departed to Formosa.[17]

14. Lowe, *Containing the Cold War*, 88, 100–102.
15. NSC 34/2; Kaufman, 'The CAT Controversy', 96.
16. James T. H. Tang, *Britain's Encounter with Revolutionary China, 1949–54* (New York: St. Martin's Press, 1992), 55.
17. James T. H. Tang, 'World War to Cold War: Hong Kong's Future and Anglo-Chinese Interactions, 1941–1955', in *Precarious Balance: Hong Kong between China and Britain, 1842–1992*, ed. Ming K. Chan (Hong Kong: Hong Kong University Press, 1994); R. E. Watson, 'The Foreign Office and Policy-making in China, 1945–50: Anglo-American Relations and the Recognition of Communist China' (PhD thesis, University of Leeds, 1996).

6

The Planes Fly In

Once the Communist armies had crossed the Yangtze river in April 1949 it would have been obvious even to the most ardent supporter of the Nationalist cause that the game was up. All of northern China, including the expanse of Manchuria, the ancient capital Peking and the vast plains to its south, was under Communist control. The industrial and commercial heartland of the country was now open to their forces. They already held Hankow and Wuchang (now Wuhan). The other major cities of central China—Shanghai, Soochow, and Nanking—were within their grasp. Recognizing this, the Nationalists moved their capital south to Canton, a relocation that had been planned since the previous autumn.

After the decisive battles at the turn of the year, there had been a pause in hostilities as both sides gathered themselves for the next stage. During the pause the Americans tried to broker a settlement, to no avail. They also held discussions with the United Kingdom and France about what attitude their countries should take towards a Communist government of China. They all decided to maintain their embassies at Nanking for the time being.

Communist leaders, views, and policy

What might be expected from the incoming masters of China? By and large the leadership of the Chinese Communist Party was from a different class to that of the Nationalists. Whilst the latter was a wealthy privileged clique, well-educated, urban and Westernized, the Communists were largely from peasant stock. However, they came from more prosperous peasant families and accordingly their education and training was better than that of the ordinary peasant. The thirteen members of the CCP politburo in 1949 had all been elected in 1945. Eight of them had studied in the Soviet Union, two in Japan, and only one in the West: Chou En-lai, the premier and foreign minister, who had been a work-study student in France after a spell in Japan. Both Chou and Mao Tse-tung (a former assistant librarian) had read widely and reflected upon China's history and current position.

Born around the turn of the twentieth century, the leaders' formative political years had seen the continuing occupation of valuable coastal pockets of China by foreign 'concessions' and settlements, the fall of the Ch'ing dynasty, Dr Sun's 1911 revolution and its subversion, the Russian communist revolution, the humiliating treatment of China at the Paris Peace Conference of 1919, and the reaction to that in the May Fourth student movement. They had experienced the results of the Russian revolution during their years in the Soviet Union. More recently they had lived through Japan's barbaric occupation of much of their country and their own long struggle against the KMT which had been supported monetarily and militarily by the USA. Inevitably, all this coloured their outlook on the world.

Communist leaders, in common with their supporters, were fiercely nationalistic and suspicious of foreigners whom they associated with imperialism and the unfair treatment of China during previous decades. They felt particularly antagonistic towards the USA which they regarded as now the principal imperialist reactionary power and the main opponent of liberation movements and workers' rights. Mao considered the USA a 'paper tiger', temporarily powerful but in the longer term vulnerable to economic and political crises and other trends of history. Nevertheless, he and fellow CCP leaders feared that the US might yet intervene directly in an attempt to thwart the communist revolution in China. If the US was the modern imperialist power, the UK was the old one which had led the encroachment upon China in the nineteenth century but was now weaker and more subtle: it had not taken sides in the Chinese civil war and had a pragmatic approach towards relations with the Central People's Government. Moreover, it ruled Hong Kong, a city which had been, and might in future be, useful to the communists.[1]

By 1949 CCP leaders had acquired administrative experience from running the 'liberated areas', those parts of China which had come under Communist control during the civil war. Chou En-lai had been a member of the left-wing of the KMT before it had been purged and during the war against Japan had been the CCP's principal representative in Chungking, Chiang Kai-shek's wartime capital, where he had dealt with ambassadors and visitors from America, Britain and other countries. Chou's assistants in Chungking were to become officers in the CPG's foreign ministry. Either in Peking or Hong Kong, they came to play a part in the saga of the Chinese aircraft at Kai Tak. However, in its early years the CPG was more concerned about its own survival and establishment than about foreign policy. This entailed giving priority to consolidation of its territory and resuscitation of the economy.

The CPG did have some principles regarding relations with other states. These had been laid down in early 1949 in the Common Programme of

1. Qiang Zhai, *The Dragon, the Lion, and the Eagle: Chinese-British-American Relations, 1949–1958* (Kent, OH: Kent State University Press, 1994), 6–15.

the Chinese People's Political Consultative Conference proposed by Mao. Concerning international matters the programme stipulated that the CPG would be prepared to establish diplomatic relations with others on the basis of equality and independence, but that foreign diplomatic missions and personnel accredited to the KMT would not be recognized, existing treaties would not necessarily be accepted, the CPG would be in no hurry to be recognized by imperialist and capitalist countries, and legal status would not be accorded to imperialists if they continued their hostile attitude. The CPG would however protect the legitimate interests of foreign nationals and be willing to trade with capitalist as well as socialist countries.

The concept underlying the CPG's approach towards relations with governments of other states was that of the 'fresh start'. In international affairs the CPG would 'lean towards' the socialist camp and it would need time to 'clean the room' before inviting guests in. The economic and cultural influence of the imperialists was felt to be still strong and would need to be eliminated.[2]

Chinese airlines

The principal Chinese civil airlines, Central Air Transport Corporation (CATC) and China National Aviation Corporation (CNAC), certainly realized the threat that the Communist advance posed to their business and their aircraft. Their main operations had been in Shanghai and Tientsin, large commercial cities with longstanding international connections, respectively on the middle and northern part of China's east coast. In January 1949 both airlines sought and received permission from the Hong Kong authorities to move their headquarters to the colony and establish maintenance depots and workshops around Kai Tak airfield.

CNAC had its roots in a Sino-American joint venture of the early 1930s. It had been re-founded soon after the Second World War by agreement between the Ministry of Communications of the KMT government and Pan-American Airways Corporation (Pan Am), the US international carrier. Well before the Second World War, Pan Am, which had been established in the USA in 1927, had identified the potential for civil airlines in China. Since 1933 it had been operating services, mainly domestic but to Bangkok and Hong Kong too, on behalf of CNAC. During the war it had been based in India. After the war, the airline moved back to Shanghai, with its operations out of Longhua Airport and staff quarters in the old French Concession. Pan Am secured a joint venture agreement with CNAC together with a 20 per cent shareholding in it and the right to nominate two of its nine directors. Pan Am trained

2. James T. H. Tang, *Britain's Encounter with Revolutionary China, 1949–54* (New York: St. Martin's Press, 1992), 28–30; Zhai, *The Dragon, the Lion, and the Eagle*, 24.

air and cabin crew and provided technical assistance for CNAC. Its fleet consisted largely of second-hand US war surplus aircraft and some new planes of American manufacture.[3]

CNAC was in form a true corporation, with shares, directors, and a memorandum and articles of association, although all the other 80 per cent of the shares were held by the government. CNAC's object was to operate on specific air routes within China, those which linked major cities such as Peking, Shanghai, Tientsin, Chungking and Hankow, and to certain destinations outside China. Its head office was in Shanghai.

In contrast CATC, despite its full name, was not a corporation at all. It was not a company and had no shareholders, although it did have a board of governors similar to a board of directors. Rather, it was a division of the government that had been set up in 1942 and was operated by the Ministry of Communications. It had close connections with the Chinese Air Force. It too ran services between major cities and to a few overseas destinations. Those services began after the end of the Second World War. Much of CATC's fleet and equipment was military surplus, virtually new, that it had bought from liquidation authorities after the end of hostilities. Similarly, many of its pilots were former Air Force servicemen, some recruited from CNAC. There seems to have been a fairly close relationship between the two airlines and a certain fluidity regarding their staff.

There was a third, though smaller, player on the airline scene in China. This was Central Air Transport, or CAT. It operated commercial charter flights within China and to certain outside territories. CAT had been set up in 1946 by the American entrepreneurs Claire Chennault and Whiting Willauer with the support of investors in the USA and China. After collaborating in the Flying Tigers initiative, Chennault and Willauer had seen the commercial opportunities in China's fledgling post-war airline industry. By 1949 CAT's US$4 million contract from the United Nations Relief and Rehabilitation Administration had come to an end but it still operated contract flights all over China, including Hong Kong.

However, during that year CAT had been obliged by the Communist advance to abandon a succession of its mainland routes and operating bases. By June its main bases were in Hong Kong (it used the JAMCO engineering shop at Kai Tak) and Hainan. In October its office headquarters was evacuated from Canton to Hong Kong. Lately it had enjoyed a surge in business from carrying Nationalist administrators, soldiers and sympathizers from the mainland to Taipei. CAT's principals, Chennault and Willauer, feature large in the tale of the Chinese civil aircraft marooned at Kai Tak.

3. Wikipedia.org/wiki/CNAC. Pan Am was one of the largest international airlines in the twentieth century, the unofficial flag-carrier of the USA. Despite, or perhaps because of, its size it suffered hard times when competition intensified in the 1980s and ceased services in 1991.

In May 1949 when Shanghai was taken over by the Communists, CNAC's and CATC's principal flights were operated from Hong Kong. The headquarters of CNAC were then moved to Hong Kong. The headquarters of CATC was relocated to Canton in June but soon also moved to Hong Kong.

At around the same time, the British defence ministry reinforced the Royal Air Force base at Kai Tak. This had the only runways in the colony capable of accommodating military aircraft.[4] Kai Tak had housed an RAF base since before the Second World War and the military had been its principal users until the resurgence of civil aviation after the war. It had been a Royal Naval Air Station from 1945 to 1947. RAF buildings and its hangar dominated the eastern end of the airport.

Crowded Kai Tak

The land surface at Kai Tak was not extensive. The site had been reclaimed in the early twentieth century by dredging and landfill at the northern end of Kowloon Bay, an inlet from and to the north of Hong Kong's harbour (named, like so many things in the colony, Victoria). This was part of New Kowloon, the area immediately above urban southern Kowloon, which had been acquired for expansion of the colony under the Convention of Peking 1898 for 99 years from Imperial China and thus was technically part of the 'New Territories'. Originally the site had been intended for housing development by two local worthies, Sir Kai Ho Kai and his business partner Mr Au Tak (or Tack), who, along with other investors, had purchased it through their Kai Tack Investment Company in 1912. The western end of the site, close to Kowloon City, had been built upon when the speculative property boom of the early 1920s suddenly deflated and the company became insolvent. Kai and Tak did not survive but their surnames lived on in the name given to the airfield and its surrounds.

In 1924 the government stepped in with the idea of using the remaining expanse of flat empty land as an aerodrome. A grass strip was created for use by aviation schools and flying clubs. In 1927 the Royal Air Force opened a base there, though mainly for seaplanes. A concrete slipway for seaplanes was added. In 1934 the RAF put up buildings on the perimeter and in 1935 a control tower and hangar were constructed. The first commercial service was introduced during 1936. The strip was hardened and lengthened in 1939. The facilities initially provided were somewhat rudimentary since there were few flights. Apart from RAF planes, the aircraft that landed on the strip in the early years were predominantly regional in origin. Long-range flights were

4. The only other airstrip was a small grass field at Shatin for recreational flying which in 1949 was being adapted for military use. An RAF airfield at Sek Kong was approaching completion.

not introduced until the late 1930s and were anyway usually by flying boat ('clipper'). The craft landed in the waters of Kowloon Bay; passengers and crew were ferried to a tented 'terminal' on the edge of the airfield.

Initially there was just one relatively short landing strip. It ran from west to east (or east to west depending upon the winds) across the top of the bay with Kowloon Peak looming close behind. As it stood, Kai Tak was not a long-term proposition as an international airport. Its inadequacies for future military and commercial aviation were recognized as early as 1938. Plans for a second runway were drawn up and sites for another airport were considered. The RAF investigated the Kam Tin Valley as the location of an alternative for its use: ground at Pat Heung was actually levelled off and an access road built but work was taken no further once Japanese forces advanced into Guangdong because the site was within artillery range of the border.[5] In October 1941 the Governor, Sir Mark Young, asked a visiting RAF expert to consider the suitability of Stonecutters Island, used by the Royal Navy, for adaptation into a base for fighter planes. Stonecutters had the attraction of not being within the territory leased under the 1898 Convention. But that turned out to be about its only attraction. The advice was that the island was not suitable because of the direction of the prevailing winds, the short runway and logistical problems of supplying a 'remote' island.[6]

During the Second World War the Japanese, who occupied Hong Kong for almost four years from December 1941, added a second hard strip at Kai Tak using prisoners of war, many of them RAF personnel who had been serving at the airport, as slave labour.[7] The second runway cut diagonally across the first, giving the runways a scissors-shape. Whichever runway was used, the safety margins were tight. Planes approached over high ground, suddenly sighted the airfield and descended steeply, often encountering winds from the hills on three sides. One passenger remembered that landing on a blustery day in the 1950s

> seemed like an all but suicidal exercise, the aircraft lowering itself crab-like, wobbly with gusts of cross-wind, nervously racing its engines and feathering its propellers, on to the small runway that ran parallel with the sea.[8]

---

5. The site is still largely vacant, an incongruous flat area of weeds and concrete at the foot of the Kai Kung Leng hill behind the villages of Sheung Che and Ha Che.
6. Hugh Farmer, 'Stonecutters Island Airport Proposal – pre and post WW2', The Industrial History of Hong Kong Group, 10 October 2020, https://industrialhistoryhk.org/stonecutters-island-airport-proposal-post-ww2/.
7. In the course of this the wall of Kowloon Walled City and a huge boulder carrying an ancient Chinese stone tablet commemorating the last Sung dynasty emperor (Sung Wong Toi) were destroyed for construction material. The tablet was retrieved and is displayed at a park at Ma Tau Chung, Kowloon City.
8. Jan Morris, *Hong Kong: Epilogue to an Empire* (Harmondsworth, Middlesex: Penguin, 1988), 155.

There had been many advances in aviation during the Second World War. Afterwards, larger and longer-range, multi-engined, propeller-driven passenger and cargo aircraft were introduced. The flying boat services dwindled, to be replaced by land-based aircraft from the growing airline industry.

One of the tasks of the Hong Kong Planning Unit in London during the war had been to draw up plans for a new airport. They considered a number of possible sites, including ones at east Lantau, north Lamma and Deep Bay, as well as at Kam Tin and Stonecutters again. But they alighted upon a valley in the Ping Shan district to the west of Yuen Long in the northwestern New Territories as the most desirable location. It so happened that one of the ships diverted to join Admiral Harcourt's task force that arrived to take over administration in September 1945 had on board a team from the RAF airport construction wing that had been destined for Okinawa. Instead they swiftly found themselves at work in Ping Shan.

The site was actually closer to the district of Hung Shui Kiu than Ping Shan. It covered an area of 7.5 square miles which provided for a runway more than a mile long and 55 feet wide capable of extension by another half mile and to double in width. It ran from Nai Wai village in the south, northeast through the settlements of Sun Fung Wai, Chung Uk Tsuen, Tin Sum and San Lee Tsuen to Shek Po and beyond. The southern part of the runway would have crossed the line of the Castle Peak Road and then would have proceeded roughly parallel to and east of today's West Rail line between Tin Shui Wai and Lam Tei. The air approaches to the runway would have been over the sea and a flat valley of padi fields, with hills (including Castle Peak) on either side. The project would have displaced hundreds of villagers and cut into their traditional hillsides and burial grounds.

The site for the new airport was surveyed; formation work began; construction workers were recruited; rock was cut from a nearby quarry; a small hill was removed. The villagers became alarmed about losing their fields, ancestral homes, temples and graves. Air Chief Marshall Sir Keith Park visited from England and inspected progress. Then in March 1946 work stopped. The villages affected by the project were dominated by the Tang clan whose elders had been ringleaders of the resistance to the British takeover of the New Territories in 1899.[9] Their current elders had protested about the proposed airport to the Nanking government which in turn had complained to the Hong Kong and British governments, pointing out that Britain had pledged in the 1898 Convention that there was to be no expropriation or expulsion of inhabitants from their land. The Convention was ambiguous because it

9. See Malcolm Merry, *The Unruly New Territories: Small Houses, Ancestral Estates, Illegal Structures, and Other Customary Land Practices of Rural Hong Kong* (Hong Kong: Hong Kong University Press, 2020); Patrick H. Hase, *The Six Day War of 1899: Hong Kong in the Age of Imperialism* (Hong Kong: Hong Kong University Press, 2008).

also said that land might be taken for fortifications and like official purposes provided fair compensation was paid. It seems that the RAF had not thought about compensation. The District Commissioner for the New Territories, John Barrow, sympathized with the villagers. So too did the Colonial Secretary, David MacDougall, who, ironically, had proposed the project when a member of the wartime Planning Unit. However, it was not sensible to antagonize the Tangs who were capable of making life difficult for local administrators, nor was it sensible to defy the Nationalist authorities since the site was only three miles from Chinese airspace.

A further reason for the cessation of work was that representatives of the British Overseas Airways Corporation found the planned airport would be unsuitable for its future aircraft, as well as being far from town. Under new agreed international civil airport standards the southern approach through a valley would be too confined and the initial runway too narrow. Although the RAF said that the airstrip would be adequate for its purposes, the final blow was dealt by the government in London which decided that it could not afford the scheme. The work at Hung Shui Kiu was not entirely wasted: the RAF placed mobile radar units on the site during the 1950s. Since the 1980s the area has been developed with blocks of flats, village houses and other facilities.

Nevertheless, it was foreseen that Hong Kong could become an important civil aviation hub, connecting the East with the West, if it had a good airport. In March 1947 visiting technical representatives of air ministries and airlines concluded that conversion of Kai Tak for modern aircraft was impracticable and recommended reclamation at Stonecutters as an alternative. But this proved prohibitively expensive. Instead, attention turned to Deep Bay, a few miles to the northwest of Ping Shan. Along the coast of the bay an airport might be built, partly on reclaimed land, which would be larger than Kai Tak and the aborted Hung Shui Kiu site and would have safer approaches. But it would be much more expensive and even further from town. It too fell victim to the prevailing austerity.

So Hong Kong had to continue to make do with Kai Tak. In fact, it was to make do with Kai Tak for more than 50 years, mainly by building a long and extendable new runway on reclamation into Kowloon Bay. But in 1949 that runway was a decade away. Instead, to accommodate new aircraft, one of the existing runways was extended across the road (then called Clearwater Bay Road, now Kwun Tong Road) which arched around the northern end of the apron: barriers were installed across the carriageway, bringing traffic to a halt whenever a larger aircraft was about to take off.[10] Direct services to Hong Kong, with many intermediate stops, began from London and Sydney.

10. The long runway protruding into the waters of Kowloon Bay, at right angles to the original landing strips, was not added until large jet aircraft became prevalent in the late 1950s; it was later extended to take ever-larger passenger planes.

The introduction of dozens of mainland aeroplanes based at the airport over the spring and summer of 1949 made for a crowded apron. Eventually more than 80 airliners were parked there by CNAC and CATC, together with a large amount of spare parts and other equipment. CNAC built and operated a workshop on the airport perimeter. The aircraft were placed near the maintenance hangars of HAECO and JAMCO.[11] Some were coated with substances to deter rusting. The planes included the latest types of passenger and freight transports: Douglas DC3s, Convair 440s, Curtiss C46s and Douglas DC4 Skymasters, all US-made and alleged by William Donovan to have been acquired on lend-lease terms using finance supplied from America.[12] Actually, only 45 had ever been US government property. These had been sold as surplus, not leased or lent, to the Chinese airlines or government for less than a tenth of their original cost. The US government had no financial interest in them. Sixteen had been acquired new from the manufacturer. The rest had been purchased second-hand from US airlines. One of the planes was for training and one other was an amphibious craft suitable for patrol duties.[13] In addition to the planes, each airline had workshop facilities for repair and maintenance and for storage of spare parts at the airfield. These all occupied space: conditions were becoming difficult.

The authorities object

The expansion of the RAF presence afforded an opportunity, or perhaps an excuse, for the Hong Kong administration to request the Chinese airlines to remove their planes and operations from Kai Tak. It was suggested that Formosa (Taiwan) would be a more appropriate home for them. The Governor, Sir Alexander Grantham, did not want the embarrassment of harbouring the planes if and when there was a change in regime in China. He could foresee the potential for difficulty if staff of the airlines within the colony were to transfer allegiance from Nationalist to Communist. With refugees from the civil war pouring into Hong Kong and many bringing with them loyalties to one side or the other, he also feared the potential for disputes that would disrupt the peace of the colony. 'I remember well', Grantham later wrote,

> recommending to two vice-presidents of Pan-American, who were on the Board of CNAC, that the aircraft should be taken to Formosa since most probably the British government would be giving *de jure* recognition to the Peking

11. Hongkong Aircraft Engineering Company and Jardine Aircraft Maintenance Company.
12. According to evidence given by Livingston Merchant of the State Department to a Senate sub-committee in March 1950 there were 23 Douglas DC-3s or C-47s, 36 Curtiss C-46s, five Douglas DC-4s, five new Convair 440s, one North American AT-6 and one PBY.
13. State Department evidence to Senate Appropriations Committee, March 1950.

regime, and then we should have no option but to hand over the planes to the Chinese government should they claim them, as they were likely to do.

However, the vice-presidents would not agree to do this, claiming that the civil airports in Formosa would not be able to accommodate the planes and that, if they did take them there, it would be resented by Peking. In fact, Pan Am was hoping to recommence flying in China. Grantham described their claim about the inadequacies of Taiwanese airfields as 'nonsense, because that is where they finally went', but in this he was mistaken.[14]

The requests for the airlines to relocate were nevertheless made several times as Communist forces moved closer to Hong Kong. The Governor repeated the request and a warning of difficulties ahead directly to William L. Bond, the vice-president of Pan Am in charge of local operations, but with no success. Eventually notice to quit Kai Tak had to be expressly given to CNAC.

It has been claimed that in addition to commercial reasons the planes were not moved in mid-1949 probably because of a wish (presumably American) to embroil Britain and China in an argument.[15] No evidence had been suggested in support of this theory and the proponent seems confused about the course of events, stating that the Peking government demanded that the planes be handed over to them and that this was resisted by 'the Civil Air Transport Corporation'. However, the demand and the resistance came well after the middle of 1949, for Chennault and Willauer of the CAT airline did not intervene until the end of November that year and their corporation CAT, Inc. (together with the US government) did not enter the scene until December. It was the executives of the two airlines who refused to move the planes. At that stage, the contestants for control of the aircraft and of the airlines were the rival regimes in the Chinese civil war.

Half of the CNAC accommodation at the airfield was requisitioned for other uses by the Kai Tak authorities. CNAC found replacement facilities for their workshop, equipment and parts at nearby Bailey's Yard which its shareholder Pan Am purchased, but left its aircraft on the airfield. Pan Am foresaw that once conditions became settled in China, the market there would be even more lucrative than it had been before and thought that if their operations were at a neutral venue rather than Formosa, the new government in China would be better disposed towards their airline. They were neither the first nor the last Western businessmen to fall victim to the mirage of the China market. The CNAC Operations Manager at Kai Tak, Mr Alison, 'bitterly resisted the instructions to move out'.[16] Replacement storage space was found by CATC

14. Alexander Grantham, *Via Ports: From Hong Kong to Hong Kong* (Hong Kong: Hong Kong University Press, 1965), 162; the fate of the planes is dealt with in Chapter 19.
15. Peter Lowe, *Containing the Cold War in East Asia: British Policies towards Japan, China and Korea, 1948–53* (Manchester: Manchester University Press, 1997), 159.
16. Foreign Office memorandum, 'Chinese Aircraft at Hong Kong', 18 March 1950, chronology.

close to the airfield, at the premises of the New Asiatic Chemical Company, a mainland pharmaceutical manufacturer.

Meanwhile, US Secretary of State Dean Acheson and British Foreign Secretary Ernest Bevin met to discuss Far Eastern policy. The question of what to do in the event of a Communist takeover in China would have been pressing. Britain, supported by France, favoured early recognition of the impending Communist government. The Americans chose to differ. They supported the Nationalist sea blockade of Chinese ports now under Communist control. They began to withdraw their diplomats from China, closing all their consulates except for a reduced presence at Shanghai and Nanking.

Emergency regulations

In August 1949 the Governor promulgated new regulations for the control of ships and aircraft. Using a measure designed for emergencies, he took power to detain disputed aircraft 'if it appears to him to be necessary or expedient in the public interest to do so'.[17] The regulations were not prompted by the influx of Chinese aeroplanes to Kai Tak but by the proximity of the Chinese civil war to Hong Kong. As their name, the Emergency (Control of Ships and Aircraft) Regulations, implies, the rules were directed as much at sea vessels as at aircraft. They were intended as a safeguard against infringement of the colony's neutrality by naval ships or military planes of one side or the other. The local authorities were particularly concerned that Nationalist forces might attempt to use Hong Kong as a refuelling base.

These precautionary regulations reflected the determination in Whitehall and at Government House that both the United Kingdom and Hong Kong should remain neutral as between the warring sides in China. The legislation under which they were made, the Emergency Regulations Ordinance, was a ruler's dream for it enabled the Governor to make any regulations whatsoever that he may consider desirable in the public interest. The only pre-requisite was that he perceived there to be an emergency or public danger. There was no need to obtain legislative consent to the regulations, either before or after they had been made. There was no limit as to their subject matter. There was even no requirement to declare a state of emergency. The Ordinance had passed through the government-controlled Legislative Council in the course of one day in February 1922.

It may well be imagined that some unusual circumstance gave rise to this dictatorial legislation. This was so, for it was occasioned by the first successful mass industrial action in the history of Hong Kong or indeed China. This

17. Emergency (Control of Ships and Aircraft) Regulations (21 August 1949), made under the Emergency Regulations Ordinance, Cap 241.

was a strike by seamen protesting against poor pay and conditions, the value of their static wages having been eroded by inflation and deductions during and after the First World War. The seamen attracted sympathy and support from other workers. Sir Reginald Stubbs, one of the least impressive of Hong Kong's colonial leaders, mistakenly perceived the strike to be politically motivated. When intimidation occurred and a call to make the strike general went up, Stubbs and the employers panicked and introduced the Emergency Regulations Ordinance. It proved futile, for the workers simply withdrew to their homes in Guangdong, on foot because the government suspended the rail service, disdaining sometimes violent attempts by police to stop them. The employers, though well represented in the corridors of power, had to give in. The regulations were withdrawn but the Ordinance was too valuable to the authorities to be abolished. It was used regularly in subsequent decades to deal with political and economic threats as well as war, disease and natural disasters. It remained, even into the era of Human Rights Conventions and constitutionally protected liberties, to be activated whenever the government feared it might be overwhelmed, the most recent occasion being during the civil unrest of late 2019.[18]

In 1949 there was of course no question of using the new regulations to detain the aircraft that had flown in from the mainland. On the contrary, Sir Alexander Grantham wanted the aircraft to leave. But there was to come a time during the saga surrounding those aircraft at which his masters, if not the Governor himself, wished to detain the aircraft. It was then that the Control of Ships and Aircraft Regulations might prove useful.

18. *Kwok Wing Hang v Chief Executive in Council* [2021] 1 HKC 120, CFA.

7

Insurrection

Moving towards recognition

By the beginning of September 1949 the air fleets, equipment, machinery, workshops and offices of CNAC and CATC were safely in Hong Kong, along with general managers and hundreds of staff and their families. The directors and some senior management were in Taipei.

Western governments had been anticipating the communist takeover of China for some months and debating how to respond to it. They had been discussing this both internally and between each other. A Foreign Office paper produced for the British Cabinet in December 1948 had recommended that Britain should co-ordinate its China policy with allies and consider the effect of that policy on British colonies in the Far East. The paper reflected upon the effect of a communist victory on Britain's commercial interests in China, the future of Hong Kong, and nationalist movements in southeast Asia. There was particular concern about the effect that any acceptance of a communist government would have upon the emergency in Malaya led by local communist Chinese. The British High Commissioner for Southeast Asia, Malcolm MacDonald, and the Governor of Singapore, Franklin Gimson, opposed early recognition because they feared it would give a communist government the power to appoint consuls throughout the region and thereby embolden the insurgents.

The State Department in Washington accepted the need for caution and the desirability of international co-ordination, and if possible a common front, in the acceptance of any new government in China. Like the Foreign Office, the department saw the Chinese nationalism of the CCP as presenting an opportunity to separate it from Soviet communism and agreed that cultivating contact with the communists would be helpful in achieving this. But the USA did not have the commercial and colonial interests to protect that Britain had, and Britain did not have a domestic political faction vehemently advocating against recognition like the China lobby in the US. Furthermore, the British attitude towards recognition was narrower and more pragmatic than the

American which tended to be moralistic and emotional. Acheson laid down three conditions or principles for US recognition of a new Chinese government. First, the new government must have factual control over the territory of the nation. Second, it must have the ability and willingness to discharge the nation's international obligations. Third, it must have the general acquiescence of the people of the nation. Britain and the Commonwealth countries had little dispute with the first and third of these principles but the second was not universally accepted. Furthermore, to many American politicians the principles did not go far enough.

In August 1949 Sir Alexander Grantham in Hong Kong had received through intermediaries a message, purportedly originating from Chou En-lai, to the British government to the effect that Chou was in favour of establishing relations with the West although there were conflicting views within the Chinese Communist Party. At about the same time similar assurances had been given by senior communist officials in Shanghai.

Upon the declaration of the People's Republic on 1 October 1949 diplomatic representatives of other countries, mostly still in Nanking, were invited by the CPG to recognize the new government. Only Russia and its acolytes promptly obliged. Ironically, they alone had followed the Kuomintang government to Canton earlier in the year. The US, which had already closed its diplomatic missions in China, ignored the invitation. Britain, determined to be neutral in the continuing Chinese civil conflict, held back from formal recognition too. However, the British government hoped for friendly relations with the new regime so as to revive UK business and trade with China.

During 1948 and 1949 Peter Scarlett of the Foreign Office's Far East Department had been encouraging British consuls in China to attempt to make contact with the new authorities as their areas came under communist control. Their efforts to do so had been largely in vain. Nevertheless, in Peking the British consul W. G. Graham thought it would be a good idea to respond to the newly declared government's invitation by approaching the communist authorities who had been in charge of the city for some months prior to the declaration. On 5 October he sent a diplomatic note to Chou En-lai, whom he addressed as the Minister of Foreign Affairs of the Central People's Government, stating that the UK government was 'carefully studying the situation resulting from the formation of' the CPG, recalling the friendly and mutually advantageous commercial and political relations that had existed between Britain and China for generations and expressing the hope that they would continue in future. The note then suggested that informal relations should be established between British consular officers and 'the appropriate authorities' in the territory under the control of' the CPG 'for the greater convenience of both governments and promotion of trade between the two countries'.

At that time the usual British practice in respect of the acceptance of unconstitutional governments (i.e., those which had seized power by force) was to proceed cautiously in accepting their legitimacy. The UK government would not use recognition as an instrument of change or as a matter to be bargained over. It would react to reality so that once a new regime was in apparent control of a state or part of a state, the UK would recognize that regime as being the government in fact of that state or part. This was de facto recognition. Only once the regime was discerned to be so firmly in control of the great majority of the state's territory as to be its permanent government would formal, or de jure, recognition be extended so that, in British eyes, the new regime had replaced the former government. This approach had been used, for instance, in the case of the Spanish Civil War during the late 1930s and in the case of the communist takeover of Poland from its wartime government-in-exile following the Second World War.

The two-stage process meant that there would be an intermediate period in which Britain would recognize two governments of a country: the government de jure which had not yet been fully or formally replaced and the insurgent regime which was regarded as the government in fact of part, maybe most, of the country's territory. In early October 1949 and for several weeks thereafter, China was at this intermediate stage, as it had also been for most of the previous months of 1949.

Graham received no reply to his note, unsurprisingly, because Chou En-lai was interested in full recognition only. The British Foreign Office was later to deny that the note was intended to accord even de facto recognition and insisted that Graham had been acting precipitously and without the knowledge of his superiors. This is difficult to accept, given Scarlett's encouragement of informal relations. Indeed, the essence of the note had been set out by Sir Ralph Stevenson, the British ambassador at Nanking, in a message sent to London on 1 October, having consulted his Indian and Australian counterparts. Nevertheless, Arthur Ringwalt of the American embassy in London, who had close contact with the Foreign Office, was in no doubt that Graham was acting on his own initiative, perhaps without realizing the consequences: 'It caused a great deal of stir back in London,' he recalled, 'the British were taken aback.'[1]

As far as most countries were concerned, caution was called for. The Communists were not yet in charge of the whole of China. Five provinces remained, at least nominally, under the control of the Nationalists. Their

1. *Civil Air Transport Incorporated v Central Air Transport Corporation (Hong Kong)* [1953] AC 70 at 88; Peter Lowe, *Containing the Cold War in East Asia: British Policies towards Japan, China and Korea, 1948–53* (Manchester: Manchester University Press, 1997), 106–107; Arthur Ringwalt, 'Oral History Interview with Arthur R. Ringwalt', interview by Richard D. McKinzie, 5 June 1974, trumanlibrary.gov/library/oral-histories/ringwalt. See also Chapters 18 and 20.

government still operated from Canton. Chiang Kai-shek and many of his supporters were in Taiwan. The large southern island of Hainan was also still under Nationalist control. Most felt that at that point recognition would be premature. The British and French governments were in favour of early recognition and had discussed this with US representatives in June, but the USA demurred and asked them not to recognize the CPG until consultations had been completed. Differences of approach had begun to emerge. During August Ernest Bevin had discussed recognition, as well as trade and the evacuation of foreign citizens, with Lewis Douglas the US Ambassador in London and the differences were apparent. Britain wanted its diplomats and businessmen to stay in China and attempt to influence events; the US was closing its consulates and advising its citizens to leave. In September the British and American foreign ministers, Bevin and Acheson, and their advisers met in Washington DC to discuss Far Eastern policy but no common decision on recognition was made.[2]

It seems that behind public professions of co-operation and unity of purpose, the September meetings had been tense, if not acrimonious. Despite their disenchantment with Chiang Kai-shek and his obvious failure in the civil war, the Americans felt that they had to continue to support him, if only as a symbol of their resistance to the advance of communism. The State Department wanted to isolate the CPG and had begun to evacuate US citizens, diplomats and businesses. The US had supported the Nationalist blockade of ports and had imposed an embargo on export of strategic materials to communist areas which Britain had half-heartedly followed and which the US now wished to extend. The US saw the denial of recognition as part of that approach. Also, it thought recognition unpalatable because it would acknowledge that the Communists had won the civil war.

At that stage British policy-makers expected that the Americans would move towards recognition in tandem with them. They imagined that the US would be more realistic after the mid-term congressional elections in November and that ChiNat anger had subsided. Acheson accepted that Britain would pursue a different course from the US because of Britain's commercial interests in China and need to protect Hong Kong. Nevertheless, he thought that a joint policy was possible. The Foreign Office, convinced that its longer experience of China gave it greater insight, wished to maintain diplomatic contact and support British business to stay in the PRC to provide what it called 'a foot in the door'. It was not convinced that Chinese communism was the same as the Soviet version and harboured hopes of enticing the former away from the latter through influence and trade.

2. Evan Luard, *Britain and China* (London: Chatto and Windus, 1962), 76; Qiang Zhai, *The Dragon, the Lion, and the Eagle: Chinese-British-American Relations, 1949–1958* (Kent, OH: Kent State University Press, 1994), 39–41.

The Foreign Office's analysts concluded that the Americans, their policy of supporting the Nationalists having failed, had now no policy for China. The analysts failed to discern that a replacement US policy was in fact forming, a policy of isolating the CPG derived from the aim of containing communism. The withdrawal of US consular representatives and nationals was part of that emergent policy, as were the embargoes and continued support for the Nationalists. It was the opposite of the British approach of attempted engagement. Whereas the British were guided by pragmatism and regarded the PRC as a state with which to do business and a fact to be lived with, the Americans were driven by the ideology of anti-communism. They viewed the CCP in geopolitical terms as related to Soviet expansionism.

That ideology, coupled with the Truman Doctrine and emotional attachment to the Nationalists, pointed towards the US sustaining Chiang Kai-shek in Formosa. The island could become 'free China' and be part of a chain of territories hemming in the PRC to its east. The same ideology was to underlie the US attitude towards the fate of the aircraft at Kai Tak.

For the moment, however, both the American and the British administrations doubted whether Formosa could be saved and a decision on recognition of the PRC did not seem pressing. Bevin said there was no rush and urged closer co-operation. Acheson cautioned that recognition might not be a strong card to play to keep China away from Russia but he insisted, somewhat against the evidence, that America's differences from the UK arose from the two countries' different situations and not from their policies. Bevin thought the differences were of tactics not objectives. At the end of the meetings they agreed that everyone would watch and wait.[3]

After the announcement of the founding of the PRC, circumstances continued to evolve. On 12 October the Nationalists abandoned Canton, the original home of the Kuomintang. They retreated to Chungking, the remote bastion from which Chiang Kai-shek had defied the Japanese only a few years earlier. Voices in favour of prompt recognition began to be raised. In Britain a group of members of parliament proposed a parliamentary motion calling for recognition. In America the *Washington Post* newspaper also called for it, although the *New York Times* urged caution.[4]

'He's done it'

After a copy of the note sent to Chou En-lai by the British Consul in Peking fell into French hands, the Foreign Office was forced to reveal its existence to the Americans. The office explained the consul's 'demarche' as an unfortunate

3. R. E. Watson, 'The Foreign Office and Policy-Making in China, 1945–50: Anglo-American Relations and the Recognition of Communist China' (PhD thesis; University of Leeds, 1996).
4. Lowe, *Containing the Cold War*, 107–108.

accident and that it was not meant to amount to recognition of the CPG. Sir Ralph Stevenson, the originator of the text of the note, insouciantly argued that because there had been no reply to it, the note did not amount to recognition. This was unconvincing since recognition is a unilateral act which is not dependent on acceptance by the recipient for its existence. At the Foreign Office Sir William Strang, the Permanent Secretary, thought that delivery of the note constituted de facto recognition. Beckett, the legal adviser, when told that Graham had not intended his note to constitute de facto recognition, replied that this did not matter, 'he's done it'.

The Americans thought so, too. They were incensed about both the note and about not being forewarned of it: just a few weeks earlier at Washington the countries had agreed to consult and act together. Other allies were angered too. Foreign Office officials, whilst conceding that the consul's actions had been 'too precipitous', lamely explained that, since they knew that the CPG was not interested in anything less than full relations, the note had simply been intended to 'keep things sweet'. They argued somewhat desperately that since the note did not amount to recognition, no warning to the US had been necessary. They also said that they had sent a message to the State Department in advance but that by mistake it had been dispatched by airmail rather than cable. Sir Esler Dening put the blame on the Foreign Office's staff being short-handed and overworked. The State Department concluded that the incident was either the result of uncharacteristic British diplomatic disorganization or had been deliberate, and they were inclined to believe the second. The careful wording of the note is inconsistent with the notion that its sending was unplanned and was all the work of a well-intentioned maverick. The timing of the note also suggests that it was a deliberate response to Chou En-lai's invitation to other nations to accord recognition to the PRC. President Truman thought that Britain had not 'played very squarely'.

Acheson and Douglas protested on behalf of the US about both the content of the note and the lack of consultation. Bevin apologized to Douglas on 18 October and reprimanded his officials. That same day Sir Ralph Stevenson left China for 'consultations' in London.[5] This was a prelude to the withdrawal of recognition from the KMT. But Britain wanted any change to be in consultation with its Commonwealth partners and other friendly governments. A conference of British diplomatic and colonial representatives in the Far East was due to be held in Malaya in November where the question of recognition of the Communist government was bound to be discussed.

5. Luard, *Britain and China*, 77.

Apprehension

One can well imagine the thoughts which occupied the minds of the hundreds of Chinese staff in Hong Kong of the two airlines CNAC and CATC as summer turned to autumn in 1949. They would have had little to do once the aeroplanes had been decommissioned—no passengers to attend to, no cargo to deal with, no baggage to check, no tickets to issue, no manifests to draw up—and so plenty of time in which to contemplate and discuss the future. Any excitement of being based in Hong Kong would have soon dissipated. So would the attraction and prestige of working in a new and glamorous industry. They were far from their families in a British colony on the edge of, but outside, their homeland.

What was to happen to that homeland? A complete takeover by the Communists, almost unthinkable only three years previously, now seemed inevitable. What sort of people were these Communists? They seemed very patriotic and to want the best for China. Rumour suggested that they treated people well. But the people in question were the poor peasants and the industrial proletariat, not well-paid employees in a modern, Westernized industry.

The aircrew and other staff would have realized that the likelihood was that their airline would not be able to stay in Hong Kong. It was known around Kai Tak that the Hong Kong government wanted both CNAC and CATC to leave. The most obvious alternative would be Taipei, to which many Nationalist enterprises and civilians were in the process of decamping. The prospect of living on a besieged island, cut off from their relatives and friends, was not appealing. Their families might even be held hostage as punishment for their going there and as an inducement for their return. Sixty-five years later one of the workers' representatives, ninety-year-old Xie Jingwan, recalled: 'At that time more than 2000 employees saw the war of liberation and felt there was no future in moving to Taiwan. Some resigned and found a ship to return to Shanghai and home.'

The airlines' staff would have taken some solace from being employed in state-owned enterprises. The new government would surely simply take the airlines over and continue to run them. There would be new people in charge at the top but that would probably be the only change. In China there would be more opportunities to expand an airline industry and more job opportunities to go with it. Airlines there would need their talent. The Nationalists, having fled to Chungking and Taipei, would be out of the picture. But that assumed that the airlines and their aeroplanes returned to China or at least remained in Hong Kong.

On 11 September 1949 a trade union was founded for airport workers. The Hong Kong and Kowloon Aviation Workers Union was affiliated with the communist-inclined Federation of Trade Unions. Initially it had 400 members, mainly working for CATC and CNAC. Union leaders were in touch with Peking. According to Xie, Premier Chou En-lai's instructions at that time were to 'refuse to move to Taiwan, strive for talent, and strive for an uprising'. The union found the airlines' discontented employees to be a ready source of new members. Its leaders formed an action group of airport employees to organize support for an uprising. Xie was one of them. They managed to sign up more than 2000 of the workers. 'People felt hopeless at the prospect of relocating to Taiwan and fighting to earn a living,' Xie explained, 'many wanted to return to China.'

When on 1 October Mao proclaimed the People's Republic of China, he had declared that China had at last stood up. Airline employees in Hong Kong, especially those who were members of communist-infiltrated trade unions, might well have believed this to be welcome. One of the first acts of the new regime in Peking was to issue a decree dismissing all the Nationalist ministers, including the Minister of Communications who was responsible for CATC and influential with the board of CNAC. New people were in charge of the air ministry, too. Yet senior management in Hong Kong was still taking orders from the old bosses. Rumours of discontent among staff at CATC and CNAC, which had been circulating for some time, intensified.[6] There was a division of opinion among the staff as to which regime to support.

Middle and lower-level employees were easily persuaded by the union's action group. Senior members of management and many of the pilots felt loyalty towards the Nationalist government which had employed them. This feeling was more intense among pilots who had served in the Chinese Air Force. The CPG sent agents to lobby the general managers of the airlines.

Insurgency

Most of the staff eventually took matters into their own hands. During October about 300 of them refused to take orders from the senior staff and declared allegiance to the new regime. They included the general managers (or managing directors), some of the other directors, CNAC's expatriate American operations manager Mr Alison, and many of the aircrew. Most of the American staff at CATC agreed with Alison. The majority was supported by the trade union of airport workers. They seized the planes and prevented the old management and its supporters from having access to them.[7] The defecting employees took out an advertisement in newspapers listing their names and announcing the termination of their employment.

6. William M. Leary, *Perilous Missions: Civil Air Transport and CIA Covert Operations in Asia* (Tuscaloosa: University of Alabama Press, 1984), 91.
7. Foreign Office memorandum, 'Chinese Aircraft at Hong Kong', 18 March 1950, 2 and chronology.

To the rebels the point was simply that the planes belonged to the government of China and the government of China was now communist. The attitude of Alison and the expatriates was coloured by Pan Am's desire to continue in business on the mainland. It has been suggested that the general managers received monetary inducements to change allegiance and that they may also have been encouraged to do so by the threat of exposure of financial irregularities in their airline's accounts.[8] One cannot rule out, however, that the suggestions originated in rumours put out by Whiting Willauer or some other pro-Nationalist source.

In Peking on 1 November the new Minister of Communications in the Central People's Government purported to appoint replacement directors of CNAC and declared that the airline's head office was to be in Shanghai again.

The China National Resources Commission faced a similar uprising. It held a stockpile of minerals in Hong Kong which was taken over by defecting employees. The revolt spread to other institutions of the Chinese government, including China Merchants and the Bank of China.

A daring departure

Matters took an unexpected turn a week later. On 9 November, C. Y. Liu of CNAC and the general manager of CATC, Colonel Chen Cheuk Lin (C. L. Chen), took a dozen of the planes, all transports with crews, to northern China. Two were CATC planes, the rest belonged to CNAC. One aircraft, a Convair 240 piloted by Gordon Poon (Pan Guoding), flew to Peking. The others went to Tientsin. Their journeys took seven hours. They were pursued part of the way by KMT fighters but were protected by low cloud.[9] Altogether there were about 40 crew members on the twelve planes.

The Convair that went to Peking was met with great ceremony. The next day, Chou En-lai declared all the aircraft to be the 'sacred property' of the People's Republic of China.[10] The defections had obviously been arranged with PRC contacts in advance. Permission to take off had not been sought from the Kai Tak authorities.

Typical of the pilots who took part in this daring operation were Captain T. L. Chan (Dali Chen) and Captain C. H. Tang (Tang Chong Huang).

8. Martha Byrd, *Chennault: Giving Wings to the Tiger* (Tuscaloosa: University of Alabama Press, 1987), 335.
9. Judgments of Sir Gerard Howe CJ in *Civil Air Transport Incorporated v Central Air Transport Corporation* (1951) 35 HKLR 22, 37–43, and Gould J in *Civil Air Transport Incorporated v Central Air Transport Corporation* (1951) 35 HKLR 162, 172–175; Luard, *Britain and China*, 157; Victor S. Kaufman, 'The United States, Great Britain and the CAT Controversy', *Journal of Contemporary History* 40, no. 1 (2005): 95–113; Byrd, *Chennault*.
10. William M. Leary, 'Aircraft and Anti-Communists: CAT in Action, 1942–52', *China Quarterly* 52 (1972): 654, 656. The Convair, with one engine missing, is displayed at a military aviation museum in Beijing.

Both had graduated from the Chinese Air Force Academy in the late 1930s, both had served as pilots in the air force, both were married with family on the mainland. They were firm friends. Each had flown over the Hump hundreds of times during the war with Japan. In 1943 they both had joined CNAC. Contemporary photographs show them as handsome, fit, confident individuals.[11]

C. L. Chen had left an emergency committee of executive and technical staff to manage CATC's affairs whilst he was away. The committee members included the directors of the business, finance and operations departments of the airlines. Chen was particularly concerned that the committee should guard against Nationalist representatives sabotaging the remaining aircraft or gaining control of them and flying them to Formosa.[12] Once he arrived in the mainland, Chen reported to the Civil Aeronautical Administration of the CPG.

Chen and C. Y. Liu must have been in touch with Peking for some time before the daring flight, for the planes were expected and welcomed on arrival. Chen rather skated over this in the evidence he later gave to the court in Hong Kong. There he said 'on 9 November, 1949, I accepted the orders of the Central People's Government of the People's Republic of China and went to Peking with the intention of continuing to carry out the objects for which' the airlines' property was to be used—in other words, to continue to operate air routes within China and to Hong Kong and Bangkok. But there was probably more to his and Liu's visit to Peking than this. They needed to discuss with the new authorities how to move all the other planes back to the mainland, along with the tons of valuable equipment stored at and around Kai Tak.

One of the twelve planes later returned to Hong Kong, so 71 remained on the ground at Kai Tak.[13] Why did all of the planes, or at least a greater proportion, not fly off to Tientsin? This may be because the operation was clandestine and the perpetrators calculated that a dozen was the maximum number of aircraft that would be able to get away before the airport authorities intervened. Or perhaps they felt that a small number had a better chance of surviving the long flight intact and unmolested. A third possibility is that twelve was the greatest number that could be adequately crewed with a navigator and wireless operator as well as a captain and co-pilot from those willing to go. In fact, according to Xie, initially the crew of 20 CATC craft agreed to participate but within two days the number had halved and in the end only two CATC planes participated. Xie attributed this to CATC's being under the

11. See cnac.org/tlchan01.htm and cnac.org/chtang01.htm (accessed 9 September 2021).
12. Howe CJ, *CATI v CATC*, 22 and 36.
13. Different sources provide differing numbers but 71 is the likeliest. Steve Tsang gives 71, as does Leary and as did the State Department. Luard gives 73; the British Foreign Office, 70. Some accounts do not allow for the one aircraft that returned to Hong Kong, others have an enlarged impression of the original number.

control of the Air Force. Most of its pilots had been in the force and they were reluctant to revolt.

Certainly not all pilots wished to make the journey. It would be hazardous and the prospect of living under totalitarian government may not have appealed. Personal circumstances would influence the decision. For instance, Moon F. Chin, an older pilot who had flown for CNAC during the war and joined CATC after the war, chose to stay and serve the latter in Taiwan. He was, however, Chinese-American with family in the USA. Also, by the late 1940s he held a position at CATC with executive responsibilities: he chose and bought aircraft on the airline's behalf. Moon Chin was not the only pilot to refuse to move back to the mainland. There were in all 37 American citizens among the pilots of the two airlines, most of whom were also reservists in the US armed forces. They resisted invitations to join their colleagues in China, despite attractive financial offers.[14]

A hearty welcome

The insurgency may have been expected around Kai Tak and in Peking but elsewhere it came as a shock. The Communists hailed it as a feat of patriotism that had prevented the airlines from moving to Taiwan. Chairman Mao sent a personal message of congratulation to the defectors. On 12 November the Premier, Chou En-lai, addressed a letter to both Liu and Chen and 'All Officers and Workmen' of the two airlines. 'My hearty welcome to you who rise gloriously to uphold the cause under the guidance of the two General Managers Liu and Chen,' it began. Chou continued:

> I hereby accept in the name of the Cabinet of the People's Central Government of the Chinese People's Republic the telegraphic request made by you on 9.11.1949, declare the China National Aviation Corporation and the Central Air Transport Corporation to be the property of the Chinese People's Republic and exercise control of the said China National Aviation Corporation and the said Central Air Transport Corporation on behalf of the People's Central Government.

Chou then reappointed Liu to be General Manager of CNAC and Chen to be General Manager of CATC.

Chou went on to express the hope that the staff remaining in Hong Kong would 'unite in a body under the guidance of the two General Managers, heighten their precautions, shatter the secret plots of the reactionaries, bear the responsibility of protecting the assets and wait for further instructions'. The living costs of all officers and workers would be borne by the CPG, the letter promised. It closed by expressing the hope that 'you will stick to the

14. Karl Lott Rankin, *China Assignment* (Seattle: University of Washington Press, 1964), 20.

position of patriots, strive to make progress and exert yourselves in the cause of establishing the civil aviation enterprise of New China'. Apparently the CPG intended to operate the airlines through CATC and CNAC rather than to set up new structures.

In the end some 1700 employees of the airlines returned to China, including pilots and technicians who would be vital to the establishment of an aviation industry in the PRC. Xie was among them: he 'resolutely flew north and returned to embrace the motherland'. It was however a struggle to set up airlines there. This partly explains the subsequent efforts to extract from Hong Kong not only the planes but also the great and valuable amount of other stock, plant and equipment that both airlines had there.

Whitey springs into action

The dissent among the staff at CNAC and CATC in Hong Kong during October and early November 1949 had been viewed with mounting concern by Whiting Willauer. He had been working long hours himself running CAT's services to, from and within the mainland. Those services were in high demand from passengers fleeing the Communist advance.

The sudden flight of a dozen of the airliners from Kai Tak on 9 November was a shock to Willauer and Chennault. It showed that all the planes might easily be lost to the Communists unless action was taken. Furthermore it undermined morale amongst those CATC and CNAC staff who had remained loyal to the old set-up.

Given his onerous duties and the fact that the planes belonged to rivals of his airline, it might seem strange that Whitey Willauer was concerned about the departure of CNAC and CATC planes. But both he and Chennault had been doing all in their power to resist the Communist advance. For some time Chennault had been urging his contacts in Washington DC to do more to help the Nationalists. He and Willauer feared that the aircraft might be used in an invasion of Formosa. Intelligence suggested that the Communists were training paratroops for such an invasion. Willauer later said that he and Chennault felt that if the PLA 'got those transport planes and put them together with the Red paratroops, considering the chaos which existed on Formosa at that time, it would have been a pushover for the Reds to have taken Formosa'.[15] It might be added that a Communist invasion would have jeopardized their business links with the Nationalists and undermined American security. Perhaps more realistic is the suggestion that was made at a US Senate sub-committee hearing

15. Leary, 'Aircraft and Anti-Communists', 656.

that once invaders had secured an airfield in Formosa, the planes could be used to ferry troops to and from there and to other areas of the island.[16]

Certainly in November 1949 invasion of Formosa was a logical next step for the CPG. In fact during the summer of 1949 Mao had instructed the PLA to prepare such an invasion. Chou En-lai had suggested purchasing aircraft from the USSR and sending recruits there to receive air training with a view to an invasion in 1950. In November 1949 Mao decided to develop a navy for coastal defence against an anticipated Nationalist-US assault from Formosa and for a possible PLA attack on the island. He intended to ask the USSR for air and naval supplies during his forthcoming visit to Moscow.[17]

Willauer realized that if something was not done soon, all the aircraft would be lost. He determined to go to Taipei immediately and talk to those now responsible for the airlines. He expected to find confusion and indecision there. He wanted to obtain authority to represent the Nationalist government in Hong Kong and to do whatever he considered necessary in order to 'neutralize' the planes, as he put it.

16. By Senator William Knowland (R, California) based on 'what I believe to be competent authority': meeting of sub-committee on appropriations, 27 March 1950.
17. Zhai, *The Dragon, the Lion, and the Eagle*, 96–97.

8

The Tussle for Control

Willauer flew to Taipei on 10 November 1949. There he found General Chow, commander of the Nationalist air force, in a state of distress. Willauer's plan was to seek authority to represent the Nationalist government in matters concerning the two airlines, including their aeroplanes, in Hong Kong. He had prepared a memorandum for Chiang Kai-shek.

The memorandum warned that the defections of employees and loss of all the planes would place Taiwan in danger of invasion and undermine the morale of loyal staff and of Chiang's remaining supporters who would see that their last means of escape had disappeared. As a result, panic might spread in the parts of China remaining in Nationalist hands, it claimed.[1] Willauer asked to see the Generalissimo to explain the gravity of the situation. An appointment was made for 8:30 the next morning.

Willauer duly met Chiang, delivered the memo and requested permission to 'neutralize' the remaining airplanes on behalf of Chiang's government. He outlined his plan then began negotiations with government representatives.

Flurry of activity

Meanwhile in Peking Chou En-lai was declaring all the aircraft to be the 'sacred property' of the People's Republic of China. On or about 12 November, the CPG's Minister of Communications purported to appoint C. L. Chen general manager of CATC and C. Y. Liu general manager of CNAC, the same posts that they had held under the Nationalists. Directors were appointed and instructions given.

That same day Chen and Liu were dismissed by the Nationalist government whose Minister of Communications came to Hong Kong urgently from Taiwan. Next day the minister appointed a loyal senior local employee, Ango Tai, as both a member of the Board of Governors of CATC and as Vice-President

1. William M. Leary, 'Aircraft and Anti-Communists: CAT in Action, 1942–52', *China Quarterly* 52 (1972): 654–699, 656; Victor S. Kaufman, 'The United States, Great Britain and the CAT Controversy', *Journal of Contemporary History* 40, no. 1 (2005): 95–113, 99.

and Acting President of the Board and instructed Tai to regain control of the remaining planes. All employees were suspended until they had been vetted for loyalty.

The flurry of activity continued as the Nationalists' Minister of Foreign Affairs, George Yeh, informed the Hong Kong government that the certificates of registration of all the aircraft had been suspended by the aviation authorities in Taipei and that the licences of all the aircrew had also been suspended. Yeh asked the Hong Kong authorities to immobilize the remaining aircraft and suspend the Kai Tak identification permits of all CNAC and CATC employees. In reply, Governor Grantham suggested that Yeh arrange for the collection and return of the permits. The 71 aircraft remained under the control of the airlines' (ex-)employees. Ango Tai and his colleagues could not reach the planes. Tai made efforts to regain control. He sought the advice of a firm of solicitors who in turn consulted counsel. Several legal actions were begun in Hong Kong with the intention of freeing the planes from the recalcitrant employees and their supporters.

On Tuesday 15 November the Central People's Government began to pay the staff of CATC, just before Ango Tai dismissed the defecting employees. Tai also appointed William R. Parker, an employee of CAT, to take charge of security and arrange for the planes to be guarded. Parker engaged a squad of Sikhs as guards. They took up position around the aircraft. This alarmed Grantham who feared that violence would break out between the guards and the defectors, each with support from political sympathizers and consequent risk of escalation. He ordered that the Sikhs depart, which they did, leaving employees loyal to Peking to retake control. Those employees expressed the intention to stay until the British government recognized the CPG.

Grantham also announced that the aircraft would not be permitted to depart until an air agreement had been made between the Hong Kong government and the new authorities in China. This ensured that the status quo would remain for the time being.[2]

Stand-off

An impasse had been reached but it favoured the communists since they held the aircraft on the ground. Willauer was alarmed. Although the Nationalists were preparing for legal action, he feared that before any court ruling more of the planes would participate in unauthorized departures or that the workers

2. William M. Leary, *Perilous Missions: Civil Air Transport and CIA Covert Operations in Asia* (Tuscaloosa: University of Alabama Press, 1984), 656–657; Kaufman, 'The CAT Controversy', 99–100; Foreign Office memorandum, 'Chinese Aircraft at Hong Kong', 18 March 1950, 2; Gould J in *Civil Air Transport Incorporated v Central Air Transport Corporation* (1951) 35 HKLR 162, 172–175, 177–179; Howe CJ in *Civil Air Transport Incorporated v Central Air Transport Corporation* (1951) 35 HKLR 22, 36–43; *Civil Air Transport Incorporated v Central Air Transport Corporation* [1953] AC 70, 83.

would start to dismantle the planes preparatory to shipping them out by sea or road. So one evening he led a group of CAT employees on a foray to Kai Tak in which they let down the tyres of some of the planes. He also spread rumours that trucks would be driven across the path of any aircraft attempting to take off.[3]

On Thursday 24 November legal actions were started by Ango Tai for CNAC, by CATC and by the China National Resources Commission against 20 named former employees of those organizations who were believed to be communist sympathizers. The writs sought injunctions restraining the defendant ex-employees, their servants or agents from disposing of or dealing with the plaintiffs' assets, and damages for trespass. The solicitors for the plaintiff organizations were a long-established (and still existent) law firm, Wilkinson and Grist.

The matter was handled by Mr Blake, the senior partner of the firm. A survivor of military service in the First World War and internment in the Second, Denis Henry Blake was a pillar of the expatriate colonial establishment. He had been with Wilkinson and Grist for thirty years, since shortly after returning from the First World War during which he had been wounded and then chosen to undertake a speaking tour of the United States in an effort to stimulate army recruitment. He had been trained before the war as a solicitor in the office of the Town Clerk of his native Great Yarmouth in Norfolk. In Hong Kong, the firm promoted Blake to partner within five years. During the 1920s he had handled the legal side of the development of the country club, golf course and 23 'taipan houses' with out-buildings and grounds at Shek O on the then-remote southeastern promontory of Hong Kong Island. Blake had extensive business and community involvement, having been chairman of the Hong Kong Club and of the Automobile Association and serving on numerous councils and committees including those of the Law Society, the General Chamber of Commerce, and the Yacht Club. He held directorships of large companies.[4] He was a member of a Masonic Lodge much favoured by judges, lawyers and policemen.

No number of contacts or amount of influence, however, could readily solve a practical problem that faced Blake and his clients. This was the difficulty of identifying who was actually preventing access to the aircraft. Since Willauer and the Nationalist sympathizers could not get close to the planes and since those now in charge on the Nationalist side had not been involved with the airlines before in Hong Kong, they could not name all the people who were actually holding the aircraft. So the 20 names stated as defendants

3. Leary, 'Aircraft and Anti-Communists', 657; Martha Byrd, *Chennault: Giving Wings to the Tiger* (Tuscaloosa: University of Alabama Press, 1987).
4. Carl T. Smith, *History of Wilkinson and Grist*, unpublished manuscript; this and other information was kindly provided by Mr John Budge of Wilkinson and Grist.

on the writs were somewhat speculative. Anyway, it is likely that those holding the planes changed from time to time.

Wilkinson and Grist promptly used a procedure designed for emergencies by which, without first giving notice to the defendants, they asked an available judge for an interim injunction, that is to say, an urgent provisional order preserving the current position until trial or further court order.[5] Their application was heard by the Chief Justice, Sir Leslie Gibson, who made a decision prohibiting the ex-employees from removing the airlines' planes or equipment from Kai Tak and from entering the airlines' property there. Sir Leslie set a date, 21 December, for all parties to come back to court and argue about whether the injunctions should be continued.

Next day, the defendants, or some of them, retaliated. Probably stung by the letting-down of the tyres, they engaged lawyers who asked another judge, Mr Justice Gould, for a similar order directed at the three plaintiffs. (Presumably Sir Leslie Gibson was not available.) These applicants were all believed to be communists or their sympathizers. The injunction was granted, so both sides were forbidden by law to touch the aircraft.

A few days later Wilkinson and Grist asked the Attorney-General, John Griffin, for government assistance in identifying those in control of the remaining aircraft. They were concerned that the injunctions would not be obeyed, for the defendants named in the proceedings did not seem to be those actually in control. They suggested that court bailiffs and the police had a duty to assist. The suggestion has the mark of Chennault and Willauer about it, for the Hong Kong solicitors would have been aware that the police would not be involved in helping parties to a civil dispute, especially one of such sensitivity, and that bailiffs are relevant only after a court judgment has been given. Griffin rejected the suggestion but, lest there be a breach of the peace, did arrange for the police to attend at Kai Tak to protect representatives of the plaintiffs as they questioned those guarding the aircraft and warned them of the terms of the injunctions. The police appeared at the airfield at the appointed time but the airlines' representatives did not. Presumably the representatives were afraid of being publicly identified as anti-communist. This may also explain why representatives of the plaintiffs did not act upon the Governor's suggestion, in response to George Yeh's request of 13 November that employees' permits to enter Kai Tak be suspended, that the airlines themselves collect employees' passes to enter the airfield so as to deny them access to the aircraft.

In their efforts to bar the Nationalists from the planes the dissident employees could call upon the support of trade unionists and other communist sympathizers working at the airport or living nearby. Just across the

5. Now under Order 29, rule 1 of the Rules of the High Court.

road that skirted outside the airport's apron, between Kai Tak and the Walled City, lay a recently developed area of four- and five-storey buildings known as Kowloon City. The post-war expansion of population had turned this into a crowded residential and commercial area. During the war Kowloon City, with its ready access to the Sai Kung peninsula infested by Communist guerrillas, had been an urban centre for those resisting the Japanese. After the war a significant number of residents retained those sympathies. They were readily mobilized by trade unions to support the airline rebels.

The dissident employees could expect support from another source, the CPG. On 3 December 1949 Chou En-lai issued a statement that the right of his government to the two airlines' property in Hong Kong deserved respect and proper protection by the Hong Kong authorities. The statement was surprisingly mild and made no claim that the dissidents or their supporters were acting on behalf of the CPG.[6]

The US steps in

With the legal route leading nowhere for the time being, Willauer and Chennault were keen to find a way to break the impasse. They had been agitating for action in Washington DC and through their friends at the CIA, emphasizing the potential of the aircraft for use against the large islands still in KMT hands, Formosa and Hainan. This led the US State Department on 1 December to inform the British Foreign Office of its concern. Although aware that legal processes must be allowed to take their course, they asked whether there might be some 'extraordinary measures' that the Governor could take to prevent the aircraft falling into Communist hands. The next day Livingston Merchant, the Deputy Assistant Secretary of State for Far Eastern Affairs, fortified the concern by orally telling the counsellor at the British Embassy in Washington DC of the importance of not allowing the Communists to have the planes. He requested that the UK government take all feasible and necessary steps to prevent that.[7]

This began a period of mounting agitation and complaint by US interests aimed at putting pressure on the British government, and also the Hong Kong government, to do something to help them. It continued throughout December 1949 and January 1950 until and beyond the hearing of the substantive legal issues by the Chief Justice in February. Arthur Ringwalt, the China specialist at the US Embassy in London, recalled going over to the Foreign

6. Shao Wenguang, *China, Britain and Businessmen: Political and Commercial Relations, 1949–57* (Basingstoke: Macmillan, 1991), 77, fn 66.
7. Foreign Office memorandum, 'Chinese Aircraft at Hong Kong', 2; Kaufman, 'The CAT Controversy', 101; record of proceedings of the US Senate Sub-committee on Appropriations for 1951, 272 and 718.

Office almost daily: 'We talked endless hours at the Foreign Office. I sat in these conferences and took notes.'[8] The British, and Hong Kong, attitude throughout this period was that the matter was in the hands of the judiciary and that the legal process could not be interfered with. 'Every time I'd go to the Foreign Office they'd say, "Of course you know this has nothing to do with politics."' Ringwalt remembered. 'The decision is a legal decision and a legal decision only,' he would be told. Ringwalt was not convinced.

The anxiety of Chennault and Willauer was not just that, despite the injunctions, the remaining planes might be flown away surreptitiously. They feared that the United Kingdom would soon recognize the Central People's Government as the legitimate government of China and that this would deliver the planes in the British colony to the new government. The Communists had continued to gain territory since Mao's declaration of the PRC on 1 October. The Nationalists had abandoned Canton on 12 October and Communists had taken it over at the end of that month. Early in November they had taken over Kunming too.

Paving the way for recognition

Discussion within diplomatic circles as to whether and when the CPG should be recognized had been continuing since the second quarter of 1949. The meetings between US and British foreign service representatives in mid-September 1949 had highlighted their differences of approach. In October the declaration of the PRC and the invitation to Chou En-lai to establish informal relations by the British consul in Peking brought the issue to the fore. Whereas the US and other states tended to regard recognition as a political matter, a gift of approval to be bestowed upon a new government once the recognizing state was ready to do so, the British view was that it was a matter of fact and law. That is to say, once the new authorities had established a sufficient degree of control and permanence (questions of fact), recognition would follow as a matter of law and diplomatic relations could be established. Accordingly, official (or de jure) recognition should be automatic once the requisite facts were present and there should be no element of bargaining or any question of approval involved. Recognition was acknowledgement of reality, not an indication of support. As Winston Churchill pithily put it, 'the reason for having diplomatic relations is not to confer a compliment but to secure a convenience'.[9]

That certainly was the view of Sir Eric Beckett, the Foreign Office's principal legal adviser. On 20 October 1949 he advised his seniors that, given the

8. Arthur Ringwalt, 'Oral History Interview with Arthur R. Ringwalt', interview by Richard D. McKinzie, 5 June 1974, trumanlibrary.gov/library/oral-histories/ringwalt.
9. Qiang Zhai, *The Dragon, the Lion, and the Eagle: Chinese-British-American Relations, 1949–1958* (Kent, OH: Kent State University Press, 1994), 45.

ostensibly hopeless position of the Nationalist government, de jure recognition of the CPG was legally justifiable. Nevertheless, the policy-makers were reluctant to cede the decision to the lawyers. On 29 October a Foreign Office memorandum noted that the Nationalists were no longer representative of anything but their ruling clique and the CCP was the only alternative; the success of British policy was now dependent on recognition which should be sought on political and practical grounds, the writer advised. In other words, if Britain was to salvage something from its previous investments in China and to entice the CCP away from the Soviets with trade and friendship as had been planned, now was the time to manifest a friendly demeanour by officially recognizing it as the proper government of all China. The attitude of seeking advantage by recognition died hard.

Beckett would not have this. He linked recognition of a government with its admission as the representative of a state at the recently established United Nations organization. The UN was not a private club to which new governments might apply for membership and be accepted on condition of good behaviour or not at all. If a government was in effective charge of a state, it must be admitted whether existing members liked it or not. Beckett disapproved of a speech by Acheson to the UN General Assembly on 4 October in which he had suggested that since China had entered into certain international obligations, the new regime must honour them in order to be recognized. It was not customary to make conditions of this nature preliminary to recognition, Beckett observed, before embarking upon a long written minute in which he ventured the opinion that the predominant and right view was that recognition depended upon whether the regime fulfils the qualifications laid down by international law. Political considerations should be limited to the formation of an opinion as to whether those qualifications had been fulfilled. Beckett had to accept however that many states had not followed this approach and that even his own Secretary of State, Ernest Bevin, had appeared to depart from it when he had said that there would be no recognition of the Communists as the de jure government until they accepted Chinese international obligations.[10]

The difficulty about laying down conditions of this sort is that they are presumptuous and humiliating. They presume that the government to be recognized would break its international obligations despite those obligations being implicit from the fact of recognition as a national government. For that reason such conditions are insulting to it and to require an undertaking from it is humiliating. Consequently Beckett resisted a suggestion from Peter Scarlett of the Foreign Office who was preparing a memorandum for a Cabinet meeting which was to discuss recognition of the CPG in December 1949. Scarlett had

10. Anthony Carty, 'The Practice of International Law', in *Routledge Handbook of International Law*, ed. David Armstrong (London: Routledge, 2008), 89.

suggested that a note could be sent to the new Chinese government saying His Majesty's Government was now ready to accord de jure recognition and going on to say that it assumed the new government would respect the international obligations of its predecessor; alternatively the note might recite the CPG's expressed willingness to establish relations on the principles of equality, mutual interest and mutual respect for territorial sovereignty and argue that these principles implied a general assurance of decent behaviour. Such statements, Beckett responded, invite an awkward answer and you gain nothing by them. No change in the international obligations of a state is brought about by a change of regime, Beckett explained, and therefore it was not necessary to insist upon express acceptance of this by the new regime, as the United States appeared to be doing. 'Indeed to insist on such an explicit statement has its disadvantages because it opens the way to the argument that the new regime is only bound by the previous obligations of the country if it expressly says that it will.'[11]

In early November 1949 Bevin told Acheson that Britain was inclined to recognize the new People's Republic since it was in control of three-quarters of China. Acheson continued to urge Britain to hold off. One of the reasons for this was apprehension as to the effect that formal recognition would have on the question of ownership of the aircraft at Kai Tak. But he was also receiving advice from his Far East specialists not to be over-eager to recognize the communist regime.[12]

What held the British government back from extending recognition once the legal advice had given the all-clear was a desire to co-ordinate the move with that of other states, particularly those in the Commonwealth. In the first week of November there was a conference of British diplomatic and colonial representatives in the Far East at Bukit Serene, a resort overlooking the Johore Strait and Singapore island in Malaya, at which recognition of the CPG was discussed under the chairmanship of Malcolm MacDonald, Britain's Commissioner-General for Southeast Asia. The representatives, who included Alexander Grantham from Hong Kong, concluded that recognition was desirable as soon as possible.

Grantham, looking at the question from Hong Kong's viewpoint, regarded the colony as vulnerable to the new regime and urged that recognition be immediate. So did Stevenson, the British Ambassador to China, for different reasons: he suggested a pragmatic approach and emphasized the importance of trade. India, Pakistan and Ceylon also favoured immediate recognition. Nehru, the Indian Prime Minister, had been pressing the Labour government in Britain for weeks to recognize the PRC. MacDonald and the Governor of Singapore, Franklin Gimson, feared that recognition would

11. Carty, 'The Practice of International Law', 90.
12. Ringwalt, 'Oral History Interview'; Zhai, *The Dragon, the Lion, and the Eagle*, 43.

encourage communist insurrection in Malaya, Singapore and Borneo and lead their Chinese populations to make accommodation with the insurgents and with PRC consuls who might subsequently be appointed. New Zealand and Canada, wary of breaking with the Americans, advocated delay. Australia and South Africa wanted guarantees of good behaviour to be sought, although Ben Chifley, the Australian Prime Minister, thought that realities should be faced. They all supported proposals to stem the advance of communism in Asia and thereby appease the United States. Britain also took soundings from its European neighbours. Belgium, Holland, Italy and Scandinavian countries wanted recognition to come soon. France, concerned about the effect of a communist takeover of southern China would have on its neighbouring colonies in Indo-China, urged Britain to postpone and re-consider.[13]

Sir Esler Dening recommended that the UK take the plunge and accord recognition as soon as possible. Bevin decided to seek Cabinet approval to extend recognition without conditions. The substance of Beckett's advice appeared in the memorandum that was prepared for ministers to discuss. To refuse recognition when no other effective authority exists in China, the memorandum argued, was to imply a boycott which would be negative for long-term relations. Politically, recognition meant willingness to enter into diplomatic relations, not approval of ideology, it explained: 'we cannot afford to ignore, however much we may disapprove its political orientation, a government which has effective authority over a vast territory and population'. Without relations, Britain would be in no position to exert influence on China's further development, it asserted.

Purchasing the planes

Aware that formal British recognition of the PRC was growing ever closer and frustrated by the setbacks in Hong Kong, in late November Willauer decided upon a different tack. However, he needed time to hatch his plan, which was to transfer ownership of the 71 aircraft to himself and Chennault and thus put them outside the legal ownership of either Chinese party. He feared that the plan would be nullified if the planes were removed or if Britain formally recognized the CPG and withdrew recognition from the Nationalists before the transfer could be carried through. He needed financial support to carry out the plan so turned to his old colleague Alfred T. Cox at the Office of Policy Co-ordination. Cox strongly recommended to Washington that covert support be given to the scheme with the Chennault-Willauer partnership acting as a front. The answer, however, was that the Office would not get involved,

13. James T. H. Tang, *Britain's Encounter with Revolutionary China, 1949–54* (New York: St. Martin's Press, 1992), 59–62.

although the pair's efforts should be encouraged. Willauer turned instead to Tommy Corcoran who took soundings and replied that it was felt to be in the national interest to deny the airplanes to the Communists. Corcoran set about devising a scheme to gain title to the aircraft in an efficient manner with a view to selling them and dividing the proceeds between investors in the scheme.[14] He sought the help of William Donovan.

Chennault and Willauer spent two weeks obtaining backing in Washington, consulting with lawyers and negotiating with Nationalist ministers. On Monday 5 December 1949 they wrote to the Nationalist Minister of Communications in Formosa to confirm the agreement that had been reached. The length and formality of the letter indicate that it was drafted by lawyers, probably by Donovan's firm, maybe with some input from Corcoran. The letter was addressed to 'His Excellency the Minister of Communications, National Government of China, Taipeh, Taiwan'. It began with a recital of half-a-dozen background facts or justifications: that the national government was the owner of the 'share stock' of all of CATC and 80 per cent of CNAC; that Chennault and Willauer desired to purchase and operate the assets and shares of those airlines; that the assets, the majority of which were in Hong Kong, were the subject of injunctions that had forced the airlines to cease operations and the assets had decreased in value; that the government was unwilling to sell except on binding assurances that the assets would not be used for the benefit of and within the communist areas of China; that the government was concerned to secure the future of the airlines' loyal staff members; and that the government was anxious to sell to Chennault and Willauer because of the trust and confidence it reposed (the letter said 'imposed') in them 'by reason of their loyal and devoted services during the war of liberation in China and the cause of the United Nations' and because the pair had amply demonstrated their ability to operate air services.

These recitals were quite unnecessary unless the letter's authors anticipated that the genuineness of the sale would come under scrutiny. They contained two inaccuracies, for CATC was not a corporation in law and so had no shares or stock and the two airlines had ceased operation before the court injunctions had been imposed. The assertion that the assets had decreased in value begged the question, compared with what and when? But it was designed to justify the price recorded later in the letter. Calling the Sino-Japanese conflict a war of liberation was something of an exaggeration. That and the reference to the UN seem to have been a sop to American sensibilities. The final recital showed that Chennault and Willauer were anxious to explain why the government was selling to them rather than to others. What was missing was

14. Leary, *Perilous Missions*, 93–94.

any acknowledgement of the Nationalist government's real aim, to keep the aircraft away from the Communists.

After those preliminaries, the letter got down to business. In clause 1 the government agreed to cause CATC and CNAC to sell and Chennault and Willauer agreed to buy all the assets of CATC and CNAC, including the aircraft and material in Hong Kong, free of encumbrances. The price for CNAC's assets was to be US$1.5 million; for CATC's assets, US$2 million. This was almost certainly an undervalue for the assets included aircraft which had cost collectively millions of dollars and valuable equipment and parts as well as real estate in the form of yards and godowns (housing the equipment) and office leases.

Even at an undervalue, the pair did not have that sort of cash so they offered promissory notes payable to bearer (bearer bonds) instead: in other words they were to be given credit on the strength of their promise to pay later. No mention was made of payment of interest. Willauer it seems had an idea as to how the purchase might be financed. He and Chennault undertook to form a corporation or other legal entity to take over the assets and shares and to issue new promissory notes to replace those that they would issue to the Nationalist government for the initial purchase. They and their advisers foresaw that investors in this new entity might take the promissory notes as security for the money they put into it, that money being used to discharge the debt to the Nationalist government. So the agreement provided for holders of the notes to have the option of taking shares in the new entity, instead of cash, in discharge of their loan. The agreement also allowed for the Ministry's taking shares in the new entity in exchange for release or reduction of the debt. It was stipulated that any holder of the notes be free of connection with Chinese communists, represent 'the true forces of Anti-Communism in China' and be designated to exercise the option by the government.

Aside from the sale, the agreement provided for the fate and use of the planes. Chennault and Willauer pledged to use their best efforts and do everything within their power to gain possession and control of the airline assets. The government pledged to assist them in that endeavour. The pair were to have a management contract with the new entity and gave an assurance that the aeroplanes would not be used, directly or indirectly, for the benefit of or for carriage to and from or within the communist areas of China. They also promised to use their best efforts to continue the employment of as many loyal staff members of the airlines as was reasonably possible and to dispose of the rightful claims of Pan Am.

In Taipei on 12 December the terms were accepted by Mr Liu Shao Ting, recently appointed by the Nationalists as chairman of the board of directors (or governors), representing CATC. Liu was also the Nationalist Vice-Minister of Communications. The terms were accepted for CNAC on 13 December by

Mr Nih Chun-sung, the chairman of the board of directors. The contract was ratified on 31 December at a board meeting of CNAC in Hong Kong at which representatives of Pan Am, which at the time of the contract had still held a 20 per cent interest in CNAC, were present. The Nationalist Premier, Yen Shi-san, wrote from Formosa to Chennault and Willauer also accepting their offer.[15] The decisions and acceptances were made and formalized in rather a hurry. This was understandable in the circumstances, but it was to lead to difficulties later when the sale came to be considered by the courts.

The British Foreign Office was informed of the sale on 15 December during a visit to Whitehall by the US Chargé d'Affaires, Julius Holmes, and Arthur Ringwalt. The visit had been arranged by the Embassy at the request of the State Department. The diplomats were accompanied by lawyers representing CAT, the airline of Chennault and Willauer. The lawyers were William Donovan, now in private practice in New York after his wartime exploits, and his law partner Colonel Heppner. The two had served together in OSS, the US secret intelligence organization. It was probably Donovan who had asked the State Department to set up the meeting. Holmes emphasized the official American interest in the fate of the aircraft. He asked that precautions be taken against their transfer to the communists. The two lawyers told the FO that the 71 aircraft would be registered in the USA. They hoped that this would influence the Hong Kong court's decision at the hearing scheduled for 21 December.

That hope, however, was forlorn. The forthcoming hearing would consider the continuation or otherwise of the injunctions granted in November which had frozen the planes at Kai Tak. It would not decide the question of their ownership. Donovan, Heppner and the diplomatists were anxious that this question should be decided before any recognition of the Communist government. They pressed for the proceedings to be expedited.

Once news reached Peking, the sale and on-sale of the aircraft were renounced by the Head of the PRC's Civil Aviation Bureau. On 23 December he declared the transactions null and void, then brought the PRC's claims to the attention of the UK government. However, the Head did not declare that the planes were under his bureau's control. It was not until 13 January 1950 that he instructed the new general managers of the airlines to take over the assets of the airlines.[16]

15. Gibson CJ in *Civil Air Transport Incorporated v Chennault and Others* (1950) 34 HKLR 358, 367; Howe CJ in *CATI v CATC* (1951) 35 HKLR 22, 34–35; Gould J in *CATI v CATC* (1951) 35 HKLR 162, 178–183; *CATI v CATC* [1953] AC 70, 82; Leary, 'Aircraft and Anti-Communists', 659.
16. Shao, *China, Britain and Businessmen*, 77, fn 66.

Recognition imminent

Donovan and Heppner were conscious that an announcement by Britain to recognize the CPG was imminent. Rumours to that effect were current in political and diplomatic circles in London. Speculation was rife in Hong Kong amongst the host of diplomatists who had fled there from the mainland, including Karl Rankin whose efforts to take up the US consular post in Shanghai had been frustrated.[17] Holmes, the US Chargé who had accompanied Donovan and Heppner to the Foreign Office, would have been well aware of the move for it had been signalled for some time. In fact Bevin's recommendation concerning recognition was to be considered at a Cabinet meeting that very day, 15 December. The US diplomatic representatives might even have been discreetly told this during their visit.

As advised by Beckett, ministers in effect had no choice but to recognize the new authorities once satisfied that the CPG had effective control over most of China and that its control was so established as to be permanent. The decision to recognize was at last taken. The exact date upon which recognition would be accorded was left to Bevin to decide. A public announcement was not made immediately however since the date for recognition had yet to be fixed. Bevin wanted to wait until after a forthcoming conference of Commonwealth Foreign Ministers in Columbo and after elections in Australia and New Zealand. Initially he nominated 2 January 1950, then changed his mind. On 23 December he settled upon the end of the first week of January.

US moves

Meanwhile in the USA urgent steps were being taken to have the 71 planes registered as American. On Saturday 17 December a State Department official met an officer from the Civil Aeronautics Administration to discuss how the registration could be hurried up. An obstacle was that Pan Am partly owned CNAC. Two days later Livingston Merchant, the Deputy Assistant Secretary of State with responsibility for Far Eastern Affairs, met William Bond of Pan Am, a prominent figure in CNAC, and urged that Pan Am co-operate.

So it was that on 20 December, Bond and T. V. Soong of the Nationalist government negotiated the sale to that government of the Pan Am shares in CNAC for US$1.25 million. The same day the CAA waived the requirement of airworthiness inspections and granted US registration of the aircraft.

American efforts to have the matter resolved outside the law continued on 21 December with a visit by the new US Consul General in Hong Kong, Karl Rankin, to Governor Grantham. Rankin had been instructed by the State

17. Karl Lott Rankin, *China Assignment* (Seattle: University of Washington Press, 1964), 17.

Department to give every assistance to CAT. Rankin was accompanied on the visit by Willauer and Chennault. They showed Grantham a document signed by the Nationalist Prime Minister certifying the sale of the two airlines' assets to CAT. Grantham was unmoved. Adhering to the line taken by the British and the Hong Kong governments, Grantham told his visitors that title depended entirely upon the outcome of the legal proceedings. He did not tell them his view that any action he might take to put the aircraft in their hands would lead to violence. Security remained Grantham's over-riding concern. Later that day he informed his masters in London that executive action to place American interests in possession of the aircraft would precipitate 'disturbance and sabotage'.

By then the aircraft had a new owner. On 19 December 1949, just a week after they had acquired the planes, Chennault and Willauer sold them to a company newly incorporated in the US State of Delaware, a jurisdiction known for its special, business-friendly corporate law. This allowed the structure of companies to be flexible, afforded them greater privacy and lower taxes, and provided a specialist company court. So there was no need to reveal the names of directors or office-holders. The new company was called CAT, Inc. This is not to be confused with CAT, Civil Air Transport, the airline which had been operated by Chennault and Willauer for some years.[18] The pair certainly had roles in the new entity but there was a hidden background as well. Chennault (in Taipei) was nominally the company's chairman and Willauer (in Hong Kong) its president. CAT, Inc. was however entirely held by a Panamanian corporation called CAT SA. The shareholders in CAT SA were Tommy Corcoran, his brother David, William Youngman and James Brennan, as well as Chennault and Willauer: they had all been behind China Defense Supplies. Panama afforded secrecy and lenient tax treatment. Donovan and Heppner had been engaged by Tommy Corcoran to represent CAT, Inc.[19]

Return to court

On 20 December Chief Justice Gibson began the hearing to consider the fate of the interim injunctions that had been granted a month earlier. The hearing was complicated by an application taken out on behalf of Chennault and Willauer a few days earlier to be joined as additional plaintiffs in the actions. As far as they and the airlines were concerned, CNAC and CATC no longer owned the planes and other assets so no longer had any interest in the continuation of the injunctions or in the outcome of the litigation. If the planes

18. The abbreviations, the comma and the full stop were all part of the proper name of CAT, Inc.
19. Byrd, *Chennault*, 338.

were to continue to be held at Kai Tak by court order, it was Chennault and Willauer who would have to ask for that.

But their Hong Kong lawyers, perhaps pushed by Donovan, had made a mistake. The appropriate application would have been to substitute Chennault and Willauer as plaintiffs in place of the airlines, not to add them. Either that, or Chennault and Willauer should have started a separate action. Their case, and that of the Nationalist directors, was that ownership had been transferred, not that they were now all owners of the aircraft. On the face of matters, their interest conflicted with that of the airlines since both sides were claiming ownership. So the Chief Justice had no difficulty in rejecting their application.

The application for joinder seems doubly misconceived, for, the day before the hearing began, Chennault and Willauer had sold the aircraft and assets on to the Delaware company. Doubtless there was not enough time to reflect this change of circumstances in the written evidence which had to be put before the court prior to the hearing and it may even be that, due to the time difference between Hong Kong and the USA, the on-sale did not actually take place before the start of the hearing.

In any event, there was no change from the original plaintiffs. This meant that the plaintiff airlines had no standing to oppose, and no interest in opposing, the defendant employees' application for discharge of all the injunctions against interference with the aircraft. However, the airlines had also claimed damages for trespass so there would have to be a trial and there would probably be a dispute as to whether the injunctions had been properly granted in the first place. At the conclusion of the hearing on Friday 23 December the Chief Justice decided that the issues would turn on facts and law that could only be decided at trial.[20] He continued the injunctions until then or until the making of a further order. It was a pragmatic, if legally doubtful, decision: he would have anticipated that the new owners would launch separate proceedings and apply for a fresh injunction. He would also have realized that it would please the authorities both in Hong Kong and London if the injunctions remained.

Activity unrelenting

There was to be no relaxing holiday weekend for those involved in the saga. On Christmas Eve the US State Department instructed its London embassy to re-iterate to the Foreign Office its interest in the matter and views as to what should be done. The department also repeated to Rankin in Hong Kong its instructions to help CAT, Inc. to obtain possession of the aircraft.

Cox at least was able to have dinner in Hong Kong on Christmas Eve with two former OSS colleagues. One of them was Heppner: he was in town

20. Foreign Office memorandum, 'Chinese Aircraft at Hong Kong', chronology, 4.

to represent Willauer, Chennault and CAT, Inc. in their quest for the planes. They expected to be joined shortly by another old hand, Bill Donovan. Willauer however was preparing to fly to the USA in an effort to attract financial support for his airline CAT. The airline's loss of business within China, and the costs of repeatedly relocating its bases there, had been devastating. CAT was now operating from Formosa. On 15 December 1949 it had dismissed its local staff and sent most of its aircraft to Taipei. The last of its planes, and Chennault, flew off from Kai Tak the next day.[21]

21. Leary, *Perilous Missions*, 98–99; memorandum, J. F. Nicoll, Colonial Secretary, to Colonial Office, 16 December 1949, FO 371/84782.

9

The US Ramps Up the Pressure

The outcome of CAT's application to join the legal proceedings may have seemed like a defeat to the Chennault-Willauer partnership but at least the Chief Justice had continued the injunctions which froze the planes at Kai Tak. This gave the pair an opportunity to rethink their tactics, with the assistance of Bill Donovan, the lawyer for CAT, Inc., who was shortly to arrive in Hong Kong.

Donovan's advice must have been to attack on all fronts, political, diplomatic, practical, as well as legal, and in all places, Hong Kong, London, Washington, New York and Taipei. That would have been Chennault and Willauer's inclination anyway.

Donovan in his element

The dispute must have seemed idyllic to Bill Donovan. It combined elements in which he was experienced and with which he was comfortable. The international legal aspect was only a subsidiary part of it. The Truman Doctrine and the US policy of containing communism gave it an exciting geo-political dimension. The CIA's indirect involvement through CAT, Inc. provided the skullduggery which he relished. The political and diplomatic dimensions recalled his time as a political candidate and presidential adviser. The military angle harked back to his earlier career as a soldier. The shuttling between ministries and offices in cities on three continents satisfied his restless soul. More than anything, finding a satisfactory solution to the dispute was a challenge that he could not refuse, a challenge in which he could exploit his contacts in the corridors of power. It was a game in which he was playing not just for his clients but also for America.

In truth, Donovan was not much of a lawyer. He was more of a fixer, a man of action, interested in the result and in the thrill of seeking it. So in December 1949 and January 1950 he was intent upon an extra-judicial solution to the problem of the planes stranded at Kai Tak. This was diametrically opposed to the approach of the British and Hong Kong authorities who saw the legal system as an instrument by which to find a way out: an independent arbiter whose view would be accepted by all the contestants.

We have seen that US concerns had been building since the beginning of December, with the request by the State Department to the Foreign Office on the first of the month that undefined 'extraordinary measures' be taken to keep the aircraft from the Communists, the visit of Donovan with his partner Heppner and US embassy officials to the Foreign Office in the middle of the month, and the discussion between the US Consul-General and the Governor on 21 December. The pressure stepped up in scale after Christmas.

The continuation of the injunctions had given Donovan and his clients, Chennault and Willauer and their companies, breathing space in which to try to arrange an extra-legal solution to the impasse. Donovan had been called in at the behest of Tommy Corcoran, who was ostensibly an adviser to CAT, Inc. but secretly and in reality one of its financial backers. The breathing space would be short since the announcement of British recognition of the PRC would surely come soon.

One of Donovan's pre-occupations was with proof of a valid sale of the aircraft by the Nationalist interests to Chennault and Willauer earlier in the month. This was rather a technical matter, involving Chinese company law, the powers of directors and correct formalities. As Donovan saw it, the technicalities could all be cut through and obstacles avoided simply by evidence from the Nationalist authorities that they accepted that the sale had taken place.

Turning up the heat

On Thursday 28 December the Foreign Office received a note from the Chinese (Nationalist) embassy in London informing the Office that the sales had taken place and that a Mr Sing, Assistant Secretary General of the Executive Yuan, had been authorized to act for the government in all matters relating to the CNAC and CATC. Later that day the text of a letter by the Nationalist Chinese Premier to Chennault and Willauer accepting their offer was sent as well, with a request that the Colonial Secretary in Hong Kong be informed. The letter stated that Chennault and Willauer were now the owners of the two airlines' assets.[1] The letter did not mention the onward sale to CAT, Inc. It may have been composed before that sale or the Premier may have been unaware of the sale.

The concern about recognition was underlined during a visit to the Foreign Office the same day by the US Civil Air Attaché in London, accompanied by a New York lawyer, Malcolm Fooshee, a colleague of Donovan. They reiterated

1. Foreign Office memorandum, 'Chinese Aircraft in Hong Kong', 18 March 1950, 4; Howe CJ in *Civil Air Transport Incorporated v Central Air Transport Corporation* (1951) 35 HKLR 22, 35.

the anxiety that ownership would still be unresolved when the Communist government was formally recognized. Fooshee observed that the planes were now registered as American yet the courts had refused to allow Chennault and Willauer to join in the litigation. He received the standard British reply: the matter was all sub judice and no extra-legal action could be contemplated. Fooshee also complained that the Governor was unco-operative and was discriminating against CAT, giving the example of CAT's radio rights being cancelled. The FO promised to look into this; it turned out to be nothing to do with the 71 aircraft. The US parties and their lawyers were throwing everything into the argument without discrimination.

This was a time of almost daily visits to the Foreign Office for Arthur Ringwalt of the American embassy in London. The embassy was being pushed to lobby harder about the planes by the State Department which in turn was being pushed by politicians in Washington DC. Ringwalt reckoned that for weeks he spent about half of every day just handling the planes case. Apart from telegrams and letters from Washington, lawyers from Donovan's office in New York 'would come to see me about once every other week trying to take more vigorous action and pound more tables at the Foreign Office'.[2]

The Americans put pressure on the Hong Kong authorities too. On 29 December Governor Grantham received Carl Rankin, the US Consul-General, accompanied by Willauer and his lawyer, Heppner. They informed Grantham of the sale that had taken place on 12 December and asserted that US markings should accordingly be put on the exterior of the planes, though they would await recognition of the validity of the sale by the government in London. The Governor told them that he had been informed of the sale but the matter was still before the court.

Next day in London the US Chargé d'Affaires (diplomatic head of the embassy) Julius Holmes complained to Sir William Strang, the Permanent Secretary (administrative head) of the Foreign Office, that American representatives had no access to the planes whilst communist employees did. Holmes also said that sabotage was occurring and vital parts were being removed. He asked if the legal proceedings could be expedited and for a statement which could be sent to Washington that Britain shared the concern of the United States government that the aircraft not fall into communist hands. Would recognition of the CPG affect the outcome of the legal proceedings?

These questions and the mounting US agitation caused a high-level meeting to be convened in Whitehall on New Year's Eve, Saturday 31 December 1949, to take stock of the whole matter. Senior officials from both the Foreign Office and the Colonial Office were present. So were the legal advisers of both offices. The meeting's conclusions were that recognition might affect the

2. Arthur Ringwalt, 'Oral History Interview with Arthur R. Ringwalt', interview by Richard D. McKinzie, 5 June 1974, trumanlibrary.gov/library/oral-histories/ringwalt.

court's decision, but then again it might not; that they could not comment on the validity of the sale to CAT, Inc., although they could make a copy of the Chinese ambassador's note affirming the sale available to the American government if it wished; that they would ask the Governor about the allegations of sabotage; that they should warn the Americans that they could do nothing to forestall or frustrate the court's decision, although either side might prolong the proceedings by appealing and thereby continue the immobilization of the aircraft; and that the expediting of the proceedings was in the hands of the plaintiffs. These conclusions were consistent with the prior British attitude that ownership would be adjudicated by the courts but they were bound to be seen as unhelpful by the men in a hurry, Donovan, Chennault and Willauer.

The meeting was timely for two other reasons. First, the previous day, 30 December, a set of questions for the Foreign Secretary had arrived from Sir Leslie Gibson, the Chief Justice of Hong Kong. These were about recognition of the CPG and would need earnest consideration shortly. Second, the dispute had implications for Britain's relations with both the USA and China. It had moved so far up the foreign policy agenda that a full briefing, incorporating the meeting's conclusions, had to be prepared for British government ministers to read and consider immediately after the New Year holiday.

Consequently, the Head of the Foreign Office's General Department, William Frederick Montagu Pollock, gave up part of his holiday weekend preparing a long memorandum summarizing and commenting on events since the beginning of the year and recounting relevant policy considerations. The tall, enthusiastic and eccentric Bill Pollock was a flamboyant dresser with a penchant for unusual cars, avant-garde music and the Swedish delicacy gravadlax. He was marked out as a high-flyer but he was a Scandinavian, not a China or Far East, specialist, having served for several years at the British embassy in Stockholm. He entitled the paper 'Chinese Civil Aircraft at Hong Kong'. It formed the basis of the brief to ministers and of accounts later circulated to British and Commonwealth missions overseas.

On the first working day of 1950, Monday 2 January, the brief was considered by Arthur Creech Jones, the Secretary of State for the Colonies, by Hector McNeil, the deputy to Bevin at the Foreign Office, and by Clement Atlee the Prime Minister. The brief recounted a delicate situation. Britain was caught between the demands of the Communists, whom it was about to recognize as the legitimate government of all China, and those of its great, wealthy and powerful ally the USA, supporting the Nationalists. The ministers agreed on four points to put to the American authorities. First, they would assure the US government that they sympathized with US anxiety to prevent the aeroplanes falling into communist hands. That should ameliorate the most fundamental American concern. However, second, they would remind the Americans that it was not proper to interfere with the course of justice. This was a point that had been made repeatedly in answer to US imprecations to take some executive action to secure the planes. Third, they stated that if the verdict about ownership in the Hong Kong courts went against the US claimants, an appeal to the Privy Council would cause a further 12 months' delay. Finally, they assured the Americans that if and when it became legally possible for the aircraft to be flown out, the UK would do everything to facilitate their departure. These points were swiftly communicated to Holmes at the US London embassy orally and were followed up by a telegram to Washington next day.[3] In all probability they were also communicated to Moscow, for the secretary to McNeil was the louche Guy Burgess, one of the 'Cambridge Five' ring of spies within the British government working for the KGB. The indolent, alcohol-loving McNeil was in the habit of delegating all the hard work, such as drafting meeting notes, to Burgess who promptly made copies for his secret masters.

A point not included in the four agreed by Atlee, Jones and McNeil, but one which motivated the British government and which was made orally to Holmes and in the telegram to Washington, was concern about British investments in China. The Foreign Office did not want to give the about-to-be-recognized Communist government a weapon with which to damage Britain's large business interests in the country. Exports continued to be a priority for the recovering British economy.

Big Bill wades in

The ever-active General William Donovan must have spent his new year travelling to Hong Kong to see his clients Chennault and Willauer, join his partner Heppner and keep appointments with important people whom he expected would help him save those aircraft for America. It was a long journey, for in the early 1950s the air route from London's new Heathrow Airport took three to four days, with half-a-dozen intermediate rest stops—typically at Rome, Cairo, Karachi, Calcutta, Rangoon and Bangkok. It was also an expensive journey, but that would not have bothered Donovan who had indulgent habits and the means to pay for them. It is not known whether he paused on arrival at Kai Tak to view the seventy-one disputed airplanes from a distance.

On Wednesday 4 January 1950, Donovan teamed up with Rankin, the US Consul-General, to visit Government House. There Donovan played what he seems to have regarded as a trump card in proving that title to the aircraft rested with his clients. He informed Grantham that sale of the planes to CAT, Inc., had been certified by a note from the Nationalist government. Grantham smoothly replied that he had heard something of that, but the question of

3. Foreign Office memorandum, 'Chinese Aircraft at Hong Kong', 6 and 7; Victor S. Kaufman, 'The United States, Great Britain and the CAT Controversy', *Journal of Contemporary History* 40, no. 1 (2005): 95, 101.

title to the planes was sub judice and he would be advised by his Attorney General whom the visitors would be seeing later. The General then tried some moral suasion, claiming that the planes had been paid for by American taxpayers and had been supplied to China on lend-lease terms. He complained that, although the aircraft were now US-registered, American officials had not been allowed to paint US registration markings on the aircraft. The Governor patiently explained that officials of the US Civil Aeronautics Administration were being allowed to enter Kai Tak but they would not be allowed to interfere with the aircraft. This was because of Grantham's fear that violence might break out if American representatives tried to approach the planes. With the Governor proving unmoved, Big Bill turned into Wild Bill. The security of Hong Kong and Formosa was at stake, Donovan asserted. He did not accept that the issue had to be decided by the courts. Without American help, Britain would have lost the war, he said, adding that if the Governor did not co-operate, it would mean the ending of Marshall Aid to Britain and he would make things hot for Grantham in London.[4] Donovan had misjudged the calm and cautious Grantham, a veteran of both the First World War and the colonial administrative service. 'Donovan's bullying attitude neither impressed nor offended me,' Grantham was to record in his autobiography. 'No doubt he had found it successful on other occasions, so thought he might as well try it in this case.'[5]

The General and his team's next stop was at the office of the Attorney General, Mr John Griffin. They were joined by Dennis Blake, the solicitor from Wilkinson and Grist. It was, in the words of Montagu Pollock's memorandum, 'a long and far from pleasant interview'. Donovan explained, in answer to enquiries from Griffin, that the three original actions by CNAC, CATC and Chinese Resources were no longer being proceeded with because all of the airlines' assets, which were the subject of the litigation, had been sold to CAT, Inc. The main point that Donovan was anxious to put across to Griffin was that the certificate from the Nationalist government ought to be regarded as conclusive evidence of all legal issues, including title to the planes. The certificate was so conclusive, claimed Donovan, that the Governor could disregard the court injunctions and hand the planes over to the representatives of CAT, Inc., using the police if necessary. Griffin asked Blake how such action could be done consistently with the law but the solicitor could not assist. When Griffin explained his and the Governor's concerns about the risk of breaches of the peace, Wild Bill again surfaced. He said he did not believe that the judiciary could not be influenced by the executive. He again warned of the adverse effects on Marshall Aid of failure to oblige America, and told Griffin to be

4. Foreign Office memorandum, 'Chinese Aircraft at Hong Kong', 6–7; Alexander Grantham, *Via Ports: From Hong Kong to Hong Kong* (Hong Kong: Hong Kong University Press, 1965), 162–163.
5. Grantham, *Via Ports*, 162.

practical. According to Montagu Pollock's memorandum, 'General Donovan then terminated the meeting by an abrupt departure, informing the Attorney General in so doing that he would report to the State Department that the Attorney General was obstructive and non-co-operative'.[6]

Wild Bill may have left in a hurry but he had not finished. That evening he continued his campaign to get the planes by holding a hastily arranged press conference. He told the eager journalists his version of what had happened earlier in the day with the Governor and the Attorney General. He complained that they had been uncooperative. He said he was pressing hard for executive action. He revealed that two officials from the US Civil Aeronautical Department had been refused permission to inspect the planes that day. The newspapers, Chinese as well as English, gave the event full and gleeful coverage, with photographs of the General to the fore. Of course it was all part of Big Bill's attempts to lean on the colonial authorities.

What Donovan did and what he said to the press was a gross breach of the confidence that the Hong Kong government representatives might reasonably have supposed to have attached to the two meetings. Donovan had not forewarned them of his intentions. His conduct appalled members of the Foreign Office.

This forced the Hong Kong government to issue a statement the next day. The statement confirmed their refusal to take executive action. The reason, it explained, was that the matter was sub judice. The statement did not say, but officials at the Foreign Office reflected, that Donovan's revelations had made it harder for them to do anything to help him even if they had thought it right to do so. They may also have reflected that the revelations showed their sincerity in seeking a judicial solution and would have done their credibility no harm in the eyes of Chinese Communists.

The following day Donovan wrote to the Attorney General suggesting that the court be moved to take account of new facts, namely the certificate by the Nationalists that the assets had been sold. He suggested that the Attorney General intervene in the litigation, either on behalf of the government or to assist as a friend of the court (amicus curiae). By doing so, Donovan was revealing his weakness as a civil litigation lawyer (he had been a criminal prosecutor) and his fixation with the Nationalist certificate. He then returned to another obsession, executive action, by adding that CAT, Inc. was ready to explore with the government any suitable method of enabling the company to obtain possession by such action. This might be possible, he suggested, if British recognition of the Communists was expressed not to be retro-active. The letter made no headway with Griffin who merely acknowledged its receipt and said that he was not willing to continue the discussion.

6. Foreign Office memorandum, 'Chinese Aircraft at Hong Kong', 6–7; William M. Leary, 'Aircraft and Anti-Communists: CAT in Action, 1942–52', *China Quarterly* 52 (1972): 654, 659.

The General's suggestion about non-retroactivity of recognition again exposed his limitations as a lawyer. The effect and extent of recognition are matters of law for the courts, not for the government. An administrative declaration that the recognition was not retro-active would have had no impact. Donovan's persistent pleas for 'executive action' may also have undermined his case, for to British ears during that era the phrase held connotations of performing arbitrary, even authoritarian, acts. In American usage it simply meant acts by the administrative branch of government.[7]

Donovan's tactics were to squeeze the authorities both in Hong Kong and London, using his influence in political and diplomatic circles. He fired off a telegram to his law colleague Mr Fooshee in London giving his version of the interview with the Governor, emphasizing that ownership was essential and instructing Fooshee to attend the Foreign Office to insist that Britain recognize the sale and that recognition of the Communist government should not be retrospective. So, on Thursday 5 January, the same day as Donovan's letter to Griffin, Fooshee and US embassy representatives were at the Foreign Office armed with the telegram. They pressed for the UK to recognize the validity of the sale and asked that the Governor be instructed to provide certified copies of a second note which the Foreign Office had received two days' earlier from the Chinese ambassador stating that Pan-Am's 20 per cent interest in CNAC had been transferred to his government and that all the assets of CNAC and CATC had been sold to CAT, Inc. Fooshee complained that Grantham had been uncooperative. The Foreign Office stuck to the line that the validity of the sale was a question for the court but undertook to make available a certified copy of the ambassador's new note for use in the litigation. This was delivered on the following Wednesday.

Two new writs

On the Friday two writs were issued in Hong Kong on behalf of CAT, Inc. claiming delivery of the planes and other assets and damages for their wrongful detention. One writ concerned the assets of CNAC, the other the assets of CATC. The defendants were not the airline workers or Communist sympathizers thought to be in control of the aircraft, however. Rather they were Chennault and Willauer themselves. In other words, the defendants were two of the principals behind CAT, Inc., the plaintiff. This was not as eccentric as might at first appear, since it was Chennault and Willauer in their personal capacity who had sold the airline assets to CAT, Inc. The company's lawyers

7. Dean Acheson, *Present at the Creation: My Years at the State Department* (New York: W. W. Norton, 1969), 391–392.

were no doubt anxious to launch the proceedings before the change in recognition by Britain.

CAT, Inc. immediately filed an application for the appointment of a receiver for the disputed assets. This is a procedure whereby property which is the subject of litigation may be placed in the custody of an independent person so as to preserve it until the outcome of the dispute is decided. The application was fixed to be heard on 1 February 1950 by the Chief Justice.

As things stood, the people with actual custody of the planes, the Communist sympathizers, were not parties to the new litigation. The defendants, Chennault and Willauer, were being sued to hand over the assets they had sold but not delivered to CAT, Inc. They could not deliver them because they did not have custody or control of the assets. They needed to bring the sympathizers into the two actions. So on 21 January they applied for and obtained permission to serve notices joining as third parties the employees who had been defendants in the previous, now discontinued, case. When those employees acknowledged service of the Third Party Notices, appointed a team of lawyers to rival the Americans, and filed affidavit evidence opposing the appointment of a receiver, the scene was set for a legal showdown over who owned the 71 planes.

Recognition is announced

The US embassy representatives would have known before their visit to the Foreign Office that UK recognition was imminent since it was common knowledge among diplomatists and around Whitehall. The announcement duly came at midnight on 5–6 January that His Majesty's Government had withdrawn de jure recognition of the Nationalist government of the Republic of China as the government of China and that the Central People's Government of the People's Republic of China was now recognized as the government of China de jure. The Foreign Office addressed a note to Chou En-lai:

> I have pleasure to inform Your Excellency that His Majesty's Government . . . having completed their study of the situation resulting from the formation of the Central People's Government of the People's Republic of China and observing that it is now in effective control of by far the greater part of the territory of China have this day recognised that Government as the de facto Government of China.

The note then stated that His Majesty's Government was ready to establish diplomatic relations 'on the basis of equality, mutual benefit and mutual respect for territory and sovereignty'. The note was circulated to British diplomatic representatives around the globe.

Pending the establishment of diplomatic relations, Mr J. C. Hutchison was appointed British Chargé d'Affaires ad interim in Peking. Premier Chou En-lai accepted Hutchison's appointment on 9 January and suggested negotiations for the establishment of diplomatic relations.[8]

Ceylon and Norway immediately accorded de jure recognition to the CPG. Other countries swiftly followed. India and Pakistan, as well as the Soviet Union, had already recognized the new Chinese government.[9]

The British announcement caused anger amongst members of the China lobby in the US Congress.[10] This stoked mounting concern in the Congress and the administration about Communist China. Republican senators sensed that the anger was a weapon that might be used against the Democrat administration, especially the Secretary of State, Dean Acheson, whom they suspected of being a dangerous liberal, if not a covert socialist.

Admission to the UN

One week after the announcement of recognition, on 13 January 1950, the Soviet Union placed motions before the Security Council of the United Nations organization for the expulsion of KMT representatives from the council and the admission of CPG representatives instead. Five of the thirteen council members voted in favour but the majority voted against, so the motions were lost. The Soviet representative, Mr Malik, walked out in protest and the USSR decided to absent itself from the council. This boycott had been agreed a few days earlier in Moscow between the Soviet Union's foreign minister Vyshinsky and Mao Tse-tung, as had the tactic (implemented the following week) of the PRC appointing a UN representative anyway.[11]

Britain abstained on the vote despite its earlier withdrawal of recognition from the KMT, its consequent recognition of the CPG, and the view of Beckett the FO's legal adviser that recognition of a government was linked to the qualification of its state to membership of the UN. Why? The diplomatic answer was that Britain had ascertained that there was no majority for the Soviet motions and so had decided that to support them would be futile. The blunter political answer was that the UK did not want to antagonize the US and did not wish to appear over-eager for PRC admission. The US was against the CPG's admission and had exerted its influence on the governments which did not support the motions in order to defeat them. At the time, it seemed likely that Taiwan would soon fall to the Communists and resolve the question of KMT

8. Evan Luard, *Britain and China* London: Chatto and Windus, 1962), 83.
9. Luard, *Britain and China*, 79.
10. Kaufman, 'The CAT Controversy', 103.
11. Qiang Zhai, *The Dragon, the Lion, and the Eagle: Chinese-British-American Relations, 1949–1958* (Kent, OH: Kent State University Press, 1994), 99–100.

participation at the UN anyway. But it made Britain appear ambivalent, if not duplicitous.

State in a state

The reaction from politicians in Washington to London's announcement provoked more representations, exhortations, and entreaties from the Department of State. The American mood was further darkened by reports from Kai Tak that the communist employees were removing Nationalist emblems from the fuselages of the aircraft and painting the PRC flag in their place. This had probably been prompted by an order given to C. Y. Liu on Monday 13 January by the head of the CPG's Civil Aviation Bureau to take over the assets of CNAC.

On 10 January the American embassy in London forwarded to the Foreign Office a message from the department that it had been officially informed by the government of the Republic of China that it had sold its interests in CNAC and CATC to Chennault and Willauer, that the State Department recognized that government, and that the validity of the sale was questioned only by communist elements in the companies. Copies of various telegrams from the US Consul-General in Hong Kong to the US Embassy in London were handed over in an effort to persuade the Foreign Office to recommend executive assistance to US interests. The suggestion of both the embassy and the Consul-General was that since CAT, Inc. was not a party to the injunctions granted in the earlier litigation during November, the Foreign Office might possibly recommend executive assistance despite the opposition to it from Hong Kong. The Foreign Office response was that this would be deciding the legal question of to whom the aircraft belonged at the time of the sale.

This was followed up by another visit by the US Chargé d'Affaires Holmes to Sir William Strang, the Permanent Secretary. Strang used the opportunity to express concern about the unscrupulous threats used by General Donovan in Hong Kong, observing that the presence of the US Consul-General at those meetings seemed to give official blessing to the General's actions. Although diplomatically expressed, this was withering criticism from such an eminent foreign policy mandarin. Holmes described the General as 'a difficult man to curb'. Then he asked whether, if the court judgment went in favour of CAT, Inc., British authorities would facilitate departure of the aircraft and whether, if the question of ownership was left undecided, they would recognize the corporation's ownership on the strength of the Chinese embassy notes. Strang said he would reply in writing.

Before he could do so, a message arrived from Hong Kong stating that Donovan proposed to discontinue all legal actions so that the court injunctions would be discharged, but before doing so he wanted assurance from the Governor that if the injunctions were lifted, executive action would immediately be taken to place CAT, Inc. in possession of the aircraft. It is difficult to know what the General's reasoning must have been here. The original actions would have to be discontinued if they had not been already, since on the American case the plaintiff airlines no longer owned the property at issue. The General had acknowledged this in the interview with the Governor the previous week. So abandonment of the plaintiffs' injunctions in those actions was inevitable. As yet, no replacement injunctions had been sought or imposed in the two fresh actions by CAT, Inc. Hence Donovan was proposing really to give up nothing. Perhaps he reasoned that the prospect of there being no legal restraint on the communists in charge of the planes would alarm the British and Hong Kong authorities and galvanize them into action. If so, it was another miscalculation on his part.

Donovan and Chennault were using their political contacts in Washington to good effect. On 14 January Chennault wrote to Clark Clifford, who had the ear of President Truman, at the White House, setting out what he saw as the strategic importance of the aircraft. In desperation to emphasize this, Chennault asserted that they constituted a modern fleet which in the Far East was the equivalent of the British or French naval fleets during the Second World War. Using the planes, the Communists could consolidate their power in China, attack Taiwan or support guerrilla warfare against the Philippines, Indochina and Indonesia, he wrote.

Donovan lobbied members of Congress to push the Truman administration to help Chennault. On 25 January Congressman Mike Mansfield wrote to President Truman expressing his worry about the lengthy court processes. During the delay the Chinese Communists might 'be able to make off with these planes,' he said and urged the President to do all in his power to prevent this.[12]

Strang's written replies to the American Chargé Holmes were delivered in London on 14 January, together with a written response to the earlier allegations of sabotage and of discrimination against CAT. Holmes was dissatisfied with these, so he was back at the Foreign Office on 20 January, this time for an interview with Sir Eric Beckett, the legal adviser. The US diplomats were accompanied by Malcolm Fooshee, Donovan's colleague. The atmosphere was becoming febrile as 1 February, the date of the next court hearing, approached. Again the Americans asked whether, if the actions were to be discontinued, His Majesty's Government would be willing to authorize executive action to place the aircraft in the hands of CAT, Inc. Sir Eric was non-committal: if there were no injunction applicable to the planes and no proceedings before the court relating to them, and there were no judgment deciding to whom the planes belonged, any action the executive might take

12. Zhai, *The Dragon, the Lion, and the Eagle*, 106.

to facilitate the departure of the planes would depend upon the manner in which the factual situation developed, he said, adding 'and it is not possible to forecast how it would develop'. As if that was not discouraging enough, he observed that the hypothesis on which the question depends 'seems rather an improbable one'. Fooshee repeated the allegations of unhelpfulness and delaying tactics by the courts, presumably at the insistence of Donovan. He was asked to give an instance of this but was unable to do so.

A further symptom of consternation at the State Department came next day, 21 January, with messages sent to the FO via the US embassy and to the Governor in Hong Kong asserting that the airlines' assets had been transferred to Chennault and Willauer and that the certification of this should be acceptable under accepted principles of international law. The message described the assets as 'an American interest' and requested their protection. Diplomatic back channels revealed that the pair were worried that the injunctions might be lifted by the Hong Kong court after the forthcoming hearing and the planes flown away before an appeal could be lodged.[13] Chennault was in Hong Kong in late January where during a reception at the US Consul-General's residence he met the US Ambassador at large, Dr Philip Jessup, who was on a tour of US diplomatic posts in the Far East prior to a conference with all US regional representatives in Bangkok.

Jessup, a long-serving professor at Columbia University in New York and an international lawyer of repute, was a calm analyst who was thought to favour early recognition of the Communist government by the USA and therefore to represent one strand of opinion within the State Department. The evidence of this is, however, flimsy and probably originates in Jessup's joint authorship of the White Paper, a massive recent State Department reassessment of US policy in the Far East, in which the Nationalist regime had been criticized and a policy of non-intervention in the civil war advised. The paper hoped, rather unrealistically, that democratic elements within China could still provide a third option. Jessup seems to have kept his own counsel and listened to the range of opinions within Hong Kong, including no doubt Chennault's ardent anti-communist views. There was in fact a range of views within the State Department about recognition of the CPG. Those in favour of prompt recognition were said to include Acheson, the Secretary of State, himself, although he gave off contradictory signals at various times. In any event, the prospect of the US following Britain in recognizing the PRC was receding by early 1950 for political reasons.[14]

Shortly before the hearing on 1 February, London asked the Governor for copies of any pleadings and injunctions that he could get hold of. He was also asked to notify the Foreign Office as soon as possible if a judgment

13. Foreign Office memorandum, 'Chinese Aircraft at Hong Kong', 10.
14. Karl Lott Rankin, *China Assignment* (Seattle: University of Washington Press, 1964), 23 and 109.

seemed imminent, especially one likely to favour the Communists. There were no spare copies of the pleadings (it was before the days of the photocopier), so the Foreign and Colonial Offices had to make do with a summary.

Once the hearings started, US concern heightened. Although the hearings were in private, the State Department had a back-channel through the lawyers for CAT, Inc. and thence Chennault, Willauer and Donovan to the Consulate-General in the colony, as to how the applications for appointment of receivers were going. Reports about observations and reactions by the Chief Justice Sir Leslie Gibson and about submissions by opposing counsel would filter back. On Monday 6 February the American Assistant Secretary of State Mr Perkins called at the British embassy in Washington to reiterate the seriousness that the US attached to the entire episode and the importance of preventing the properties from falling into communist hands. Three days later the State Department instructed Rankin in Hong Kong that in the event of an adverse ruling he should formally notify the colonial government that the planes were US-registered but lacked airworthiness certificates so it would be contrary to British obligations under the Chicago Convention to permit the planes to take off.

New attitude in USA

Anglo-US diplomatic relations were at a low point.[15] This was the consequence of American unwillingness to accept the British view of the importance of seeking a judicial solution to the dispute and of British failure to appreciate the strength of anti-communist feeling among influential people in Washington DC. The UK aimed for good relations with the new Chinese government in the hope of salvaging some of its trade and investment in China and continuing its position in Hong Kong. It trusted that Chinese communism might prove distinct from the Soviet Russian version. Consequently, it preferred that independent judges decide the issue of ownership and did not want to take 'executive action' or do anything that suggested lack of even-handedness towards the two sides or that jeopardized the reputation of its judicial system.

The United States by contrast regarded the matter as political, not legal, so in its eyes there was no obstacle to imposing an administrative or even a military solution. Communism was communism wherever it existed and world communism, inspired by the USSR with Red China its satellite, was now the enemy. That attitude had been growing throughout the Cold War. In early 1950 there seemed to be an upward step-change in its growth, eradicating any temptation to view Mao Tse-tung's regime with goodwill.

15. Chi-Kwan Mark, *Hong Kong and the Cold War: Anglo-American Relations, 1949–1957* (Oxford: Clarendon Press, 2004).

10

Waiting for Judgment

The hearings

The applications for appointment of a receiver for the airline assets were presented at long hearings held at Hong Kong's elegant Edwardian-era Supreme Court building during the first 10 days of February 1950. The application concerning CNAC took more than three days, from Wednesday 1 February to Saturday 4 February. That concerning CATC was shorter, since many of the facts and arguments were the same as for CNAC, and occupied only 8 and 9 February in the following week. The evidence was entirely in the form of affidavits (sworn written statements), as is usual for such applications. The essential facts were not in dispute anyway.

During the interval between the two hearings, Chief Justice Gibson had other business to deal with, including an application for the appointment of a provisional liquidator for CNAC. The airline had not been in operation since the suspension of its aircraft and the High Court injunctions the previous November. In the confusion and difficulty, it had not been paying its bills. On 12 January 1950 a group of 67 creditors had petitioned for the now communist-controlled CNAC to be wound up by the court on the basis that it could not meet its debts. The petitioners and a group of others who were owed money by the airline then invoked an unusual procedure for the appointment by the court of a provisional liquidator, an independent person to take charge of the business of the airline pending the outcome of the winding-up petition. No doubt some of the applicants were supporters of Chennault and Willauer who would have seen this as another way of ensuring that the planes were kept at Kai Tak.

The airline certainly took the provisional liquidator application seriously, deploying to oppose it the full team of counsel that had been arguing its cause in the application for appointment of receivers the previous week. CNAC wanted to pay its debts, they argued, but was prevented from doing so by the court injunctions. The corporation had plenty of assets in Hong Kong, including cash at the bank, book debts, the planes, equipment, land and buildings.

These were worth millions of dollars, far more than the claimed debts. There was no danger of CNAC being insolvent.

The Chief Justice had no difficulty in batting away this application. He pointed out that the court would appoint a provisional liquidator only in exceptional circumstances and would be particularly slow to do so if the winding-up petition was opposed and its outcome uncertain. Here, the petition was opposed and the outcome was uncertain. An appointment would cause great inconvenience to the corporation by interfering with its activities. Although it intended to move the planes and equipment back to China, the corporation had considerable immovable property in Hong Kong.

Actually, CNAC's ownership of land and buildings and the rarity of appointing a provisional liquidator should have been reasons enough not to appoint one. Another good reason was that the dispute with CAT, Inc. about the ownership of the assets and the claim by defecting employees that the planes and equipment were now held on behalf of the CPG meant that a liquidator would have had an impossible task trying to take them over. Yet the Chief Justice betrayed his anxiety to please those now controlling the corporation and the Hong Kong authorities by resorting also to a weak reason, that a liquidator would impede the airline's operations. CNAC had not been transporting passengers or goods for months. Gibson acknowledged this and that its only operations were the maintenance of the aircraft. Yet, he asserted implausibly, this was a big task to entrust to a provisional liquidator.[1]

Once the question of a provisional liquidator had been disposed of, the Chief Justice could turn back to the main event, the appointment of receivers. The hearings of this application would have been held in chambers, that is to say in private. The courtroom would have been closed to the Press and other members of the public. Only the parties and their legal representatives would have been allowed to attend. This is standard practice for incidental procedural matters prior to trial, what lawyers call 'interlocutory applications'. The court would give and publish written reasons for important interlocutory decisions, as was to happen in this instance.

The seriousness of the outcome of the applications to the parties is evident from the eminence of the barristers who were engaged. The plaintiff, CAT, Inc., deployed two King's Counsel and one junior counsel. The fifteen allegedly communist employees who were third parties, the real opponents of the application, engaged one King's Counsel and two juniors. The nominal defendants, Chennault and Willauer, were represented by one junior counsel. The nine barristers thus employed would have amounted to a good proportion of those then practicing at the Bar in Hong Kong.

1. *South China Morning Post*, 8 February 1950.

The lead counsel of each real protagonist was the best that could be found in the colony. Leo D'Almada KC, who led for the American interests on the instructions of Wilkinson and Grist, was of Hong Kong Portuguese descent and had made his name at the Bar before the Second World War.[2] He was relatively young for leading counsel but stood out in the small pool of barristers then practicing. Local administrators certainly regarded him highly: after the war he served as a judge of the military war crimes tribunal and chaired a committee to consider whether rent controls should be continued (always a controversial subject in which the administrators liked to defer to 'experts') and he became a member of the Executive Council, the Governor's 'cabinet'. Appearing with D'Almada was another KC, recently appointed but no less well-regarded. He was John McNeill, from an old Scottish family, who had been practicing in Shanghai, mainly representing the local authorities there, but transferred to Hong Kong after the Second World War. McNeill had quickly built up a strong practice in the colony and in turn was asked by the government to head a committee to consider the future of rent controls in the 1950s. Both D'Almada and McNeill chaired the Hong Kong Bar Association during that decade. They were supported by Leslie Wright, an Irish lawyer who had come to Hong Kong with the military administration at the end of the war and stayed on to enjoy almost half-a-century of prosperous practice, mainly in the area of company law. So prosperous indeed was Wright's practice that in later years he could afford to live permanently at the Hilton Hotel and dine daily at its grill.

Similarly, the second junior barrister engaged for the employees had arrived with the British military and stayed on. Brook Bernacchi was to practice for almost 50 years. He was a man of liberal social and political attitude who later became a thorn in the side of colonial administrators when as chairman of the Reform Club he pressed for more representative government. Bernacchi became as known for this as he was for his ownership of a tea plantation and a bus company on then-remote Lantau Island.

Even more radical was the employees' first junior, Percy Chen. One of the few Chinese barristers in post-war Hong Kong, Chen was in fact from the West Indies. He was the elder son of Eugene Chen, a lawyer of Hakka descent practising in Trinidad, and a French Creole mother whose family owned a large plantation on that island. Although Eugene Chan hardly spoke Chinese and loved Western art and literature, he became fired by the Chinese Nationalist ideas of Sun Yat Sen whom he had met in London. Eugene followed Sun to China and joined the left-wing faction of the Kuomintang. In 1926 young Percy abandoned his practice in Port-of-Spain to join his father whom Sun had appointed foreign minister of China. Percy accompanied the KMT's Soviet

2. His full name and title was the Honorable Leo D'Almada e Castro, CBE, KC.

adviser Borodin back to Moscow when Chiang Kai-shek threw off Russian assistance (see Chapter 3) and stayed there for six years. Like his father, Percy grew sympathetic to communism, later writing from Tientsin for left-wing newspapers including *Ta Kung Pao* in Hong Kong. Although Eugene died in captivity in China during the war, Percy survived and came to Hong Kong in 1947, setting up as a barrister in Princes Building. In 1949 he founded the Hong Kong Chinese Reform Association to advocate elections for the municipal council which had been proposed three years earlier as part of the Young reforms. This alarmed Sir Alexander Grantham who could foresee a democratic council being a political cockpit between Nationalists and Communists with the likes of Chen becoming elected and agitating against British rule.

Bernacchi and Chen's leader was Eldon Potter, KC, the doyen of the local Bar who had been appearing in the Hong Kong courts for more than four decades, initially as a prosecutor. Potter's roots were in southwestern County Cork in Ireland. By 1950 Potter was 68 years old and had survived internment during the Japanese occupation. He had been chosen by his fellows as the first chairman of the Hong Kong Bar Association on its foundation in 1948, with Percy Chen as its first secretary.

These three were all instructed by a relatively new firm of solicitors, Ford, Kwan and Company. In a profession dominated by expatriates, Ford Kwan stood out for its Chineseness, so it was a natural choice for the communist side in the litigation. Seventy years later the firm's website was still boasting that it was among the first to serve clients from the mainland.

There had in fact already been an application for appointment of a Mr Hunt, a chartered accountant, to be receiver of the assets of the two airlines. This had been made in early January 1950, almost immediately after the launching of the new actions by CAT, Inc. At that stage the only parties had been the corporation and Chennault and Willauer. The application had been heard by Mr Justice Williams. He had rejected it on 9 January. No record of his reasons is available—he may well have delivered them only orally—but it seems that he thought that CAT, Inc. had not sufficiently established its title to the property.[3] That would not have been surprising given the haste in which the application had been made. There would have had to be proof that the sales in Taipei by the two airlines, presumably governed by Chinese law, had been valid and then that the on-sales by Willauer and Chennault, governed by US or possibly Hong Kong law, had also been valid.

Williams J may also have been mindful that the persons with sole access to the planes, the communist employees and sympathizers some of whom at least had been defendants in the earlier action started by Chennault and Willauer, were not before the court. Since these individuals would have been affected by

3. Foreign Office memorandum, 'Chinese Civil Aircraft at Hong Kong', 8; Gibson CJ in *Civil Air Transport Incorporated v Chennault and Others* (1950) 34 HKLR 358, 364.

any order that the receiver take possession of the property, they should have been given an opportunity to state their position.

The applications

The February applications before Chief Justice Gibson were for the appointment of joint receivers of the assets of the airlines. Mr Hunt was again proposed, this time with his colleague and fellow accountant, a Mr Ross. The communist employees and sympathizers had been joined as third parties and served with the evidence. They resisted the appointment of receivers. The defendants, Chennault and Willauer, naturally consented to the appointments.

The role of a receiver appointed by the court is to take charge of property which is the subject of a lawsuit so as to preserve that property pending the outcome of the suit. The property may need protection from some danger which threatens it or a receiver may be required so as to enable someone who possesses rights over the property to obtain the benefit of those rights and preserve the property where ordinary legal remedies are defective. The receiver does not become owner of the property. He or she is the custodian of the property who exercises the property rights as an officer of the court and subject to its supervision.[4]

The court's power to appoint a receiver is given by rules of court, which in 1950 were contained in the Code of Civil Procedure.[5] A receiver may be appointed where it appears just and convenient to do so. Accordingly the judge has a wide and flexible discretion. However, it is a judicial discretion, that is to say its exercise should be based on reasons which emerge from and are consistent with considerations in other similar cases. Those considerations might include whether there is a risk of assets being dissipated, whether the assets can be protected in some other way, and whether there is a risk of uncompensatable damage to a party if a receiver were to be appointed. A dispute over ownership of the assets may be a relevant consideration but is not in itself a bar to the appointment of an interim receiver.

A receiver appointed by the court is usually a professional person, as the proposed receivers were in the present application. He is subject to directions given by the court. He is entitled to remuneration at professional rates approved by the court. Consequently, the proposed appointment of the accountants Messrs Hunt and Ross, although interim (until after trial), would have been an expensive undertaking.

---

4. *Parsons v Sovereign Bank of Canada* [1913] AC 160, 167.
5. Section 587 of the Code. The rules should be underpinned by legislation but this provision in the Code does not seem to be based on any Ordinance. The current power is in s 21L of the High Court Ordinance, Cap 4, and Order 30 of the Rules of the High Court.

The evidence in the applications was in the form of affidavits again. There had been more time to prepare these than for the hearing before Williams J. Although affidavits are supposed to deal solely with factual evidence, parties often (improperly) include in them arguments, opinions concerning the issues, and assertions of law. In this case the third parties had used the affidavits to warn the court and the other parties that they intended to raise the point of sovereign immunity.

Sovereign immunity

Foreign heads of state and governments have immunity from the jurisdiction of the municipal courts of other states. Consequently it is an absolute objection to a lawsuit that the claim impeaches a sovereign foreign government. Only if that government chooses to submit to the other jurisdiction will the case be heard. The immunity is based upon the comity of nations and their respect for each other's equality and independence. Courtesy, civility and consideration towards the governments, laws and customs of other countries underlie the doctrine. The government in question here was the new Central People's Government, or CPG, in China.

Two years earlier in the High Court of Hong Kong an objection founded on sovereign immunity had been raised in a dispute about some rice owned by a trading enterprise belonging to the Nationalist government of the Republic of China. The parties in that case had been represented by two of the counsel engaged in the present dispute, so it is quite possible that the idea of raising the point came from them.

At first blush sovereign immunity would have seemed an issue upon which the third parties were unlikely to succeed. They were all individuals, not governments or members of any government. So far as is known, they were residents of Hong Kong not accredited to the CPG. They were merely sympathetic to that government. Furthermore, the planes and other assets had all belonged to commercial airlines, one of which was a limited company.

There was even a question mark over whether the CPG was relevant. The aircraft and other property were located not in China but in a Crown Colony, on British territory and within Hong Kong's jurisdiction. Britain had not recognized the CPG officially until January 1950. That was after the planes arrived in the colony, after the sale to Chennault and Willauer, and after their onward sale to CAT, Inc.

The executive certificate

However, the effect of British recognition of the CPG could well become relevant to the Chief Justice's judgment. Fortunately he had already taken steps to ascertain the proper position regarding recognition. In the earlier sets of proceedings, those between Chennault and Willauer on the one hand and the employees and their sympathizers on the other, he had, with the consent of the parties' lawyers, in late December 1949 framed a number of questions to be put to the British authorities concerning which government was regarded as in charge of China and when. This was the proper procedure. There was high authority that any question as to the sovereignty of a foreign state is one upon which British courts are to be guided by the UK government: 'Our State cannot speak with two voices on such a matter, the judiciary saying one thing and the executive another.'[6]

Since the early nineteenth century the practice had been for the court to request assistance from the Foreign Office which in response would provide a certificate stating the executive's position regarding recognition of the entities in question. Normally the contents of the certificate would take the form of a statement although in this instance, since the request consisted of a number of questions, the certificate was framed in the form of answers. The Foreign Office's policy advisers disliked this since it reduced the scope for evasion and obfuscation, although Sir Eric Beckett, the FO legal adviser, urged that the replies be precise and explicit. The questions were finalized and sent to the Foreign Office several weeks before the beginning of the hearing in early February 1950. The answers, which had to be considered by ministers and their advisers, were not settled and sent until after the hearing had concluded. Kenneth Younger, the new Minister of State, was primarily responsible for the drafting, but Beckett would have contributed too. According to Younger, their sole concern was that the answers should be accurate and informative.[7] It would later emerge however that they had been economical in both aspects.

As a result of the number of questions and the preciseness of the answers, the certificate was unusually long and complex. It was quite normal for the certificate to be cautiously worded so as to avoid unintended consequences. However, the contents in this case have been described as the ultimate in temporizing.[8]

The answers were finalized on 14 February 1950 and arrived in Hong Kong the next day. This must be one reason that it took Gibson CJ almost two weeks to complete the reasons for his decision on the application for appointment of a receiver. A copy of the answers was immediately sent to the US embassy in London, reaching it before the answers reached Gibson.

---

6. Lord Atkin in *Arantzazu Mendi* [1939] AC 256, 264.
7. Victor S. Kaufman, 'The United States, Britain and the CAT Controversy', *Journal of Contemporary History* 40, no. 1 (2005): 95, 102; Peter Lowe, *Containing the Cold War in East Asia: British Policies towards Japan, China and Korea, 1948–53* (Manchester: Manchester University Press, 1997), 159.
8. D. P. O'Connell, *International Law*, 2nd ed. (London: Stevens, 1970), vol. 1, 114–115; James Crawford, *The Creation of States in International Law*, 2nd ed. (Oxford: Oxford University Press, 2006), 198–200.

Questions and answers

The first question asked of the Foreign Office was whether His Majesty's Government recognized the Republican government of China (the Nationalist government) as the de jure government of China. In December 1949, when this question had been asked, the answer would have been yes. But by the time of the hearing and at the time that the question was answered the answer was no: HM Government does not recognize the Nationalist government as the de jure government of the Republic of China. This was actually slightly ambiguous, for by that time the Republic of China had been reduced to the islands of Formosa and Hainan plus a few other dependencies. The Republic as it had been no longer existed, the greatest part of it having become the People's Republic of China. But the Foreign Office did not descend into such detail.

The Chief Justice's second question was: if HM Government does not recognize the Republican government, when did it cease to recognize that government? The answer to that had become well known between the time that the questionnaire had been delivered and the time that it had been answered: up until midnight on 5 January/6 January 1950. Until that point, the answer elaborated, the British government recognized the Nationalists as the de jure government of the Republic of China and as from that point the British government ceased to recognize them as the de jure government of the Republic of China.

Similarly, the answer to the third question (really two questions) had become well known by the time that it was answered. Is the Central People's Government or any other government recognized as the de jure government and, if so, from what date? The answer was that as from midnight on 5/6 January 1950 the British government recognized the Central People's Government as the de jure government of the Republic of China.

The fourth question (again, really two questions) was more difficult. It was, has the Republican government ceased to be the de facto government (either at the time of moving the seat of government to Formosa or otherwise) and, if so, from what date? The FO's response was that the British government recognized that the Nationalist government had ceased to be the de facto government of the Republic of China. As to when it ceased so to be, the response was that it ceased to be the de facto government of different parts of the territories of the Republic of China as from the dates on which it ceased to be in effective control of those parts. The response to the latter part of the question was not helpful, but it could hardly be put any other way since the answer to who was the de facto government by definition depended upon the facts.

The second part of the fourth answer troubled both the Chief Justice and the American embassy, for it was pregnant with a further question: if the Nationalist government had ceased to be the de facto government of various parts of China when it ceased to be in effective control of them, who was regarded as their de facto government after that? The implicit answer was, the CPG, at least after its declared formation on 1 October 1949. So Sir Leslie Gibson set about drafting a supplementary sixth question: whether HM Government recognized the CPG as the de facto government of China between 1 October 1949 and 5 January 1950. That question was sent off on 17 February but Sir Leslie decided not to delay his judgment to await the answer. This was perhaps just as well since it took four weeks to receive a reply.

The fifth question was: Is any other government recognized as the de facto government and, if so, from what date? Given the response to the latter part of the previous question, some subtlety was required in answering this. The formula which the FO came up with was that 'HM Government does not recognize any governments other than the Central People's Government of the People's Republic of China as the de facto Government of the Republic of China', but then added: 'Attention, however, is invited to the 2nd sentence in answer to question 4'. In other words, who is the de facto government is a matter of fact and the Nationalists may still be in effective control of parts of China irrespective of recognition.

Both the fifth question and its answer were really addressing the complication that Formosa was still under the control of the KMT. This was raised directly in the sixth and last question. What, it asked, is the status of Formosa? Is it part of China or is it foreign territory vis-à-vis China? The answer was necessarily somewhat convoluted. In 1943 Formosa was part of the Japanese Empire, the answer began, 'and HM Government consider Formosa is still de jure part of that territory'. The reference to 1943 is because of the conference of the allied powers at Cairo on 1 December that year at which it was agreed that all territories that Japan had 'stolen' from the Chinese, including Formosa, should be restored to the Republic of China. That declaration had been confirmed at the Potsdam Conference in July 1945. Three months later, with allied consent, Japanese forces on Formosa had surrendered to Chiang Kai-shek and administration was thereafter undertaken by the government of the Republic of China. At present, the answer added, so far as HM Government are aware, the Governor of Formosa, Wu Kuo Cheng, had not repudiated the superior authority of the Nationalist government. This was all a cautious and roundabout way of saying that for the moment Formosa was regarded officially as still part of Japan but that in reality it was under the control of someone who answered to the Chinese Nationalists. The formal retrocession of Formosa by Japan to China had not yet taken place. That would require a peace treaty between the two countries. But which government could make such a treaty, which would affect Formosa, on behalf of China?

The answers concluded gratuitously that the effect of the British government's recognition as set out in the answers, in particular its retroactive effect if any, 'are questions for the court to decide in the light of those answers and of the evidence before it'. Here the hand of Sir Eric Beckett can be detected, setting out the legal position. He and his ministerial superiors did not want the judiciary to put the issue back to the executive by saying in their judgments that whether and to what extent the recognition was retrospective was a matter for the government or by asking yet another question to be answered prior to the judgment. The question of retroactivity of recognition had caused much anxiety to the American side which feared that the court would say that although Great Britain had not officially recognized the CPG at the time of the sale in mid-December 1949, once that recognition had taken place it could be regarded as effective from the founding of the PRC on 1 October 1949 or, in areas in which the Communists had exercised effective control, even earlier.

As it transpired, the answers were not greatly relevant to the outcome of the proceedings. Their main point, that recognition was withdrawn from the Nationalists and given to the Communists on 5/6 January 1950, was so notorious that it hardly needed stating. The answers' approach to the question of de facto recognition in effect moved the enquiry back one stage to ask who, if anyone, was in charge at a particular place at a particular time. That is why it so concerned both the Chief Justice and the US embassy. If a relevant part of China was under the control of the Communists at the relevant time, they would be recognized as the de facto government of that part and that might affect the outcome of the case.

The answer that was eventually received to the supplementary question was that HM Government recognized that in the period between 1 October 1949 and 5/6 January 1950 the Central People's Government was the de facto government of those parts of the territory of the Republic of China over which it had established effective control. The answer added that if control was established after 1 October 1949, the CPG was the de facto government from the dates when it so established control. In other words, being the de facto government remained a matter of fact even in the case of a government that was newly recognized as the de jure government. This answer arrived in Hong Kong in mid-March, too late to be included in Sir Leslie's reasoned judgment.

Donovan's late suggestion

The arguments in the application concerning the forty CNAC aeroplanes and other assets were concluded by the weekend of 4–5 February. On Monday 6 February Bill Donovan made another of his sudden initiatives. He suggested to Sir Alexander Grantham that the United States government might intervene in the case on the basis that the assets were all lend-lease material.

Donovan had made the lend-lease allegation before, at the conference that he suddenly threw for the press after his fruitless meetings with the

Governor and the Attorney General in early January. What he was saying was that the planes and equipment belonged really to the United States and were merely on loan to the airlines. Whether there was any basis for his assertion is difficult to say. The planes were certainly of American origin, having been made by US manufacturers. Some of them at least had been purchased at discounted rates as US wartime military surplus, but that did not make them part of a lend-lease scheme. The Nationalist authorities undoubtedly regarded them as having been purchased outright, for they sold them to Chennault and Willauer.

However, whether the General's allegation was correct or not is somewhat beside the point. Simply by making the allegation and suggesting that the US might intervene, Donovan was aiming to disrupt the smooth judicial resolution of the dispute. He was in effect telling the British and Hong Kong authorities that their idea of leaving things to the courts could become complicated. Even if the court decided that title now vested in the CPG, the US government, which was not explicitly involved in the litigation, might assert a better title.

What prompted Donovan to make the allegation only once the application was being heard? He had been influential in, and possibly in command of, the American side of the litigation for two months. He had raised the lend-lease point more than a month earlier. An application to join the communist workers and sympathizers as parties had been made and granted in late January. Why had no similar application been made in respect of the US government's alleged interest?

The answer probably is that the General was frustrated at the way in which the hearing before the Chief Justice was going. He would have been privy to the information concerning the submissions and the judge's reactions which had prompted the US embassy's complaint of 10 February based on messages from their Consul-General in Hong Kong who in turn must have been briefed by the lawyers in court for the American parties. This information indicated that Sir Leslie was not persuaded by the American arguments. As a great believer in private intelligence, the General would surely have accepted the information as reliable. As a man of action, he would have wanted to do something about it.

As it happened, the threat to intervene did not materialize. It was far too late for the US government to be heard. It would have had to launch a separate application, if not a separate suit. Anyway, such an intervention might well have backfired, convincing the Chief Justice that title was doubly in dispute, thereby providing an additional reason for denying CAT, Inc.'s application.

More agitation

Instead, the US returned to exerting diplomatic pressure with visits, notes, representations and telegrams throughout the period that the Chief Justice was considering his decision and composing his reasons. On 6 February, even before the hearings had concluded, Assistant Secretary of State Perkins called at the British embassy in Washington to reiterate to the Chargé d'Affaires the seriousness that the US attached to the affair and the importance of preventing the property from falling into communist hands. On 10 February, after the hearings had concluded, the Consul-General Karl Rankin sent a telegram to Washington stating that the application for receivership had been denied on the grounds that the aircraft needed to be maintained. This must have been a garbled account of one of the submissions on behalf of the third party employees to which the Chief Justice had reacted positively in court. No decision was in fact announced for another two weeks.

The telegram also protested that the court seemed about to decide serious questions of title and international law on affidavit evidence alone. This was misconceived: the use of affidavits in cases which turned on questions of law was perfectly normal since the hearing was not a trial and affidavits were the usual means of presenting evidence of facts in procedural matters; the parties' advocates could make submissions of law, supported by case citations, for consideration by the judge. The Consul-General asserted in another telegram that CAT, Inc.'s lawyers, both American and British (presumably meaning Hong Kong counsel and solicitors), thought this 'a denial of the process of law'. Copies of these telegrams were given to the Foreign Office. Officials in Washington were so concerned that they had telephoned the US embassy in London and said that President Truman was personally interested in the matter. Rankin's complaints, misconceived though they were, drew praise from Willauer for the support he was receiving from US diplomats in Hong Kong.[9]

On Monday 13 February the Governor replied by letter to the Consul-General's earlier allegations of sabotage and lack of co-operation. He explained that the aircraft could not fly away because their ailerons (the hinged surfaces on the trailing edge of the wings) had been removed and the planes had been allowed a minimum amount of fuel, sufficient only to start the engines in the course of routine maintenance. He denied any partiality. He had no objection to visits by US officials, he said, but would not allow US markings to be painted on the planes for to do so would be to prejudge the issue.

The Governor's reply did not deter the US embassy from making further allegations of favouritism towards the Communists by Hong Kong authorities

9. Foreign Office memorandum, 'Chinese Aircraft at Hong Kong', 11; Livingston Merchant, evidence to US Senate Sub-committee on Appropriations, 725.

in a long note delivered by the Chargé d'Affaires Holmes to Sir William Strang on 14 February. The note reminded the FO of the assurance given at the beginning of January that HM Government sympathized with US anxiety to prevent the aircraft falling into Communist hands. It then alleged that Communist representatives had been permitted to pack spare parts and prepare the aircraft for rapid departure. It repeated the misconceived point about the use of affidavit evidence and returned to the familiar refrain about executive action: unless there was a firm instruction from London to the Governor requiring him to take such action the Communists would remove the planes and US interests would be irretrievably prejudiced. The note went on to suggest that, as an alternative to executive action, the Hong Kong Attorney-General should ask the court to issue an injunction restraining the disputants from moving the aircraft pending the court decision. The note reached a climax by claiming that if the aircraft fell into Communist hands, that must have repercussions damaging to 'our mutual positions in the Far East' and requesting 'as of extreme urgency' that the instructions be sent to Hong Kong so that American interests in the case would be adequately protected.

The complaints were added to orally by Holmes who told Sir William that the American parties had not been given an opportunity of putting their case to the court as they would have wished and, if the Communists were permitted to fly the planes off, they would not feel they had received full justice. He asserted that the authorities in Hong Kong could take a strong line, as they had done recently in facing down a tramway strike. In response, the Chargé was reminded of the Governor's concern about the danger of breaches of the peace and that Hong Kong was not ruled from Whitehall. Although the Governor was fully aware of HM Government's concern and attitude towards the dispute, it was the latter's policy to leave the Governor to determine his own administrative actions.

Exasperation

Whitehall's exasperation with US persistence is evident from a further salvo from the Foreign Office the next day. This informed the US embassy that it would be more helpful if their representations were made in Hong Kong and that it appeared remarkable that the American Consul-General there was not in a position to satisfy the State Department on questions of sabotage, access to the airfield, court procedure and so on, upon which the State Department had found it necessary to make continual representations in London. Having constantly to repeat US allegations to the Governor implied that the FO lacked confidence in his ability to act in accordance with the policy of HM Government, whereas in fact they had full confidence in him, the reply went on.

Having thus diplomatically told the Americans to stop pestering it and to use their own resources to find the answers to their questions, the Foreign Office closed by telling them that they had only themselves to blame for the current mess. In the FO's own words, the US embassy was 'reminded that the whole of the present legal tangle was due to the past refusal of Pan-American Airways to use their influence to move CNAC out of Hong Kong when so advised by the Governor'. That was an exaggeration, but it no doubt made the FO mandarins feel better.

The salvo did not deter the US embassy from one more effort to push the Foreign Office. On 22 February it sent another representative to complain that the Governor of Hong Kong frequently seemed to be without clear and immediate guidance on the legal issues and that his administrators were leaning over backwards in endeavour to please the Communists.

That very day, just as the Foreign Office was dealing with the latest set of allegations from the US embassy, came a flash from Hong Kong. Judgment was due tomorrow.

11

Sir Leslie's Surprise

The alert is sounded

The telegram from the Governor of Hong Kong which arrived in London on Wednesday 2 February 1950 informed the Foreign Office that it was likely that the cases would be dismissed. The injunctions holding the aircraft at Kai Tak would lapse, the telegram said, and there would be no legal obstacle to removal of the aircraft by the communists.

How did the Governor know this? Sir Leslie Gibson was not due to deliver his reasoned judgment until the next day. One possibility is that Sir Leslie, aware of the political sensitivity of his ruling, had informed the Governor. In the small, closed, expatriate world of the upper echelons of the Hong Kong establishment this was quite likely. The information may well have passed between the Chief Justice and the Governor or their assistants over lunch or drinks. Another possibility is that the Governor had informants in the administration of the Supreme Court: the reasons would have had to be typed up prior to delivery and it would have been impossible to keep them secret. A third possibility is that word had leaked out through lawyers involved in the litigation, an advanced copy of the reasons or a summary of the result having been provided by the Chief Justice's clerks to the lawyers on a confidential basis to enable counsel to prepare submissions, such as on costs, consequential to the outcome of the application. Anyhow, the Governor's source was accurate.

Reasons given

Next day the Chief Justice announced that the applications to appoint receivers were indeed dismissed. The injunctions were consequently removed. The injunctions had been imposed in the earlier action, the one brought by the partnership of Chennault and Willauer before they sold the planes on to CAT, Inc. That action was now inactive. The onward sale meant that the partners no longer had an interest in the property so they had nothing relevant to preserve. Their solicitors had 'gone off the record' of the court as representatives of the partners.

The outcome was hardly unexpected by those involved. The feedback from the lawyers in court as to how the arguments had been received would have revealed the way in which Sir Leslie's mind was working. The judge would have been no less anxious than the Governor to avoid offending the new authorities in China. This is reflected in the respectful language used in the judgment. There he calls the new regime 'The Central People's Government' rather than 'the Communists', 'the Peking regime' or 'the Mao Government', and Mao Tse-tung himself is referred to as 'General Mao'.

What was surprising though was the approach that Sir Leslie deployed. Giving judgment first in the case concerning the forty CNAC aeroplanes, he selected reasons which made it unnecessary to reach any conclusion about ownership of the planes and associated equipment. It was as if he was intent upon avoiding making a decision on the issue of title, even though that was the issue which everyone wanted resolved. The principal means by which he did so was by fastening on to the issue of sovereign immunity. This would provide an absolute block on delving into the merits of the case.

Any decision concerning title to the planes and other assets would violate the sovereign immunity of the Central People's Government, Sir Leslie declared. He acknowledged that the CPG was not a party to the proceedings and had made no formal claim to the assets, and also that it was not the owner of them. CNAC, which was or had been the owner, was an entity separate from its shareholders, including the majority shareholder the Chinese government. Nevertheless, the Chief Justice reasoned, the proceedings did involve property of which that government was in possession or control. It was in possession or control through employees of CNAC who recognized the authority of that government, accepted orders from its high officials and were paid by them, he said.

There was here though an inconsistency which had evidently eluded Sir Leslie. If the individuals who were third parties were employees of CNAC, then surely they represented CNAC, not any government. Just because those individuals had declared that they preferred one political party over another did not alter for whom they worked, nor did the fact that one of the competing governments chose to discharge CNAC's obligation to pay the individuals and purported to give them orders in the name of CNAC. In fairness, this point does not seem to have been squarely put in front of the judge by those representing CAT, Inc. or the Chennault-Willauer partnership. Nor does an associated point seem to have been put to him. This is that the employees could not by mere self-declaration become agents of a particular government or of the Communist-controlled entity called CNAC and that, even if they were accepted as employees by that entity, it would not destroy their duty of loyalty to the enterprise which had engaged them, the Nationalist-controlled CNAC.

The question of the effectiveness of the defectors' representation of the CPG was raised before Sir Leslie but it was set in the context of the legality of that representation. Counsel for the American interests submitted that the employees' acts were in breach of the injunctions which had been awarded in late November 1949 in the course of the earlier proceedings and also of the Representation of Foreign Powers (Control) Ordinance, legislation which had been enacted on 4 November 1949. The injunctions had prohibited the removal of the planes and equipment from Kai Tak and entry to the airline's property there. Section 3 of the Ordinance provided that 'no person shall function on behalf of any foreign power without the consent of the Governor'. In fact the argument entangled two separate points. One was the legality of the employees' acts at the airport (breach of injunction and contempt of court), the other was legality of their purported representation of the CPG.

The Chief Justice brushed the points aside: the CPG did not have to rely upon the actions of persons in contempt of court, he asserted, and when a question of sovereign immunity based on de facto possession is raised, there was authority that the court is not concerned to enquire whether the possession is valid under municipal law. It is unclear what Gibson meant when he said that the CPG did not have to rely upon persons in contempt: perhaps he meant that the workers had not removed the planes after the injunctions had been imposed, or perhaps he meant that their pledge of allegiance was nothing to do with the injunctions. Whichever he meant, the reason seems sound. However, his point about validity of possession under municipal law being irrelevant misses the nub of the second point which is concerned with whether there was de facto possession on behalf of the government (and therefore immunity) in the first place. How could there be government possession through agents when by virtue of law they could not be empowered to act for the government? They could have actual possession but only on behalf of themselves. So no occasion for immunity of a sovereign arose.

Sir Leslie seems to have been uneasy with his answer to the submission because he attempted to bolster it with another point. This was that a statute was to be construed as far as its language permits on the presumption that the legislature did not intend any inconsistency between it and international law, namely the doctrine of sovereign immunity. He concluded that there can have been no intention to displace the doctrine. He added that there was plenty of scope for operation of the Foreign Powers (Control) Ordinance outside the ambit of sovereign immunity. But here again the judge had missed the point, that the Ordinance goes to validity of representation and invalid representation prevents involvement of the sovereign through the representative in the first place.

An associated point about representation which was not made by counsel is that an agent of one principal cannot unilaterally declare himself no longer the agent of that principal and now the agent of another principal. Nor does it make a difference that the second principal accepts the offer of the agent to be his representative. Before any change of agency can arise, the original principal must consent. If the law allowed such a unilateral change, or a change provided that the second principal agreed, there would be nothing to prevent the staff of one employer from announcing that they were now working for a rival employer though using the first employer's name, premises, stock and goodwill. It would make no difference that the second employer was a foreign government since, again, the point is concerned solely with the validity of the agency.

The Chief Justice had more reasons up his sleeve in case his reasoning about sovereign immunity were to be faulted on appeal. His further point was that not all the proper parties were before the court. The real dispute was between the plaintiffs and the defendants (together, the Americans) on the one side and the CPG and CNAC on the other, he said. An order to appoint a receiver would accordingly deprive a party of possession of the property without making him a party to the action. This reasoning was somewhat bizarre in that the judge had just found that the employees (who were party to the proceedings) were in possession as agents of the CPG. Consequently, although the CPG itself was not a party, its agents, those through whom it was found to be acting, were parties. If they had not been so acting, then the CPG would not have been in possession, the CPG would not have been impleaded and the claim to sovereign immunity would not have stacked up. As for the position of CNAC, whether it was a proper party or not depended upon which set of directors, the Nationalist one or the Communist one, was accepted as relevant: that could be resolved only by delving into the merits of the case, something that the judge studiously avoided doing for fear of causing offence.

The Chief Justice's next reason was that the plaintiffs had not established a sufficiently strong case. An applicant for an interlocutory order does not have to show that he will definitely succeed at trial but does have to show a reasonably arguable case, or as it is now termed that there is a serious issue to be tried. The reason for this requirement is the risk of doing irreparable harm to the other party if it should turn out that the applicant's claim fails. In this instance the Chief Justice reasoned that the appointment of a receiver would lead to immobilization of the airline for a protracted period. Yet this overlooked the undoubted fact that CNAC was already immobilized (hence the order would have simply preserved the status quo) and that where the subject of receivership is a functioning business, the role of the receiver is to keep that business in operation. The judgment fudged the issue of whether the case was reasonably arguable by jumping to the effect of an injunction on the airline. Since there appeared on paper to be successive sales of the assets culminating in CAT, Inc., its case seemed sound and there was undoubtedly a reasonably arguable case.

Finally, the Chief Justice detected defects in the plaintiff's case, or rather purported to do so. He picked out three objections of a technical nature: first, that there was no evidence of who were directors of CNAC at the date of the meeting on 31 December 1949 to approve retrospectively the sale of its assets to Chennault and Willauer and as to whether those directors had been properly summoned to the meeting; second, there was no evidence as to who were CNAC's shareholders (who, under Chinese law, had to approve the sale); and third, that the affidavit setting out the Chinese law regarding the validity of the sale was inadequate.[1]

But here again the judge was applying an exacting standard which, whilst it might be appropriate at trial, was harsher than necessary on an interlocutory application aimed at preserving the disputed property in neutral hands rather than awarding it to one of the disputants. All that was required at that stage was that the plaintiffs have a prima facie case. Could it seriously be contended that the Nationalist-controlled CNAC had not wanted to sell the aircraft and equipment? They obviously had been motivated to keep them from the Communists and their government had certified the validity of the sale. Reading the judgment, it is difficult to avoid the impression that his lordship had set course for a certain destination and was searching for reasons to justify the route.

On the same day Gibson CJ gave judgment also in the application concerning the CATC assets. His reasons were short since the only material difference between it and the CNAC case was that CATC was a government department not a company. This difference did not affect the main point, sovereign immunity, so Sir Leslie did not dwell upon it. State immunity was an absolute answer, so he dismissed the CATC application as well.[2]

Widely misunderstood

Both at the time and subsequently, exactly what Sir Leslie Gibson had decided was not correctly grasped. Press and politicians, eager to simplify, declared that the PRC had won or that the planes had been awarded to China rather than to the Americans. More surprisingly, administrators and diplomats also gained that impression. More surprising still, historians have perpetuated the inaccuracy. According to four American authors, seemingly aping each other, the court 'ruled that the aircraft were the rightful property of the People's Republic'. In similar vein a British historian has written that 'it was decided

1. *Civil Air Transport Incorporated v Chennault and Others* (1950) 34 HKLR 358, 372–383.
2. *Civil Air Transport Incorporated v Chennault and Others* (1950) 34 HKLR 384.

that the aircraft were indeed the lawful property of the People's Republic of China'. Hong Kong historians have suggested that the courts found in favour of the PRC too.[3]

The Chief Justice did none of these things. He did not rule on the issue of who owned the planes. He did not need to do so because he decided the application on the principle of sovereign immunity. This meant that the Chinese parties were not subject to the jurisdiction of the court. He did go on to consider briefly other aspects of the case but these did not include the question of ownership. Had he considered that question, his views would have been what lawyers call *obiter dicta*, literally remarks made by the way, and so not determinative.

The hearing was not a trial but an interlocutory application for appointment of a receiver to preserve the property until trial and determination of the question of ownership. Consequently what Sir Leslie was doing was considering the exercise of his discretion. Ownership would not have been determinative of the direction in which the discretion was to be exercised even had he ruled upon the question.

To the American applicants the result was undoubtedly a defeat, but if they had been confident of success beforehand, they would have been deluding themselves. In the Hong Kong of 1949 it would have required a judge of extraordinary boldness and fortitude to rule against PRC interests. The government and administration would have been sternly against the courts doing so, as would the population at large. No one knew what fate awaited the colony at the hands of the new masters to the north. No one dared antagonize them, not least the Governor who advocated that Hong Kong keep its head down and get on with its work. Sir Leslie Gibson was not a man of boldness and fortitude: he was an imperial time-server approaching retirement. He plainly did not want to decide the question of ownership. That is why he latched onto an issue, sovereign immunity, which provided a pleasing, quick and simple solution. He couched his reasons in respectful terms, bordering on the obsequious, so as to appease the CPG.

The result left the aircraft in the control of the communist employees and sympathizers. Accordingly, it might have seemed that they had 'won' since they had successfully resisted the appointment of receivers. In reality there was

3. Victor S. Kaufman, 'The United States, Great Britain and the CAT Controversy', *Journal of Contemporary History* 40, no. 1 (2005): 95, 102; William M. Leary, 'Aircraft and Anti-Communists: CAT in Action, 1942–52', *China Quarterly* 52 (1972): 654–699, 660; Martha Byrd, *Chennault: Giving Wings to the Tiger* (Tuscaloosa: University of Alabama Press, 1987), 339; *William M. Leary, Perilous Missions: Civil Air Transport and CIA Covert Operations in Asia* (Tuscaloosa: University of Alabama Press, 1984), 97; Frank Welsh, *A History of Hong Kong*, rev. ed. (London: Harper Collins, 1997), 448; Priscilla Roberts and John M. Carroll, eds., *Hong Kong in the Cold War* (Hong Kong: Hong Kong University Press, 2016), 35–36; James T. H. Tang, *Britain's Encounter with Revolutionary China, 1949–54* (New York: St. Martin's Press, 1992), 188; Chi-Kwan Mark, *Hong Kong and the Cold War: Anglo-American Relations, 1949–1957* (Oxford: Clarendon Press, 2004), 97.

no change in the status and location of the aircraft. In practice, they could not be flown off because they were not in a fit state to fly.

An embarrassing position

On the very day that Britain's Labour government was re-elected, the judgment threw their strategy into disarray and extended the agony of Hong Kong's government too. In addition to surviving on a much-reduced parliamentary majority, Attlee's administration would have to assuage the anger of its greatest ally and attempt to salvage something from the wreckage. All along their mantra had been 'let the courts decide' who owns the planes, pretending that it was solely a legal question to be resolved by judges. They had every confidence in the judges, they intoned; the course of justice must not be interfered with. Now, the first time the question had been put to a judge (and the most senior one at that), he had avoided giving an answer. His Majesty's government was, as a Foreign Office internal memorandum put it, in an embarrassing position.[4]

The immediate reaction of the Foreign Office was to blame the plaintiffs. HMG had always assumed that there was the possibility of an appeal, they cabled to the Governor: why was there no appeal yet? The answer was that the application had just been dismissed and the plaintiff's legal advisers needed to scrutinize the judgment and frame grounds of appeal. But the officials were not concerned about practicalities, nor did they care about the intricacies of legal procedure. They were concerned about blame. As they candidly told the Governor: if anything went wrong, it was essential that HMG should be able to demonstrate that it was the fault of the United States parties to the case.[5]

One participant who may not have been so dismayed at the decision was Sir Alexander Grantham. If the outcome meant that the aeroplanes could fly off, that would be one problem fewer for him to deal with. He was in the midst of a full-blown refugee crisis as a result of hundreds of thousands of Chinese flooding into the colony during the previous six months. Peace and good order were under threat from squabbling Nationalists and Communists vying for influence within the colony. Housing shortages, price and rental inflation and suppressed wages were causing tensions: he had just seen off a strike by tram workers by standing firm. China trade, the lifeblood of the colony's economy, was under threat from the Nationalist blockades of Shanghai and the Pearl River delta.

The one thing holding up departure of the planes was that they had two conflicting registrations. The American registration had been expedited in

4. Foreign Office memorandum, 'Chinese Civil Aircraft at Hong Kong', 4–5.
5. Memo, Chinese Aircraft at Hong Kong, 18 March 1950, 13.

late December 1949. The CPG had issued registration certificates for them at the beginning of February 1950, just as the court hearings had started. The certificates were presented to the Governor at the end of that month. Grantham would have been quite content to let the planes fly back to China but his masters in London had other ideas.

Sir Leslie Gibson was well aware of the impact his decision would have and that his reasoning would not be welcome to governments as well as to the main parties. Immediately after he had delivered judgment he called counsel into his chambers and told them that he was taking steps to facilitate a speedy hearing of an appeal in case it was decided that there should be one. He had ordered that the record of proceedings in front of him should be prepared with the utmost dispatch and he would arrange for a full (appellate) court to sit at any time after an appeal had been lodged.

Consternation

In the United States the reaction to the decision was sharp. On receiving the news in Washington DC, Livingston Merchant, the man in charge of the State Department's Far East desk, telephoned the British embassy at midnight to say that he was astonished. The Secretary of State, Dean Acheson, fired off protests to London and Hong Kong. The State Department told the British Ambassador, Sir Oliver Franks, that there was apprehension at the effect release of the aircraft would have on US opinion. The embassy in turn asked the Foreign Office to issue a statement as soon as possible in view of the effect on US-British relations. Franks warned London of US congressional anger and the consequent threat to Marshall Aid and the Military Assistance Programme.[6] The day after the judgment, Acheson told a press conference that the US had vigorously protested about it to London. Meanwhile Chennault and his allies such as Senator Knowland made loud public complaints that the planes had been awarded to 'the Reds'. It was 'one of the greatest blows to the non-Communist world,' said Knowland.[7]

In Hong Kong Carl Rankin, the US Consul General, told the government that any recognition of the registration of the aircraft by others would amount to confiscation of US property. The Governor formally informed London of the outcome of the hearing and stated that there was now no obstacle to the departure of the aircraft other than the question of registration. He was instructed to accept no registration of the aircraft pending a legal decision on the merits.

---

6. Evidence by Merchant to Senate Appropriations sub-committee, 27 March 1950, 280–281; Kaufman, 'The CAT Controversy', 103.
7. Leary, *Perilous Missions*, 97.

On Monday 27 February a Foreign Office spokesman made a statement. It held to the previous line, declaring that the British government would not interfere with the workings of the Hong Kong courts. This probably was not quite what Sir Oliver Franks had had in mind and certainly was not what the Americans wanted to hear.

Next day in London, at their request, the British Foreign Secretary, Ernest Bevin, saw US diplomatic representatives. Since Ambassador Lewis Douglas was not available, Julius Holmes, the US Chargé d'Affaires, attended. To emphasize US concerns, Holmes was accompanied by Walton Butterworth, the Assistant Secretary of State responsible for Far Eastern Affairs, who happened to be passing through London. Bevin was joined by Sir Eric Beckett, the FO legal adviser, to discuss Gibson's judgment.

Later in March, Butterworth recounted the meeting to a US Senate subcommittee at which the State Department had been accused of not doing enough to reflect American concern that the planes not fall into communist hands. 'We went to see Bevin and made very strong representations on instructions from the State Department,' Butterworth told the senators. 'The Foreign Office chief legal adviser was there who concurred that the judgment was very inadequate and cause for concern,' he went on. Although the State Department had no wish to interfere with the independent processes of the courts, Butterworth explained, it was anxious that the decision be reviewed on appeal and if necessary in the Privy Council. Bevin had replied that this was feasible.[8]

Meanwhile, all legal steps would be taken to prevent the departure of the aircraft until the position had been reviewed in consultation with a law officer from Hong Kong, Bevin reassured his American visitors. This was markedly different from the public British line which pretended that the fate of the aircraft was entirely a matter of law and was therefore in the hands of the courts, in which there was utmost confidence and with which it would not be proper to interfere. At the turn of the year British officials, including Bevin's deputy, had gone no further than sympathizing with US anxiety about the planes falling into communist hands and emphasizing that, if initially judgment went against the US claimants, appeals were possible and would take months. Publicly there was no mention of government lawyers reviewing the question or of the planes being stopped from leaving Kai Tak. One might have expected Bevin to say that all legal steps would be taken to prevent departure of the aircraft until a final determination of the merits of the case, but now he seemed to be hinting at active administrative steps to help the claimants.

The law officer that Bevin was referring to was the colony's Attorney General, John Griffin. He arrived in London on 1 March, so must have already

8. Department of Defense Appropriations for 1951, evidence of Walton Butterworth to Senate Appropriations Sub-Committee, 30 March 1950, 706.

been en route as Bevin spoke to the American diplomats. But what light might Griffin cast upon the events and the legal position that was not already known to London?

Bevin also told the Chargé that he hoped registration formalities would afford an opportunity for delaying tactics by the executive.[9] That very day, however, in Hong Kong representatives of the communist interests presented to Governor Grantham certificates of registration for the aircraft in China issued by the Peking authorities. On 3 March the Governor informed London of this and also that the American Consul-General had told him that to accept any registration certificates except those of the United States would amount to confiscation of the aircraft. Grantham added that he expected the communists to ask for permission to conduct test flights and sought London's guidance on what to do. The answer he received the next day by emergency secret telegram was, in short: you have power to ensure no aircraft takes off; refuse any flights on the basis that the Chicago Convention on Civil Aviation prohibits double registration; we are going to submit the whole case to the Law Officers for their opinion shortly.[10]

The FO's analysis, evidently by Beckett, was that the Governor's acceptance of either one of the certificates of registration would be tantamount to deciding the issue in favour of the holder of the certificate. The case was not specifically provided for in any article or regulation, so the line that Grantham was advised to take was that he was not in a position to determine which registration was valid and therefore was not able to be satisfied that any flight would not be in contravention of Article 18 of the Convention, which provided that an aircraft cannot be validly registered in more than one contracting State, and therefore in breach of provisions of the Colonial Air Navigation Order. Under Article 60 the Governor had the power to prevent any flight, even for test purposes. The Foreign Office saw this as a means of ensuring that the aircraft could not leave until the question of ownership had been resolved and of carrying out Bevin's wishes. But it was an unconvincing argument and transparently a temporary tactic. The Convention was to do with the safety of aeroplanes in flight, not their registration.

The instruction caused consternation in two quarters. First, the Colonial Office, which was responsible for Hong Kong, viewed the FO reaction as contrary to agreed and settled policy.[11] Second, Grantham regarded it not only as a change in policy but also as detrimental to British and Hong Kong interests. Both had their focus on the effect that the action proposed by the FO would have on China and in turn upon Hong Kong.

9. Foreign Office memorandum, 'Chinese Aircraft at Hong Kong', 15.
10. Ibid; Telegram 307, Colonial Office to Grantham, 4 March 1950.
11. CO537/5628, 7 March 1950.

Alarming possibilities for trouble

In a note of 7 March 1950, John Paskin of the Colonial Office stated that the FO view seemed to be that Hong Kong should take any legal steps open to it regardless of its effect upon Anglo-Chinese relations. But this, he noted, was contrary to established policy, held out 'the most alarming possibilities for trouble' in Hong Kong, and showed the undue influence of America. What established policy was the note referring to? Paskin did not expand, but the common line from both the Foreign and Colonial Offices had been that title to the assets of the airlines was a legal question which would be answered independently of government by the courts in litigation between private parties, so it would be improper for either government, British or Hong Kong, to intervene. It had been hoped that this 'hands off' approach would placate the other governments, American, Communist Chinese and Nationalist Chinese, interested in the fate of the planes. Now the Foreign Office seemed to be siding with the Americans and abandoning the policy.

The 'alarming possibilities for trouble' which Paskin foresaw must have been a reference to the risks of civil disorder which Governor Grantham had been concerned about ever since the Chinese civil war came to Hong Kong's doorstep. If it were known that the British, and therefore the Hong Kong, authorities were siding with the Americans in the dispute over the planes, communist elements within the colony might start protests which Nationalist sympathizers would feel compelled to oppose. Paskin had visited Hong Kong a year earlier and had travelled with Grantham to a regional conference, so the Governor would have had an opportunity to impress upon the Colonial Office's senior Far East man his concerns about the risk of civil unrest.

For his part Grantham wanted rid of the aircraft and the Chief Justice's decision seemed to open the way for that. Months earlier Grantham had warned the airlines of trouble if the planes remained in Hong Kong. After they had remained and trouble had indeed erupted, he took the position in accord with the Colonial Office that the courts would decide the matter and that it would be improper for him or his officials to intervene. That was why he had rebuffed entreaties to take 'executive action'. Now that the court had, it seemed, decided that the planes were to remain with the communists, they could be flown to the mainland and would cease to be a problem. Twice Grantham mentioned in telegrams to London that as a result of the judgment there was no obstacle to their removal except the question of their dual registration. Now suddenly the Foreign Office was reneging on the agreed approach. It was urging him to act to keep the planes in Hong Kong by any available means. That could only be because it did not want the communists to have the planes and, by deduction, wanted the Americans to have them instead.

Grantham's reaction to the FO instruction was to protest about the effect this would have on Hong Kong's position and upon the UK's reputation. On 5 March he told the Colonial Office that 'the strength of our position in Hong Kong' required his government to treat the KMT and the Communists exactly similarly and absolutely according to law. He stressed the importance of not becoming involved in political issues. He feared that Hong Kong would suffer if China did not get the planes. 'I have no doubt,' he pointedly cabled a few days later,

> that further consideration is being given to irreparable harm that would be done to Britain's prestige in China and Hong Kong if we were ourselves to infringe 'rules of law'. It is our respect for this law that has contributed as much as anything to our good name in the world. It would not seem worth jeopardizing this for the sake of seventy aircraft in order to please Americans.

The judgment and American pressure had opened up a schism between two government departments, the FO and the CO, and between the British and Hong Kong governments. Uncertain as to how to proceed, they put the matter before the British Cabinet on Saturday 11 March 1950. Ernest Bevin was in hospital that weekend for injections to help his failing heart, so Kenneth Younger deputized for him.[12]

Obdurate China

What motivated the more accommodating attitude struck by Bevin and the FO towards American concerns? There seems little doubt that the persistent pressure exerted by US administrators, diplomatists and politicians played a part. Britain did not want to choose a side to favour. It wanted friendly relations with both the US and China, for self-interested reasons. But as 1950 wore on it became apparent that this would not be possible. The new regime in Peking was proving less tractable than had been hoped, whilst in the US anti-communist opinion had been gaining ground.

The CPG had shown itself obdurate about the establishment of diplomatic relations. British leaders assumed that an exchange of ambassadors would as a matter of course follow their recognition of the CPG in early January 1950, for this was the usual diplomatic practice. At first the assumption seemed justified for on 9 January Chou En-lai accepted the appointment of an interim British Chargé d'Affaires, John Hutchison, and suggested discussion of preliminary matters for the establishment of diplomatic relations. On 13

12. Allan Bullock, *Ernest Bevin: A Biography* (London: Politico's, 2002), 744; Geoffrey Warner, ed., *In the Midst of Events: The Foreign Office Diaries and Papers of Kenneth Younger, February 1950–October 1951* (London: Routledge, 2005), 9–10.

February, Hutchison and embassy staff arrived at Peking from Nanking ready for negotiations.[13]

At first the Vice Foreign Minister Zhang Hanfu told Hutchison that the Chinese government was not ready for discussions. Then a week later Zhang started to hint at pre-conditions to accepting the British offer. He asked whether Britain would vote to oust the representatives of the Nationalist Republic of China at the United Nations and for clarification of Britain's position regarding Chinese national property on British territory, by which he mainly meant: who did the British government regard as entitled to the aircraft standing at Kai Tak? Later Zhang also asked whether Britain would remove its consulate from Formosa. To Communist leaders these were tests of whether the UK government was sincere. They detected ambivalence if not duplicity in the British attitude. On the motion for expulsion of the Nationalists from the UN the UK had abstained rather than voted in favour. The British consul continued to be present in Formosa and KMT agencies continued to operate in Hong Kong. The administrations in London and Hong Kong refused to express a view on the future of the CATC and CNAC planes and other Chinese national property in the colony.

Those who had studied what Communist leaders had said about engagement with Western powers would not have been surprised that the CPG was in no rush to accept the British offer, nor that it would use agreement upon diplomatic relations as an occasion to set pre-conditions. The CPG had stated that it would establish relations with any government that was willing to observe the principles of equality, mutual benefit and mutual respect for territorial integrity and sovereignty. The Common Outline of Chinese Policy which had been adopted at the founding of the People's Republic had declared (in Article 56) that if a nation severed relations with the KMT and adopted a friendly attitude to the CPG, the PRC would negotiate and establish diplomatic relations with them. The history of Chinese humiliation at the hands of Western powers meant that the CPG would be cautious and difficult to satisfy on the counts of equality and respect. The three questions touched on issues upon which the Chinese were sensitive. Respect and equal treatment for the CPG lay behind all of them. Consequently, the answers assumed greater importance in the minds of CPG leaders than they did in those of the more pragmatic British leaders.

The British reply was delivered by Hutchison on 17 March 1950. Diplomatic relations with the KMT had been severed and KMT organizations in Hong Kong had no official status, the reply explained, and the UK had abstained at the United Nations because there had been no likelihood of a majority decision so any acceptance of CPG membership would have been premature.

13. Evan Luard, *Britain and China* (London: Chatto and Windus, 1962), 83; Tang, *Britain's Encounter*, 74–75.

The right of the CPG to Chinese state properties was accepted, the reply went on, but if the CPG's claims were disputed they must be settled by the courts. Zhang said that the Chinese authorities would have to study the reply before responding. In fact they did not accept that the courts should decide their claims and that the CPG should be treated as a mere party to litigation. In their eyes, the matter was political and should be resolved politically. To this at least, ironically, the Americans agreed.[14]

Hutchison was optimistic that relations would be formalized quickly. The day before he had delivered the reply, the CPG had agreed to establish relations with India. In April the CPG agreed to relations with Sweden and Denmark. Britain had already begun to take soundings at the UN with the aim of forming a majority on the UN Security Council for CPG membership which it would then support. However, the US and France remained opposed.

British interests clung to the fond belief that China needed Western investment and trade and so would become amenable to closer ties. The China Association, the influential pressure group of British companies with large businesses in the mainland and Hong Kong, argued that economic self-interest dictated that the new government would come to an accommodation with the capitalists. So long as the CPG controlled its form, trade and investment by overseas Chinese and foreign concerns would be allowed, they suggested.

CPG leaders did indeed perceive that international economic relations would be useful. They took over and continued KMT trading and financial enterprises that had been doing business abroad. They established state trading agencies to co-ordinate the supply and distribution of basic commodities and raw materials. However, they did not regard such relations as vital and they saw the need to keep those enterprises under tight control and their business at arm's length from the general population. Hong Kong was a perfect instrument for that. The city's trading role goes a long way to explain why the anti-imperialists tolerated the continuation of a British colony on the shores of China after 1949. The existence of Hong Kong was another reason that the CPG was relaxed about a timetable for the creation of diplomatic relations with Britain. Liaison with London could be conducted indirectly, through PRC informal representatives at the Xinhua news agency and the Governor there. This led Grantham later to suggest that a Foreign Office diplomat join his staff as an adviser.

The Chinese response to the British reply regarding pre-conditions to diplomatic relations did not come until 7 May 1950. The response was that the reply had been unsatisfactory: Britain must support Chinese admission to the UN, and impounding the Chinese aircraft in Hong Kong pending court adjudication of ownership was not respectful of China. By then Kenneth

14. Tang, *Britain's Encounter*, 77; Wenguang Shao, *China, Britain and Businessmen: Political and Commercial Relations, 1949–57* (Basingstoke: Macmillan, 1991), 82–83.

Younger had accepted that there would be no prompt establishment of diplomatic relations. 'It seems clear that in the short run we are not going to get much change out of the Peking Government,' he noted in his diary on 11 May. 'British interests in China are likely to have a very thin time and we will probably not get an exchange of Ambassadors.' Bevin was unwilling to give ground in negotiations. His trade union experience told him that this would be interpreted as a sign of weakness and lead the other party to increase its demands. There was growing scepticism in Whitehall as to the CPG's sincerity about wanting relations.[15]

The pre-conditions suggested by the three questions raised by the Chinese may indeed have been convenient excuses for delaying the establishment of diplomatic relations. Both Mao Tse-tung and Chou En-lai had indicated that they were not anxious to allow foreigners back in to China. 'We should not be in a hurry to solve the question of recognition of our country by the imperialists,' Mao had said. It seems it was at Mao's direction that the response to Britain's initial request to establish relations had been delayed for two months.[16] 'We prefer to wait for a time,' explained Chou. In the aftermath of the revolution, they wished to purge the PRC of foreign influences. Those influences ran deep, for the elite of China's population had been Westernized and the domestic economy had been dominated by overseas enterprises. Those influences had to be eradicated before an independent, truly socialist and truly Chinese society could be built, was the thinking.

The bulk of Communist supporters were peasants and not at all internationalist in outlook. They were parochial and inward-looking, suspicious of foreigners, rural and traditional, and on the whole less educated than town-dwellers. Consequently, nationalism was a powerful force which PRC leaders and propagandists did not hesitate to exploit. Populist, jingoistic diatribes were the order of the day. British hopes of resuming their commercial interests within China were doomed. The imperialists were to be taught a lesson.

Hardening of US attitude

Meanwhile in the US, attitudes towards the CPG had been hardening. At the beginning of 1949 when the question of whether and when to recognize the likely communist government of China began to move up the foreign policy agenda, opinion in the US administration appeared to be not greatly different from that of their counterparts in the UK. Bevin expected Britain to extend recognition once the new Chinese government had become established and thought that the US would follow suit after a reasonable time. The Secretary

15. Warner, *In the Midst of Events*, 15; Tang, *Britain's Encounter*, 80; David Clayton, *Imperialism Revisited: Political and Economic Relations between Britain and China, 1950–54* (London: Macmillan, 1997), 19–20.
16. Shao, *China, Britain and Businessmen*, 34.

of State, Dean Acheson, and his department were better disposed towards the Chinese communists than most other relevant organs of government and politics in the US. In 1949, however, Acheson had described the communist takeover of China as ominous. Anyway, he had to be cautious. Although personally inclined to recognize the new government, he and President Truman had the China lobby to consider. The advice of Sir Oliver Franks to Bevin was that US recognition would occur once US public opinion had been prepared for it. The FO expected recognition after the US mid-term congressional elections in November 1950.

That this did not happen was due to a gradual but distinct change in the way that the Chinese Communist Party was perceived in the US during the final months of 1949 and the early months of 1950. The change was the consequence of a confluence of factors. Most fundamental was the equating of Chinese communists with Soviet communists. The Truman doctrine and the policy of containment dictated that America would oppose totalitarian regimes and resist their expansion. Recent Cold War episodes such as the Soviet blockade of Berlin and the Soviet-sponsored coup in Czechoslovakia heightened the general distrust of communism in the US. The Department of Defense and the US military, notably but not solely General Douglas MacArthur, were alarmed by the communist threat. The new regime in China seemed inherently hostile to foreign influences, particularly those perceived to be imperialist. These certainly included the US which had poured money and arms into assisting Chiang Kai-shek and his Nationalists. After the formation of the CPG, Communist propaganda became strongly anti-American. In January and February of 1950 there were attacks on US citizens in China. A US consular building at Peking was seized. Then on 14 February 1950 a treaty of alliance was announced between the USSR and the new Chinese government. This cemented the impression that all communists were the same: the onerous terms extracted by the Russians and the personal rivalry and jealousy between Stalin and Mao exhibited during negotiations were overlooked or not known. Exaggerated reports by the CIA and by McConaughy, the US Consul-General in Shanghai, led the US government to believe that the new regime was floundering and deeply unpopular.[17]

Meanwhile at home Senator Joseph McCarthy had begun his campaign against leftist influence within the US government. In January a former State Department officer, Alger Hiss, was sentenced to five years in jail for perjury in denying in court that he was a communist. The only connections between Hiss and Acheson were that they knew each other and that Hiss's brother had once been a law partner of Acheson.[18] Exploiting the fervid atmosphere, on

17. Clayton, *Imperialism Revisited*, 23–28.
18. Dean Acheson, *Present at the Creation: My Years in the State Department* (New York: W.W. Norton, 1969), 250–252; there was a false rumour that Hiss had been Acheson's assistant.

9 February 1950 the Senator denounced Acheson and declared that no fewer than 250 employees of the Department of State were secret members of the American Communist Party. Acheson was under pressure to take a firm line and seems to have given way to this. Refusal to recognize Mao's government was part of the tougher stance, as was diplomatic and rhetorical agitation concerning the aeroplanes at Kai Tak.

The firmer attitude towards communism was reflected in National Security Council Directive 68 issued in the Spring of 1950. This secret internal document adopted the philosophy of containment, advocating a programme of re-armament in response to the perceived Soviet threat to Europe and support for anti-communist movements and governments throughout the world. Applied to east Asia, this meant no diplomatic or trading links with the PRC and renewed economic and military aid for Chang Kai-shek in Formosa. It certainly did not envisage that 71 aircraft and valuable spare parts would be given to the communists.

12
Detaining the Planes

The Chief Justice's surprising basis for denying the application for appointment of receivers meant that the communist sympathizers were in effect immune from any action to deprive them of the planes and equipment. Although the aeroplanes could not fly, they might be dismantled and sent to China, and moveable spare parts and other stored equipment could be sent off by road or sea at any time, points that Grantham had made in messages to the Colonial Office. There was in fact a large amount of valuable equipment at the airfield and in adjacent stores and yards.

Moreover, the detention of the aeroplanes themselves could be only temporary. The Governor could not pretend indefinitely that their double registration meant he could not allow them to leave. The Chicago Convention required merely that an aircraft be registered with some country, not that it be registered with only one. The uncertainty as to which of the registrations was correct did not prevent one of them from being correct. Only by resorting to consequential requirements, such as that the craft bear the colours of the registering state, could the argument for non-compliance be sustained.

Preparing for departure

The CPG and its followers at and around Kai Tak regarded the Chief Justice's decision and the discharge of the injunction as, in effect, an award of the planes and equipment to them. Consequently, in early March 1950 preparations for their removal were expedited, apparently on orders from Peking. A vice-minister in the Department of Civil Aeronautics arrived to oversee the arrangements, with additional officers available if required. More than twenty pilots and other flight crew were sent to Hong Kong by train from Canton. Workers had already started to paint the 5-star red flag on the aeroplane fuselages. Engines were put through vigorous tests. Truckloads of crated equipment were removed from the airfield to Bailey's Shipyard and other storage facilities prior to shipment.

The airlines also began to pay some of their debts. Pilots, both American and Chinese, who had chosen not to go back to China were given their arrears of salary. Other, less exalted staff were not so lucky, however. The airlines said that they would need to investigate the wage claims.[1]

These events pointed to the urgency of finding a means of holding the planes at Kai Tak and the equipment at the godowns. But that means had to be viable legally, otherwise it would undermine the posture of the UK and Hong Kong that they were neutral and simply keen to comply with the law.

Stopping the spares

The fate of the stored equipment and machinery, referred to as 'spares', came into focus when intelligence sources told the Commander, British Forces Hong Kong, that these parts were being prepared for loading aboard a British ship, the SS *Empire Dirk*, which was to leave on the afternoon of Tuesday 14 March 1950. There were said to be 900 packing cases of them. The Hong Kong government was exploring ways to delay the shipment, the Commander informed his superiors on the British Defence Co-ordination Committee for the Far East. He requested authority to take steps to prevent the parts' departure. The committee supported the request, but they were not the ultimate decision-makers. Every possible step should be taken to delay the departure, they told Whitehall. The committee urged that an embargo be imposed on removal of the equipment.

For the decision-makers in London the question was: on what legal basis might the steps be taken? The Colonial Air Navigation Order which the Governor had been told to use was confined to aircraft. It did not cover loose equipment. An embargo on the export of military equipment to China had been agreed between Britain and the USA. That covered arms and fighter planes but not civilian planes and spare parts for them. At least that was the British view; the American ambassador Lewis Douglas argued otherwise.

That question, and the wider issue of whether the spares really merited such attention, was urgently considered on 14 March 1950 by SEACOS, a joint committee of senior figures from the ministries concerned with east Asian matters: Defence, Foreign Office and Colonial Office. After a report on the background by John Paskin of the Colonial Office, Sir Esler Dening from the Foreign Office explained that his minister, Ernest Bevin, was anxious not to appear to take sides in the civil dispute and wished to abide strictly by the law; Bevin wanted to know the degree of risk of any action before taking it and therefore would seek legal advice. If the American parties did not apply for an injunction, Dening added, there would be nothing to prevent the aircraft

1. Report, *South China Morning Post*, 3 March 1950.

from being removed. His departmental colleague Montagu Pollock said that it was not clear why there had been no application for an injunction: perhaps the Americans had difficulty in naming defendants. An injunction would hold matters up for about a year, Pollock thought, but it was probable that judgment would go against the Americans.

The Commissioner General Southeast Asia, Malcolm MacDonald (a former government minister), had announced his concern to the Colonial Office in a secret telegram from Singapore. The decision of the court seemed to be making a present of about seventy valuable aircraft to the Communists, he thought. The planes might be used to support the communist Viet-Minh against the French, he added; it was against all common sense to allow this to happen when the Colonial Office was urging further British and American support to the French on the most vital defence line in southeast Asia. The planes should be impounded, he advised.

From the military side, the Deputy Chief of the Air Staff, the one-armed Air Chief Marshall Sir Arthur Sanders, said that removal of the aircraft would provide a threat to Hong Kong and be of considerable assistance to the communists in southeast Asia. But he was doubtful that spares and stores which would render about a dozen aircraft serviceable constituted such a threat as to justify taking action. Lieutenant General Sir Nevil Brownjohn, the Vice-Chief of the Imperial General Staff, was even less convinced about the significance of the spare parts. He thought that the aircraft did not even pose a serious threat to Hong Kong. But in his view, a weak policy would invite trouble, so Britain should maintain a firm but impartial line. Air Chief Marshall Sir William Elliot, the Chief Staff Officer at the Ministry of Defence, said that from a military point of view he wished to prevent removal of the planes and parts, therefore it was in British interests to delay their removal as long as possible, by which time the legal position would be clearer.

According to the minutes of the meeting the consensus was that removal of the aircraft would be a serious matter and all reasonable steps should be taken to prevent this. No reasonable military arguments justified recommending action which might prejudice the diplomatic position. The rule of law must be allowed to prevail.[2] Translated from the language of bureaucratic diplomacy, this meant that the committee supported what the British government was doing: sitting on the fence between the parties and their factions, urging them to take the dispute to court and awaiting a judgment on the question of ownership. The authorities should maintain their present objections about registration for as long as possible, in the hope that the courts would keep the planes from flying, and seek legal advice. As for the spares,

2. Minutes of COS Meeting, 14 March 1950; CO 537/5628; Victor S. Kaufman, 'The United States, Great Britain and the CAT Controversy', *Journal of Contemporary History* 40, no. 1 (2005): 95, 104.

they could be allowed to go since they were not important enough to justify deviating from the current approach.

In the event, had the committee favoured intervention to hold up the spares, it would have been too late to take action. The ship would have already sailed, mid-morning London time being early evening in Hong Kong. Anyway, on what basis could the Hong Kong government have acted? Any technical objection, for instance wishing to check the cargo for contraband such as opium, would have held up the shipment for only a matter of hours. A trade embargo on aircraft parts would have required new regulations which, even in the colony's executive-led system, would have taken days to put in place. The same would be true of an expansion of the definition of arms (already the subject of embargo) to include transport planes which might be used for military purposes and spare parts for them. This would have been overtly anti-communist and would have risked provoking the PRC. Any use of the Emergency Regulations Ordinance would also have taken time and would have required the announcement of a state of public danger or emergency which, apart from being far-fetched, would have blown apart the pretence that the British and Hong Kong governments were merely letting the law decide.

Open intervention of this sort would have exposed the colony to the risk of communist-inspired strikes and protests and even a blockade of vital supplies from the mainland. In the view of the Colonial Office and the Governor, if not the Foreign Office, this risk was more worrying than threatened action by angry Americans. All that could be done about banning export of spare parts was to hope that the lawyers could come up with something and do so quickly.

So on the morning of 15 March the *Hong Kong Standard* reported that '1,000 tons of valuable airplane parts and engines belonging to the now Communist controlled CNAC were moved out by ship to North China last night'. Virtually all of them were on the list of goods whose export to Asia had been recently prohibited by the State Department, the report went on. They had been taken from the airline's huge stockpile at Bailey's Shipyard. Somebody sent a copy of the report to Senator William Knowland at the US Congress.

The view from America

The failure to intervene to stop the departure of the spares did indeed cause anger in America. Lewis Douglas, the US ambassador to the UK, protested about the shipment and reminded the Foreign Office of its promise that the status quo would be maintained during the litigation. ChiNat sympathizers were hard at work stirring up discontent in the press and the Congress. The attitude there towards the exodus of the stores and spares was in complete contrast with the resigned and cautious attitude in Hong Kong and Britain. The prospect of the departure of the 71 aeroplanes caused something approaching apoplexy in certain US quarters. Chennault argued that the 'Hongkong British are protecting their own property in Shanghai and elsewhere in China by paying 'squeeze' to Chinese Communists out of American property'. Chennault proposed the appointment of a supreme commander to co-ordinate economic, political and military resistance to communism throughout the Far East: a job designed for MacArthur.[3]

During the second half of March 1950 these subjects became the focus of a sub-committee of the Senate which was scrutinizing Defense Department financial appropriations for 1951. A number of Republican members of the sub-committee, led by William Knowland of California, were staunch supporters of Chiang Kai-shek. Knowland brought these subjects up on the tenuous basis that they affected expenditure on aeroplanes provided by the United States to the United Kingdom under the Military Assistance Programme. As he put it, he was 'getting a little fed up . . . of having the British aid and abet . . . Communism in the Far East while they are expecting the American taxpayer and the American Congress to furnish them equipment and funds . . . in Europe'. He had with him a document from Donovan's firm about the Kai Tak planes which was read into the record. It gave a long and at times tendentious and one-eyed account of what had been happening.

As far as Knowland was concerned, what had happened in Hong Kong was that '[t]he British Government has by a court decision in Hong Kong given to the Chinese Communists some 71 planes which were CAT planes'. This single sentence, containing three if not four inaccuracies, reflected the level of information and debate at the sub-committee hearings. His colleague Senator Ferguson was even further from the mark: 'the British prevented by their action the Nationalist Government from getting these 71 planes,' he declared. Knowland told his colleagues more than once that he had visited Hong Kong and seen the planes at the end of 1949. Ferguson had too, for they were part of a Far East tour by American politicians. On the tour Knowland had met both Chennault and MacArthur. Knowland took pride in the accuracy of his sources there. He did not name those sources but they must have included Chennault and Donovan, neither of whom was a disinterested witness or a paragon of veracity. Knowland's arguments bore more than a little resemblance to those deployed by Chennault in his letters and circulars and to the account of the litigation put together by Donovan's firm.

The sub-committee was told by Knowland that the aircraft at Kai Tak were being maintained and their engines run so that they would be ready for take-off in short order. Knowland announced melodramatically that he

3. Peter Lowe, *Containing the Cold War in East Asia: British Policies towards Japan, China and Korea, 1948–53* (Manchester: Manchester University Press, 1997), 160.

was seriously considering putting forward amendments to the legislation governing the Military Assistance Programme to prevent the further delivery of airplanes to Britain under it unless steps were taken to stop the engines of the planes from being turned over in Hong Kong.

According to Knowland, the British were 'more concerned about the loss of their investments in Red China than they are in what the United States may do' and were 'holding the planes as bargaining points until China agrees to exchange ambassadors—using them as leverage to work out their other problems with the Chinese Communists'. In fact it was the Communist government that was withholding exchange of ambassadors until the planes were handed over but this neat inversion of the truth suited the senator and his informants. 'Let us be practical about the matter,' intoned Knowland. 'As soon as the Chinese yield, the titles will be transferred and the planes will be free to fly off.' In vain did Livingston Merchant, the State Department official sent to assuage the senators' wrath, assure them that no, the retention of the planes was a delaying tactic designed to enable the plaintiffs' lawyers to get an injunction. Knowland bracketed the holding of the aircraft as a bargaining chip along with British recognition of the Communist regime, their court's award of the planes to China, and British diplomatic efforts at the United Nations to replace the Chinese Nationalist government with the Communist government. There was no assurance, he declared, that next week the British would not 'eliminate the logjam and permit the planes to fly off'.

Knowland and his Republican colleagues were of course keen to denounce the Democrat administration's foreign policy as soft on communism and weak on China. The Labour government in Britain was also suspect in their eyes. The senators had no idea of the tensions which had arisen within that government and also between that government and the Governor of Hong Kong. The Republicans were keen to punish Britain by withholding mutual defence assistance despite the latter being concerned with resisting Soviet expansion in Europe. The senators saw a striking symmetry between American provision of bombers to Britain to fight communists and what they thought of as Britain's provision of aircraft to communists in China. Knowland rounded off with a threat:

> We are going to find out if these people are on our team or whether they are playing 'footsy' with the Communists in Asia while they are expecting help from the US in Europe. I think they have to make up their mind pretty soon.

It was useless for John Ohly, the State Department official responsible for US military assistance to Europe, to protest that this would amount to the US cutting off its nose to spite its face. For the China lobby, communists everywhere were communists even when they had Chinese characteristics. They thought of the PRC as just another satellite of the Russians.[4]

The rough treatment of State Department representatives over the planes issue by the Senate sub-committee prompted Acheson to speak to the British ambassador in Washington, Oliver Franks, a few days later. Franks related to Bevin that Acheson had said that the Governor of Hong Kong 'had shown himself, perhaps understandably so, to be particularly preoccupied with the local situation and relations with his immediate neighbors' and suggested that perhaps the Governor 'had not been made sufficiently aware by London of the importance of the larger issues involved, including US-UK relations'. This was a veiled warning to Whitehall that US patience was running out, a reminder of where British interests lay and a hint that the UK government should be more decisive.

Acheson also complained to Franks about the shipment to China earlier in the month of hundreds of tons of spare parts and machinery on board a British ship. The Communists had been allowed access to the equipment but the Americans had not been, he complained. Acheson ended by cautioning that some Congressmen were talking of opposing further assistance to the UK and opposing State Department appropriations. He predicted that the subject of the grounded planes would 'become even hotter' and 'we are in for a great deal of trouble'.[5]

Appeal and injunction

On 8 March 1950 CAT, Inc. lodged notice of its expected appeal against Sir Leslie Gibson's judgment. In the view of impatient British mandarins this was not before time: they had been asking why there was no appeal almost since 23 February. But then they were unschooled in the deliberate ways of lawyers and in the generosity of procedural time limits. The rules gave 14 days for the lodging of notice of appeal. It took all that time to decide whether to appeal. The corporation's Hong Kong lawyers had been understandably pessimistic about the prospects for an appeal against the exercise of discretion by the head of the judiciary. No doubt their confident American clients took a more bullish view.

Those impatient mandarins had also been asking why there was no application for another injunction to keep the planes on the tarmac. Although the Colonial Office had speculated that the reason was the difficulty in identifying and naming the people holding the planes, it is more likely that the company's legal advisers had been negative about the chances of obtaining such

4. US Senate, minutes of the meeting of the Sub-Committee on Appropriations for 1951, 272–289.
5. Chi-kwan Mark, *Hong Kong and the Cold War: Anglo-American Relations, 1949–1957* (Oxford: Clarendon Press, 2004), 97–98.

an injunction and that Chennault and Willauer had been wary of incurring more costs on a futile exercise. Certainly there could be no injunction without an appeal, but even after 8 March CAT, Inc. hesitated.

The Chief Justice had shown his reluctance to offend the CPG and its supporters in the reasons for his refusal to appoint receivers given two weeks earlier. He had held that the employees were agents of the CPG and therefore immune from court process. He had said that appointing receivers would prevent the airlines from operating. These points could certainly be appealed. But issuing an injunction to prevent movement of the aeroplanes would be contradictory to one basis of his decision, namely that they were being used by functioning airlines.

Accordingly, there was no surprise when on 28 March applications for such injunctions by CAT, Inc. were refused. The Colonial Office noted that the Americans were very unhappy. But at the Foreign Office Kenneth Younger entered in his diary, either ruefully or gleefully, that 'the whole trouble flowed from the refusal of the Nationalists and the US to take our advice and remove the planes while there was time'.

A long self-justification

Stung by three months of American and Chinese pressure and criticism, the British government felt the need to defend itself. Diplomacy dictated that this could not be done openly by press release but only by background briefing to those who might be called upon to deal with concerns based on the criticisms. So at the end of March the Foreign Office circulated in the diplomatic bag confidentially to British ambassadors and representatives throughout the world a 21-paragraph, 4500-word paper outlining the history of the affair and dealing with points that had arisen during it. This was intended as background that could be used for replies to enquiries. But, the paper cautioned, 'it is important that no inference should be given that political considerations have in any way influenced the handling of this case by His Majesty's Government or by the Government and courts of Hong Kong'. The representatives were to emphasize that this was 'a purely legal dispute, in regard to which we are determined to act with the strictest impartiality'.

The briefing was of course drafted from the British government's point of view and designed to justify their actions and position. It incorporated much of what had appeared in Montagu Pollock's earlier memoranda and must have been approved by Younger, for it placed the blame squarely on the Nationalists and the Americans.

The briefing summarized the embarrassment in which the UK found itself. 'Whatever the eventual outcome of this dispute may be,' the circular conceded, 'its consequences cannot fail to be harmful to the interests of His

Majesty's Government and of Hong Kong'. If the Chinese obtain possession, the paper explained, the planes would doubtless be used for purposes detrimental to Anglo-American defence interests in the Far East and relations with the US would suffer. Yet if the American parties obtain possession, UK relations with the Chinese government, on which the welfare and security of Hong Kong largely depended, would suffer and retaliation may be taken against British commercial interests in China, it warned.

The circular suggested that the Americans were inclined to exaggerate the military usefulness of the planes and hoped that the US government would come to appreciate the injustice of laying the blame on HMG. Rather, the paper continued, the fault lay on the shoulders of 'the American aircraft interests,' evidently a collective name for Pan Am and Chennault and Willauer, their companies and associates. Despite frequent warnings, these interests had failed to remove the aircraft to Formosa before the other parties could lay claim to them, the briefing explained, adding 'the United States Government cannot be absolved of all responsibility in this respect'. On this the circular was more prescient than perhaps its authors realized, given the secret backers of the American claimants. Strangely, the circular attributed no responsibility to the Nationalists who had ordered the aircraft to go to and remain in Hong Kong.

The paper made a bold prediction about the eventual outcome of the case. If the courts were somehow allowed to decide the question of ownership, the Chinese would be granted the 31 CATC aircraft while CAT, Inc. would have the 39 (in fact 40) CNAC ones, it suggested. (Though not stated, this was based on the opinion of the departmental legal advisers.) The Americans would react strongly to that outcome, the circular conceded, but if it could be postponed for some months, Sino-American relations may have entered a new phase. Again the authors proved prescient, but not in the way they had intended. Also, the circular added hopefully, after those months, the Americans may have adopted a more realistic attitude towards the case and the part played by HMG and the courts.

The courts were not the only aspect of Hong Kong's involvement that deserved some recognition and the authors duly mentioned another. Apart from the strain on Britain's international relations caused by the dispute, 'the continued presence of the aircraft in the over-crowded colony of Hong Kong presents the Government of the colony with already formidable and steadily increasing problems'. HMG sympathized with the US desire that the aircraft should not fall into communist hands, the circular explained, but 'we have a greater interest: to safeguard the world-wide reputation of British courts for impartiality'. So Grantham's arguments had made their mark.

The briefing concluded by commenting on ten demands or complaints that had been made 'by the American side' against Britain during the dispute.

To suggestions that the Hong Kong or British governments attempt to influence the courts or their procedure, the response was that the courts were independent; the government could intervene only if the court requested and had no power to expedite the procedure which anyway had not been unduly protracted. To allegations that the courts had displayed partiality, the answer was that this was not so: injunctions had been granted to both sides and each had been allowed to state its case. To assertions that the Hong Kong government had been uncooperative, the riposte was that it could not give assistance whilst a case was sub judice. To requests that the governments recognize the validity of the sale, the response was that its validity was a matter for the courts, not governments. To the accusation that the authorities had failed to take steps to prevent sabotage of the planes, the reply was that if sabotage was confirmed, it was for the parties to request an order for protection from the courts. To the allegation that US officials had been denied access to the aircraft whilst the Chinese had been allowed access, the explanation was that this was the fault of the Nationalists for failing to cancel the employees' passes and that US officials had been allowed to visit the airfield under arrangements which would prevent a breach of the peace. To the question of whether recognition of the CPG would affect the court's decision, the answer had been given that it might or might not. To the request that any recognition be made not retrospective, the answer had been that this was a matter for the courts. To the assertion that acceptance of any registration certificates other than US ones would amount to a confiscation of the property of US citizens, the reaction was that the Governor had been instructed to decline to recognize either set of certificates pending the advice of government Law Officers.

All eyes on the attorney

After it had been decided to seek the advice of the Law Officers of the Crown about the whole affair in the hope of finding a solution in the law, the legal advisers to the Colonial Office and to the Foreign Office, respectively Sir Kenneth Roberts-Wray and Sir Eric Beckett, set out to draft a set of instructions to the officers. 'Gentlemen,' the instructions began in the high Victorian style used by senior British civil servants well into the twentieth century: 'We have the honour, by the direction of Mr Secretary Griffiths and Mr Secretary Bevin, to request that you will favour them with your opinion on certain questions that have arisen consequent upon the presence at Hong Kong of civil aircraft . . . to the number of 70 belonging to Chinese operating organisations.'

The questions came at the end of the instructions. The most immediate were whether the action that the Governor had been authorized to take to prevent the aeroplanes from flying (on the basis that the Chicago Convention, as applied by the Colonial Air Navigation Order, did not allow double registration) was legally proper and whether it would be justifiable to continue that action until the pending appeal had been decided. These were followed by the question: if there were a further appeal to the Privy Council, what attitude ought the government to take while that appeal was pending? Finally, the brief asked if the courts were unable to decide on title to the planes because the plea of sovereign immunity continued to be successful, what course of action should the government of Hong Kong then take? The legal advisers' suggestions focused upon the Convention and the Air Navigation Order. They did not mention the Governor's powers under the Emergency Regulations Ordinance, nor did they suggest use of his embargo powers under import-export regulations. Presumably they thought neither set of regulations was applicable to civilian aircraft.

In fact, on the international legal aspects of the case there were no greater authorities than Roberts-Wray and Beckett themselves. They had each served many years as legal advisers in their respective departments and by virtue of Britain's world-wide empire they had in the past had to consider many practical issues of public international law. Major universities in Britain and throughout the globe had academic experts in that field but the external affairs departments of no country could boast more experienced advisers.

Accordingly in their instructions the legal advisers shared with the Law Officers their views on the merits of the dispute. They summarized the history of the matter, enclosed Montagu Pollock's detailed chronology of events and set out the British and Hong Kong interests which were at stake. Then they described the Chief Justice's judgment of 23 February and interposed their thoughts about the merits of the judgment. It appeared that an appeal against the finding of sovereign immunity in the judgment was likely to be successful at least as regards the CNAC aircraft, they said, since there was no evidence that the Chinese People's Government had excluded CNAC from possession of them and indeed the CPG had appointed a communist managing director of the company through whom it seemed they intended to control the aircraft.

The instructions concluded by stating that the ministers 'would be grateful for any observations that you may feel disposed to offer generally on the case' and that, as would be apparent, the situation was one of great urgency so 'an early reply would be very gratefully appreciated'. They were marked 'secret' and signed off on 18 March 1950, precisely two weeks after Grantham had been told to hold the planes whilst legal advice was sought.

Grave repercussions

Although 'the Law Officers' meant both the Attorney General and the Solicitor General, it was Sir Hartley Shawcross, the Attorney General, alone who responded.[6] His opinion was rendered on 3 April 1950. In between times the difficulties for London and Hong Kong only became worse.

On 21 March Grantham, apparently uncomfortable with his orders to use the Colonial Air Navigation Order to detain the planes, sought clarification of his rights under it. He informed the Colonial Office that he had been told that the Communists 'are beginning to suspect that the British merely want the aircraft to lie and rot until useless to anybody'. If those suspicions were confirmed by events including deterioration of the planes or loss and damage by typhoon, he warned, 'the repercussions on relations between Hong Kong and the CPG and upon British-China relations generally are bound to be most grave'. This was an unusually strong expression of resistance by a colonial governor to instructions from London. In predicting repercussions for relations between Britain and China, Grantham was going outside his proper remit and trespassing upon that of the Foreign Office, a trespass which had led to reprimands for his predecessors. But he must have felt that the foreseeable impact upon Hong Kong justified this and it is perhaps a measure of the sympathy in Whitehall for his position that there was no reprimand this time.

Two days later Sir Eric Beckett minuted his view that the Colonial Air Navigation Order gave power to stop aircraft from flying from a territory if it was not properly registered. Proper registration was, he said, based on ownership. So 'where, as in the present case, there are conflicting claims to ownership and in fact registrations in different countries, it is not possible to say which is the right registration while the issue of ownership is undecided'.

That same day the hostile Senate sub-committee hearings began. The US mood darkened further when CAT, Inc.'s applications for injunctions were dismissed on 28 March and when more equipment was moved out to China. By early April about 10,000 tons had been shipped away. Could the same happen to the remaining planes? Perhaps the English Attorney General would provide an answer.

Sabotage

Before the Attorney's opinion was available someone decided to seek a more immediate remedy. On Sunday 2 April 1950, time bombs were surreptitiously set on seven of the planes. The explosives used were light. No one was injured and the damage was not extensive. Even so, it was enough to disable the aircraft from flying.

There had been much talk of sabotage previously, particularly from the Americans, but the only known earlier instance was the midnight foray led by Whiting Willauer the previous December following his return from Taipei.

6. The SG was another Labour MP, Sir Frank Soskice.

The perpetrators of the 2 April sabotage were described as 'Nationalist sympathizers' or 'Nationalist agents'. However, it must be doubted whether they were acting on behalf of the Nationalist government for it had sold the planes. Only if the Nationalists felt there was a real possibility that the aircraft would be used to invade Formosa would they have had cause to disable the planes. Willauer and his allies are more likely suspects. Whoever perpetrated the incident must have been motivated by desperation after the courts' refusals to put the planes under the care of receivers and to grant further freezing injunctions.

Chou En-lai blamed the British and Hong Kong governments. By this he did not think they had set the bombs but that they had not protected the aircraft and they had impeded the aircrafts' departure. He declared that they 'must be held fully and directly responsible for the present losses incurred by China' and demanded the immediate transfer of the remaining aircraft.[7]

Keeping CAT aloft

During the battle for the planes at Kai Tak, Willauer and Chennault's little airline CAT had been neglected. Its old work on routes within China had disappeared with the Communist takeover of the mainland. Most of its new work, ferrying soldiers and prosperous refugees to Formosa, also disappeared once the Nationalists had settled down there. Since December 1949 the airline had been operating from Formosa and Hainan. It had been kept alive financially by regular infusions of cash from Cox at the OPC for whom it ran little projects, mainly covert in nature. Willauer had returned from his New Year investment-raising trip to the United States with a promise of more support. He had made a proposal to his contacts there which was receiving earnest consideration.

The proposal was that the Central Intelligence Agency should buy CAT. Willauer had made quite a strong argument for them to do so: the alternative was to sell to the Communists. By the end of March 1950 the agency was making funds available to run the airline and Willauer was anxiously awaiting an official response to his proposal.[8]

7. *New York Times*, 4 April 1950, quoted by Qiang Zhai, *The Dragon, the Lion, and the Eagle: Chinese-British-American Relations, 1949–1958* (Kent, OH: Kent State University Press, 1994), 107.

8. Kaufman, 'The CAT Controversy', 101; *William M. Leary, Perilous Missions: Civil Air Transport and CIA Covert Operations in Asia* (Tuscaloosa: University of Alabama Press, 1984), 96; Martha Byrd, *Chennault: Giving Wings to the Tiger* (Tuscaloosa: University of Alabama Press, 1987), 340.

13
Two Opinions

First thoughts

Attorney General Sir Hartley Shawcross' written opinion was sent to the Foreign Secretary and the Secretary of State for the Colonies on 3 April 1950. For the recipients, it must have been disappointing reading. The opinion found no ready legal solution to the dilemma in which Great Britain found itself. 'From a political if not also from the military point of view this matter is obviously one of great difficulty and embarrassment,' Shawcross lamented, then added:

> Unfortunately, it is not one for which any obvious legal solution can be found since it is not covered by any precedent and the existing powers are not such as to indicate any course of action which the Executive authorities in Hong Kong can pursue without fear of legal repercussions or the charge of political discrimination.

Nor could he be confident of where the title to the planes rested, and anyway not much was to be gained by canvassing this aspect because a decision as to title by the executive, whether on the advice of the Law Officers or not, would be of no legal effect and would not entitle the executive to detain the aircraft as against one claimant or the other. Anyway the executive could not intervene without statutory power or court order.

Shawcross rehearsed the present position. The Supreme Court of Hong Kong had decided that all the planes were in the possession and control of the CPG which enjoyed the jurisdictional immunity of a sovereign state. The immunity prevented the trial of the issue of title to the aircraft. The decision was under appeal but it would be improper for the government to act as if it was not at present binding, still less that it may be reversed by a superior court. The previous injunctions had been discharged and CAT, Inc. had failed in its recent attempt to obtain an injunction, but Shawcross nonetheless thought it should appeal even though he did not know enough of the facts to express a view on the chances of the Full Court granting such an injunction. Why was he of that opinion? Simply because if an injunction were granted, it would keep the matter in suspense for some time 'and it may be that this is the most that can be hoped for'.

On that pessimistic note, the Attorney turned to consider whether there was any way in which the executive could intervene to prevent the planes being removed to China. The only suggestion was to take steps under the Colonial Air Navigation Order 1949. By that order aircraft may not be flown without a certificate of airworthiness valid according to the law of the country where the craft are registered. Since they had been registered both in America and China and Article 18 of the Chicago Convention 1944 contemplated that an aircraft be registered in one state only, one of the registrations must be invalid and the Governor was in no position to judge which was the valid one. Consequently, he could not be satisfied that the various regulations would be complied with and therefore was entitled to act under Article 60 of the Order, which empowered the Governor to detain an aircraft to prevent a flight which would be in contravention of the Order.

Shawcross could see the weakness of this reasoning. It was not as if the aircraft had no registration and no certificate of airworthiness: they had two. The Air Navigation Order was concerned with safety of aeroplanes in flight; its object was to promote safety in the air and the mere fact of dual registration did not affect safety. But, having acknowledged this, Shawcross wrote that he thought the powers in the Order were wide enough to permit their exercise for another purpose. He did not explain why he thought so and he immediately undermined the thought by stating 'it is desirable not to advertise the fact that the Governor may in fact use them for an entirely collateral and political purpose which has nothing to do with safety'.

The use of administrative powers for collateral purposes would be subject to attack in the courts. Shawcross forecast that if the Governor did use the Order in this way, the CPG would be faced with two options: either bringing a court action alleging that the detention was illegal or dismantling the aircraft and transporting them to China by land. It is somewhat shocking to find a government legal adviser advocating the use of a power for a collateral purpose but this was politics, not law. The object was to buy time, waiting for the outcome of the appeals. Shawcross was evidently not convinced of the soundness of his suggestion for he went on to say that action by the Governor on the pretext of the uncertainty was not politically plausible because the craft had originally been registered in China, their registrations there had been merely suspended, they bore Chinese markings, and they were in the possession and control of the Chinese.

As for the legal plausibility of the pretext, Shawcross thought that 'the Governor is, I think, though I cannot be quite sure', legally entitled to say that in view of the two registrations and of the fact that an airworthiness certificate should exist only in relation to one of them, he was not satisfied that the Colonial Air Navigation Order would be complied with. Shawcross warned that the Governor might then be made the defendant in an action in which it might eventually be held that he did not possess the power he claimed or in which the validity of the registrations would be settled in favour of the Chinese. Any decision to use the Order in this way, where no question of safety in the air was concerned, would be a political decision, explained the Attorney. The expediency of doing so would be a matter of policy for decision by the Cabinet.

Grantham resists

The Attorney-General's lukewarm and hesitant endorsement of the use of the Colonial Air Navigation Order was enough to satisfy London. It enabled ministers to stick to the strategy of letting the courts decide. The planes would be retained at Kai Tak whilst the politicians and diplomats waited for the appeals to work their way through the legal system. During that time, tempers would subside and the planes would rot—and who knew what else might happen?

One man, however, was not happy to wait and see. That was Sir Alexander Grantham. On 5 April he protested to London that it was most questionable whether he was legally entitled to use Article 60 of the Air Navigation Order to stop the aircraft from flying away. The Chinese might take action against him in the courts and that would undermine his position in the colony and he would be liable to a heavy claim for damages. Furthermore his attorney general Mr Griffin would, he warned, resign.

This was a strong stand for any colonial governor to make but the more so for such a conventional character as Grantham. It is not clear whether he was aware of Shawcross' advice of two days earlier when he uttered his protest or whether his reaction was simply the hardening of the attitude which he had displayed during March in response to instructions not to allow the planes to take off.

Grantham's objections had an effect. Eric Berthoud, the Assistant Under Secretary at the Foreign Office, recommended that the Governor be given latitude in implementing his instructions. Moreover, Shawcross changed his mind about the appropriateness of using the Air Navigation Order.

Cabinet meeting

On Thursday 6 April Sir Hartley Shawcross attended a meeting of the British Cabinet. It was unusual for an attorney general to do so. In order to maintain his independence as the government's principal legal adviser, the Attorney was not a member of the Cabinet. He would be invited to attend its meetings only if some difficult legal question had arisen and it was considered desirable to hear from him directly. Shawcross' attendance attests to the level of importance that the matter of the Chinese planes, the handling of which had strained relations with the USA and antagonized the new government in China, had reached.

Younger, on behalf of the Foreign Office, and Jim Griffiths, the Secretary of State for the Colonies, together presented for consideration at the Cabinet meeting a joint memorandum on the background concerning the planes. It was dated 3 April 1950 and entitled 'Chinese Civil Aircraft at Hong Kong'. It was an updated version of the paper of the same name authored by Montagu Pollock of the Foreign Office in January and of the paper entitled 'Chinese Aircraft at Hong Kong' of 18 March which had been enclosed with Shawcross' instructions and circulated to British diplomatic representatives. The memorandum asserted that 'the strength of our position in Hong Kong depends largely on our not becoming involved in Chinese political issues, the maintenance of an impartial administration and on insisting that the rule of law must prevail'. It expressed fear of strikes, disturbance, sabotage and an economic embargo in the colony if executive action partial to the US were to be taken. Such action would, it said, 'stultify the whole of our policy towards China'. Grantham's views had evidently made an impact.[1]

However, Acheson's veiled warning about keeping an eye on the bigger picture and the effect upon US-British relations of the planes issue had struck home with Bevin. He warned his Cabinet colleagues that public opinion in the US was highly charged and that 'if the impression gained ground in the US that American interests had not been fairly treated, the effect upon Anglo-American relations would be out of proportion to the particular issues here involved'. This would also affect Dean Acheson's personal position which was 'somewhat precarious'.[2]

The Cabinet members would have seen Shawcross' written opinion and would have expected to be asked to approve the use of Article 60 of the Air Navigation Order by the Governor to keep the planes in Hong Kong. But they were in for a shock. Sir Hartley told them that he now thought that using Article 60 would be inappropriate. Action under it would 'be something of a subterfuge' since it would have involved a not-very-plausible use of powers created for a different purpose and therefore of doubtful legality. Moreover, it was arguable that in acting under Article 60 the Governor would have had to be satisfied affirmatively that either the Chinese or the American registration was invalid and that uncertainty as to which was valid would not be enough.

1. James T. H. Tang, *Britain's Encounter with Revolutionary China, 1949–54* (New York: St. Martin's Press, 1992), 188.
2. Chi-kwan Mark, *Hong Kong and the Cold War: Anglo-American Relations, 1949–1957* (Oxford: Clarendon Press, 2004), 98.

That would have been unexpected enough. Moreover, what he proposed instead was quite radical.

Instead, he proposed that the British government should change the law of Hong Kong. They should do it not through the obedient Legislative Council of the colony but by Order-in-Council, that is to say by using the Royal Prerogative through His Majesty's Privy Council. In form it would be implementation of a decision by the King's advisers on a matter to do with one of his colonies. In modern reality it would be an executive act of the UK government. It would by-pass the legislatures both at Westminster and in Hong Kong. This route would avoid any embarrassing questions from members of those legislatures and absolve the Governor of Hong Kong from any responsibility for the amendment. It would be clear that the alteration was the work of the British government.

What had prompted Shawcross' sudden change of heart? Certainly, as shown by his written opinion, he was not confident that use of Article 60 was convincing or that it would survive legal challenge. But he had nevertheless recommended it as a pragmatic, short-term expedient. Maybe he had learnt of the Governor's deep misgivings and Griffin's threat to resign, although this is not certain and alone is unlikely to have caused such a radical turn. More likely he had been reflecting upon those issues which previously he had carefully avoided as irrelevant to the immediate question of how to justify stopping the planes from flying, namely which party had title to the aircraft and how to overcome the plea of jurisdictional immunity.

The two issues were interlinked, for to obtain a judgment on the merits of the claims to ownership of the planes, one had first to persuade the judges to accept that they had jurisdiction over the dispute. The sovereign immunity of the CPG constituted a complete blockage to obtaining a judgment on the competing claims. An apparently sound way around it had been suggested by Beckett and Roberts-Wray, the international law experts: one of the airlines, CNAC, was a private company not a government entity, so immunity did not apply to it and if the claim concerning its, rather than CATC's, assets were to be pushed forward, the appeal courts might accept this and decide the issue. Yet there was no guarantee that this argument would succeed, especially not with the Full Court in Hong Kong. Two judges there (Gibson CJ and Williams J) had already shown themselves averse to offending the PRC. The politician in Shawcross must have seen that it would be unrealistic to expect any court in Hong Kong to take a different attitude. On further appeal the Judicial Committee of the Privy Council, far removed from the influence of the PRC and more sensitive to the American arguments, might well hold that sovereign immunity did not apply to the CNAC assets but the case would take months to reach that level and the Judicial Committee would have to send it back to Hong Kong for consideration of the merits of the opposing claims. Once there, the question of whether to appoint liquidators would remain one of discretion and the local court could easily find new reasons to rule against the appointment.

The only answer therefore was to bulldoze the obstacle out of the way. This could be done by a precisely crafted Order-in-Council which in effect provided that sovereign immunity would not apply in any case about the Chinese airlines' assets only. The application of the doctrine of sovereign immunity would therefore generally continue but not in this particular sort of case. Although it would be a strange order, the damage to the integrity of Hong Kong's constitution and courts, and to international legal principle, would thereby be limited. The trouble was, such a move would not only be questionable in international law but would also brazenly disadvantage the Communist parties to the litigation and be naturally interpreted by them as intended to favour the American claimants. Presumably for that reason, when Shawcross proposed it, there was opposition from some Cabinet members. The Cabinet being divided, a decision was deferred. Meanwhile, Shawcross set about writing a second opinion.

A deceptive tactic?

On 8 April Grantham replied to a message, sent by the Secretary of State a few days earlier and before the Cabinet meeting, instructing him to use the Air Navigation Order. He was still politely yet firmly resisting the instruction. In the course of the reply he mentioned two measures alternative to the Order which might form a basis for restraining departure of the planes. One was the Control of Ships and Aircraft Regulations which had been made six months earlier under the Emergency Regulations Ordinance. The other was regulations for the embargo of certain types of goods under the Import and Export Ordinance which were had also been made quite recently.

It has been suggested by one historian that in not mentioning to his masters in London the Control of Ships and Aircraft Regulations earlier Grantham was deliberately concealing a power which he knew to be more convincing to stop the aircraft than the Air Navigation Order because he did not want to prevent the planes from departing and that this was an instance of a Governor promoting the interests of Hong Kong over those of Great Britain where the two clashed. It has also been said that Grantham did not inform or remind the policy-makers in London of all his powers.[3] That may be so, but it is doubtful that Grantham's actions towards his superiors in London were deliberately deceptive or underhand. The Ships and Aircraft Regulations made under emergency powers were not secret and indeed they were known in Whitehall.

3. Steve Y. S. Tsang, *Governing Hong Kong: Administrative Officers from the Nineteenth Century to the Handover to China, 1862–1997* (Hong Kong: Hong Kong University Press, 2007), 175.

In mid-March they had been mentioned during a joint defence committee meeting at which both Foreign Office and Colonial Office representatives were present. There it had been remarked by John Paskin of the Colonial Office how far-reaching those regulations were. They had been made fewer than six months before April 1950 when Grantham is alleged to have avoided mentioning them. In his opinion of 3 April, Shawcross had made an oblique reference to them. Consequently, it would have been natural for Grantham to assume that they were also in the minds of those to whom he reported.

It is possible that, distracted by the many problems on his plate, Grantham simply forgot about the emergency regulations, but a more likely innocent explanation is that he did not think that they applied to civilian aircraft which were the subject of a legal dispute about ownership. The regulations had been enacted when the civil war was still raging, with military aircraft in mind. Grantham was concerned not to offend Peking and sensitive to the threat of legal challenge which, if successful, would undermine his authority. Any such challenge would lead to judicial review of the Ships and Aircraft Regulations which would certainly entail scrutiny of their application to the present circumstances and might also raise questions as to whether the prerequisites to the enactment of the regulations had been satisfied. Before emergency regulations such as these could be made, an occasion of emergency or public danger had to exist and the regulations had to be desirable in the public interest. Whilst the Ordinance under which the regulations had been made placed assessment of these matters in the hands of the Governor, his assessment was not immune from attack. The conclusion that there is an emergency or danger must be reached in good faith and must be reasonable, in the administrative law sense of being rational. One can see that the government might have struggled to make a convincing argument that a civil war on the mainland which by 1949 had been continuing for several years was an emergency or posed a special danger to Hong Kong and that, even if it did, that regulations aimed at impounding aircraft which were not engaged in that war were made for a purpose relevant to the danger or emergency and were in the public interest.[4]

The suggestion of using the Air Navigation Order appears to have come from Beckett, the legal adviser to the Foreign Office. He would have been familiar with both the Order (applicable to British colonies generally) and the Chicago Convention on civil aviation, having no doubt had to advise on matters of international aviation in the recent past. He was less likely to have been aware of domestic emergency regulations peculiar to Hong Kong. The latter are not touched upon in the instructions to the Attorney General which he and Roberts-Wray drafted. The instructions do however dwell upon the Air Navigation Order and specifically ask the Attorney for advice about it.

4. Emergency Regulations Ordinance, s 2(1); *Kwok Wing Hang v Chief Executive in Council (No 6)* [2021] 1 HKC 120, 142–143.

Since officers from both the Colonial and Foreign Offices had discussed the Control of Ships and Aircraft Regulations, as well as the Import and Export Regulations, in mid-March, shortly before Beckett advised on the scope of the Governor's powers, the likelihood is that Beckett considered both sets of regulations and dismissed them as inapplicable to civilian aircraft. It was Shawcross who first considered that the Control of Ships and Aircraft Regulations provided an answer but he did not say so until later in April.

As Shawcross was backtracking on using the Colonial Air Navigation Order and a decision about an Order-in-Council was awaited, there was little point in insisting that the Governor use a procedure with which he was uncomfortable. The new Secretary of State for the Colonies, Jim Griffiths, told Grantham to do everything that he could to prevent the planes from leaving but not to use the Air Navigation Order. The Attorney General was going to compose another opinion giving his revised views.

Important but tiresome issue

On Easter Saturday, 8 April 1950, Kenneth Younger reflected in his intermittently kept diary on his new job as Minister of State at the Foreign Office. He found the job exhausting and badly needed a rest. There was a steady flow of important issues, he noted. 'The most tiresome item has been a dispute about 70 Chinese aircraft now in Hong Kong whose ownership is in dispute between the Americans and the Chinese Communists.' He had had to see Lewis Douglas, the American ambassador, about it, and had also been to Cabinet (on 11 March) about it. To Younger, it was just one of a number of 'relatively small issues which raise the question of our relations with the US and our capacity to resist undue pressure from them'. He felt that the aeroplanes issue highlighted the fact that Britain and the US were running inconsistent policies towards the Far East. 'I anticipate a great deal of friction in coming months,' he concluded.[5] Younger's attitude towards this 'small' and 'tiresome' issue suggests that he did not appreciate quite how important the fate of the planes was to the Americans, to the Chinese and to Hong Kong.

With a decision about what to do in abeyance, the diplomacy continued. On 14 April 1950 whilst the second opinion was in preparation, Younger met Lewis Douglas again. Younger, who was less sympathetic to the American position than his superior Bevin, told the ambassador that he did not think that the planes could be held much longer: not to release them undermined the United Kingdom's impartiality. Douglas responded that releasing them whilst they were the subject of competing claims to ownership made no sense. He

5. Geoffrey Warner, ed., *In the Midst of Events: The Foreign Office Diaries and Papers of Kenneth Younger, February 1950–October 1951* (London: Routledge, 2005), 9–10.

also warned of the effect on US public opinion of giving the planes to the Communists. If these points did not impress Younger, they do seem to have had an impact elsewhere in the British government.

Second thoughts

Hartley Shawcross' second written opinion concerning the dilemma of what to do about the Kai Tak planes is notably shorter than his first. Dated 17 April 1950, it begins by acknowledging that the Governor may not be able to continue the delaying tactics much longer and that instructions will have to be given as to the action he is to take. Shawcross then focuses upon the Emergency (Control of Ships and Aircraft) Regulations which, he says, have now come to light. These regulations, Shawcross explains, empower the Governor to prevent aircraft leaving the colony when it appears to him 'expedient in the public interest to do so'. In his view the Governor was 'clearly entitled to detain the aircraft under these Regulations if he considers it in the public interest so to do'. By contrast, the legality of acting under Article 60 of the Colonial Air Navigation Order was, as he had pointed out in his earlier opinion and repeated at the Cabinet, doubtful. Here the opinion was heavy on assertion and light on analysis. It does not seem that the Attorney paused to reflect upon why the Foreign Office legal experts had not relied on the emergency regulations in their brief to him if those regulations provided so obvious an answer.

Sir Hartley was in a hurry to get to the point which he regarded as key and in no mood for reflection. There could be no doubt, continued his opinion with misplaced confidence, that it would be proper for the Governor to detain the aircraft under the emergency regulations if he considered it in the public interest to do so, and it might be in the public interest to act so as to prevent the aircraft being disposed of pending adjudication as to their title. So, if action was to be taken under existing legislation, it should be under the emergency regulations and not the Air Navigation Order.

Whether it was actually in the public interest to detain the planes was essentially a political question, said Shawcross, which addressed a policy dilemma. Was it better to meet the United States' representations by using the regulations, or some ad hoc legislation, at the cost of prejudicing the chances of establishing friendly relations with the Communist government of China? Or was it preferable to leave the parties to their own legal remedies, if any, in the hope that the Communists may thereby be conciliated although Britain's relations with the United States may be embarrassed?

On this question of policy, Shawcross declared modestly, it was not for him to express a view; and he did not do so, at least not directly. But he did nudge his readers in a certain direction. He achieved this, first, by two suggestive parenthetical qualifications: the chances of friendly relations with the Communists were '(perhaps already very slender)' and the hope of conciliating them was '(perhaps remote)'. Second, he set out nine considerations which, he ventured to think, should be kept in mind. At least five of these considerations can be said to point towards intervention so as to enable the airline assets to be awarded to the Americans; four appear to be neutral and none of them point towards leaving matters as they stood so that the planes might remain in communist hands.

The first public interest consideration was that the aircraft had been transferred to the United States company (CAT, Inc.) with the approval of the Chinese Nationalist government at a time when that government was recognized by Britain as the de jure government of China. Here Shawcross seemed to assume the validity of the sale despite its having been questioned by the Chief Justice. Somewhat inconsistently, his second consideration was that it was at least probable that the title to some, if not all the aircraft, had in law been transferred to the United States interests. Presumably Shawcross was here allowing for a distinction to be drawn between the CNAC and the CATC aeroplanes.

The third consideration was that the aircraft had been flown to Hong Kong by servants or agents of the Chinese Nationalist government or a corporation controlled by it. Shawcross did not add that the purpose of doing so had been to keep the planes from the communists. His focus however was upon the role of the employees, as is brought out by the fourth point, that the planes had come into the possession and control of the Communist government only owing to the defection of those servants or agents at a time when Britain continued to recognize the Nationalists as the de jure government.

The fifth consideration was that whilst the executive should stand aside and let the law take its course, the jurisdictional immunity of a State prevented law from taking its normal course of settling the rights of the parties according to the justice of the case. In other words, the worthy intentions of the UK government had been frustrated by one side in the dispute happening to be connected with a government. This tied in with another point, which Shawcross presented as the eighth consideration, that where the law could not take its course and decide the parties' rights owing to jurisdictional immunity, it may be proper for the executive to intervene to see that those who, on one view, might be regarded as being in illegal possession of the aircraft should not be able to dispose of them to the prejudice of other claimants. The opinion does not refer to sovereign immunity as a long-established principle of public international law, nor the reasons for it. Still less does it advert to the possibility of the effect upon Britain's reputation of a failure to observe that principle.

The Attorney's sixth policy consideration was that the decision of the Hong Kong court as to possession and control was not final and might eventually be reversed by the Privy Council. Of course no part of the decision had been final for it had been made only in an interlocutory proceeding but Shawcross had obliquely acknowledged the weakness of Gibson CJ's reasoning, notably the judge's reliance upon the employees' self-declaration of agency for the Communists. Shawcross did not mention the possibility of the Chief Justice's decision being reversed by the appeal court in Hong Kong, presumably because he was aware of the political realities in the Colony.

The seventh consideration was that the Hong Kong court had not granted an injunction to preserve the status quo in the meantime. Such an injunction could have prevented the removal of the planes and parts without resort to administrative or legislative manoeuvres, but the implication was that in its absence such measures would have to be resorted to so as to ensure that any eventual decision on the merits was not academic.

The final point made by the Attorney concerning public interest was that, in any event, if the aircraft were to be flown away, this would in effect involve the Governor's acceptance of the American or Chinese registration, as the case may be, as valid. The implication here was that title, and thus validity of registration, could only be decided by a court decision on the merits.

One-sided selection

Having set these public interest factors out for his colleagues to consider, the Attorney again forswore having any view. 'I mention these matters not in order to point to one conclusion,' he insisted, 'but merely to indicate that the merits may not be entirely on one side.' But Shawcross' selection of considerations pointed discreetly to a conclusion in favour of intervention, not just by the points he made but also by those that he left out. He had not mentioned that the aeroplanes had been the property of state-controlled entities in China, nor that Hong Kong was dependent upon China for food, water and other vital supplies. He had not alluded to the volume of trade between Hong Kong and China, nor to the preservation of British and Hong Kong investments on the mainland. He had not even suggested that the view of the Governor might be relevant. Yet these were all factors which pointed to the public interest lying in allowing the planes to return to the north, if not by executive action then by doing nothing and allowing the Hong Kong courts to decide the case.

Moreover, Shawcross did not consider whether the Ships and Aircraft Regulations were really made on an occasion of emergency or public danger or had been made merely as a precaution or convenience in case the powers in them might be needed. At the time that they were made the civil war had not suddenly erupted and it was not obvious what danger the war posed to the public. The detention of Chinese civilian aircraft in Hong Kong so that adjudication upon their ownership might be made by the local courts was hardly a purpose relevant to any threat from the civil war. Shawcross' ready conclusion that the regulations empowered the Governor to stop the planes from flying seems to have been based simply upon the apparent width of their wording rather than any consideration of their purpose or legitimacy. He assumed that the regulations had been properly made and that the exercise of their powers would be appropriate and jumped to an assessment of the public interest.

The reason for his ignoring any question of the legitimacy and application of the emergency regulations and for his one-sided selection of public interest considerations became apparent in the final section of the second opinion. There Shawcross advised that if it should be decided that policy required the executive to intervene then, despite the availability of the regulations, 'the more straightforward and satisfactory course would be for His Majesty's Government in the United Kingdom to accept responsibility for an Order-in-Council' providing for the aircraft to be detained pending adjudication as to title. This was a real departure from previous thinking. An Order-in-Council is a decree nominally by the monarch by and with the advice of the Privy Council. Historically the making of such an order is part of the Royal Prerogative but in modern practice it is used as extra-parliamentary legislation by the executive branch of government. It is sparingly employed in domestic matters since legislation by parliament is preferred. It is largely used to legislate for the establishment of Crown colonies and as a means of giving effect to an act of parliament which empowers the issuing of Orders-in-Council. The Colonial Air Navigation Order is an example of such a use, applying to British colonies UK legislation designed to give effect to the Chicago Convention on International Civil Aviation. Shawcross was proposing an extraordinary use of an Order-in-Council, in effect to legislate for Hong Kong even though the colony had its own legislature.

Why did he do so? Why not simply use the emergency regulations? One explanation is that Shawcross wanted to make plain that the UK was responsible for the decision to retain the planes at Kai Tak, thereby deflecting Communist Chinese anger from Hong Kong to London. That is suggested by his stating that HMG would accept responsibility for the measure and has found favour with one leading historian.[6] But it must be doubted that this was the Attorney's main reason. Rather, an Order-in-Council would enable the British government to dictate the terms upon which the courts would consider the merits of the dispute. Shawcross could see the disadvantage of using regulations to detain the planes and allowing the appeal to go ahead on its present terms in the hope that it would resolve the issue. Even if use of emergency regulations was proper as Shawcross assumed (implicitly Beckett and Roberts-Wray had thought it would not be), the argument that those in charge of the

6. Tsang, *Governing Hong Kong*, 164.

planes had sovereign immunity was an almost insurmountable obstacle to the courts' adjudicating upon the question of ownership. As Gibson CJ's judgment showed, it would be easy for other judges to dismiss the appeal on the basis of the immunity without touching on the merits of the case. Furthermore, even if the courts somehow avoided that obstacle, the case remained a discretionary decision about the appointment of receivers, not a proper trial. A well-crafted Order-in-Council could overcome these difficulties.

Hence Shawcross devoted part of the final paragraph of his second opinion to the contents of such an order. It should begin by reciting that the question of the possession of the aircraft was still the subject of litigation, that the aircraft were registered both in the United States and China, that both the Communist government and certain United States corporations claimed to be owners of the aircraft and certain spares, he advised, and then recite that in these circumstances the Governor's right to accept one registration or the other as valid was in doubt and that the equities of the case demanded that the title to and ownership of the aircraft should be settled by normal process of law. After that, the order should provide that the aircraft be retained pending an adjudication as to title, and it should set up machinery for the trial of this issue. The duty of protecting and maintaining the aircraft in the meantime should be impressed upon the Governor, he added.

Change of direction

This conclusion proposed a change of direction by His Majesty's Government. The proposal amounted to interference in the court process, something that they had hitherto resolutely refused to do. True, it was not direct executive action of the sort pressed for by Donovan and American diplomats and it retained the veneer of allowing the court to decide the issue. But it certainly was not 'normal process of law' even if the suggested recital declared that it was.

Shawcross' advocacy of a subtle capitulation to American pressure found favour with the majority of the Cabinet. They were uncomfortable with the existing policy which did seem set to leave the planes in the hands of the Communists even if it was not intended to do so. They knew that Hong Kong's interests had to make way for the preservation of Anglo-American relations. They could feel the heat blowing across the Atlantic.

14

A Most Unfriendly Attitude

Cabinet confirmation

On Monday 24 April 1950 the British government's senior ministers met in Cabinet and agreed to the course of action which the Attorney General had proposed in his second opinion. An Order-in-Council would be issued ensuring that the case would be decided on its merits. Left-wing members of the Labour Party were still unhappy that their government seemed to be giving way to American pressure, but they were a distinct minority in the parliamentary party. Their views were shared by several junior ministers but by hardly any of the Cabinet.[1]

Another person who was displeased was Sir Alexander Grantham. He had been arguing against the use of domestic regulations to hold the planes for weeks. Now an Order was being imposed from London which would achieve the same object. 'Who was I, a mere governor of a colonial dependency to complain, and what good would it have done if I had?' lamented Grantham in his memoirs.[2] But he was there downplaying his earlier resistance which led to the decision being taken out of his hands and the benefit which he and Hong Kong received from being distanced from the decision.

The Commonwealth Relations Office, the department responsible for communications with countries within the British Commonwealth of Nations, told its representatives overseas that they should discountenance any suggestion that the UK was yielding to the US on this issue. 'The Order is destined only to maintain British standards of impartial justice in this case to meet requirements of international law,' the Office's telegram explained. 'Its primary function will be to ensure that [the] dispute over ownership is in fact brought before the Court, and that meantime the aircraft remain in

1. Aneurin Bevan in the Cabinet and Kenneth Younger, John Strachey, George Strauss (Minister of Supply) and Hector McNeill, all juniors, harboured reservations: see Geoffrey Warner, ed., *In the Midst of Events: The Foreign Office Diaries and Papers of Kenneth Younger, February 1950–October 1951* (London: Routledge, 2005), 54.
2. Alexander Grantham, *Via Ports: From Hong Kong to Hong Kong* (Hong Kong: Hong Kong University Press, 1965), 162–163.

Hong Kong.'[3] Since the Order specifically over-rode the principle of sovereign immunity, the assertion that it met the requirements of international law was disingenuous. It seems that ministers and senior civil servants did not think about the requirements of international law. The only requirements they considered were their own.

Agreement to disagree

The US Secretary of State Dean Acheson visited London in the second week of May 1950 for a number of international meetings mainly concerned with European security. Acheson had bilateral discussions with Ernest Bevin. These proved futile and served only to emphasize the widening division between British and American policy. Acheson put the lack of progress down to Bevin, who was recovering from a medical operation, having to take sedatives. Younger put it down to Acheson having been disconcerted not only by Bevin's condition but also by a 'vicious campaign' against him in the US and as a result not daring to put forward a constructive policy. Right-wing Republicans in Congress had constantly attacked Acheson as having 'lost' China and being 'soft on Communism'.[4]

In such circumstances, during the meetings there was minimal discussion about China and the Far East and none about the planes at Kai Tak. Presumably the State Department was resigned to the law taking its course on the latter. The two countries' positions were well known to each other and there seems to have been a tacit agreement to disagree on this and other divisive issues such as recognition of the Communist government, continuation of trade and commerce, establishment of diplomatic relations, PRC membership of the UN, and the attitude to take towards Taiwan. Younger noted on 11 May 1950, 'presumably for the next few months we are to pursue our present policy with the object of "keeping the door open" in China without paying too much attention to American susceptibilities' whilst the Americans will 'carry on their relations with the Nationalists in Formosa without much regard to its effect on our position'. Younger was not optimistic as to the immediate prospects for British policy, however. On diplomatic relations it seemed clear to him that 'we are not going to get much change out of the Peking Government' and that British interests in China were 'likely to have a very thin time'. Nevertheless, he thought that the 'decision over the Chinese aircraft in Hong Kong' was correct.[5] Presumably by that he meant the decision not to hand them over to the Communists rather than the decision to make use of an Order-in-Council.

3. FO371/84791. The word 'destined' may be an error for 'designed'.
4. Dean Acheson, *Present at the Creation: My Years in the State Department* (New York: W.W. Norton, 1969), 384–385, 390; Warner, *In the Midst of Events*, 14–15.
5. Warner, *In the Midst of Events*, 15.

Drafting challenges

The proposed Order-in-Council was a novelty, being directed to a specific type of case about a specific matter in a specific jurisdiction. The drafting of the Order presented quite a challenge. It had not to be too wide so as inadvertently to affect other future cases, yet it had to be wide enough to deal with all eventualities that might occur in future litigation concerning the aircraft. Shawcross had already set out some guidelines towards the end of his second opinion. He had suggested recitals that would give the background to the Order (the existing litigation, the double registration of the aircraft, the competing claims to ownership, the doubt as to which registration was valid, the need to settle the question by legal decision) and the substance that should be dealt with by the Order: detention of the aircraft pending adjudication on the title, machinery for trial of the issue, and protection and maintenance of the aircraft until that adjudication.

But there were other possibilities which Shawcross had not anticipated and which had to be catered for. What if the PRC government took offence and refused to participate in the trial? How then could a regular, full trial with written pleadings of the competing cases, framing of issues and calling of witnesses to give evidence take place? Normally in those circumstances the plaintiff would be entitled to judgment without any consideration of the merits of the claim, so the question of ownership would not be adjudicated upon and the whole British strategy of letting the court decide would be frustrated.

The appeal is heard

While the draftsmen got to work on the text of the Order-in-Council, the expedited appeal from the decision of Gibson CJ refusing the appointment of receivers was approaching a hearing in the Full Court. Only the CATC decision was appealed. This was somewhat surprising since, although the issues were almost entirely the same in the two cases, the argument that sovereign immunity did not apply to the assets of CNAC, a private company, appeared to be stronger than in the case of CATC, a government department.

CAT, Inc. had pursued the appeal against the advice of its Hong Kong lawyers. The lawyers were concerned solely with the slim chance of success. Donovan, Chennault and Willauer had a wider perspective, however. Not only were they by disposition gamblers, they also felt they had to respond to imprecations from the British government, conveyed through American diplomats and Hong Kong officials, to exhaust all legal avenues. They also wanted to keep the case in the public eye in America so that politicians there would maintain the pressure on the administration to prevent the Communists from having the planes.

Apparently in the hope of increasing the chances of success they brought in a new lead counsel. He was Harold Sheldon KC, a former chief magistrate and experienced barrister of only slightly less seniority than the defence's Eldon Potter. He joined the two King's Counsel and one junior counsel already engaged by CAT, Inc. They identified the main weakness in the Chief Justice's reasoning, the finding that the defecting employees were representatives of the Central People's Government. If the employees' possession of the assets was illegal, how could they be said to possess them on behalf of the CPG? Indeed, how could they be said to be in possession of the assets in the eyes of the law at all?

The judges who heard the appeal were all High Court judges brought together specifically for the purpose to comprise the Full Court. The president was Ernest Hillas Williams, the judge who four months earlier had rejected one of the Americans' applications for appointment of a receiver. In the absence of Gibson, Williams was acting as Chief Justice. In common with many at the top of the legal and administrative hierarchy in the colony, he was Irish, from a Protestant family in County Cork. He had been in the colonial civil service attaining the position of Secretary for Chinese Affairs (equivalent of the modern Secretary for Home Affairs) before turning to the law and becoming Assistant Attorney General, then a magistrate and later a puisne judge. His colleagues for the hearing were Mr Justice Scholes and Mr Justice Gould, the latter a New Zealander and former Crown Counsel. As they heard the appeal they would probably have been aware that their decision was about to be rendered irrelevant by a change in the law imposed from London.

The council makes the order

Before the Full Court delivered its decision, on 10 May the Privy Council made the Supreme Court of Hong Kong (Jurisdiction) Order. Its content was quite extraordinary for it set aside the law of sovereign immunity but did so for one narrowly circumscribed type of case only, that concerning the planes and equipment at and around Kai Tak. Moreover it was directed at a case that did not yet exist. It did not affect the existing actions and the interlocutory proceedings which had already progressed through the Hong Kong courts, with judgment imminent on the appeal from Gibson CJ's decision of 23 February refusing to appoint receivers. Since the trial of the substantive claims in those actions had yet to be heard, it would have been possible to apply the Order to them but evidently it was thought more seemly to alter the law for future claims only, so as to avoid differing decisions about sovereign immunity at different stages of the same case. The authorities in London may also have been aware that Gibson was due to retire soon and a fresh action would be unlikely to come to adjudication during his tenure.

The name of the Order was misleading, for the jurisdiction of the Supreme Court was only part of its subject-matter. After reciting that 70 aircraft (in fact there were 71) at Kai Tak were registered both in the USA and China, that dual registration was contrary to the Chicago Convention, that ownership of the aircraft was in dispute and that it was just and desirable that their ownership and the right to their possession should be decided by a court of law before they be permitted to leave Hong Kong, the Order provided that '[i]n any action or other proceeding concerning the aircraft which may be instituted in the Supreme Court of Hong Kong after the date of coming into operation of this Order, it shall not be a bar to the jurisdiction of the Court that the action or other proceeding impleads a foreign sovereign State'.[6] That was not merely procedural: it amended the law of state immunity and deprived the communist employees and supporters of their trump card. What if they therefore decided that the whole contest was stacked against them and refused to participate? That possibility was anticipated, for the Order went on to state that if a defendant in any such action or proceeding failed to appear or put in a defence or take any other step which he ought properly to take, the court would, notwithstanding any rule enabling it to give judgment in default in such a case, 'enquire fully into the matter before giving judgment'. So the normal court processes in claims which are unopposed were to be ignored. There would still be a judgment about ownership but after a full enquiry rather than a traditional trial. In case the other claimants also refused to participate, the Order also permitted the government to refer the matter to the court after 21 days.

Seemingly what was contemplated was more akin to an investigation than a trial. The court was given power to hear evidence, summon witnesses, call for documents, give directions and provide for service of documents. In the common law system court proceedings are generally adversarial: they depend upon the parties to an action presenting competing cases which are argued out by their representatives before a judge who may ask questions about what is presented but not seek evidence himself. There are, though, exceptions in which a more inquisitorial approach is adopted, for example a Coroner's enquiry into the cause of death. Administrative or political enquiries chaired by judges are also held, though these were not as common in 1950 as they are now. It seems that the Order envisaged a combination of trial and enquiry. The facts were hardly in dispute and had already been laid out in prior judgments based on affidavits filed by the parties. The main task of the judges in any future action would be to rule on the law.

---

6. Supreme Court of Hong Kong (Jurisdiction) Order in Council, 1950, s 1(1). The aircraft were defined to include any spare parts, machinery and equipment for use in relation to them and the Governor could give directions particularizing the aircraft etc in case of doubt: s 6(2).

Whatever was envisaged, it was not a normal Supreme Court trial so the usual route of appeal would not be open unless this was spelt out. Accordingly the Order stipulated that anyone claiming the planes 'may appeal therefrom to the Full Court and . . . thence to His Majesty in Council'. As a precaution it added 'and such an appeal shall lie notwithstanding such person has not taken any part in previous proceedings'.[7] This would enable the Chinese government and its supporters, and for that matter the American claimants, to participate in an appeal even if they had not been named or joined as parties to the proceedings and even if they had chosen to stand aloof from the contest initially. It would also have enabled the US government, or indeed the British one, to take part.

The provision for appeal and further appeal was an important part of the UK government's tactics. Its insistence that the courts decide the question of ownership was predicated upon the ultimate judicial decision being manifestly independent and of the highest possible calibre. Shawcross had no doubt detected the reluctance of the judges in Hong Kong to reach a decision adverse to the new government in China. It was therefore imperative that any route of appeal terminate outside the colony. The easiest way to do that was to stipulate that any appeal could be heard by the Judicial Committee of the Privy Council, just as all Hong Kong appeals might then have done.

The Order next dealt with the question which had vexed the authorities in London and Hong Kong: how to preserve the planes and parts at Kai Tak whilst the inquiry and appeals were taking place? The Order empowered the Governor to 'give such directions and take such steps, whether by way of detention of the aircraft or otherwise, as shall appear to him necessary to prevent their removal and to ensure their maintenance and protection'. There was even provision for what would happen after the final judgment. Once the Governor had been satisfied that ownership or the right to possession had been finally determined, he was empowered to give directions and take steps as appeared to him necessary to give effect to the court's decision. Failure to comply was an offence incurring liability to a fine not exceeding HK$5000 and up to six months imprisonment or both.[8]

Sharp reaction

The course had therefore been set by the Order for a series of judicial decisions about the ownership of and right to possess the planes. But to those who considered that the Hong Kong courts had already decided these matters

7. Ibid., s 1(3).
8. Ibid., s 5(1), (2), and (3). The text of the Order is set out in the law reports: *Civil Air Transport Incorporated v Central Air Transport Corporation* (1951) 35 HKLR 162, 167–170 and *Civil Air Transport Incorporated v Central Air Transport Corporation (Hong Kong)* [1953] AC 70, 79–80.

in favour of the new Chinese government, including that government, the American interests and the press, the contents of the Order made sense only if the intention was that the existing decisions on those matters be reversed and that the reversal would take place in London by the Privy Council. Since the distinction between the Privy Council's role as an advisory and legislative body under the control of the British government and its role (through the Judicial Committee) as an independent court was semantic and rather esoteric, many were unconvinced by British protestations that the law would take its course and the courts would decide. They assumed that the outcome was ordained in advance.

The Central People's Government in Peking certainly thought so. In early April Chou En-lai had denounced Britain for impeding the departure of the planes and failing to protect them, adding that the Hong Kong authorities would be held responsible for any damage to the craft and that a favourable settlement was a condition for the establishment of full diplomatic relations. The Order-in-Council cemented his suspicions. By co-incidence, the Order was made just two days after the Chinese foreign ministry had delivered a note to the UK Chargé Hutchison asking for further clarification concerning Chinese government property in Hong Kong and PRC representation at the UN as part of the negotiations for establishment of diplomatic relations. Reaction to the Order came on 21 May. In Peking Chang Han-fu (Zhang Hanfu), vice-minister of Foreign Affairs, gave Hutchison a note declaring that Britain was exhibiting 'a most unfriendly attitude' towards the CPG and warning that unless the Order was rescinded the PRC would have reason to doubt Britain's desire to establish diplomatic relations. As far as the CPG was concerned, the Order was an example of the use of judicial procedures for political purposes.[9]

The Order-in-Council was just one of the manifestations of the unfriendly attitude in the eyes of the CPG. The others were Britain's abstention on the question of admittance of the Communist government's representatives to the United Nations as successor to the Nationalists and Britain's continued maintenance of a consul at Tamsui in Taiwan.[10] Both seemed inconsistent with the recognition of the CPG in January. Both were undoubtedly awkward, the result of trying to please the Truman administration which remained stalwart in its refusal to recognize the Communists and, as the UK's efforts to persuade the CPG to establish diplomatic relations became frustrated, ever more convinced that the refusal was correct.

9. William M. Leary, 'Aircraft and Anti-Communists: CAT in Action, 1942–52', *China Quarterly* 52 (1972): 654, 661–662; William M. Leary, *Perilous Missions: Civil Air Transport and CIA Covert Operations in Asia* (Tuscaloosa: University of Alabama Press, 1984), 98; Wenguang Shao, *China, Britain and Businessmen: Political and Commercial Relations, 1949–57* (Basingstoke: Macmillan, 1991), 79.
10. Evan Luard, *Britain and China* (London: Chatto and Windus, 1962), 83.

The CPG's expression of displeasure was, however, confined to the verbal. Its supporters in Hong Kong organized no demonstrations, incited no strikes and instigated no disturbances. There was no show of force or embargo of trade. The CPG was determined to be pragmatic.

Breach of international law?

The Order-in-Council removing the bar of sovereign immunity was effective in domestic Hong Kong law, but was it a breach of public international law? One eminent writer, teacher and practitioner in that field has suggested that it was.[11]

The immunity from suit of overseas governments in the courts of a jurisdiction is an almost universal practice and is a cornerstone of relations between states. International law doctrine holds that foreign sovereigns may be impleaded in (sued in or affected by the decisions of) the courts of another nation only by their consent. So unless the sovereign power in question submits to the jurisdiction of another, any suit which impleads it in the courts of the other will be arrested and barred. In that way respect is shown for the dignity, independence and equality of that power by the state which extends immunity to it. It would be undignified for a state to have to engage in litigation with ordinary citizens of another country—and embarrassing for that other country, carrying the risk of damaging their relations.

This practice has been explained by a number of principles the most cogent of which is comity: a sovereign enjoys immunity from suit in its own courts and extends that immunity to other sovereigns in the interests of good relations between them by waiving its jurisdiction over them. It does so not only to show friendship and respect but also in order to obtain reciprocal immunity for itself in the courts of other states. Consequently good faith and self-interest may be said to be the foundations of the immunity.[12]

By the late nineteenth century reciprocal jurisdictional immunity had become such a common practice between states that it had been recognized as an international legal custom. Not to accord it to a recognized state or, worse, to remove it was almost unthinkable. That would be a breach of the custom and, since custom is one of the sources of public international law, a violation of the law. As developed by the English courts the immunity was automatic and absolute.[13] It remained so in 1950, although that was later to change. So well-accepted was the custom that sovereign state immunity later became the subject of a UN treaty in which it was embodied.

---

11. Professor D. P. O'Connell during lectures at the University of Oxford, 1975 (author's notes).
12. Lord Wright in *The Cristina* [1938] AC 485, 502.
13. The classic statement of the English law is by Brett LJ in *The Parlement Belge* (1880) PD 197, 214.

Accordingly, in removing the immunity the British government can be said to have been dealing a blow to the dignity of the CPG. It was refusing to accept the CPG as an equal, reducing it to the level of a common litigant. The content and effect of the Order-in-Council could be construed as discourteous and uncivil, demonstrating an absence of goodwill towards the new government of China. Yet none of these considerations seem to have weighed in the calculations of the Cabinet or of the Attorney-General. Certainly they do not appear explicitly in the advice given by Shawcross to his colleagues. The closest to recognizing the nature of what was being proposed by him is the provision in the Order for the possibility that the CPG would boycott the consequent proceedings.

The likeliest response of a government treated in this inconsiderate and demeaning way would be to protest and to refuse to respond to any suit which is allowed to proceed against it as a result of the lifting of the immunity. That is precisely what was to happen in this instance.

The Full Court decision

Three days after promulgation of the Order-in-Council the judges of the Full Court gave their reserved judgment on the appeal by CAT, Inc. Their attitude towards the CPG was far from unfriendly. As expected, they followed the same line as had the Chief Justice. After spending ten pages reciting the facts as found by Gibson CJ, acting Chief Justice Williams on behalf of the whole court, turned to the doctrine of sovereign immunity and the attack made by Harold Sheldon for CAT, Inc. on the finding that immunity applied.

Sheldon's first argument was that the property concerned was not of a type to which immunity attached because the planes and equipment were not dedicated to public uses. Previous decisions concerning publicly owned trading vessels had contained differing views from appellate judges on this. Williams, like Gibson, preferred those which held that the doctrine did apply to state ships engaged in trade. In this both judges chose a view which held sway in international law until the mid-1970s when the growth of state trading enterprises led to a revision of the scope of the immunity, at least in Western courts. In any event, Williams, again like Gibson, thought that the property in the present case was for public use: 'They are essential and substantial parts of airlines used for the carriage of passengers, mails and freight in the interior of China.' China was a country of vast area, wrote Williams, and 'still backward in development so far as roads and railroads are concerned,' so such services were 'of immense importance and serve . . . essentially a public purpose'. It was not a wholly convincing conclusion, for the airlines charged for their services and traded for profit.

The appellants' second argument was a forlorn attempt to distinguish the present case on its facts from previous ones on sovereign immunity. In the present case a British court was being asked to decide a dispute between litigants from one foreign country and the government of another whereas previous instances had been claims either between British nationals or interests and a foreign state or between subjects of a foreign state and their own government. The Full Court was undoubtedly correct to dismiss this as having 'no bearing whatsoever on the principles being applied' since application of the doctrine arose from the status of the foreign sovereign and was not affected by the identity of the person seeking the aid of the court.

Then the appellants sought to draw a distinction based on the timing of the gaining of possession by the CPG. This argument relied upon the date of recognition of that government by Britain. Although the communist employees had control of the planes from the autumn of 1949, the argument ran, since the property was in a British Crown Colony, they had no right to take possession on behalf of the CPG which had no standing until it had been recognized by Britain. That had not occurred until the first moment of 6 January 1950—and by then the property had been sold to the claimants (on 12 December 1949) and their writ had been issued (on 5 January). In answer, the Full Court pointed out that, although not recognized de jure until 5/6 January, the CPG had been recognized by Britain as the de facto government of most of China before that date and indeed prior to the sale in December, and de facto recognition was sufficient for the doctrine of immunity to apply. Anyway, the court added, the important date concerning possession is not so much the date when the writ is issued as the date upon which the claim to immunity is made, which in the present case was the date of the hearing for appointment of receivers, which had been in February 1950.

On the findings that actual possession and control of the aircraft was held by persons purporting to act on behalf of the CPG and that the CPG intended to possess them through those persons, Sheldon chose to concentrate upon the legality of the acts of those persons. He reprised the argument that they had not obtained the consent of the Governor to function on behalf of the CPG in Hong Kong, in violation of section 3 of the Representation of Foreign Powers (Control) Ordinance 1949. In response, the judges of the Full Court set out the reasons given by Gibson CJ for rejecting it, described in Chapter 11, and said that they thought those reasons were correct. They quoted passages from several appellate judgments in the UK to the effect that the courts are not concerned with the legality of a government's possession of the property in dispute and that municipal law is irrelevant to sovereign immunity once the property is in the sovereign's possession.

Sheldon does not seem to have argued that the illegality was relevant to the prior question of whether the property is actually in the possession of the government for which immunity is claimed. If he did, the judges must have misunderstood the point, for the judgment does not deal with it. The argument would have been that the Ordinance, and indeed the common law, prevented the employees from unilaterally changing from one employer to another and therefore from acting on behalf of the CPG, with the consequence that their possession of the planes and equipment was not possession on behalf of that government. Could servants of one master become the servants of another by declaring allegiance to the other simply with that other's acceptance after, or even before, the declaration? This was pivotal to the imposition of state immunity on the basis of possession by the CPG and it seemed a rather dubious answer to say that they could. The change of allegiance was a finding of fact and appeal courts usually refuse to overturn facts as found by the judge at first instance. But it was a conclusory fact, that is to say one deduced from other, primary facts concerning the events which had happened and which were not in dispute. Appellate judges are readier to disagree with a factual conclusion of this sort since they are in as good a position as the earlier judge to make a deduction drawn from undisputed or indisputable primary facts. Also, the effectiveness of the change of allegiance was a question of law. However, it would have been an uphill battle to persuade the three judges to accept that their chief had been mistaken: not only because he was their superior but also because they lived in a community which was disposed to give the new Chinese government the benefit of the doubt both out of wishful thinking and out of self-preservation. In social and official circles the judges brushed shoulders with government officials who would have shared the Governor's desire to be rid of the planes.

Nor does any argument appear to have been run that the employees were not fully in control of the assets. The planes and some of the equipment were not on their property but at the Hong Kong government's airfield. Access to the airfield was controlled by the airport authorities: workers and managers required passes to enter. The employees could not fly the planes away since some had vital parts missing and all had insufficient fuel, which was rationed by the authorities. In addition, departure of the aircraft was forbidden by order of the Hong Kong government and it was unclear with which country they were properly registered and therefore whether they complied with relevant national regulations. Rather than having control, what the third-party employees had was access and the means to bar others from access. That was more than the appellant CAT, Inc., had but it was debateable whether it amounted to the physical possession and control necessary to found a claim to sovereign immunity.

Perhaps sensing the weaknesses of the Chief Justice's finding that the CPG was in possession through the employees and with an eye to any further appeal, Potter and the Communists' representatives sought to uphold sovereign immunity on grounds additional to the CPG's possession of the disputed assets through the workers. They argued that the CPG claimed an interest in the assets of both airlines through requisition or other decree. In the case of CATC they also said that the assets were owned by the CPG in consequence of the change of government. This last contention happened to coincide with the view of Beckett, the Foreign Office's legal adviser. The appeal court side-stepped these arguments, however, on the basis that it was unnecessary to decide them given their acceptance of the argument that the CPG had possession through the employees.[14]

Finally, for good measure, the Full Court agreed with the Chief Justice that anyway the applicants had not shown a sufficiently strong case to justify appointment of receivers. At the time of the contracts of sale between the airlines and the Chennault-Willauer partnership in December 1949 most of mainland China, including Shanghai, was under Communist control, the judges pointed out. Although not yet recognized by Britain de jure, the CPG was the de facto government and therefore, they reasoned,

> It follows that any acts done by the Nationalist Government as regards that part of China under de facto control of the Central People's Government are to be regarded as a mere nullity in that area by the Courts of this country.

The sales were such acts. The appellants accepted that this would be true of any acts done within areas controlled by the CPG but suggested that it did not apply to acts done in Hong Kong and elsewhere outside CPG control. 'It seems illogical,' the court reflected, 'to say that the agreement is binding upon the Central People's Government as to some things and a nullity as regards others.' However, the appellants were not saying that. They were saying that what is important is where an act is done, not what is done. Their point was that where the CPG had no actual control, as in Hong Kong, the relevant Chinese government was that recognized by the sovereign power there, the United Kingdom, at the time of the relevant acts, the sales. Their point was illogical only if one accepts that the distinction between recognition de jure and recognition de facto is illogical.

Undeterred that their conclusions upon international law were unnecessary, the Full Court plunged in further, utilizing the principle of succession between governments. 'It would seem,' they declared, 'that the right of succession of the Central People's Government to these assets must be deemed to have arisen before the purported dealing in them' on 12 December 1949. Once de jure recognition had taken place, the right of succession was to relate back to the date upon which de facto recognition took place, they said. Moreover, the CPG, the government of the area to which the assets belonged, had already dismissed the officials who entered into the agreements by the

14. (1950) 35 HKLR 386, 403–409.

time that they had been made, and the purchasers Chennault and Willauer knew this.

A further difficulty in the case of CNAC, the court said, was that of the authority of those who attended the purported directors' meeting on 31 December 1949 to ratify the agreement. They had been appointed by a government which had no power to appoint them. 'The purported sale appears to be quite contrary to the constitution of the corporation,' the court concluded.

The effect of the Full Court's judgment was to leave matters where they stood before its decision. But by the time it had been delivered, the judgment had been sidelined anyway.

15
Change in Mood

International law issues

Although the Full Court's decision had been rendered academic by the intervention of the Order-in-Council, the judges' reasoning did bring into focus a number of issues of public international law that arose from the dispute and which might be expected to be raised, if not decided, in any new phase of litigation occasioned by the Order. There was of course the question of sovereign immunity, although that had been pushed out of the way by the Order and so would not be considered in future. In addition, there were issues of recognition, of succession and of international treaties.

Recognition in public international law may concern recognition of new states, of new governments, of territorial changes, of belligerency and of insurgency. The recognition in question concerned recognition of governments by other governments and particularly the retrospectivity of that recognition. In the case of the aeroplanes the focus was upon the effect of the British government's recognition of the Central People's Government as the de jure government of China, and the concomitant withdrawal of de jure recognition from the (Nationalist) government of the Republic of China, in early January 1950. What was the effect of that? Was it retrospective and, if so, to what extent? The Communists had been in control of most of China long before their formal recognition as the government. The Foreign Office certificate had indicated that before de jure recognition Britain had accepted them as the de facto government of those parts of China over which they had had control from the beginning of that control. Did the formal recognition relate back to then? Or did it relate back to 1 October 1949, the date upon which the PRC had been declared? Or did it relate back to later in 1949 when the UK government decided that it would recognize the PRC but had yet to decide upon a date for doing so? Or was there no relation back at all?

Another aspect was the role of the UK government's executive certificate concerning recognition, issued at the request of the Chief Justice in accordance with British practice which, unlike American practice, regards it as impermissible that the courts should adopt a view of recognition different to that of the government. The issuance of such a certificate to a court was by no means the first time that this procedure had been used. The justification for judges asking for this guidance was that there should be no inconsistency between the views of the government and the conclusions of the courts. In this instance, the certificate was in the form of a number of answers to questions raised by the court rather than a statement by the Foreign Office of the position regarding recognition. The certificate was accordingly rather fuller than might have been expected. In the event, the answers given were artfully crafted and directed precisely to the questions. But what if the government had declined to answer the questions posed by the court, or had answered them incompletely or obscurely? The certificate in this case deliberately threw back the question of the retrospectivity of recognition to the court.

The doctrine of succession of governments in international law concerns the responsibilities that an incoming government 'inherits' or takes over from its predecessor. The Chinese Communist leadership had caused apprehension by its adamant statements to the effect that it would not be bound by unfair treaties and other obligations of past Chinese governments. In general, however, because of the desirability that there should be continuity of administration, the succeeding government is taken to accept what has been done by its predecessor. In the case of the Chinese planes the succession was specifically that of succession to property, namely the assets of the two airlines. Assuming that those assets had belonged to the Republic of China, did the CPG succeed to them, and if so, when? Again, there were a number of choices of date. If that date had been before the sale and transfer of title to the assets to Chennault and Willauer, the ROC would have had nothing to transfer to them.

The relevant international treaty in the planes case was the Chicago Convention on Civil Aviation 1944. As we have seen, this required that a commercial aeroplane be registered with the relevant authorities of its home state. Uncertainty as to the meaning of this had been the excuse for the Hong Kong government to detain the planes at Kai Tak. Might the uncertainty about their proper registration have a bearing on the outcome of the dispute?

A further aspect of international law was to be raised in the new phase of litigation. This was the concept of trusteeship, specifically of a government as trustee of state assets for the people of the state. Did it apply and if so, was it relevant to resolution of the legal issues?

Litigation again

Chennault and Willauer lost no time in launching fresh proceedings to take advantage of the abolition of sovereign immunity for any future actions concerning the aircraft. On 19 May 1950 CAT, Inc. issued a new writ against

CATC for a declaration that the 40 aircraft which formerly belonged to it were the property of CAT, Inc. CATC was now undoubtedly controlled by the CPG and its representatives had undoubtedly been appointed by the CPG. Consequently, there was no need to sue the employees or others holding the aircraft as well.

The new Communist governors of CATC evidently had decided that it would be wasteful of time and money to become engaged in this new litigation. They refused to accept service of the writ. Normally service of a writ upon a foreign government or its agencies is arranged through diplomatic channels, in the case of Hong Kong in 1950 by the Colonial Secretary. That route having failed, CAT Inc.'s solicitors received permission from the court to use an alternative form of service, by leaving a copy of the writ at CATC's office in Hong Kong's Central district. This too was ignored. CATC did not acknowledge service or enter an appearance on the court record. The scenario envisaged by the Order-in-Council was unfolding.

Alterations in attitude

During 1950 attitudes toward the new regime in China underwent significant changes. In Hong Kong, initial admiration for the success of the Communists in both winning the civil war and unifying the country, and a feeling that their government could only be an improvement on the Nationalist one, gave way to trepidation. In the course of 1949 the optimistic view that the Communists were at heart more agrarian reformers than hardcore communists had yielded to a no less deluded expectation that after some turmoil China would settle down and normal business and cultural relations would be resumed and even that the Communists would be unable to cope with all of China's problems and their regime would soon collapse. The only evidence to support this had been that the Communists had behaved better than expected towards British nationals and interests in the parts of the country which they had so far taken over.

The belief that relations would return to normal once Britain recognized the new regime was particularly prevalent in the business community. It was shared by American and Shanghainese, as well as British, taipans who viewed recognition as an inevitable if distasteful step and therefore better taken sooner rather than later. Speculation about early recognition was rife by late October 1949 after the declaration of the creation of the PRC.

Once recognition had taken place and the new year had progressed without any discernible change for the better, all that wishful thinking gradually was replaced by a more realistic assessment. A disruptive and bitter tram workers' strike which broke out at Christmas 1949 and lasted several weeks was thought to be backed by Communists, both local and from the mainland.

Waves of refugees continued to pour into the colony, increasing the pressure on housing and rents and also the number without work, as well as heightening fears of rises in crime, instability and communist infiltration. In response, the border was closed. The internal policies of the CPG were proving more repressive and nationalistic than anticipated. Many among the mass of ordinary Chinese inhabitants in the colony continued to identify with the CPG and were buoyed by the legitimacy given by international recognition of the new government. Others accepted communism in order to safeguard their livelihoods. The attitude among the colony's elite, however, was more sanguine. Business on the mainland was being hampered by restrictions and impositions, mainly by the new authorities but also by the Nationalist blockade of the China coast. The outlook for mainland trade deteriorated. A mood of gloomy foreboding descended. No one could be sure of the CPG's intentions regarding Hong Kong: perhaps they would decide to take it over. The outbreak of war in Korea, with the North being supported by China and the South by the USA and Britain, only heightened the anxiety.[1]

Similar disillusion struck the United Kingdom. The Labour government was disappointed and somewhat taken aback that what it saw as the realism and generosity of extending recognition did not lead to an immediate exchange of ambassadors. British recognition of the PRC had been at some cost to its relations with the USA. Establishment of diplomatic and political relations normally automatically followed recognition and were not matters to be haggled over, but all the Chinese would accept Hutchison's delegation for was preliminary discussions. Britain assumed that the discussions would be about formal and technical matters such as diplomatic immunities and facilities for consulates, so was further taken aback when the Chinese began to raise questions of policy and demand substantial concessions. Chinese radio broadcasts hinted that British properties and interests on the mainland would be raised at the talks, as would the position of Hong Kong. British business continued to experience difficulties in China. The nationalization of British-owned enterprises there caused further disappointment, although it would have come as no surprise to those who understood the Chinese Communist frame of mind. The regime's repeated denunciatory rhetoric, dogmatic, intransigent and directed at Britain as well as America, was a constant irritant.[2]

The idea of driving a wedge between Moscow and Peking received a blow when Mao visited Moscow for seven weeks from 16 December 1949 (ostensibly to celebrate Stalin's 70th birthday) and, among other things, negotiated a

1. David Clayton, *Imperialism Revisited: Political and Economic Relations between Britain and China, 1950–54* (New York: Macmillan, 1997), 105; James T. H. Tang, 'World War to Cold War: Hong Kong's Future and Anglo-Chinese Relations 1941–1955', in *Precarious Balance: Hong Kong between China and Britain, 1842–1992*, ed. Ming K. Chan (Hong Kong: Hong Kong University Press, 1994) 107; Karl Lott Rankin, *China Assignment* (Seattle: University of Washington Press, 1964), 38.
2. Evan Luard, *Britain and China* (London: Chatto and Windus, 1962), 83–85.

treaty to replace the one that the Nationalists had made with the USSR in 1945. It was Mao's first visit to any foreign country. He was joined by Chou En-lai for part of the negotiations. The main object of this Treaty of Friendship and Alliance, made in mid-February 1950, was to give the parties security against a threat which each perceived from the USA and Japan. It also reflected ideological solidarity and included agreements on economic matters, such as loans and railways, and territorial matters, such as Soviet control of Port Arthur (Loshun). This marked the end of a phase of strained relations between the two parties. Previously Stalin had cultivated Chiang Kai-shek, an ally during the Second World War. The presence of Nationalist armies had protected the USSR's eastern flank from Japanese incursions. During both that war and the Chinese civil war, Stalin had been indifferent if not suspicious towards the Chinese communists. The USSR's embassy had even followed the KMT government to Canton and Chungking as the Communists took over China. Stalin had acknowledged that he had been mistaken in supporting Chiang but never apologized to Mao, whom he regarded as a rival, for the mistake. Even after the likelihood of Communist triumph became apparent, Stalin postponed Mao's visit for almost a year.

In reality, relations between Mao and Stalin were strained and formal. After arriving, Mao was made to wait weeks before discussions began and sulked in his dacha far from town. He regarded the eventual terms (which were secret at the time), under which the PRC agreed not to allow foreigners to live in or pursue business ventures in Manchuria and Sinkiang and gave the USSR the right to occupy two Chinese ports and run the Manchurian rail line, as humiliating and redolent of imperialism. Even the Soviets' low-interest loan of US$300 million to buy Russian industrial equipment was less than Mao had hoped for. But all this was overshadowed in Western eyes by the threatening prospect of cooperation between the dictators of two giant, communist, totalitarian states.[3]

British diplomatists tended to attribute the CPG's cool response regarding diplomatic relations to the Chinese complaints made in preliminary negotiations concerning establishment of formal relations. These were about the UK's abstention in January 1950 on the Soviet motion for the admission of the CPG to the United Nations, its maintenance of relations with the Nationalists in Formosa, and its retention of the planes and other Chinese assets in Hong Kong. However, these complaints may well have been excuses deployed to disguise ideological hostility and an isolationist policy and also to strike a pose of nationalistic anti-imperialism for domestic consumption. The Chinese Communist Party's attitude towards recognition of its government by foreign powers had been set in March 1949.

---

3. Peter Lowe, *Containing the Cold War in East Asia: British Policies towards Japan, China and Korea, 1948–53* (Manchester: Manchester University Press, 1997), 112–114.

Early entry into diplomatic and political relations had been part of Britain's strategy of 'keeping a foot in the door' for commercial opportunities in China and of attempting to integrate the PRC into world affairs so as to lure it away from the influence of the USSR. PRC membership of the UN and replacement by it of the Nationalist delegates on the Security Council had also been part of the strategy. However, British ministers and advisers had been diverted from supporting the Soviet motion to admit the PRC to the UN by concern not to alienate the Americans. They said that they wished to ensure that a motion for PRC admission had majority approval before Britain would vote for it. This was not mere excuse, for they did take steps privately to obtain more support for PRC membership despite American misgivings.

Abstention pleased nobody: at the Foreign Office, Younger described it as an attempt to ride two horses at once, Dening said it brought no benefit, and Strang thought it substantiated Chinese criticism of Britain as double-faced; from Peking, Hutchison pushed for change. In June 1950, ministers revised their view and decided to support PRC membership, but the damage had been done. American opposition and the outbreak of war in Korea led to delay in implementing the decision. Eventually, in September Britain voted in favour of the PRC's admission to the UN, but it abstained on a Soviet proposal to expel the KMT. To the CPG, this conduct confirmed suspicions that the UK was an American acolyte whose offer of friendship was insincere and motivated only by self-interest.[4]

Self-interest certainly played a part, as it always does in international relations. Britain had two fundamental and related concerns: restoration of its trade with and investment in China and protection of its valuable colony, Hong Kong. Britain's economic stake in China, however, continued to dwindle during 1950. Despite recognition, British businesses encountered grave difficulties. Early optimism that the new authorities would allow foreign operations to continue had disappeared. There was said to be a feeling of hopelessness in Shanghai where changes in tax and labour laws and forced purchase of bonds, added to the KMT blockade, had reduced the mercantile life of the city to a shadow of its former self. Businesses were closing down or surviving on subsidies from their British parent. The value of these remittances was eroded by unrealistic official exchange rates. Imports to China were hampered by controls. The imposition of governmental monopolies for bulk goods, enjoying the advantages of scale, state subsidy, transport facilities and favourable exchange rates, took away export opportunities for small and foreign traders. Western institutions found competition with the giant new People's Bank and the Chinese People's Insurance Company difficult. Labour unrest and militancy (unrealistic and obdurate wage demands, verbal abuse and lock-ins of

4. Tang, 'World War to Cold War', 82, 90, 130–136.

managers), often backed by local Communist cadres as part of the revolution, made normal operations impossible. Costs were heightened by increased business taxes (usually locally levied and backdated), government-dictated wage increases, severance payments and compulsory wages for no work. The China Association complained to Bevin in March 1950 about business conditions in China, as did Members of Parliament, but with no formal relationship as yet, there was little that he could do except exhort the association's members to hang on.[5]

The securing of formal government relations was hardly vital to the continuation of commerce in Hong Kong so there was little pressure from the colony to speed up diplomatic negotiations. It became apparent that the Communists were willing to participate in foreign trade through new state enterprises and had no objection to foreign firms being involved. Hong Kong benefited from that. Trade within China, however, was a different matter. The Communists had no wish to perpetuate foreign domination of the domestic economy.[6]

Members of the British government began to regret its unconditional recognition of the PRC and its open offer to establish diplomatic and political relations. The CPG's demanding response to the latter brought frustration to policy-makers. Its continued intransigence during negotiations seemed designed to humiliate Britain. The episode led to derision from some quarters, especially in America.

In the United States there had been fewer illusions about the Chinese Communists. The souring of attitudes towards the PRC which had set in even before 1950 (noted in Chapter 5) continued, as did support for Chiang Kai-shek. Visiting the Far East in January 1950, Philip Jessup, the State Department's ambassador-at-large, issued a statement opposing communist theory and practice and emphasizing the United States' support for equality and independence for China. The meeting of US diplomatists that Jessup chaired at Bangkok that February was dominated by discussion of the communist advance in Asia and the risk of war in southeast Asia. China's new treaty with the USSR confirmed the diplomatic concern. The US National Security Council produced a paper advising the President that it was important for US security that all practical measures be taken to prevent further communist expansion in southeast Asia and propounding the 'domino theory' that unstable states in the Far East would fall prey to communism, one after the other. The paper advocated both overt and covert action to resist communist

5. Wenguang Shao, *China, Britain and Businessmen: Political and Commercial Relations, 1949–57* (Basingstoke: Macmillan, 1991), 47–50; James T. H. Tang, *Britain's Encounter with Revolutionary China, 1949–54* (New York: St. Martin's Press, 1992), 49–52.

6. Tang, *Britain's Encounter*, 148–152; Shao, *China, Britain and Businessmen*, 41–47.

expansion.[7] At the end of March the emollient Butterworth was transferred and replaced by the tough-minded Dean Rusk as Assistant Secretary of State for Far Eastern Affairs. The Department of Defense began arguing for a harder line to be taken with China, an attitude which found favour with President Truman and his policy of containment.

One seasoned US diplomat with 25 years of experience behind the iron curtain, Karl Rankin the US consul in Hong Kong, detected a strikingly close similarity between the methods he saw in communist China and those he was familiar with from the Soviet Union: infiltration, sabotage, propaganda, guerrilla warfare and seditious movements. Russia and China were both vast territories with widely divergent regions and an enormous population. In both, the people had a low standard of living, all but a fraction were ignorant and politically inert, and political power was highly centralized. He predicted to the State Department that efforts would be made to place communist regimes in charge elsewhere in Asia, using China as a springboard. Instead of a direct military assault, the communists would continue to infiltrate neighbouring countries, particularly those to the south, utilizing the large Chinese populations resident there. The Chinese were the most numerous and capable people in Asia and China had the potential to become a dominating power there. Rankin advocated that the US extend economic, military and technical assistance to the countries under threat and that steps be taken to prevent strategic materials reaching the communists: that included 'rearguard action' in Hong Kong to prevent them getting the planes and aviation equipment.[8]

ChiNat interests became ever more vociferous and ever more suspicious of what they saw as British duplicity. The State Department, though understanding of British concerns, thought Britain was bending over backwards to placate the PRC. Any inclination on the part of Dean Acheson to propose US recognition of the CPG had been forgotten by the middle of the year. Yet remnants of the previous attitude of engagement lingered within the State Department. In early October 1950 the US put out feelers through Indian diplomats to arrange a direct link with the CPG. These were turned down by the Chinese, an indication of the CCP's enduring enmity towards the Americans but also of planned Chinese initiatives in Tibet and Korea.[9]

7. NSC 64 (March 1950); Martha Byrd, *Chennault: Giving Wings to the Tiger* (Tuscaloosa: University of Alabama Press, 1987), 339–340; Victor S. Kaufman, 'The United States, Great Britain and the CAT Controversy', *Journal of Contemporary History* 40, no. 1 (2005): 95, 101; Rankin, *China Assignment*, 23–24.
8. Rankin, *China Assignment*, 35–36, 39–41.
9. Tang, *Britain's Encounter*, 92.

The Korean War

The simmering difficulties came to the boil with the outbreak of war in Korea. On 24 June 1950 North Korean troops crossed the 38th Parallel, the line of latitude at which American and Russian forces had divided their occupation of Korea upon the evacuation of Japanese troops at the end of the Second World War. This line subsequently had demarcated the border between the satellite regimes of the USSR and the USA in, respectively, North and South Korea, neither of which were yet members of the United Nations. The North Korean dictator Kim Il-sung thought he could swiftly conquer the South and effect unification before any Western intervention. He spuriously claimed that his armies were responding to a South Korean attack. They made rapid progress against poor South Korean defences. Chinese broadcasts and official statements supported the North Koreans, although it is doubtful Kim had informed Peking of his intentions in advance. China had long regarded Korea as within its sphere of influence, treasured the countries' historical connections and valued Korea as a buffer against Japanese and American influences. The Japanese had invaded China through Korea three times in the past, including twice in the last 55 years.

President Truman immediately ordered the US Seventh Fleet to patrol the waters between Formosa and mainland China. He said this was to prevent fighting between the Nationalists and the Communists. In fact, intelligence informed him of hundreds of thousands of PLA troops in southeast China poised to invade the island. The US Department of Defense, which now had US military advisers in Formosa, feared that the Communists would use the commotion in Korea to cover an invasion. The Truman administration had decided that Formosa must be kept from the Communists, in effect a reversal of its previous policy of non-intervention in the Chinese civil war. Since the status of Formosa was to be addressed in the forthcoming peace treaty with Japan, the Americans did consider whether achieving their aim would be enhanced by the replacement of Chiang Kai-shek and the imposition of a new constitutional arrangement for the island, such as a US trusteeship under the United Nations, but eventually decided to stick with Chiang.[10]

The deployment of American warships annoyed the Peking leadership even more than did American support for the South Koreans since it frustrated their plans to complete the conquest of all China. Chou En-lai denounced the deployment as designed to obstruct the liberation of Formosa, 'armed aggression against Chinese territory', and a violation of the UN Charter.

British policy-makers were also displeased with the American bracketing of Korea with Taiwan. They thought that the interposition of the Seventh Fleet risked driving China towards the USSR, as well as widening the Korean

10. Lowe, *Containing the Cold War*, 118.

conflict and alienating allies. The Colonial Office was particularly concerned about the consequences for Hong Kong, fearing that China would react to the American move, and to the continued detention of the planes at Kai Tak, by bringing pressure to bear upon the colony. Embargoes upon the export of oil and strategic materials to the PRC added to this risk. As Grantham observed, all these decisions decreased the value of Hong Kong to China. The British government was careful to give no support to American policy towards Formosa.[11]

Truman, Acheson, and Clifford thought it imperative that the US react to North Korean aggression swiftly and do so through the United Nations. The policy of containment demanded it and the absence of Communist China and the Soviet Union from the UN Security Council made it possible. Ironically, the Soviets had absented themselves from the Council in protest at the rejection in January of their motion for exclusion of the KMT representatives there. On 25 June the Security Council passed a resolution calling on North Korea to withdraw and stating that all members should provide South Korea with such assistance as may be necessary to repel armed attack and restore international peace and security. On 27 June, since the North had not withdrawn, the Council recommended that UN members assist South Korea. American forces from Japan responded promptly. Ten days later the Council put UN forces under the command of the United States.

Although 22 countries eventually sent military or medical units to Korea, the involvement of soldiers from nations other than the US was minor. The United Kingdom dispatched a battalion from its closest garrison, the recently strengthened forces at Hong Kong. (Ironically, the British government had already decided to cut down its forces there as an economy measure.) General Douglas MacArthur hurried from his vice-regal duties in Japan to command the UN effort. They arrived just in time to prevent a North Korean victory.

During the next few months the fortunes of war flowed to and fro. South Korean and UN forces were beaten back to a portion of territory around the southeastern port of Pusan. Then, following a bold sea-borne landing by UN forces near Inchon on the central west coast of the Korean peninsula, North Korean troops were out-flanked and forced back. As the UN troops advanced to the 38th Parallel the question arose: should they cross it and invade North Korea? The fear was that if they did, China would intervene. In fact Chou En-lai had already sent an observer group to North Korea and had directed PLA troops from the southeast coast to the Yalu River on the border with North Korea under the command of Peng Dehuia, the general who had recently successfully invaded Hainan. The small Chinese navy had been ordered to concentrate upon defending the northeast coast instead of the shore opposite

11. Chi-kwan Mark, *Hong Kong and the Cold War: Anglo-American Relations, 1949–1957* (Oxford: Clarendon Press, 2004), 100–102.

Formosa. Since the middle of the year Chinese state enterprises had been buying essentials such as metals, cotton, pharmaceuticals and electrical goods and stockpiling war materials (steel, wire, petroleum, tyres, wireless and telephone equipment) to the benefit of Hong Kong and British exporters.[12]

The head of the Foreign Ministry's Asian Division, Chen Jiakang (who had been with Chou in wartime Chungking), regarded the US's actions as linked both to Taiwan and Asia in general: the US was planning an economic resuscitation of the region and was pushing its allies to co-operate with this, he concluded. Chen thought that the detention of the aircraft at Kai Tak was part of that strategy.[13]

Despite the preparations, debates were going on within the CPG's Central Committee about the merits and risks of entering Korea. Some argued that the PRC was not yet firmly established and was not ready for another conflict. Others feared it would spark a world war. The majority, however, including crucially Mao and Chou, thought that the USA was so aggressive and the North Koreans (who lacked air and sea forces in a country with poor road and rail connections) so vulnerable that China would have to become engaged, and the sooner the better. Aside from securing China's borders and heavy industry in its northeast, intervention would discharge a favour which was owed to the North Korean communists who had helped the CCP during the Chinese civil war and would prevent a humiliating setback for international socialism.

In late September, Chou said that should the imperialists invade her neighbour 'China could not stand aside'. On 2 October he told the Indian ambassador that US troops should not cross the 38th parallel. MacArthur brushed these warnings away as bluff. Peking radio stated that a 'serious situation' would be caused by a US invasion. There were incursions by the US Air Force into Chinese airspace in Manchuria. Visiting the US to attend a session of the United Nations in the autumn of 1950, Younger detected a 'strong war psychosis' and feared that MacArthur was a 'dangerous megalomaniac' and a gambler.[14]

Acheson thought that the PRC would not become involved so long as the USSR feared a world war. Stalin did indeed fear war with the US and was reluctant to help the Chinese whose advance was delayed by the USSR's logistical problems and unwillingness to provide air cover. Eventually Chou En-lai had to travel to Sochi on the Black Sea to meet Stalin and obtain his assistance.[15]

12. Shao, *China, Britain and Businessmen*, 53, 59, 91–93.
13. Qiang Zhai, *The Dragon, the Lion, and the Eagle: Chinese-British-American Relations, 1949–1958* (Kent, OH: Kent State University Press, 1994), 66–67.
14. Geoffrey Warner, ed., *In the Midst of Events: The Foreign Office Diaries and Papers of Kenneth Younger, February 1950–October 1951* (London: Routledge, 2005), 46–48; Qiang Zhai, *The Dragon, the Lion, and the Eagle*, 69–71.
15. Qiang Zhai, *The Dragon, the Lion, and the Eagle*, 81.

In the event, American and British forces halted at the parallel; South Korean forces, not bound by UN resolutions, pressed ahead. On 1 October, MacArthur called on North Korea to accept a ceasefire. British military chiefs wanted the UN to halt north of the parallel, at the 'waistline' of the peninsula which would be easier to defend and might not be thought as threatening to China as having foreign troops on her border. Others, including MacArthur, wanted to finish the job of unifying the whole of Korea which had been discussed ever since 1945. The UN forces thereafter occupied most of North Korea, including the capital, Pyongyang.

Soldiers from the Chinese Northeast Frontier Army eventually began crossing the Yalu on 18 October. They did so surreptitiously and in the guise of 'The Chinese People's Volunteers'. A week later they first engaged in battle. On 27 October came the first reports of Chinese troops in North Korea, soon confirmed by MacArthur. By 2 November, UN forces were in retreat. Peking claimed that the troops were 'Chinese people volunteering to resist American aggression to aid Korea and to defend their country'. There were so many 'volunteers' that UN troops were pushed back over the 38th Parallel by the turn of the year. Only on 21 January 1951 was the communist advance halted. At the end of that month the UN passed a resolution declaring that the PRC had engaged in aggression in Korea.

That resolution was described by Chou En-lai as 'illegal, slanderous and void' but New China's undoubted intervention in the conflict changed profoundly the way in which the PRC was perceived. It had become an aggressive, totalitarian, militarist dictatorship in the eyes of many in the West who had previously been sympathetic or willing to give it the benefit of the doubt. Allowing it to have the detained planes now was unthinkable.

CIA buys CAT

On 28 June 1950, just three days after the outbreak of fighting on the Korean peninsula, the Director of the CIA approved the purchase of Chennault and Willauer's airline CAT. This was separate from the other investment, CAT, Inc., which had been used by the pair and their supporters to buy the Chinese airline assets in December 1949. Those supporters had close links with the CIA too.

Two Delaware companies were used to disguise the purchase of CAT. Willauer transferred the CAT business to the first company, which had directors who were all CIA office employees, and the first in turn transferred the business to the second company. The latter was called CAT Incorporated, a name designed to be confused with both CAT, Inc. and CAT. The majority of the directors of CAT Incorporated were from the CIA.

As far as the agency was concerned, the purchase was a temporary measure. It required an airline for short-term, operational reasons. The purchase had been presented to US authorities as necessary for covert operations in resisting the advance of the communists and preventing the fall of dominoes in east and southeast Asia. Assurances were given that the new owners would not compete with commercial American airlines. Under the terms of the deal Willauer was given an option to re-purchase CAT from the agency within three years. He and Chennault remained with the airline so that outwardly little had changed. They still regarded it as their enterprise and Willauer at least was active in its day-to-day running.

Formalizing the sale to the CIA took almost two months. Willauer and Chennault received only a modest return on their investment (Tommy Corcoran and William Youngman took a handsome slice of the price in legal and consultancy fees), but they were relieved to get what had become a loss-making concern off their hands. They could now concentrate on their mission with CAT, Inc. to keep the Kai Tak planes out of Communist hands. The airline would continue to be used by the CIA for its transport needs, including for clandestine missions.[16]

Stores

Despite the shipments of parts and equipment in the spring of 1950, hundreds of tons of CNAC and CATC goods remained in Hong Kong. They were stored at Kai Tak, at Bailey's Shipyard and at the premises of the New Asiatic Chemical Company, guarded by staff of the airlines. In turn, they were watched over by Hong Kong government agents, anxious that the equipment be not spirited away to China.

In mid-September a consignment of parts was intercepted by investigators of the Department of Commerce and Industry. It was found aboard the Chun Sang, a Jardine Matheson steamer, listed in the manifest as typewriters and furniture.[17]

A new chief

At the beginning of 1951 Hong Kong acquired a new Chief Justice. After little more than three years in the job, Sir Leslie Gibson departed to become a legal adviser to the Colonial Office, a task for which he had no obvious credentials.

---

16. William M. Leary, *Perilous Missions: Civil Air Transport and CIA Covert Operations in Asia* (Tuscaloosa: University of Alabama Press, 1984), 110; Byrd, *Chennault*, 341.
17. Report, *South China Morning Post*, 18 September 1950.

It may be that Sir Leslie was ill and was given a pre-retirement sinecure. He was replaced by Sir Gerard Howe.

The new chief justice was in his early 50s and was another Irishman who had been a long-term colonial servant. After attending an eminent Protestant school in Ulster, he had graduated from Trinity College at the University of Dublin, been called to the Bar there and entered the colonial legal service. He served mainly in Africa, ending as attorney-general of Nigeria, before appointment to Hong Kong.

Howe's experience would have been largely in criminal law, as magistrate, Crown counsel and attorney-general. It was hardly good preparation for deciding a case of public international legal importance.

16
Back to Court

The law's delays

Why were the Americans taking so long to bring their new case to court? That was the question that senior staff at the Foreign Office were asking as 1950 drew to a close. They could not understand the delay and speculated that the Americans were not pursuing the case with seriousness for political reasons. A Foreign Office official minuted: 'In view of the Korean situation it was considered that any decision would inevitably prove most embarrassing politically and it was therefore decided to make no attempt to expedite the litigation so long as the Korean Crisis lasted.'[1] The perplexity was increased by a decision of the Federal Court of California in January 1951, concerning CNAC assets in San Francisco, that the sale to Chennault and Willauer had been valid, a decision which the American embassy in London lost no time in communicating to the Foreign Office.

CAT, Inc. had begun the latest rounds of its contest for the aircraft, this time with Communist-controlled CATC, in mid-May 1950, secure in the knowledge that sovereign immunity could not be used this time. By July that year it had become apparent that the corporation would have a clear run in the courts because CATC would not be contesting the claim. Why not just apply to court and obtain unopposed judgment?

One obstacle to doing so was that the Order-in-Council had ruled out the normal procedure in uncontested cases whereby a plaintiff applies for speedy judgment, whether that be judgment in default (of acknowledgement of service or of defence) or summary judgment without trial. The Order directed the courts to inquire fully into the case. In addition, the Central People's Government had refused to accept notice of the writ on behalf of CATC even though the latter was one of its departments controlled by its Civil Aeronautical Administration. This meant that CAT, Inc.'s lawyers had to apply to court for permission to use a form of service in substitution for the usual personal service (handing over of the writ to a senior officer of the company),

1. R. F. G. Sarell, 'Statement of the Present Position', 16 February 1951.

in this case by leaving a sealed copy of the writ at CATC's offices in Hong Kong. This required the making of affidavits and the issuing of summonses, which took up much of the autumn.

The Order-in-Council had created a hybrid sort of proceeding but did not specify the extent to which normal procedure would apply. Being uncertain and cautious, the plaintiffs applied unilaterally (ex parte) for leave to proceed without CATC. Leave was granted by the court on 4 December 1950. The case was set down for argument in front of the new Chief Justice beginning on 28 March 1951.[2]

Divergence

The new year found Kenneth Younger worrying gloomily in his diary about the international situation. His boss, Ernest Bevin, was perpetually ill and seemed broken and drifting with no stamina. In Korea, the Chinese had begun a new offensive, below the 38th Parallel. Could UN forces hold on? The morale and quality of most US troops was poor, according to Younger's brother-in-law, an officer with the Argyll and Sutherland Highlanders fighting in Korea. In Younger's opinion the US had played into the hands of the Russians and had hardly done a sensible thing for months. The Americans had refused to recognize the Peking government, clung to Chiang Kai-shek, linked Formosa with Korea, pursued a rash military policy through MacArthur and had been unable to fight properly. Now they wanted UN sanctions, such as a blockade and withdrawal of diplomatic representatives, against China and condemnation of it as an aggressor.[3]

The British government was indeed concerned that the US seemed determined to widen the conflict. Attlee told Truman that a UN resolution calling the PRC an aggressor would jeopardize ceasefire prospects and that sanctions would damage Hong Kong. The UK Foreign Office thought that sanctions would be futile and contradict Britain's policy of engagement with the PRC. Worse, sanctions could precipitate trouble for Britain in the Far East. They would split the Commonwealth whose premiers were meeting in London. The newer members such as India regarded the Communist Chinese as a nationalistic independence movement. The Foreign Office was particularly concerned about the effect of sanctions upon Hong Kong. It told the State Department that UK support for the US proposal should not be assumed.

British concern about the colony and inclination to appease the CPG, demonstrated also in their attitude towards the planes dispute, irritated the

2. *Civil Air Transport Incorporated v Central Air Transport Corporation* (1951) 35 HKLR 22, 26.
3. Geoffrey Warner, ed., *In the Midst of Events: The Foreign Office Diaries and Papers of Kenneth Younger, February 1950–October 1951* (London: Routledge, 2005), 52–54.

Americans.[4] Younger's prediction of the previous July that US and British policies in the Far East would increasingly diverge seemed to be coming true. The last thing that Whitehall wanted was that the issue of the aeroplanes at Kai Tak should blow up again.

At the same time, Britain's relations with the PRC were deteriorating. It could hardly be otherwise given that their forces were facing each other in Korea. Naturally, the CPG resented Britain's eventual support for an American proposal at the UN branding the PRC as an aggressor, even if that support had been given grudgingly (the Cabinet had been divided on the issue) and even though the PRC had been resisting peace initiatives. The PRC accused colonial authorities in Malaya of 'frenzied persecution' of overseas Chinese there, three thousand of whom had been 'repatriated' as suspected communists or their dependents. Two British diplomats were expelled from remote areas of China, allegedly for spying, in January 1951. On his retirement from the negotiating mission to Peking, John Hutchison was given a coldly formal farewell. The quest for diplomatic relations had been going nowhere for months and the Foreign Office had lost enthusiasm for it. Hutchison's successor, Leo Lamb, was instructed not to press for formal relations. Lamb was also told that if the Chinese asked about the Hong Kong aircraft or their UN membership, he should say that he had to consult the Foreign Office.[5]

The UN motion condemning Chinese aggression was eventually passed. Statements emanating from America such as one from Chennault calling for the overthrow of the Communist regime in China through sabotage, guerrilla warfare and uprisings were as inflammatory as they were unrealistic. Tensions were such that in January 1951 the US Consul-General advised US nationals to leave Hong Kong. In May an American resolution for a selective embargo against China was adopted at the UN and acted upon by Britain the following month with licence controls on exports to China and Hong Kong. The Chinese foreign ministry called the UN resolution 'a malevolent attempt to extend aggressive war' and said that the UK had 'revealed its determination to be the enemy of China'. Also, Britain agreed with an American suggestion to postpone further any discussion of PRC representation at the UN. There was no prospect of any British business in China. The foot in the door had been reduced to barely a toe.[6]

4. Chi-kwan Mark, *Hong Kong and the Cold War: Anglo-American Relations, 1949–1957* (Oxford: Clarendon Press, 2004), 104–106.
5. Peter Lowe, *Containing the Cold War in East Asia: British Policies towards Japan, China and Korea, 1948–53* (Manchester: Manchester University Press, 1997), 129.
6. James T. H. Tang, *Britain's Encounter with Revolutionary China, 1949–54* (New York: St. Martin's Press, 1992) 107–111, 181; Qiang Zhai, *The Dragon, the Lion, and the Eagle: Chinese-British-American Relations, 1949–1958* (Kent, OH: Kent State University Press, 1994) 108–109.

Contingency plans

As the date for the new hearing drew closer, thoughts in the Foreign Office turned to the question of what to do if Sir Gerard Howe CJ were to follow the example of his predecessor and rule in favour of the communist parties despite their seeming lack of interest in opposing the case. The feeling among officials was that after the Chinese intervention in Korea the previous winter it would be undesirable politically to allow any aircraft into Chinese hands. If the case involving either airline went in favour of China 'we shall have to consider administrative action', such as export controls, to prevent the aircraft being handed over, one official noted. The aviation expert at the Colonial Office, W. T. Bigg, suggested that the Hong Kong government could detain the planes by using emergency regulations or an export prohibition order.[7]

But the British government hoped to avoid taking such action. They stuck to the argument that entitlement to the airline assets was solely a matter for the courts, so it would be better to get the Americans to appeal, if necessary to the Privy Council. The loser had six months to appeal, the Foreign Office noted, though of course the Chinese side would not do so since that would be to acknowledge the jurisdiction of the Hong Kong courts. We want the Americans to appeal, John Shattock, the Head of the Foreign Office's Far East Department, minuted on 16 March 1951, because 'up to now we have maintained both publicly and with the Central People's Government of China that the Hong Kong aircraft case is a judicial matter for the courts to decide and therefore not one on which we can express any opinion'.[8] In Hong Kong, Sir Alexander Grantham was less sanguine. Reporting to the Colonial Office at the end of the hearing in front of Sir Gerard Howe that judgment would be delivered in about ten days, he asked what he should do if the aircraft were to be awarded to China.

London Silk

There was a new leader of CAT, Inc.'s team of lawyers for the new case. He was Sir Walter Monckton KC, an eminent member of the English Bar renowned for his charm and persuasiveness. Monckton's engagement for this case must have been one of the first instances of a phenomenon which was to become common in Hong Kong courts later in the twentieth century, that of the 'London Silk' who is flown in specifically to appear in a particular case. Frequent air services between London and Hong Kong had made this feasible. Even so, Monckton would have had to endure a journey with half-a-dozen stopovers over three or four days. CAT, Inc. and its American backers must

7. FO 371/93126, Minute, 1 March 1951; Bigg to Sarell, 13 March 1951.
8. FO 371/93126, note, 16 March 1951.

have calculated that the expense would have been justified by the international law aspects of the dispute upon which expertise would not have been available at the Hong Kong Bar. They may also have thought that colonial judges would be more likely to be swayed by arguments made by an advocate of Monckton's credentials. Those credentials were indeed impressive. After Harrow School and Balliol College Oxford, where he had been President of the Union and played cricket for the University, Monckton not only survived the First World War as an officer in the regiment of his native West Kent but won a Military Cross too. At the Bar, he had risen quickly to earn the silk gown of King's Counsel and then was appointed Attorney-General to the Duchy of Cornwall. The Duke of Cornwall being also the Prince of Wales and heir apparent to the throne of England, Monckton's duties included giving legal advice to Edward, Prince of Wales. In 1937, after Edward had succeeded to the throne, Monckton advised Edward over the latter's abdication as King. During the abdication crisis Monckton met another of the King's advisers, Winston Churchill, who was so impressed by the KC's emollient and sure touch that on becoming Prime Minister three years later he brought Monckton into government. Monckton held senior positions at the Ministry of Information and later the Foreign Office, then in 1945 served briefly as Solicitor-General until Churchill's election defeat. Monckton returned to practice. He became legal adviser to the Nazim (ruler) of Hyderabad before it was absorbed into independent India. By 1950 he was in demand as a fashionable silk. His establishment status and foreign policy experience made him an ideal choice as lead advocate in the latest round of the case of the Chinese aircraft.

There was one other new member of CAT, Inc.'s courtroom team, R. I. Threlfall. The other members remained as before, Leo D'Almada KC and John MacNeill KC, all instructed by Denis Blake of Wilkinson and Grist.

Another judgment

The hearing in front of Sir Gerard Howe CJ lasted three days, 27 to 29 March 1950. An initial question for the judge was what form the hearing was to take. The Order-in-Council had instructed him to enquire fully into the matter. However, only one party was represented so there was no written defence summarizing the defectionist employees' case, no contending submissions to be considered, and no cross-examination of witnesses. Furthermore, no independent counsel to assist the judge had been appointed, as is common in public enquiries. No amicus curiae, or 'friend of the court', was there to present evidence and put arguments in opposing directions either.

Sir Gerard seemed a little perplexed about what he was required to do but eventually settled upon an approach which considered not only the plaintiff's case in the present proceedings but also the cases of the applicants, respondents and third parties in the previous cases concerning the aircraft and other assets of both airlines. He interpreted the Order-in-Council as disallowing any reliance upon the law of sovereign immunity and therefore permitting the court to proceed despite that the proceedings impleaded a sovereign state, but as otherwise leaving the substantive law untouched. He thought the reference to steps which a defendant 'ought properly to take' related only to a state's failure to put in a defence or otherwise comply with proper procedure after having initially put in an appearance. This approach allowed him to take into account all that had gone before concerning the aeroplanes.

Sir Walter Monckton's submissions ('put with great ability' according to Howe CJ) were in outline that on 12 December 1949 CATC was wholly owned and controlled by the Nationalist government; on that date there was a valid sale by that government to the Chennault-Willauer partnership on condition that the partnership was to organize a corporation to which the assets were to be transferred; the partnership duly transferred the assets by valid sale to CAT, Inc.; the Nationalist government was empowered to enter into this transaction as it was then recognized de jure by the British government; a change of government is by succession and the incoming government is bound by the acts of its predecessor so the CPG was bound by the transaction; the doctrine of retroactivity of recognition did not affect the transaction.[9]

Given his conclusion that all the background to the case was to be considered by his inquiry, the first pages of Howe CJ's judgment were devoted to a review of already well-trodden ground. He recounted there the two corporations and their air services, the transfer of their enterprises to Hong Kong, the successive relocations of the Nationalist seats of government, the grounding of the aircraft at Kai Tak and suspension of their registrations, the declaration of the PRC, the dismissal of Nationalist ministers, the rebellion by most of the airlines' staff, the payment of the wages of those staff by the Communist government, the injunctions, the sale of the airline assets to the Channault-Willauer partnership by the Nationalist government, the applications for appointment of receivers, the court's questions and the Foreign Office's answers about recognition of the contending governments of China, the further sale of the assets by the partnership to CAT, Inc. and the judgments by Gibson CJ and the Full Court relying on sovereign immunity.

Howe then quoted at length from an affirmation made in the earlier proceedings by Chen Cheuk Lin, the general manager (or managing director) of CATC who had defected to the PRC in November 1949 with pilots and planes and who had been re-appointed by the CPG authorities to manage CATC. This affirmation of course gave a one-sided view of matters, particularly in its assertion that CATC was a department of the CPG, its statement that those assets

9. *CATI v CATC* (1951) 35 HKLR 22, 33–34 contains a summary by the judge of Monckton's submissions but this seems to be incomplete. The judgment contains a number of minor inaccuracies.

were managed, possessed and controlled by himself and his staff on behalf of the CPG, and his reference to the airline assets as 'state property'. Chen, or rather the lawyers who drafted his affirmation, painted a picture of CATC as one continuous entity which had been under his direction throughout on behalf of whatever was the government of China: 'I say that from its organization in 1942 the Corporation had been administered and controlled as a department of the Ministry of Communication and I say that the Corporation is still a Department of the Central People's Government.' He added:

> the possession, control and management on behalf of the Central People's Government of all the assets . . . belonging to the Central Air Transport Corporation has been at all material times in myself as Managing Director and in the members of staff of the Corporation appointed by me and acting under my instructions and orders to retain and maintain possession, control and management of this property as State Property.

Chief Justice Howe seemed to regard these statements as entirely factual and containing no element of opinion or assertion. They formed the basis of part of his summary of the position as at 12 December 1949, the date of the sale by the Nationalist government to the partnership of Chennault and Willauer. In the summary he said that the members of staff and employees had 'attorned to' the CPG, that is they had acknowledged that they were now the agents of the CPG, and that, as 'rightly held' in the earlier litigation, the aircraft were in the possession and control of the CPG. That conclusion assumed the legal validity of the asserted agency: Howe did not pause to question that.

The judgment then quoted two special provisions in the agreement of sale. One stipulated that the Nationalist government was unwilling to sell the airline assets except upon binding assurances that afterwards they would not be used in any way for the benefit of or for the carriage of passengers or goods within, to or from the communist areas of China. In the other, the partnership agreed that the assets would not be used directly or indirectly in that way. In reliance on these and 'normal diplomatic usage' (meaning, presumably, the practice of most governments of according formal recognition to authorities actually in control of a country), Howe CJ inferred that the Nationalist government must have been fully alive to the probability of the withdrawal of recognition by HMG in the near future. He might have added, although did not, that Chennault and Willauer were alive to the probability as well. After referring to the actual withdrawal of recognition on 5/6 January 1950, Howe CJ concluded that the sale was a transaction entered into by both parties by which it was hoped that the aircraft might be prevented from passing to the CPG on its recognition de jure.

So it was, but what was the relevance of that? This emerged in the next paragraph in which the Chief Justice roundly declared: 'It is a transaction inimical to the Central People's Government and indeed, as the aircraft were used for a public purpose within and without China, inimical to the interests of the Chinese people.' This was an extraordinary outburst from a judge, quite out of keeping with the tone of the judgment as a whole, a moral or political rather than judicial statement. Presumably some Chinese people, those who supported the Nationalists, would have disagreed with the last part of it.

There was, however, a purpose behind the outburst. It paved the way for Howe CJ to rely upon a judicial statement in the case of the Polish seamen, *Boguslawski,* which was then proceeding through the English courts. The case concerned the effect of a change in the government of Poland soon after the end of the Second World War. During the war the recognized Polish government had been in exile in London. Although it controlled no territory because Poland had been occupied by Germany and Russia, the government-in-exile did control part of the Polish merchant fleet. On 25 June 1945 a new communist Provisional Government was established in Lublin and had de facto control over Poland. The Provisional Government was recognized de jure by the UK government at midnight on 5–6 July 1945 in place of the government-in-exile. Just before the change in recognition, on 3 July the Minister of Commerce in London, as supreme manager of Polish shipping companies, informed representatives of the Polish seamen's union that any crew who left their ships on account of the change in government would be offered and entitled to a gratuity payable by their employers. Boguslawski was one of the men who accepted the offer. When his employers, the appellant shipping line, refused to pay, he sought compensation through the English courts. The employers argued that recognition of the Provisional Government had retroactive effect so that the offer by the government-in-exile had been ineffective.

All the courts held that recognition of the Provisional Government had been retrospective only so far as acts within its own territory were concerned. Acts by the government-in-exile outside that territory were valid so long as it remained the government de jure. So the offer had been effective and the employer was obliged to pay the gratuity.

By the time of the hearing before Howe CJ, *Boguslawski* had reached the Court of Appeal and the judgments there had recently appeared in the All England Reports, which were faster than the official reports to cover the latest cases. One of the three appeal judges was a relatively new Lord Justice, Alfred Thomas Denning, whose modest background (he was one of four high-achieving sons of a shop keeper and his wife) and rasping Hampshire accent hid an incisive mind of great learning. This and a talent for pithy expression had already led to Alfred Thompson Denning's speedy promotion from the High Court. His knowledge of case law and ready grasp of fundamentals led him to deliver confident summaries of relevant principles and bold suggestions as to future legal developments. His decisions were often ground-breaking, though his views were sometimes controversial.

In *Boguslawski* Denning LJ had set out the principle of continuity in the law of State succession. Continuity requires that the new government stand in the shoes of the old one in all respects, he explained, so the law presumes that established law survives a change in government and that the contracts of the old government bind the new one.[10] But Denning qualified this with two exceptions, on the second of which Howe CJ sought to rely: except in respect of acts of members of the old government which are ultra vires, or acts which were done by them not in good faith as trustees of the state but for an alien and improper purpose. In stating, or creating, these exceptions Denning had in mind an extreme case such as that of the dictator who seizes state property on the eve of his downfall and exile. Judges are always careful in stating principles, which may come back to haunt them, too widely, hence their use of guarded language and casting of qualifications and exceptions when setting out principles. But in this instance it was the exceptions which were expressed in an unguarded way and so the exceptions gave Hong Kong's judges, intent on the avoidance of antagonizing the PRC, an opportunity of escaping the application of the principle.

Sir Gerard Howe seized the opportunity emphatically:

> In the transaction before this Court, I have no hesitation in reaching the conclusion that not only was it one designed to embarrass the Central People's Government, but it was against the interests of the Chinese people and that it was a transaction incompatible with that trusteeship which every government must assume.

What were the reasons for this conclusion? Howe explained that in a country so large and with such poor communications as China, the loss of the aircraft would be severe. The majority of the staff had already attorned to the CPG at the time of the sale, he observed, the Nationalist government only ever owned the aircraft in the capacity of trustee and it had not sold them for the purposes of fighting in the civil war to retain its territory.[11] So, in the opinion of the Chief Justice the sale by the Nationalist government was not an act done in good faith as trustees but one done for an alien and improper purpose. Hence it was not valid or enforceable in court and there was no obligation to which the new government might succeed.

Howe CJ then turned to consider the question of retrospectivity of the UK's recognition of the CPG. This arose because Sir Walter Monckton had argued that the sale by the Nationalist government must be accepted by the court since at the time of that sale the Nationalists were recognized by the UK,

10. *Boguslawski v Gdynia Ameryka Linie* [1953] AC 11, [1950] 2 All ER 355.
11. *CATI v CATC* (1951) 35 HKLR 22, 42.

and thus Hong Kong, as the government de jure of China. When a government ceases to be officially recognized, to what extent are its previous acts rendered illegitimate? Similarly, when a new government of a country is officially recognized in place of a previous government, the new government will usually have been the de facto government of at least part of the country for some time. Does recognition of it as the government de jure mean that all the acts of the new government before it was so recognized are accepted by the recognizing state as having been legitimate? CPG officials had dismissed the Nationalist officials in charge of the airlines in October 1949 and had claimed the airlines' assets as belonging to the PRC in November 1949, both acts being prior to recognition of their government de jure in January 1950.

Here again Howe CJ relied upon the succinct judgment of Denning LJ in *Boguslawski* in which the latter explained that the retrospective effect of recognition must be confined to its proper sphere. This meant past acts of the new government in the territory over which it exercised effective control. In addition, a nation's ships were regarded as extensions of home territory, so if a ship was registered in the country and the captain of the ship accepts the authority of (attorns to) the new government, that government's past acts concerning the ships are recognized too.

The sale had taken place in Formosa, outside the area of China controlled by the CPG and before it had been recognized de jure. Similarly the planes and other assets were outside that area, in Hong Kong. Those facts would therefore point to the sale being effective in Hong Kong law. But no, even though the aircraft were in Hong Kong, said Sir Gerard, there was no doubt that the CPG was in possession and effective control of them, implying that the planes were an extension of territory under CPG control. He drew an analogy between the acceptance of CPG authority by the airline employees and the position of masters of ships abroad who had attorned to the new government to deduce that the UK recognition of January 1950 would have retrospective effect to the dismissal of the Nationalist ministers at least, which occurred on 1 October 1949, well before the sale.

So Sir Gerard had decided two important issues of public international law in a brief and bold fashion. He had applied a controversial exception to the rule that governments succeed to the obligations of their predecessors and had done so in a controversial way, and he had extended the rules about retroactivity of recognition of prior acts done on territory under the control of the new government to chattels under the control of that government located on neutral territory and also to aeroplanes under the control of people who attorn to the new government. His decision caused quite a stir amongst international lawyers in foreign ministries and university faculties.

Reaction

Upon delivery of the judgment on 21 May 1951 Sir Alexander Grantham immediately cabled the Colonial Office summarizing the result and reasons. After reading the judgment Sir Eric Beckett, chief legal adviser to the Foreign Office, was scathing. He thought the reasoning was deplorable and showed that the courts simply did not understand the international law on the subject at all. He considered that an appeal against the judgment should succeed—'provided the courts know, or can be taught, some international law'.[12]

The assessment of the lawyer at the Commonwealth Relations Office, W. L. Dale, was more temperate but no less condemnatory. Dale wrote to the Attorney General of Hong Kong, John Griffin, '[i]t does not appear that the doctrine of retroactivity of recognition has ever been invoked to set aside a transaction in regard to property not within an area of territory within the control of the de facto Government'. Dale advised that the cases about ships in which the crews had attorned dealt with immunity, not title. 'To set aside a transfer of property in a foreign country by the de jure Government, itself the owner of the property, is, so far as I know, to go much further than the cases warrant.' Dale considered that the Boguslawski case brought out clearly that the doctrine of retroactivity relates to acts done by a de facto government within territory under its control. The Chief Justice seemed, Dale said, to have based himself almost entirely on one paragraph of Denning's judgment 'about which there is much to be said on both sides' to arrive at a conclusion opposite to the decision of the Court of Appeal there. He hoped that the Americans would appeal.

Sir Gerard Howe had known of course that his decision was likely to be appealed to the Full Court just as that of Sir Leslie Gibson had been and that there was likely also to be a further appeal to the Privy Council. Perhaps that is why he dealt so briefly with the crucial legal issues in the case: there was little point in his expending energy on those issues when more and higher minds would be applied to them. He could well have silently seen his role as being to set out the facts for the convenience of the appeal courts and to expedite an appeal. The latter he achieved by giving directions at the end of his judgment under the powers bestowed by the Order-in-Council, that the appeal should be brought within two months rather than the usual six.

An appeal was one matter, but what to do about the planes in the meantime? There could be no question of releasing them to China so long as Chinese troops continued fighting in Korea. The British ministries of Air and of Civil Aviation thought that in all the circumstances it would not be feasible to get the aircraft away and they should be destroyed. Grantham considered

12. FO371/93127, minutes.

that the best solution would be to push them into the sea. The Foreign Office and the Colonial Office favoured a less physical approach.

On 14 July 1951 with the deadline for the filing of an appeal only a week away, the Colonial Office suggested to Grantham two possible courses of action: that he give directions under the Emergency (Control of Ships and Aircraft) Regulations that the airliners not leave Hong Kong or that licences for export be refused under the Exportation (Prohibition) (Specified Articles) Order 1951. The latter had been passed pursuant to the resolution of the UN General Assembly in May 1951 that members place an embargo on articles of strategic value to China and North Korea. Grantham however was still resisting intervention. He replied that there were difficulties in pursuing either course. He envisaged objections being made that it was contrary to international practice to apply export prohibitions to state-owned property in peace time and that the government would be accused of deliberately frustrating the verdict of the court.

In Korea, armistice negotiations were just starting.

17

Full Court Again

The hearing

Once the appeal had been lodged on 20 July 1951, little time was lost in placing it before the Full Court. The hearing took place almost within one month, on 21 and 22 August. That was during the court vacation, when judges would normally expect to be out of town, escaping Hong Kong's sultry summer. But with China closed and Korea in conflict, temperate holiday options in the region had become limited and a case of this importance rarely came the judges' way, so perhaps Mr Justice Gould and Mr Justice Scholes did not mind having to decide it. They were already familiar with the background since they had been on the bench for the appeal from Sir Leslie Gibson fifteen months previously. Apparently a third colleague could not be found to sit with them and provide a casting vote in case the two could not agree.

This time, however, there would be no sovereign immunity to provide an easy answer. There would also be no representatives of the Chinese interests, the CPG having continued to disdain to participate despite CATC's victory in front of Howe CJ. The persuasive tones of Sir Walter Monckton would also be missing, for he was now concentrating upon politics, having been elected a Member of Parliament in the spring. So Leo D'Almada KC was restored to the lead position, supported by John McNeill KC and Leslie Wright.

At the hearing, on behalf of CAT, Inc., McNeill objected that the Chief Justice below had referred to the affirmation made in earlier proceedings by C. L. Chen, the general manager of CATC who had defected and claimed to be holding the planes with his staff on behalf of the CPG. This would have been a valid objection had this been an appeal from a regular trial but, as Gould J presiding in the Full Court pointed out, the Order-in-Council had directed the courts to conduct an enquiry. Accordingly, the Chief Justice had been entitled to look at all relevant material. Although the affirmation gave only one interpretation of the facts, the court held that justice would be served not by excluding it but by giving the appellants a chance to file an affidavit of their own in reply on Chinese law. This the appellants did, although it is difficult to see why the objectional parts of Chen's affirmation could not simply have been disregarded.

Consideration by the Full Court was also extended by a request by the court for evidence to be provided to clarify the position regarding registration of the aircraft. The court was adjourned whilst the appellants filed a further affidavit from Ango Tai to deal with this.[1]

After the August hearing there was a long pause before judgment was delivered, in marked contrast to the speed with which the appeal had been brought on. Judgment was not given until the end of the year, more than four months after the hearing dates. This was the cause of frustration in Whitehall. November and still no decision in the appeal, a memo on a Foreign Office file impatiently noted. The delay was probably caused by the complications concerning evidence. One would have expected the court to adjourn for the preparation of the further evidence then reconvene after it had been filed. However the law reports do not indicate that there was a further hearing date after August and before delivery of judgment.

Another possible explanation for the delay is that, given the importance of the case, the judges were trying to agree on all issues so that they could write one combined judgment. In the absence of a third judge it was desirable that the conclusions of Gould and Scholes JJ be unanimous. But, as we shall see, that was not to be.

UN sanctions

During the lull in proceedings Grantham engaged in a debate with London about continuing measures to keep the planes at Kai Tak should the CATC score another unsought legal victory. A new consideration had entered the picture, sanctions recommended by the United Nations against belligerents in the Korean War. On 18 May 1951 the UN General Assembly passed a resolution recommending that every state apply an embargo on the shipment to areas under the control of the CPG and of North Korea of arms, ammunition and implements of war and items useful in their production, as well as on atomic energy materials, petroleum and transportation materials of strategic value. Individual states were urged to determine which commodities exported from their territory fell within the embargo and apply controls accordingly.

Grantham wanted to use the resolution as a reason for further detention of the planes and equipment. In July 1951, a few weeks before the Full Court hearing, he had proposed to issue a statement that so long as hostilities continued in Korea, His Majesty's Government's obligations under the resolution of 18 May made it necessary to withhold permission for the transfer to Chinese

1. *Civil Air Transport Incorporated v Central Air Transport Corporation* (1951) 35 HKLR 162, 171–175.

territory of the aircraft as state-owned property. Sarrell at the Foreign Office was resistant, for the FO did not want to make explicit its view that the resolution applied to state-owned property. But the British ambassador-designate at Peking and the Colonial Office approved, although the latter suggested that the reference to hostilities in Korea be omitted. Presumably they viewed the planes and parts as transportation materials of strategic value.

The statement was duly issued, without the reference to Korea. Grantham now had another excuse to hold on to the planes, in case the judges found in favour of the CPG again. His point of view received a further boost in the following October with the election of a Conservative government in the UK. Churchill, the returning Prime Minister, and his Foreign Secretary Anthony Eden considered alliance with the USA paramount and consequently took a firmer line on China than their Labour predecessors. They did not think establishment of diplomatic relations with the CPG or its membership of the UN priorities, although they baulked at a US suggestion of severing all relations with the Communists, for fear of jeopardizing Korean peace talks.[2]

British trade with China collapsed in 1951, not so much because of the UN embargo as because of the embargo on export on strategic materials, such as oil, chemicals, munitions and machine tools, to China which the UK had imposed a few months previously. This had been done, over the warnings of Grantham as to its effect on Hong Kong, at the behest of the American government which had set up its own restrictions in December 1950. Trade declined further in 1952. In both years Hong Kong trade likewise suffered from the embargoes and shipping restrictions, but more grievously. This brought to an end the growth in prosperity that had marked the early years after the Second World War. The colony's economy was plunged into recession.[3]

Japanese Peace Treaty

Another delicate issue which came to the fore whilst the Full Court's decision was awaited was the legal status of Formosa. A draft treaty of peace with Japan had been prepared by the Americans and the British. Stalin and Mao were not consulted on its contents. Under the draft, Japan was to renounce any claim to Formosa. But in whose favour? Who was to sign on behalf of China? Britain and the US disagreed about this since one recognized the PRC and the other recognized only the (Nationalist) Republic of China. They reached a compromise: neither Chinese government would be a party to the treaty which was to

2. James T. H. Tang, *Britain's Encounter with Revolutionary China, 1949–54* (New York: St. Martin's Press, 1992), 113–114.
3. Wengguang Shao, *China, Britain and Businessmen: Political and Commercial Relations, 1949–57* (Basingstoke: Macmillan, 1991), 64, 93–96, 106; Lowe, *Containing the Cold War in East Asia: British Policies towards Japan, China and Korea, 1948–53* (Manchester: Manchester University Press, 1997), 129–130.

be signed at San Francisco in September 1951. Japan was to decide later which China it would deal with. So under the terms of the treaty Japan renounced all claim to Formosa but did not say in whose favour it did so.

Japanese exports to the PRC, especially of manufactured products, had been growing throughout 1951. Nevertheless it was no surprise when in 1952 Japan chose to deal with the Nationalists, for American pressure to do so was so great. Chou En-lai described the treaty as illegal and invalid. It was also no surprise that Japan entered into a security pact with the Americans.[4]

Retrospectivity of recognition

Finally, on 28 December 1951 the written decision of the Full Court was published. The judges unanimously dismissed the appeal but that bare result masked a difference of opinion between them. They both concluded that the sale by the Nationalist government to Chennault and Willauer had been invalid but they disagreed about the extent to which British recognition of the CPG had been retrospective, which was the principal issue of international law at stake. The sale had taken place two-and-a-half months after the declaration of the PRC by Mao Tse-tung, weeks after nearly all of the Chinese mainland had come under effective Communist control, and days after the Nationalist government had decamped to Taiwan, yet it had also taken place almost a month before recognition of the CPG as the de jure government of China by Britain. The timing exquisitely raised the question, did that recognition have retrospective effect to the time of effective CPG control, or some other time, so as to invalidate the sale?

Gould J gave the first judgment. After becoming the fourth judge to set out the facts of the saga, he turned to the legal issues. 'The essential question,' he pronounced, 'is whether the Nationalist Government had as at 12 December, 1949, power to and did effectively dispose of and give to the purchasers a good title to the aeroplanes in question.' That was the date of the sale and on that date, according to the Foreign Office answers to the questionnaire, British recognition de jure had remained with the Nationalists although recognition de facto extended to the CPG as regards those areas of China then under its control, virtually the whole of the mainland. The Nationalist government could not therefore dispose of anything in the public domain within those areas, said the judge, for it was well established that during de facto recognition the government so recognized has full rights of ownership and control over its territory.

4. Qiang Zhai, *The Dragon, the Lion, and the Eagle: Chinese-British-American Relations, 1949–1958* (Kent, OH: Kent State University Press, 1994), 109; Lowe, *Containing the Cold War*, 131.

Regarding publicly owned moveable property which either government takes from its own to neutral territory during the period of recognition, there can be no reason to suppose that the government loses any power to alienate which it previously held, Gould J observed. The Nationalist government in retreat had sent the aeroplanes to Hong Kong. They had been entitled to do that, he said. The planes had remained in their possession until November 1949 when certain employees obtained physical control of the planes and claimed to hold them for the CPG. The Chief Justice had held that by virtue of that control the doctrine of retroactivity of recognition had operated after 5 January 1950 to render the acts of the Nationalist government of no effect.

Gould J then became the first Hong Kong judge to subject to close legal analysis the assumed agency of CATC's employees for the CPG. The judge accepted that the acts of the employees had been adopted by Chou En-lai for the CPG and noted that this had been referred to as an 'attornment' by analogy with the acts of the master and crew of a ship who accept the authority of a new home government. But he questioned the similarity between the two: ships and aircraft differ in many ways, including in their registration, he observed. Here, the general manager Mr Chen was not chairman of the governors of CATC and the aircraft ended up under the actual control of the employees, including Chen, and a number of senior officials by their forcibly taking possession from those who until then had been rightfully in possession. 'A bailee cannot by attorning to a third person against the will of his bailor deprive the bailor of any title that he may have to the goods in question,' Gould announced. If those attorning had custody of the planes, they had it (as bailees) by virtue of their employment with the Nationalist government and excluding their employer (the bailor) from possession was a breach of the law, Gould reasoned. If their acts were acts of civil war or of sovereignty, they were not in accordance with international law either, for no government may carry on its civil war on neutral territory except with the consent of the government of that territory. Acquisition of possession by a wrongful act cannot confer on the party so acquiring it any benefit that he did not previously enjoy.

The CPG could not show any superior title or right to possession. Nor could it rely upon any rights arising out of actual possession. So there was nothing for the doctrine of retrospectivity of recognition to act upon. Consequently, Gould J's view was that the issue had to be dealt with on the basis of the right to possession rather than actual possession. The person with the right to possession as at 12 December 1949 had been the de jure government, the Nationalist one.

Mr Justice Alwyn (A. T.) Scholes, however, begged to differ on this aspect of the appeal. In effect he adopted the approach of the Chief Justice in the court below. Scholes thought that the analogy between the position of ships and aircraft was strong. If in *Boguslawski* the masters of the Polish ships had attorned to the new government and, before its de jure recognition, that government had been in effective control of the ships in a neutral country such as England, he thought that Denning LJ might have held that retroactivity would have applied. That would have been similar to the position of the aircraft in this case.

On the basis of this speculation, what Scholes J was proposing was in effect an extension of the accepted position in international law. That position was that de facto governments can, in the eyes of third countries' courts, validly dispose of state property situated within such governments' sphere of effective control but, except in the special case of ships, not elsewhere. The judge thought that validity should also be accorded to disposals by de facto governments of state property situated on neutral territory provide that the de facto government has actual control over that property. This had also been the view of Howe CJ in the court below.

Scholes reasoned that on 12 December 1949 the CPG was in actual possession and effective control of the aircraft and, even though they were not on the CPG's own territory but in a non-belligerent country, they were still registered in China. On 13 November 1949 their registrations had only been suspended, not cancelled, by the Nationalists and by then the CPG was in control of most of China. Not until 12 December 1949 did the Nationalists purport to cancel the registrations. Article 17 of the Chicago Convention stated that aircraft have the nationality of the state in which they are registered. If the CPG succeeded to the aircraft on gaining effective control of them, then the craft vested in the CPG by succession before 12 December 1949 and its possession would not have been wrongful.

Scholes J expressed himself on the recognition aspect conditionally because he and Gould J agreed on the answer to the other main issue in the appeal, the validity of the sale as a disposal of state property. So it was not necessary to decide on the retrospectivity of recognition.

Breach of trusteeship

The judges still had to consider the appellant's argument that the CPG was bound by the sale as the successor to the Nationalist government, which had concluded it. The appellant relied upon the well-established rule of public international law that any government that succeeds another succeeds also to all the public property of the former government, including all the rights and obligations concerning that property by which the former government would have been bound.

The lynchpin of the reasoning of both judges on this aspect of the appeal was the obiter dicta concerning trusteeship, by which the rule was said to be qualified, made by Denning LJ in the English Court of Appeal in *Boguslawski.*

The Chief Justice Sir Gerard Howe had relied upon these dicta too. Gould J agreed with the Chief Justice that the sale was a device to prevent the aircraft falling into the hands of the CPG on its recognition de jure. Gould thought that by 12 December 1949 it had been clear that the Nationalist government had lost all but a small portion of the mainland and the inescapable inference was that it knew that it was about to lose the remainder, for by then it had moved to Formosa after retreating from, successively, Nanking, Canton, Chungking and Chengdu. Recognition had been withdrawn by the British government only 24 days later, something, Gould observed, which happens only when the position of the former government is hopeless. After examining the provisions of the contract of sale in detail, Gould agreed with the Chief Justice's conclusion that the contract was hostile to the present de jure Communist government and to the interests of the Chinese people. It was, he concluded, a breach of trusteeship and done for an alien and improper purpose.

Gould J gave four reasons for this conclusion. First, the Nationalists must have known that withdrawal of recognition 'was at least not improbable', for the state of affairs in China must have been known to the purchasers by virtue of their close connection with China. Second, the contract had been entered into at a time that the CPG was already claiming the assets which were then under court control: the CPG was then in control of almost the whole of China and the assets were peculiarly associated with China. Third, the contract not only sought to deprive the Chinese government and people of the planes but also was at pains to ensure that no possible benefit could accrue to the CPG. Fourth, under the terms of the sale agreement, the Nationalist government, whilst parting with title, could acquire a major share in the stock of the holding corporation and could conceal it by the employment of a nominee. This was a cloak to hide its continued beneficial ownership. The result of the contract, if valid, said Gould, was that the Chinese people would be deprived of a public asset of immense value to their country.

Leo D'Almada KC for CAT, Inc. had submitted to the court that the Nationalists had done no more than they were entitled to do as a belligerent government then retaining recognition: it was entitled to fight back, and the sale was consistent with the object of providing funds for the struggle and putting the aeroplanes out of reach of its opponents. But Gould J was not having that, pointing out that payment was to be by promissory note rather than cash and that the contract contained no provision for retention and operation of the planes in Formosa for the benefit of the war effort. The argument for the appellants that the object of the agreement was to put the planes out of the reach of opponents in war, whilst attractive, did not prevail in view of the fact that the contract was obviously designed to offset the consequences of a possible withdrawal of recognition, said Gould, without explaining how the latter made the argument untenable.

The judge confessed that he had come to this conclusion with hesitation because of the paucity of legal authority on exceptions to the general rule that contracts of former governments bind their successors. Like the Chief Justice below, he was forced to hang his hat on the comments 'stated with confidence by Denning LJ in the Boguslawski case'. These seemed to Gould to be allied with the domestic law as to following property in respect of which a breach of trust has been committed and to be in accordance with common sense.

Scholes J agreed with Gould J's reasons and added none of his own on the contract of sale being invalid by reason of its nature and surrounding circumstances. The appeal was accordingly dismissed. CAT, Inc. therefore did not have good title to the property against the CPG.

Resignation

Compared to the reaction to previous court decisions concerning the planes, that which followed the Full Court's second judgment upon them was muted. The Americans were by now resigned to rejection by the Hong Kong courts. In Westminster and Whitehall ministers and officials had long expected that the matter would proceed to London for resolution free from the pressures felt in Hong Kong; that was why they had been impatient with the length of time that the appeal was taking. No doubt the same expectation was held amongst the CPG leadership: that was one reason for the decision not to participate in the litigation set in train by the Order-in-Council. Sir Alexander Grantham had been resigned to the process ever since his masters had intervened to set aside sovereign immunity. He had thought that the Order-in-Council would inevitably lead to the planes being awarded to the Americans.[5] It was as if everyone accepted that the appeal to the Full Court was a necessary formality prior to the real decision which would be made after the final appeal reached the Privy Council.

By the end of 1951 changes in circumstances meant that much of the urgency had gone out of the case. Negotiations for the establishment of British diplomatic relations with the CPG remained at an impasse. Likewise the question of PRC membership of the UN was in abeyance. Progress on neither would be possible whilst Chinese troops were fighting UN forces in Korea and export controls were in place. The fate of British business in China, one of the main motives for seeking diplomatic relations, had been sealed. Although there had been hope for improvement in the treatment of foreign businesses in the summer of 1950 and some improvement in Chinese imports from the West that autumn as the CPG geared up to invade Formosa and then

5. Alexander Grantham, *Via Ports: From Hong Kong to Hong Kong* (Hong Kong: Hong Kong University Press, 1965), 163.

to fight in Korea, conditions remained adverse and it became evident that there was no substantial role for overseas enterprises in the domestic economy. It was easier for trading firms to hang on than for industrial enterprises. Yet it was not simple for the latter to withdraw: to obtain permission to leave and avoid further operating losses, they had to negotiate with the local authorities which usually led to their handing over cash and property in exchange for release from liabilities. In September 1951 the Hongkong and Shanghai Banking Corporation and the Chartered Bank decided to close their branches in Peking and Tientsin because of the worsening business conditions. The import and export trade was badly affected by the stringent UN sanctions. Hong Kong's exports to China declined markedly. HSBC withdrew altogether from China the following January. The number of British firms operating in China progressively dwindled and by the end of 1952 virtually all of them had closed down. The British Chamber of Commerce in Shanghai was wound up.[6]

Despite the waning of urgency, Chennault's campaign to influence opinion in Congress, and thus keep pressure upon the US administration, continued. 'Chennault's planes' became a cause célèbre in political circles. President Truman was briefed about the latest developments in preparation for his meeting early in the new year at Washington DC with Sir Winston Churchill who had been re-installed as British Prime Minister during the autumn. Churchill's return to power boded ill for any Sino-British rapprochement. He attached even greater importance to the Anglo-American alliance than did Attlee and readily admitted to knowing little of China. He considered that the importance of China had been exaggerated and that Britain's priorities should be the USA, the British Commonwealth (or 'Empire' as he persisted in calling it) and Europe. Churchill's foreign minister, Sir Anthony Eden, had similar views. Eden thought that the UK's China policy should not be based on the tenuous possibility of separating Peking from Moscow. Neither of them wished to reverse UK recognition of the CPG and restore the Nationalists as the de jure government, even if that were possible, now that ceasefire negotiations were under way in Korea. They would not sever ties with Taiwan either, for that would disappoint the Americans and send the wrong signal about British attitudes to freedom. The Foreign Office argued that they were dealing with the provincial authorities there only, not the KMT. The expected fall of the island had not eventuated. Britain would go along with the US policy of supporting Chiang Kai-shek and not try to appease the Communists on that. Whilst Britain might seek to moderate US behaviour, especially concerning the conduct of the Korean War, the days of divergence between the two countries' China policy seemed over.[7]

6. Tang, *Britain's Encounter*, 117, 149–157; Lowe, *Containing the Cold War*, 135–138.
7. Victor S. Kaufman, 'The United States, Britain and the CAT Controversy', *Journal of Contemporary History* 40, no. 1 (2005): 95, 108; Zhai, *The Dragon, the Lion, and the Eagle*, 114–116.

Evaluation of the Hong Kong judgments

Reflecting on the case almost a quarter of a century later Daniel Patrick O'Connell, Chichele Professor of Public International Law at the University of Oxford, described the Hong Kong decisions as 'incomprehensible'.[8] This is a little harsh. The outcomes of the application for appointment of receivers to Gibson CJ, of the inquiry by Howe CJ and of the appeals from both decisions to the Full Court are quite understandable once one appreciates the precarious position in which Hong Kong found itself and the desire not to antagonize the new Chinese authorities. That is of course a political consideration which judges are not allowed to take into account, at least not expressly. They are meant to reach a conclusion solely from the application of principle and precedent. What then of the quality of their legal reasoning?

One of the difficulties with the law of nations is the lack of precedents, as Gould J pointed out. In that law, principle and analogy play a greater part than they do in legal reasoning in domestic (or municipal) law. That difficulty was exacerbated in the final round of litigation of the planes dispute by the abolition, for purposes of that round only, of the law of sovereign immunity. Any case which involved, even indirectly, a sovereign power would normally be disposed of by that immunity, as indeed the first set of litigation was, so the court would not be called upon to adjudicate upon the merits. Any claim over property in the possession of a state would accordingly be ruled out at the threshold. No consideration of the effect of recognition and whether and to what extent it operates retroactively would be required. Consequently, by insisting upon a judicial ruling as to ownership of the airline assets, the British government was handing the courts a difficult task, and by disallowing reliance upon the law of sovereign immunity it was making the task more difficult still.

Given these handicaps, the Hong Kong judges made creditable efforts to reach reasoned conclusions. Although they were conclusions at which they wished to arrive, they were able to deploy reputable legal principles in the process. The international law experts at the Foreign and the Colonial Offices viewed the efforts of both Chief Justices Gibson and Howe with reservation, yet they seem to have had more respect for the reasoning of the Full Court.

The problem of the retroactivity of state recognition is persistent because the process of changing a government, especially changing it by force, may be protracted. During that time personal and commercial transactions continue to happen and legal interests continue to come into existence. How does a court in another jurisdiction determine whether they are valid? In principle the law is reasonably well settled: one looks at when they were carried out and

8. Author's notes of lectures on 'The Theory of International Law' by Professor D. P. O'Connell, Oxford University, Michaelmas Term 1975; O'Connell, a New Zealander, was a giant of twentieth-century public international law who died aged 58 from complications of a medical operation.

where they were carried out. Those carried out within an area then controlled by a previously unrecognized government, that is to say by the de facto government of the area which has later become the officially recognized government of it, are valid. Transactions outside that area are the responsibility of the then recognized government, the government de jure, so long as it remains so recognized.

That said, there is a multiplicity of other potential considerations which may arise from the particular facts of a case. A clear example of such a consideration concerns ships. If situated outside national territory, these are regarded as within the control of the recognized authorities, as happened in the Boguslawski case. But if the captain and crew of such a ship accept the authority of the new government, the ship is regarded as coming under that government's authority. The principle which seems to underlie this exception is one of control. Just as the insurgent government's acts are valid in territory it controls because of the reality of that control, so its acts with regard to ships which accept its authority are valid because of the reality of its control over the ship. Therefore it was not inappropriate for the Hong Kong judges to deduce the importance of control in the question of recognition.

An associated consideration in the Kai Tak case was that it concerned chattels (movable property)—aeroplanes, machinery, spare parts and so on. They were not fixed to the ground, so were not real property. They were not located within territory controlled by either party or contesting government but within neutral territory, at places under the authority of a third party, a government airfield and nearby premises in Hong Kong. Accordingly, the concept and importance of a territory or area controlled by a contesting government seemed diminished and that of effective physical control over the property seemed heightened. The analogy of aircraft with ships appeared plausible. Both had captains and crew; both were frequently operated, and carried passengers and goods, outside national territory; both had places of origin and of registration.

Another complicating factor was that the chattels in question were particularly associated with the nation claiming them, being the assets of a national airline (CNAC) and of a division of the Chinese government operating another national airline (CATC). The natural 'home' of these assets was in mainland China, where they had operated and had been based and registered prior to taking refuge in Hong Kong. At one point in his judgment Gould J referred to the opinion of one writer on international law that a state has jurisdiction over a chattel if it is habitually kept within that state but is temporarily outside it and to the opinion of another writer that all means of transport have to be attributed to a fixed resting place in which they are resident even if temporarily absent. The judge did not however pursue the point, presumably because of the difficulty of maintaining that places from which the planes and parts had been absent for more than two years (Shanghai and Tientsin) were their habitual resting places.[9]

Given the relatively recent emergence of commercial civil aviation, it would have been possible to conclude that aircraft outside their home jurisdiction formed a nascent further exception or qualification to the territorial approach to recognition and its retrospectivity. The judges seemed to be attracted towards this conclusion without mustering the courage to rely upon it in the absence of a decision elsewhere or discussion in a textbook which supported it.

The contents of the judgments dealing with the other aspect of the validity of the sale, the doctrine of succession of one government by another, were obviously attributable to the unanimous distaste of the Hong Kong judges for the motivations for the sale. The idea of government as trustee of public assets and the dicta of Denning LJ outlining an exception to the succession doctrine, provided a means of putting that distaste in legal form. A lawyer instinctively recoils when moral condemnation appears in a judgment: it seems inappropriate, belonging more to the realm of ethics or politics than law. But the judges were cultivating what Denning had sown. He had planted the seed by articulating an exception or limitation to state succession for acts of the old government which were not done in good faith and as trustees of the state but for an alien and improper purpose. This fell on fertile ground for, as Howe CJ put it, 'there must surely be . . . a limit to the scope of the acts to which this doctrine applies; a limit to the transactions into which a Government, knowing that recognition will shortly be withdrawn from it, may enter'. The Hong Kong judges gratefully seized upon the suggested exception.

Denning LJ's limitation was hypothetical and general, and therefore dangerous to rely upon. Furthermore, it seemed contrary to his declaration earlier in the paragraph containing the dicta that 'the principle of continuity is of paramount importance'. The limitation introduced the idea of trusteeship, that governments are temporary custodians of public property. Trusteeship of the sort Denning envisaged is a concept from domestic law. A different sort of 'trusteeship' is encountered in the international context, referring to the mandate of an international body such as the United Nations given to a nation to administer a certain territory. This, however, is quite distinct from the idea of trusteeship over chattels.

The trustee analysis therefore seemed a slender thread from which to hang a judgment. But everyone knew it was not going to be the final word.

9. *CATI v CATC* (1951) 35 HKLR 162, 207–208; the quotations were taken from Arnold Duncan McNair, *The Legal Effects of War*, 3rd ed. (Cambridge: Cambridge University Press, 1948) 446.

18
And so to London

A need for haste

The prolonged wait for judgment from the Full Court had made Chennault, Willauer and the other backers of CAT, Inc. impatient for progress. They had been resigned to another defeat in Hong Kong, the only uncertainty having been how the judges would rule against the corporation. If they were to be granted possession of the airline assets, it would be through the verdict of the Privy Council.

They were anxious for a speedy determination because the market in second-hand aeroplanes was volatile. Immediately after the Second World War a surplus of decommissioned transport aircraft, many of them virtually unused, had depressed prices, to the advantage of firms such as CATC and CAT, Inc. expanding or setting up an airline. Demand created by the war in Korea had revived the market. There were however continual efforts, led by India and Canada, to broker peace through the UN. The prospects for negotiations fluctuated with the fortunes of the warring sides. In the middle of 1951 talks had begun about the terms of a ceasefire. The talks had run into successive difficulties, mainly about the treatment of prisoners of war pending the onset of settlement negotiations. Even so, there was pressure on both sides to disengage from what had become a war of attrition and by the end of the year the conflict seemed to be winding down.

In the summer of 1952 the US bombed targets on the Yalu, badly damaging vital dams and power stations near the border with China. This was followed by the bombing of an oil refinery near the Soviet border. These placed pressure on Chinese negotiators to make concessions. The UN, or rather the US, seemed to be winning again.

Pot on a stove

The flood of refugees into Hong Kong had been stemmed by the imposition of border controls in May 1950. Even so, the population remained swollen and the squatter areas a constant cause of concern. Good economic times for the colony had been halted by the UN trade embargo.

Hong Kong was, in Grantham's phrase, like a pot on a stove, capable of being brought to the boil at the will of the Chinese Communist Party. Events which caused displeasure to the CPG such as the trade embargo could be occasions for increasing the heat. The continued detention of the planes at Kai Tak, despite the Full Court's ruling at the end of 1951 in favour of the mainland airlines, was another such occasion.

A fire which swept through one of the squatter encampments, at Tung Tau near Kowloon City, in November 1951 provided an opportunity to spark the flame beneath the pot. Five thousand huts were destroyed. Allegations by local communist cadres of mistreatment of victims of the fire by Hong Kong government officers led to indignation in China. Communist newspapers lost no opportunity to exaggerate the trouble.

The authorities in Guangdong proposed to send a 'comfort mission' to Hong Kong, ostensibly to assist the relief efforts, in reality to stir up discontent. This led to a riot on 1 March 1952 when thousands of communist-led workers and students attacked police, passers-by and property as they marched along Nathan Road towards the rail terminus at Tsim Sha Tsui to greet members of the mission. Grantham acted decisively: the mission was denied entry and the leader of the reception committee, Mok Ying Kwai of the Chinese General Chamber of Commerce who attempted to travel by train to the border to greet them, found his carriage had been detached at Fanling. He was deported later in the year.[1] There was a predictable, furious reaction from communist newspapers. The *Ta Kung Pao*, which reprinted allegations from the *People's Daily* that the British were seeking to turn Hong Kong into an imperialist base for aggression against China at the behest of the USA, was charged with sedition.[2]

Arranging an appeal

Everyone long expected that the planes case would be going all the way through the courts. The Full Court readily gave leave to appeal to the Judicial Committee of the Privy Council. However, the process after that would normally take months and the Judicial Committee sat for only part of the year, during term time, partly out of habit but also because of the difficulty of mustering in London enough judges of the appropriate status to man (in those days judges were all men) the five-member panel required. The principal source of senior judges was the House of Lords but first call on active judges there went to

1. Alan Smart, *The Shek Kip Mei Myth: Squatters, Fires and Colonial Rule in Hong Kong, 1950–1963* (Hong Kong: Hong Kong University Press, 2006), 2, 75.
2. Chi-kwan Mark, *Hong Kong and the Cold War: Anglo-American Relations, 1949–1957* (Oxford: Clarendon Press, 2004), 107–108.

the Lords' own Appellate Committee charged with hearing final appeals from within the UK. Consequently, the Privy Council's judicial bench had to draw upon retired senior British judges and judges from Commonwealth nations who had been admitted to the Privy Council and were in or willing to travel to London.

Chennault, Willauer and their advisers had thought of a tactic to hasten the further appeal. They would apply for an early hearing using the services of Sir Hartley Shawcross KC who was now out of government office and back in private practice following the election of Churchill's Conservative Party in October 1951 but who retained influence in the corridors of power. They would engage Shawcross for the appeal hearing as well. No counsel in Britain, except possibly Sir Walter Monckton, was as familiar with the dispute and its background as Shawcross. Monckton was not available since he had become Minister of Labour in the Conservative administration. The judges would listen respectfully to Shawcross as a former attorney-general and originator of the Order-in-Council. No one suggested that Shawcross might have a conflict of interest.

In May 1952 Chennault and Corcoran met in London. They went to see Shawcross who arranged for an urgent application to be made to the committee for an order that an early hearing be held before the end of the current term. The application was made on 11 June. Shawcross explained the urgency of a decision as to the fate of the planes and parts. A date was found towards the end of the term for hearing the substantive appeal: 21 July 1952. Later Chennault and Willauer were to claim that the early date was fixed on condition that CAT, Inc. undertake that if it won the appeal, the planes would not be sent to Formosa under any circumstances and that they would be removed from Hong Kong prior to 1 October, recently proclaimed as China's new National Day. The Privy Council registrar would have had no power to impose such conditions; neither would the judges. Possibly it would have been mentioned to Shawcross by the Foreign Office if he had sounded them out privately before making the application. But it is equally possible that it resulted from embroidery of their version of events by Chennault and Willauer, a possibility which is not diminished by the claim's appearance in a memorandum by them to Chiang Kai-shek.[3]

The registrar of the Judicial Committee had to scramble to find a panel of judges. Three of the current law lords, all fairly recent appointees, were available. Two of them were former Scottish advocates with political experience. One was Wilfred Normand, who had been Solicitor-General for Scotland and a Member of Parliament in the 1930s before becoming Lord Justice General and then Lord President of the Court of Session in Scotland. Normand had

3. William M. Leary, 'Aircraft and Anti-Communists: CAT in Action, 1942–52', *China Quarterly* 52 (1972): 654, 664.

been promoted to the House of Lords in 1947. The other was James Reid, Baron Reid of Rem, who had served more than a decade as a Member of Parliament during which time he had been Solicitor-General for Scotland and Lord Advocate as well as a Conservative front-bench spokesman. Reid had been made a Lord of Appeal, also in 1947.

The third current Law Lord was Baron Oaksey, another 1947 House of Lords appointee. Born Geoffrey Lawrence, Oaksey was the son of a judge, A. T. Lawrence, who had briefly been Lord Chief Justice in the 1920s. Oaksey had been a judge since 1932 so had the longest judicial experience of the three. He and Reid had recently participated in hearing the further appeal in *Boguslawski* so were familiar with the issue of the retrospectivity of state recognition. Shawcross would have been pleased that Oaksey would be on the bench for the appeal since Oaksey, then a Court of Appeal judge, had been the President of the 1945 War Crimes Tribunal at Nuremberg before which Shawcross had come to international attention as the British prosecutor.

To fill the final place, the clerks turned to a member of the Privy Council with judicial experience in the East, Sir Lionel Leach. Born in Lancashire the son of a barrister, Leach had been a judge of the Rangoon High Court in Burma and then Chief Justice of the Madras High Court in India for a decade until 1947. After return to England, Leach continued to be active. In 1951 he had been appointed by Sir Franklin Gimson, Governor of Singapore and wartime Colonial Secretary in Hong Kong, to head a Commission of Enquiry into the Singapore Riots. Maybe it was thought that a combination of experience of judicial enquiries and knowledge of the Far East suited Leach to dealing with the case of the Kai Tak planes. Or maybe it was simply that he was available to make up the numbers.

The board needed a heavyweight chairman, someone of sufficient political as well as judicial experience to carry conviction and to reach a fast, soundly reasoned decision. Just the man was available: Viscount Simon of Stackpole Elidor. John Simon was of Welsh heritage although he had been educated in Scotland and at Oxford. He had been a Member of Parliament for more than 30 years up to 1940. He had held three of the four political offices suited to lawyers—Solicitor-General, Attorney-General and Home Secretary—in the Liberal administrations of the early twentieth century. He was unique in having held in the course of his career all the most senior offices in government. As leader of the minority National Liberal Party in the 1930s coalition, he had been Foreign Secretary, Home Secretary again and Chancellor of the Exchequer. In 1940 he attained the one remaining, and highest, legal office when he became Lord Chancellor in the wartime coalition government. After retirement, he had remained active as a judge and in 1947 he had chaired a Commission of Enquiry into the Indian Constitution. Precise and chilly in manner and with a formidable intellect, he was better suited to the law than to politics. By 1952 he was in his eightieth year, but his mind was still sharp and his appearance spry.

In the Privy Council

The appeal to the Judicial Committee, of what had become Her Majesty's Privy Council following the death of King George VI and accession of Queen Elizabeth II earlier in the year, began on Tuesday 21 July 1952. CATC, the communist employees and the CPG maintained their boycott of the proceedings even though the terms of the Order-in-Council permitted them to intervene at any stage. Consequently Shawcross and his junior, R. I. Threlfall, had the field to themselves. The hearing largely consisted of the presentation by Shawcross of CAT, Inc.'s case and the judges' questions to him. Shawcross was eloquent but he was not brief: the hearing occupied the rest of the week and spilled over into one day of the following week.

Shawcross explained to the committee the special procedure under which the present action had been taken, established by the Order-in-Council, the object of which was to enable the courts to advise on the legal aspects. This was, perhaps unwittingly, an admission that what the British government had wanted was not really a judgment between contesting parties but rather an advisory opinion to guide the government. Shawcross emphasized the 'great importance' of the issues, not so much because of the value of the property (though, at more than one million pounds, that was not insignificant to the appellants) as because of the international implications arising from the case. Those implications were now greater because of the war in Korea, he added. The general question raised by the case, Shawcross submitted, was whether the recognition of 5–6 January 1950 could affect the proprietary rights of third parties outside China. He answered it broadly by asserting that no authority supported the view that succession by a new government can affect rights lawfully acquired from a predecessor government by people, and in relation to property, outside the sovereignty of either government.[4]

That broad answer could be broken down into three propositions, Shawcross suggested. First, if the act in question was within the powers of the state which effected it, for the court of another country to hold that the act was contrary to the interests of the state on whose behalf it had been done would be contrary to both municipal law and the comity of nations. Second, retroactivity of recognition was merely a doctrine of convenience which had to be reconciled with the ancient principle that on a change of government the rights and obligations were transferred by succession, a principle fundamental to the continuity of the state and the family of nations. Consequently,

4. *Civil Air Transport Incorporated v Central Air Transport Corporation (Hong Kong)* [1953] AC 70, 72–73.

retroactivity could operate in relation to things outside the lawful territorial control of either government only in relation to such rights and obligations possessed by the predecessor government at the moment of transfer of its de jure status. Third, where a de jure government and a de facto government had rival claims to state property situated in a neutral country which was brought into that country by the de jure government and then, contrary to the law of that country and by defection of the servants of the de jure government, the de facto government acquired some degree of control over the property, lawful possession remained in the government which had been illegally ousted from possession. No de facto government could be allowed to acquire possession by a purported exercise of sovereign powers in British territory against a government recognized by Britain as the de jure government, he contended.

Shawcross then commented on the view of the Hong Kong judges that the sale was a device to deprive the Communists of the assets and that the de jure government had not been acting in good faith as trustees but for an alien and improper purpose inimical to the interests of the people of China. Who was to say that the policy of the Nationalist government, still recognized by most of the civilized world as the government of China, in selling the aircraft was a device inimical to the interests of the Chinese people? It was purely a political matter. The object of the transaction for the Nationalists was to better carry on its fight to regain supremacy in China.

Shawcross went on to deal with the scope of retroactivity of recognition (confined to the jurisdiction of the de facto government), the degree of control the communists had over the aircraft (irrelevant but anyway limited and subordinate), and the legality of that control (wrongful, being tortious and in breach of injunction and of statute). He reiterated that the question of the respondent's possession of the assets was relevant only if the doctrine of retroactivity operated outside the territory of the governments themselves, which in his submission it did not.

It is a tradition of the Bar that when appearing at a hearing in which the other party is unrepresented, counsel should assist the court to reach a correct decision by pointing out arguments and authorities which favour the absent party. Shawcross was of course well aware of this duty. In fact a few years later it formed the centrepiece of a talk that he gave on the duties of counsel to the New York Bar Association. He discharged the duty before the judicial committee by postulating the case that, he imagined, would have had to be put forward for CATC had it been represented. 'The respondents would say,' he is recording as claiming, 'that the doctrine of retroactivity operates to divest a title acquired by, for example, one of Her Majesty's subjects from the government then recognized by Her Majesty simply because of the possession' of the property. He then criticized that proposition by pointing out that the possession would have been wrongful because it would have been adverse to the title of the government which was recognized at the time and would have been possession by a government not even proved to have been recognized de facto at the time. The proposition could be justified only by admitting the validity of an exercise of sovereign power by the de facto government outside its own territory against the de jure government. This would be in breach of the normal rules of English law in relation to property on Her Majesty's territory and over which she or her Governor had overriding control, Shawcross asserted.

The account of Shawcross' submissions in the law reports is a summary so it may be that he expounded the case for the respondents more fully but what appears in the reports hardly does justice to the position of CATC. It was inaccurate to say that the Communist government had not been proven to be the de facto government at the time of the sale or of the seizure of the assets by the employees: the Foreign Office certificate showed that since 1 October 1949 the Communists had been acknowledged to be the de facto government of those parts of China over which they had de facto control; those parts were most of the mainland, included Shanghai, Tientsin and Nanking. Also, the analogy used by way of example was inaccurate. The American claimants were not subjects of Her Majesty.

The principle behind retroactivity of recognition which appears to have been discerned by the judges in Hong Kong (Gould J aside) was one of control, that is to say control over the property in issue. They had been impressed by the fact that the communist employees and sympathizers, acting in the name of the new government in China, had taken factual possession of and control over the assets. Retroactivity of recognition is in effect acceptance after the event of practical realities. That was what the facts here seemed to call for. The judges had also been impressed by the fact that the assets had been state-owned. Although they did not put it like this, they were in effect suggesting an extension of the retroactivity of recognition of an insurgent government to cover government property situated outside national territory but in the control of the insurgents.

Shawcross did not confront this proposition directly but did so indirectly by asserting that the doctrine of retroactivity was purely one of convenience, pragmatically recognizing the acts of the new government within its territory, and must be confined to that so as to avoid conflict with the legitimate acts of the old government and the principle of succession. The British government recognizes as valid acts which the new government has previously done within its jurisdiction and in relation to persons over whom it has control but does not nullify the acts previously done by the then de jure government in relation to third parties in the territory of third states, he said. This was exemplified by the outcome of the Boguslawski case, which had been considered on further appeal by the House of Lords subsequent to the Hong Kong hearings. The observation of Denning LJ in the Court of Appeal, on which the Hong Kong judges had relied, was *obiter*, Shawcross emphasized, and if the House of Lords' decision in *Boguslawski* was correct, that really was the end of the present case because then the doctrine of retroactivity was limited to the territory of the de facto government and it therefore did not matter who was in possession of the aircraft on 12 December 1949, whether their possession was lawful, and whether the Communist government was in fact recognized at the time as the de facto government.

Instant decision

Realizing the importance of a speedy decision, at the conclusion of the hearing on 28 July 1951 the board announced the result: they would humbly advise Her Majesty that the appeal should be allowed. Lord Oaksey explained that they also advised that judgment should be entered for a declaration that the aircraft and other items which were the subject of the action were the property of the appellants. They would give their reasons later.[5] Next day, an Order-in-Council was made giving effect to the decision.

A mysterious delay

Not until 13 October 1952 did the Judicial Committee publish its reasons for allowing the appeal. After a ten-week delay and all that had happened in the meantime, politically and diplomatically the reasons were something of an anti-climax. Legally they were too, for the board in effect accepted the submissions of Sir Hartley Shawcross.

Why was there such a long delay? The likeliest explanation is that in those days by convention, and because technically the reasons for judgment were advice to Her Majesty the Queen on the disposal of the appeal and inconsistent advice to her would be embarrassing, only one judgment would be delivered. Consequently the draft judgment would have had to be circulated to and approved by all five members of the board. There may have been discussion and compromise between the members on particular aspects of the advice. A more intriguing possibility is that Viscount Simon, ever the insider, quietly took the precaution of allowing British ministers to see the draft, or a summary, of the reasons. A more mundane possibility is that the board was simply waiting for further information from the Foreign Office.

The committee discerned a slight lack of clarity in the answers which the Foreign Office had provided to the questions concerning recognition of the new government of China which had been directed to the British government by Sir Leslie Gibson, so they asked a further question. It is not stated

5. *CATI v CATC* [1953] AC 70, 79; Report, *South China Morning Post*, 30 July 1952.

in the reasons or reports at what stage this clarifying question was asked and answered. It might have been before the hearing, had the committee studied the papers and spotted the problem, but given that there were fewer than six weeks between the granting of leave to appeal and the hearing, and that during that time the members would have had to be chosen and to have read and considered the no doubt voluminous papers, this seems improbable. It appears more likely to have been during the hearing but, since that lasted only one week, there would hardly have been time to frame the question, send it to the Foreign Office and receive a considered reply before the end of proceedings.

The Privy Council's question is not mentioned in the summary of Shawcross's submissions to the board. Nor does the judgment state that the question had been framed in consultation with counsel, as Gibson's questions had been. These matters suggest that the question occurred to their lordships after the hearing, during consideration of the terms of their advice to the Crown. If so, the bulk of the delay in giving that advice must have been attributable to the process of asking the additional question and obtaining an answer to it.

Additional question

In asking the additional question, the Judicial Committee inadvertently alighted upon an embarrassing episode for the Foreign Office. The question arose out of the answer to the seventh question which had been asked by Sir Leslie Gibson weeks later than the first six, the answer to which had not arrived until 13 March 1950, after the proceedings in front of him had concluded. Consequently his judgment does not mention the seventh question or the answer to it, although the judgment of the Full Court on appeal does so.

The seventh question (called by the Privy Council the 'further question') asked whether the UK government recognized the CPG as the de facto government exercising effective control on 1 October 1949 when it had been proclaimed or any other date between then and 5 January 1950 (the date of recognition) of the part of China of which the Nationalist government had ceased to be the de facto government. The answer given was that the UK government recognized that during that period the CPG was the de facto government of those parts of the Republic of China over which it had established effective control and, if control was established after 1 October 1949, as from the date when it so established control. The Judicial Committee detected an ambiguity in this answer. Was Her Majesty's Government there saying simply that it was their view in March 1950 that during the time mentioned in their answer the question of who was the de facto government of China was to be answered by reference to the factual establishment of effective control? Or was there more to it: in reliance upon that view had there been any declaration or other formal act by the UK government on 1 October 1949 or any later (and if so, what) date recognizing the CPG as the de facto government?

Under this cross-examination the Foreign Office decided to reveal the Graham incident of early October 1949 which had so annoyed the State Department. The FO replied that the only communication relevant to the Judicial Committee's questions during the relevant period was a note which had been delivered by the British Consul-General in Peking on 5 October 1949. It then set out the text of that note (mentioned in Chapter 7) inviting the establishment of informal relations. The FO was swift to add that the note had not been intended at the time that it was sent to constitute or convey de facto recognition. The answer given on 13 March 1950 to the Hong Kong courts' final question was to be understood as meaning that HM Government answering on that date asserted the view stated in the answer.

In other words, in British government eyes, those in actual control of territory were regarded as the de facto government of that territory. Consistent with that, the note had sought to establish informal relations with the authorities in the territory under the control of the CPG. It was, however, diplomatic obfuscation to deny that the note constituted or conveyed de facto recognition. It did not amount to recognition of the CPG as the de facto government of the whole of China but it did amount to recognition of it as the de facto government of those (undefined) parts under its control. As we have seen, the legal advice of the Foreign Office's own lawyers was that the consul's actions constituted de facto recognition. But its answer to the further question did not reveal that.

19

Aftermath

Swift reaction

Word of the final decision reached Hong Kong in the early hours of 29 July 1952. At 7 a.m. that morning a force of several hundred armed police, obviously primed and ready, descended upon Kai Tak and seized and impounded the planes. They were accompanied by three truckloads of soldiers. In fact they impounded all 71 planes, not just the 40 CATC ones which had been the subject of the Privy Council case, plus any equipment of the airlines which was kept at Kai Tak. They rounded up the guards who had been obstructing access to the planes and told them to leave. Those who refused to do so were arrested and taken to a police station; they claimed that some of them were beaten up. The police also raided the yards and warehouses in which the airlines' equipment had been stored and cleared them of workers.[1]

This was not the usual means of enforcing a civil judgment. The Hong Kong government justified its action by reference to the terms of the Order-in-Council of 10 May 1950 which empowered the Governor to take steps to prevent removal of the aircraft and ensure their maintenance and protection.[2] At last the Americans had been given the executive action that they had been craving.

Squat-in

In all, about two hundred communist guards and workers were taken to either Kowloon City Police Station or Hung Hom Police Station. They were allowed to leave that evening, but many of those at Kowloon City refused to go,

1. William M. Leary, 'Aircraft and Anti-Communists: CAT in Action, 1942–52', *China Quarterly* 52 (1972): 654, 664; Wenguang Shao, *China, Britain and Businessmen: Political and Commercial Relations, 1949–57* (Basingstoke: Macmillan, 1991), 79; Report, *South China Morning Post*, 30 July 1952.
2. Supreme Court of Hong Kong (Jurisdiction) Order 1950, s 5(1); Report, *South China Morning Post*, 30 July 1952.

squatting in protest in the station compound despite the onset of rain. They remained there until the early hours, wet, hungry and dispirited.

Meanwhile, military personnel were putting high net fences, topped with barbed wire, around the aircraft and searching storage areas for explosives. The public was barred entry to the airport. Sentry boxes were erected at the entrance, manned by helmeted armed police. Only genuine passengers were allowed in. Anti-riot vehicles patrolled the airport perimeter. At night, extra lights were placed to illuminate the planes.

Throughout the day, cases of equipment and spare parts were removed by truck from the New Asiatic Chemical Works godown and Bailey's Shipyard at Tokwawan to Kai Tak for safe custody. Both premises were cordoned off, with barricades across the roadway outside and police, supported by an armoured car, patrolling outside. The parts and equipment would later be transferred to the possession of CAT, Inc. The godown was boarded up.

A week later, once all had been secured and cleared, the Commissioner of Police, accompanied by the Director of Civil Aviation, toured the airfield, yards and storehouses to inspect his force's good work. He also inspected the grounded aircraft. With the planes bundled up, the guards ejected and the public barred, Kai Tak presented an eerie spectacle, recorded by a reporter from *The South China Morning Post*:

> Within the field the great squat hulks of the 71 airliners themselves sat around hemmed in by their new barriers, many still bearing the red flag of Communist China on their tail fins. Rudders and ailerons had long been removed for protection from the elements and the craft were drab with weather resistant paint.[3]

The governor reflects

Sir Alexander Grantham might well have been relieved that the operation to reclaim the planes had gone well. He was, however, dismayed though not surprised by the result of the appeal. From his perspective, the Order-in-Council had made a new law overriding the old one and the new law inevitably led to the planes being passed to the Americans. He felt it a 'sorry business' and that Britain had reason to feel ashamed, but 'who was I, a mere governor of a colonial dependency, to complain, and what good would it have done if I had?'[4]

A dozen years later in his autobiography Grantham passed over the fact that he had in fact resisted, if not complained about, British policy and that his resistance had been one reason for the British government to issue the Order-in-Council, taking the responsibility themselves and relieving him of

3. Report, *South China Morning Post*, 31 July 1952.
4. Alexander Grantham, *Via Ports: From Hong Kong to Hong Kong* (Hong Kong: Hong Kong University Press, 1965), 163.

embarrassment. His influence as the man on the spot was actually quite strong and he had pressed Hong Kong's interests more than a 'mere governor' of a dependency might have done. In the end, though, American pressure on Britain was too great for his influence to change the outcome.

Peking's displeasure

In Peking there was a strong protest about the Judicial Committee's decision. Vice-Foreign Minister Zhang Hanfu objected that Britain had 'absolutely no jurisdiction whatsoever over the properties in Hong Kong'. He demanded that Britain 'cease its illegal acts of encroaching on the sovereign rights of the People's Republic of China', perhaps an oblique reference to China's state immunity that had been removed by the Order-in-Council in violation of international comity between nations.

Two weeks later Shanghai Dockyards, the main British-owned shipyard, and Mollers, a British-owned shipbuilding and engineering works, at Shanghai were taken over without compensation. The timing of the move and attendant publicity suggest retaliation for the Privy Council decision. However, under Communist policy they would have been nationalized anyway. Perhaps the process of seizing the Shanghai ship and dock yards had been accelerated by the unwelcome news from London. Both businesses had been losing money in the prevailing difficult economic conditions and would have had to close down if they had not been taken over by the local government.

There were no communist demonstrations on the streets of Hong Kong but the workers who had been dispossessed of the planes and equipment made their feelings known. They had been allowed back into the shipyard and the godown after all the equipment had been removed. Perhaps emboldened by Peking's reaction, the CATC workers immediately raised the Chinese Communist five-star flag at the New Asia Chemical Works (where they lived as well as worked) and posted guards outside. The CNAC workers did the same at Bailey's Shipyard. They then set about erecting a replica of the façade of Tian An Men and a portrait of Mao Tse-tung outside the shipyard as well, in anticipation of the third anniversary of the PRC on 1 October.

American pleasure

By contrast, Chennault, Willauer, Corcoran, Donovan and their supporters were jubilant and relieved at the outcome in the Privy Council. The repeated losses in earlier hearings and lower courts were forgotten. Donovan described the outcome as the first Cold War victory in the Far East. It was a phrase used by Corcoran too when writing to the US Chief Justice Fred Vinson to thank him for his support. Corcoran added that he and his supporters desperately wished that the air fleet could be removed intact from Hong Kong and overhauled for use by the French in Indochina. Chennault was wary as well as jubilant: he feared the aircraft might be sabotaged or destroyed by angry communists.[5]

The State Department was also pleased. Their persistence in nagging the British authorities seemed to have paid off. But it had taken so long that by the time the final outcome became known, most of the foreign service officers who had applied the pressure in 1949 and 1950 had moved on to other tasks.

British relief

For British policy-makers the result came as an undoubted relief. It placated the Americans but, as long intended, enabled the UK government to cling to the claim that title to the aircraft had been determined by a court. It also vindicated the government's prediction that ultimately the Privy Council would have to decide. Whether it maintained a belief in British fair play and enhanced the reputation of British justice must, however, be doubted.

Governor Grantham certainly had his doubts. The whole idea of 'leaving it to the courts to decide' relied upon the protection of the independence of those courts and the preservation of a level playing field between the parties. At first, when the matter was in the hands of the Hong Kong courts during the autumn, winter and spring of 1949–1950, those considerations seem to have been upheld. But once the politicians in London became frustrated by the refusal of those courts by resort to sovereign immunity to address the question of title, the politicians barely hesitated to contaminate the pure fount of justice.

The Cabinet decision to sweep away immunity by Order-in-Council had caused disquiet to some Members of Parliament on the left of the Labour Party and even to some ministers. Younger, for instance, thought his superiors were too deferential to American desires. He had confided to his diary at the beginning of 1951 that four other Labour ministers were unhappy.[6] But the Cold War and anti-communism, plus the need to keep close to the USA, decided the policy in the end. Communist aggression in Korea had seemed to justify the policy. By the time of the Privy Council decision, Labour was out of government anyway.

5. Peter Lowe, *Containing the Cold War in East Asia: British Policies towards Japan, China and Korea, 1948–53* (Manchester: Manchester University Press, 1997), 161.
6. Geoffrey Warner, ed., *In the Midst of Events: The Foreign Office Diaries and Papers of Kenneth Younger, February 1950–October 1951* (London: Routledge, 2005), 54.

The CATC planes

Of the 71 aircraft on the airfield at Kai Tak only 40, plus their associated equipment, had been the subject of the Privy Council appeal. They were all former CATC planes and parts. The case concerning the former CNAC planes had been started but left to one side to await the outcome of the CATC action.

Chennault and Willauer had to work quickly to get the 40 former CATC planes away before anything happened to frustrate them such as sabotage or a strike which might make the Hong Kong authorities think again. After more than three years exposed to the elements the planes were in a poor condition. Many had parts and accessories missing. Almost none was airworthy.

The pair had promised to take the aircraft away before 1 October. They planned to remove the planes to the USA or the Philippines. Flying them away was not an option. Neither was dismantling them and carting them off by road and rail, for all land routes out of Hong Kong were through China. The only way was by boat. Fortunately Kai Tak airfield was bounded on one side by a bay off the harbour. But where would they find ships large enough to take the planes? The smaller aircraft could be dismantled and crated but the larger ones would have to be shipped more or less intact on cargo vessels. The pair consulted their resourceful partner Tommy Corcoran in America.

An unexpected arrival

What happened next removed any doubt that CAT, Inc. had enjoyed official US backing in its quest for the Kai Tak aircraft. On 28 September 1950 a US Navy aircraft carrier arrived in Hong Kong to take the aircraft away. It was the USS Cape Esperance, a Casablanca class compact escort carrier built during the Second World War, named after an inconclusive naval engagement in 1942.[7] Decommissioned and put in reserve post-war, the boat had been recommissioned in August 1950, stripped of most of her weapons and given a mainly civilian crew. She had been intended to serve as an auxiliary to ferry to the Far East aircraft for use in the Korean conflict. Though designed to operate with just 27 aircraft, she could carry up to 60 planes on her flight and hangar decks.

In order to load the aircraft onto the Cape Esperance and other ships, special temporary loading facilities, docks, barges and cranes, were assembled on the seawall next to the airfield. Contractors were hired but, because of the risk of attack and sabotage, had to pay exorbitant insurance premiums which they passed on to CAT, Inc. The corporation also had to give the Hong Kong government an indemnity against liability. The largest of the 40 planes

7. Fought north of the island of Guadalcanal in the Solomon chain on 12 October 1942; also called the second battle of Savo Island.

were crammed onto the deck of the carrier. She and a freighter carrying the dismembered other aircraft sailed for California a few days later, arriving at Long Beach on 19 October.[8]

To get the carrier, Corcoran had lobbied hard in Washington, pulling strings, calling in favours and exploiting sympathies. He had argued that the planes could have been used in a war and therefore US military assistance to remove them was warranted. Chennault had written to US senators arguing that although the planes were private property there was an overriding interest in avoiding the loss of face that would be suffered if, after denying the aircraft to the Communists, they could not be removed before being destroyed by sabotage. Having denounced the British and Hong Kong authorities for so long, US politicians could hardly refuse to help now that the perfidious British courts had awarded the planes to their rightful American owners. Although only six years old, the Cape Esperance had been mothballed for four years since her last mission transporting US troops back from the Pacific. She had just been brought back into service and was available.[9]

The CNAC planes

In Hong Kong on 8 October 1952, even before delivery of the Privy Council's reasons, the trial was heard by Sir Gerard Howe CJ concerning possession of the other 31 aircraft and accompanying assets, those that had belonged to CNAC. The communist-controlled airline did not acknowledge the proceedings and was not represented at the trial.

The sale of the CNAC assets had been properly concluded, Howe held, so he made a declaration that they and all spare parts, machinery and equipment for use in relation thereto were the property of CAT, Inc. Whatever he may privately have thought, given the Privy Council ruling which was binding upon him, Sir Gerard had no choice but to make the declaration. Several minor objections about the formalities of the sale by CNAC which had been made by Sir Leslie Gibson and the Full Court on the application for appointment of interim receivers in 1950 were overcome by more detailed evidence which was used before Howe.[10] Sir Leslie did not, however, live to learn this, having passed away in late September. He would at least have known the outcome of the Privy Council case.

On 20 November 1952 the Shanghai authorities ordered the requisition of three British-owned utility undertakings, a waterworks, a gas supplier and

8. William M. Leary, 'Aircraft and Anti-Communists: CAT in Action, 1942–52', *China Quarterly* 52 (1972): 654, 664.
9. Martha Byrd, *Chennault: Giving Wings to the Tiger* (Tuscaloosa: University of Alabama Press, 1987), 346; Wikipedia, USS Cape Esperance.
10. *Civil Air Transport Incorporated v The China National Aviation Corporation* (1952) 36 HKLR 302.

an operator of trams, motor buses and trolley buses.[11] This occurred six weeks after Howe CJ's decision concerning the CNAC aircraft and assets and five weeks after delivery of the Privy Council's reasons, so the timing may again suggest retaliation. However, the takeover of such important utilities was inevitable, for an electricity company and a telephone company, both American-owned, had already been expropriated in Shanghai and a French-owned power, water and tramway enterprise there was to be requisitioned in 1953. All three British utility companies had been operating at a loss since before 1949 and surviving on loans from the People's Bank of China. Properties owned by the British firm Mackenzie & Co in Shanghai, Tianjin and Hankou were also taken over at about this time.[12]

Payment of debts

Once it had been decided that Chennault and Willauer had held title to the planes to sell to CAT, Inc. the Nationalist authorities felt that they could press for payment of the US$4.75 million due under the promissory notes that the pair had given for the aircraft and other assets in December 1949. The pair was taken aback by this, reckoning the Taiwanese authorities were ungrateful for their efforts. They threatened to counter-claim for compensation for the losses, including US$2.5 million in legal and other expenses, resulting from the government's failure to deliver the assets and to keep its promises regarding the supply of foreign exchange.[13]

In the matter of finance, Chennault and Willauer were victims of their own deceptions. They had talked up the value of the aircraft and other assets in order to attract support from political figures in the US for their efforts to save them. As a result, the Nationalist authorities thought there would be more money available than there was and rumours circulated that the pair had profited handsomely from the dispute. Willauer and Chennault had obscured the distinction between CAT, their airline, and CAT, Inc., the Delaware corporation which had bought the assets and pursued the litigation and in which the pair had minority interests. They had also hidden the holding structure behind the corporation and the existence of new owners of CAT along with the complex corporate arrangement behind them. All this may have assisted the pair in conducting the litigation but it perplexed ministers and administrators in Taiwan who regarded both organizations as one, and as one controlled by the pair.

---

11. Respectively, Shanghai Waterworks Co Ltd, Shanghai Gas Co and Shanghai Electric Construction Co Ltd. See Shao, *China, Britain and Businessmen*, 80.
12. Evan Luard, *Britain and China* (London: Chatto and Windus, 1962), 188; Victor S. Kaufman, 'The United States, Great Britain and the CAT Controversy', *Journal of Contemporary History* 40, no. 1 (2005): 95, 110; Shao, *China, Britain and Businessmen*, 80–81.
13. William M. Leary, *Perilous Missions*, 171.

Accordingly, when the question of CAT's licence to operate in Taiwan came up for consideration or some other assistance to the airline was requested, the authorities there inevitably asked about payment on the promissory notes. They could be mollified only by the establishment in late 1952 of a committee consisting of government representatives and members from CAT and CAT, Inc. to supervise the renovation and sale of the aircraft. But it took another two years for a settlement to be reached and Chiang Kai-shek was not happy with the outcome.[14]

Sale of the aircraft

The airplanes could not immediately be resold, for they were in a poor state after standing largely immobile in the open air for nearly three years. Although there had been no great typhoons during that time and protective coatings had been applied to the fuselages, the strong sun, great humidity and intense rains of the summer months had done their damage. Parts had been removed from most of the craft either in an effort to immobilize them or to protect those parts or through theft.

Reconditioning took time and cost money. By the middle of May 1953 only 15 of the 71 planes had been sold. The proceeds did not even meet the huge amounts that had been run up in legal expenses, removing the aircraft and putting them in saleable condition. The dampening down of fighting in Korea, culminating in an armistice in July 1953, reduced the demand for used transports and the prospects of selling more.[15]

A fight in Tokwawan

Alexander Grantham's great fear that the aeroplanes would become the cause of trouble on the streets of Hong Kong between the two sides in the Chinese civil war was realized soon after the workers had returned to their empty depots and security had been relaxed. In the middle of the morning of 3 October 1952 a group of about 30 men appeared outside Bailey's Shipyard at Mau Tau Wei Road, Tokwawan. They were armed with iron rods, stones and ladders. They stormed the wall of the yard, attempting to demolish the Communist National Day decorations.

Guards posted to keep watch over the exterior of the yard immediately called for help. Dozens of CNAC employees rushed out of the yard to confront

14. Leary, 'Aircraft and Anti-Communists', 667–668; Qiang Zhai, *The Dragon, the Lion and the Eagle: Chinese-British-American Relations, 1949–1958* (Kent, OH: Kent State University Press, 1994), 106, fn 74.
15. Martha Byrd, *Chennault: Giving Wings to the Tiger*, 344–349; Leary, *Perilous Missions*, 171; Leary, 'Aircraft and Anti-Communists', 668.

the raiders. A short and confused battle ensued in the street. More than a hundred men took part.

Residents called the police but before they could arrive two of the assailants had been badly beaten and collapsed in the roadway opposite the yard. They and another man were taken to hospital, one in critical condition. Two others were injured. Several of the participants were taken by the police for questioning. The assault had been beaten off. Nevertheless, nearby shops closed until the afternoon.

Bailey's Shipyard remained occupied by CNAC workers even though it had been one of the assets of the corporation which, as a result of the Privy Council decision, had been found to have been sold to CAT, Inc. It became a communist hotbed, its walls and gates festooned with slogans and flags. Not until May 1955 did the authorities have the courage to invade the yard and evict the workers. In June that year bailiffs took possession of another warehouse where more stocks had been stored. It was the final act of the saga.[16]

16. Report, *South China Morning Post*, 10 May 1955.

20
Appraisal

The Privy Council's reasons

Once the Judicial Committee had announced its decision on 28 July 1952 the reasons for the decision were of interest mainly to lawyers and diplomatists. Yet the reasons concerned aspects of public international law of some significance which resonated in the chancelleries of foreign ministries and embassies worldwide as well as amongst legal academics and their textbooks. The reasons touched on the principle of succession of one government to another, retroactivity of recognition of governments, the distinction between de facto and de jure recognition, the role of foreign ministry statements concerning recognition and the notion of the trusteeship of governments for their people.[1]

The argument on behalf of CAT, Inc. which had been rejected by both the Chief Justice and the Full Court was that the sale of the airlines' assets by the Nationalist government on 12 December 1949 had been valid to transfer title to Chennault and Willauer who in turn had transferred title to CAT, Inc. a week later; that sale and transfer had been carried out by authorities which had been recognized by Britain and thus Hong Kong as the de jure government at the time and so, on normal international law principles, the sale and transfer was binding upon the Central People's Government (and therefore its airline CATC) as successor to the Nationalist government. The Chief Justice had rejected this argument on two main grounds. The first was that the sale had been invalid and its terms unlawful because it had not been carried out in good faith as trustees for the people but was a device made for an alien and improper purpose. The Full Court had agreed with this. The second was that the subsequent recognition of the CPG operated retroactively to annul the sale. The Full Court had been divided on this. Viscount Simon structured the Judicial Committee's analysis by reference to those grounds.

1. *Civil Air Transport Incorporated v Central Air Transport Corporation* [1953] AC 70, (1951) 35 HKLR 215 (13 October 1952).

Breach of trust

In considering the first ground the Judicial Committee emphasized that the validity of the transaction must be judged as at the date when it was entered into and not in the light of subsequent events. On 12 December 1949, the committee reasoned, the de jure government of China was the Nationalist government, of which CATC was an organ; therefore the property in the aeroplanes had been then in the Nationalist government; the machines had been moved to Hong Kong and it was open to that government to sell them and thereby pass the property in them to the purchasers. The committee acknowledged that the motive for making the sale was to secure that the machines should not be added to Communist resources: the conditions of the sale contract made this abundantly clear. The Nationalist government was in retreat and by this time had been all but driven out from China, but

> it was still resisting its opponents, and in their Lordships' view the impeached sale was no more 'a device' adopted for an 'alien and improper purpose' than would have been the blowing up of a store of ammunition in an arsenal in China from which Nationalist forces were on the point of being driven out.

The Chief Justice had concluded that at the time of the contract the Nationalist government must have been alive to the probability of the withdrawal of recognition by the British government in the near future, saying that this could be inferred from the terms of the contract and from 'normal diplomatic usage'. Viscount Simon described this as a matter of speculation at best. The reference to diplomatic usage presumably pointed to the undoubted fact that by international law an established and recognized government may be so completely overthrown by insurgent forces that the recognition previously afforded to it by foreign countries may properly be withdrawn, Simon observed, 'but when and by whom only the future can show'.

The Chief Justice had denounced the transaction as being inimical both to the CPG and, since the planes had been used for public purposes, to the interests of the Chinese people. The Judicial Committee was icily dismissive of this: a government's policy in buying and selling chattels which it owns was not subject to the review of foreign tribunals and whether its action in this regard was against the interests of those it is supposed to serve was a political question. 'British courts cannot take it on themselves to pronounce whether a foreign government, recognized by H. M. Government, is acting contrary to the interests of its people.' As for the Chief Justice's suggestion that the transaction was incompatible with 'the trusteeship which every government must assume' the committee was similarly unimpressed: 'a government is certainly not a trustee in these matters in any legal sense' and the right in the domestic law of trusts to follow property which is subject to a trust into the hands of third parties 'cannot have any application here'.

It appeared to the Judicial Committee that the view of the Chief Justice and the Full Court was that on 12 December 1949 the Nationalist government knew that it was on the point of being superseded by the Communists who would be recognized as the de jure government of China and that, without any regard to public interests or any injury it was doing to the Chinese people, it got rid of these aeroplanes out of spite, merely to embarrass its inevitable successor. 'Such a view,' Simon intoned tersely, 'involves assumptions which their Lordships are not prepared to make.'

So their lordships disagreed with both the suggestion that governments are in the position of trustees and with the inference that there had been any such breach here anyway. But the suggestion had not originated in the Hong Kong courts: the judges there had based themselves on a sentence, or more precisely part of a sentence, in the judgment of Lord Justice Denning in the Court of Appeal in the Boguslawski case. What did their lordships make of that? 'That sentence was not necessary to the actual decision,' they said, adding that the sentence occurred in a passage in which Denning LJ had been emphasizing the paramount importance of the principle of a succeeding government accepting what has been done by its predecessor and if the qualification which he had introduced 'were to be read as authorizing a court to treat as a nullity political decisions and actions of a former government which have resulted in the transfer of property to third parties in circumstances like the present, their Lordships would respectfully disagree'.

This part of the Judicial Committee's advice seems to have been the subject of debate and compromise behind the scenes by the judges. Since dissent was not in those days allowed in Privy Council decisions, where one or more judges was not prepared to go so far as the majority if possible the advice would be hedged or qualified so as to reflect the view of the minority. The inclusion of the phrase 'in circumstances like the present' may well have been because one or two of their lordships did not wish to go so far as propounding that Denning's qualification to the principle of continuity would never allow a court to treat a sale to a third party as a nullity. Consistent with this, a further nuanced limitation was stated by the committee: 'At the same time, their Lordships must not be understood to reject the possibility of our courts refusing, in a conceivable case, to recognize the validity of the disposal of state property by a government on the eve of its fall.' What case had their lordships in mind? They gave the example of a sale by 'a despot, who knows that previous recognition is just being withdrawn, where it is clear that his purpose was to abscond with the proceeds or to make away with State assets for some private purpose'.

So Denning LJ's idea of a limitation upon the principle of continuity between governments and their successors was not entirely rejected, although the suggestion that the limitation originates in the concept of state trusteeship was. However, the board's opinion was focused upon the idea of a successor government recovering property sold by its predecessor by tracing it into the hands of a third party. That is not the only remedy for breach of trust in municipal law. The more usual remedy is an award of money: compensation (damages) for the breach or an account for the proceeds of sale. The possibility of such an award was not considered by the board, because it was not sought by CAT, Inc. which wanted possession of the assets themselves.[2]

Retroactivity of recognition

Had the sale been nullified by the retro-action of Britain's recognition from 5 to 6 January 1950 of the CPG as government de jure of China? This second ground for the decision by the Chief Justice, Viscount Simon observed, assumed that on 12 December 1949 the aeroplanes were the disposable property of the Nationalist government and that it validly transferred them as specific and ascertained goods by the contract of that date to Chennault and Willauer, predecessors-in-title to CAT, Inc. On that assumption, the appeal could fail only if the subsequent recognition de jure of the Communist government annulled the passing of the property.

Subsequent recognition de jure of a new government could in certain circumstances annul a sale by the previous government, the committee conceded, giving the example of a sale of goods owned by the latter but at the time of sale situated in territory effectively occupied by insurgent forces operating on behalf of what is already a de facto new government. Then, if the previous government never regains the goods and the de facto government becomes recognized de jure by the British government, purchasers from the old government will not be held to have a good title to the goods by British courts after the recognition. However, the sale may be valid if the insurgents are afterwards defeated and possession of the goods is regained by the old government.

Viscount Simon explained that retroactivity of recognition operates primarily to validate acts of a de facto government which has subsequently become the de jure government, not to invalidate acts of the previous de jure government. It might be too wide to say that the retroactive effect of de jure recognition must be limited to acts done on the territory of the government so recognized, he said, but the actual case concerned chattels, which at the time of the sale belonged to the Nationalist government, in the British colony of Hong Kong. The crucial question was whether anything that happened in Hong Kong to the aeroplanes, at the instigation or on behalf of the de facto

2. [1953] Law Quarterly Review 136, 139–141.

Communist government before the change of recognition, had been retrospectively validated so as to extinguish the title conferred by the contract.

What had happened was that the planes and other assets had been seized by employees of the airlines and others, claiming to have acted on behalf of the new government. But, Viscount Simon observed, whatever physical control over the planes they had as a result of this action was in defiance of the injunction granted by the Chief Justice on 24 November 1949, and if the employees could be regarded as having acted on behalf of the de facto Communist government their act would have been an infringement of the Representation of Foreign Powers (Control) Ordinance and would be a criminal offence. This illegal taking of control of the planes could not give ground for the principle of retroactivity, the Judicial Committee concluded.

The only Hong Kong judge to emerge from the Privy Council's scrutiny with credit was Gould J. In the Full Court he had declined to agree with the Chief Justice and with Scholes J on the issue of retrospectivity. He had said he thought that if the rights of the newly recognized government were dependent to any extent on possession of the subject matter of the dispute, acquisition of possession by a wrongful act could not confer any benefit upon the acquiring party which he did not previously enjoy. In Gould's opinion the CPG could not rely upon actual possession acquired in the way that it was, so it had no possession which could bring into effect the doctrine of retroactivity. The doctrine relates to acts of a government which has already acquired jurisdiction through possession and cannot include the act of taking possession if that act be wrongful. He therefore held that the ordinary principle of continuity had not been displaced by any consideration of retroactivity. Accordingly the Nationalist government was entitled to possession of and jurisdiction over the aeroplanes.

Gould J's views were vindicated: 'Their Lordships agree with the argument and conclusions of Gould J on this point,' said Viscount Simon. They also agreed with him on another point. The Chief Justice had attached importance to the announcement on 1 October 1949 of the formation of the PRC and to the decree of the same date in the name of the CPG purporting to dismiss the Nationalist ministers, deducing that from that date the aircraft had been owned by the CPG. Gould J had observed of this that the purported dismissal could be deemed effective only within the territory and as regards assets within the control of the CPG; elsewhere, so long as the Nationalist government retained de jure recognition, the decree would have no effect. The Judicial Committee declined to accept the Chief Justice's view and adopted Gould's opinion.

The Privy Council's consideration of the case had introduced an element that had been neglected in the earlier judgments, that of the municipal (or domestic) law. The sale of the assets was a sale of goods and such a sale, being a staple of commerce, was governed by long-established rules of domestic law. This had barely been mentioned before. In submissions to the Chief Justice, Sir Walter Monckton had suggested that the sale by the partnership of Chennault and Willauer to CAT, Inc. had been good in US law (though this had not featured in Howe CJ's reasoning, nor that of the Full Court) but no one had considered the prior sale by the Nationalist government to the partnership. That sale had been negotiated between the government then located in Formosa and the partners, who were American. However, the partners were operating in Hong Kong and the assets were located there too, although previously based and registered in China. So the law of which jurisdiction governed the sale? Apparently the contract of sale did not choose a law. The contract was a mixture of US terminology and informal language. The partnership's offer had been sent to Formosa and was accepted by the government there, which suggests that the law of Formosa (i.e. the Republic of China) would apply, although a case can be maintained for US law or for Hong Kong law instead. If it was US law, the question would then arise, the law of which state of the union?

Ultimately this hardly matters because the law of sale of goods in all the relevant jurisdictions was likely to be similar. Certainly that of the majority of US states and Hong Kong is identical in most material aspects. The Judicial Committee's reasons talk of the passing of property, an English notion adopted in Hong Kong by which the delivery of the goods may be separated from ownership of (or property in) them. The general rule is that property passes on making of the contract but it is possible that the agreement or surrounding circumstances show that the parties to the contract had a different intention. It has been said that in modern times very little is needed to give rise to the inference that the property in specific goods is to pass on delivery or payment.[3] There would seem to have been scope for argument in this case since the sellers did not have custody or control of the subject matter of the contract, the planes and other assets, and the subject matter was physically in a different jurisdiction. Furthermore, payment of the price, which normally is due on delivery, was by means of the sellers giving credit by accepting a promise to pay in the future (promissory notes). If property in the goods did not pass on the making of the contract, it may have been intended that the assets would remain in the legal possession of the Nationalist government until the assets could be handed over or even until payment had been received. So the possibility arises that ownership remained with that government after 12 December 1949 and after 5 January 1950.

The Judicial Committee deftly circumvented such complications by describing the sale as a sale of specific and ascertained goods. In other words

3. *Ward Ltd v Bignall* [1967] 1 QB 534, 535.

the subject matter was not generic, as would be the case in the sale of commodities, but particular: the very assets of the two airlines, most of which were located in Hong Kong. This makes it more likely that the parties intended an immediate transfer of ownership so that the property passed from seller to buyer on the making of the contract.[4] However, it does not make that intention inevitable, for passing of property is always a matter of the parties' intention. The fact that the assets were not within the actual possession of the seller and so could not be delivered was some indication that immediate transfer of property was not intended, as is the fact that the airlines and many of the aeroplanes were not currently capable of operation. For the general rule to apply, the goods must be in a deliverable state.

Furthermore, the Judicial Committee's assertion that this was a sale of specific and ascertained goods is open to scrutiny. The subject of the sale was described in the contract as 'all physical assets and such stock as is owned by the Government' of the airlines, so the sale was of more than the goods, for 'stock' (meaning company shares) is not goods. Indeed the term 'assets' even if qualified by 'physical' is wide enough to include matters such as money in the corporate bank accounts, which again is not goods. The assets that were contemplated were not expressly spelt out: there was no list; even the aircraft were not itemized. The location of the physical assets was not set out either, beyond stating most were in Hong Kong. They might be capable of ascertainment but to say that they were ascertained at the time of the contract seems doubtful.

The transaction was decidedly more than a sale of 71 aeroplanes. It was more the sale of the businesses of the two airlines. The contract contemplated that the purchasers, Chennault and Willauer, were to operate the airlines. Yet the sale and the right to operate was also subject to unusual restrictions: the aircraft were not to be used in the Communist areas of China and the assets were to be transferred by the purchasers to a corporation which would issue promissory notes to replace those given by Chennault and Willauer and the holder of the promissory notes was to have an option to hold stock in the new corporation. Since the holder of the notes would initially be the Nationalist government, the latter feature aroused the suspicions of the Hong Kong courts which thought that the transaction was a device by which the Nationalists could retain use and regain effective ownership of the planes.

4. Rule 1 of s 18 of the Sale of Goods Act 1893 (England): 'Where there is an unconditional contract for the sale of specific goods, in a deliverable state, the property in the goods passes to the buyer when the contract is made, and it is immaterial whether the time of payment or the time of delivery, or both, be postponed.' The relevant rule was the same under the Hong Kong Sale of Goods Ordinance.

Succession

The doctrine of state succession emerged from the Privy Council's advice unscathed. The CPG was held bound by the acts of its predecessor despite their ideological differences. The concept of continuity in administration required that the sale by the Nationalists as the predecessor government could not be repudiated by the Communists as the successor government.

The potentially wide exception suggested by Denning LJ was disapproved by the Judicial Committee. The Chief Justice's suggestion that acts done by the new government were not in good faith as trustees for the state but for an alien and improper purpose was too vague for the board to accept. It would have required separation between the government and the state which it governed and it had an unavoidably political flavour which could not be disguised by the high-sounding rhetoric of trust and impropriety. Though no doubt motivated by a desire to keep the airliners and equipment out of the grasp of enemies in war, the sale was a commercial as well as a tactical transaction.

Where the Judicial Committee may be said to have over-egged the pudding is in its dismissal of the conclusion of the Hong Kong courts that the sale was arranged and pushed through in a hurry so as to be concluded prior to recognition of the Communists as the de jure government of China. The Privy Council judges were not to know that Chennault and Willauer, the men behind CAT, Inc., were acting in close collaboration with US diplomats and other officials who knew from State Department briefings that Britain was close to deciding formally to recognize the Peking authorities. However, their dismissal as 'speculation' of what would have been common knowledge among insiders in Whitehall, Washington and Hong Kong, and what would surely have been known to the Nationalist government which agreed to sell the goods and would anyway have been easily deducible by anyone familiar with Foreign Office practice, namely that recognition was imminent, was a stretch too far. It has the appearance of an attempt by their lordships to bolster their reasoning by denigrating a perfectly reasonable deduction based upon facts known in early to mid-December 1949. The declaration of the PRC on 1 October 1949 and the continuing deterioration in the Nationalist position thereafter alone would have told any sensible observer that the chances of the imminent extension of formal recognition to the Communist authorities were high. If it was speculation, it was well-grounded speculation and that was the point.

The parties' anticipation of withdrawal of recognition would not have rendered the sale improper, however, and, as the board pointed out, acts undertaken to improve a government's position in war are not an alien purpose. The illustrations given by Denning LJ and the board indicate that what this exception is aimed at is acts undertaken for personal gain or greed. This sale did not fall into that category. It was a wartime tactic undertaken to deny assets to the enemy. The Judicial Committee's analogy of the blowing up of an ammunition dump was meant to bring this point out. The analogy was not particularly strong, however, for the aircraft and equipment were not instruments of war and they were not destroyed but alienated to a third party for money to be received by the KMT government. Moreover they were alienated on terms which permitted that government to resume an interest in them at a later date. It was this last point that had struck the Hong Kong judges as indicating that the sale was not genuine. The point was not addressed by the Judicial Committee, however.

Possession and agency

The Judicial Committee, unlike the courts below, was willing to attribute significance to the illegalities involved in the control of the aircraft and equipment by the renegade employees and their accomplices. The breaches of injunction and of the Representation of Foreign Powers (Control) Ordinance rendered their 'possession' illegitimate. This is a readily understandable and simple rebuttal to the argument of agency for the CPG that had so impressed the Hong Kong judges. But is it correct?

The conclusion that the injunctions had been broken by the employees and their sympathizers (third parties to the earlier proceedings) was in defiance of the view of the courts below that there was no evidence that the third parties themselves, as opposed to other persons who were not parties, had interfered with the planes. Dennis Blake, the solicitor for the Nationalist airlines, had experienced difficulty in identifying and serving the culprits and at one point approached John Griffin the Attorney General of Hong Kong in a vain attempt to enlist official assistance in identifying them. The culprits, whoever they were, were already in control of the planes, in the sense of barring access to them by others, at the time of the imposition of the injunction. Simple continuation of that control may not have broken the terms of the injunction.

Moreover, some at least of those holding the planes were employees of the airlines. Although their claim to represent the CPG, if substantiated, may have been in defiance of the Ordinance and constituted a criminal offence, whether they really were representing the CPG would have been, or would have involved, a matter of law. Despite their protestations, it would have seemed more likely that in taking custody of the planes they were really acting for the airlines. Viscount Simon's way around this difficulty was to say that the CPG did not purport to take over the assets until January 1950, after the sale. But this requires a narrow, literal reading of Chou En-lai's message of welcome to the employees the previous November, before the sale, as well as the attachment of no importance to the purported dismissal of the Nationalist ministers on 1 October 1949.

The answer of the Hong Kong judges to the illegality point was to rely upon authorities that said that the legality of possession, as opposed to the fact of possession, was of no relevance. As Viscount Simon pointed out, however, these authorities were concerned with sovereign immunity, an issue no longer before the courts because of the terms of the Order-in-Council. In sovereign immunity, the impeachment of a government through acts of its agents is still an impeachment of it even if the acts of the agents are illegal, but that had no application here.

Legality aside, the Judicial Committee did not examine the validity of the claims of the defectors to hold the planes on behalf of the CPG. Gould J had done so in the Full Court and had concluded that an employee of one principal could not validly transfer his agency to another principal without the consent of the first principal, a process nevertheless legitimized by two Hong Kong Chief Justices by the misdescription 'attornment'. Since their lordships were impressed by Gould's reasoning on retrospectivity, perhaps we may conclude that they agreed with him on this aspect too.

Executive certification

The use by British courts of certificates from the Foreign Office concerning recognition had been established long before 1952 but the certificate in the planes' case was notable for its length and precision. Both these merits may be attributed to the certificate having taken the form of answers to questions carefully posed by the court. Most of those answers had been framed by Gibson CJ with the assistance of counsel for use in the earlier proceedings. Gibson's initial request actually contained five questions. A further question was asked by him later but the answer to it was not given until after his judgment so was available only at the later hearings. The Judicial Committee subsequently added a seventh question.

Kenneth Younger, the deputy foreign minister and barrister who was responsible for approving the draft replies, later recalled that he and his colleagues, who must have included the senior legal adviser Sir Eric Beckett, had been keen to be accurate and helpful. If so, the answers cannot be accounted a complete success. Although precise and forthcoming about the date of formal recognition, which anyway was well known, the answers were somewhat unenlightening about de facto recognition. All that those answers told the judges was that the Foreign Office treated those who were in charge of the various parts of China as being the de facto government of those parts from the dates upon which they were actually in control of those parts. These answers however seem to assume that an area is always under the control of one government, as opposed to none, and that control, once established, is never relinquished. Also they do not elaborate upon what is meant by control.

There seems to have been an element of evasion about the answer to the extra question asked by the Judicial Committee. That question pointedly enquired whether there had been any act of de facto recognition prior to the formal recognition of January 1950. The Foreign Office was forced to come clean about the initiative taken by Mr Graham, the British Consul in Peking, on 5 October 1949 (see Chapter 7). This demarche had not been alluded to in the earlier answers even though they had been in response to questions about de facto recognition, perhaps because the initiative was embarrassing or perhaps because it would require explanation. In the extra answer the Foreign Office revealed the consul's invitation to the Peking authorities to establish informal relations but immediately added that it was not intended to convey de facto recognition. This might have been strictly accurate (who except the consul knew what he intended?) but was misleading. A truer answer would have added instead that whether the message amounted to de facto recognition was a matter for the court. Sir Eric Beckett, for one, was in no doubt as to the effect of the consul's conduct: he advised that the consul on behalf of His Majesty's Government had accorded de facto recognition to the CPG at least as regards the area of Peking. Apparently it had been British practice in China and other troubled parts of the world to try to maintain relations with the effective local authorities by appointing consuls there.[5]

The omission of an explanation in the answer to the Privy Council's question is in contrast to the willingness to supply guidance to the court about the effect of recognition. One answer stated that 'the effect of recognition by H. M. Government . . . in particular its retroactive effect (if any) are questions for the court to decide in the light of' the answers and the evidence in the case. This reply had been given before (for instance in the Boguslawski case) and was intended to head off any attempt by the court to seek executive assistance on the effect of recognition.

Conclusion

Although the impression given by the Privy Council's reasoning is one of certainty and analytical precision, closer inspection suggests that their lordships did not deal fully with the points which had impressed the Hong Kong courts. Nor were all arguments which might have been made in favour of the Chinese airlines addressed. This is no doubt partly the consequence of those airlines absenting themselves from the litigation. That said, it is doubtful whether the arguments which might have been raised on their behalf would have made any

5. Note, [1953] International and Comparative Law Quarterly 136, 143.

difference to the result. Although the sale to the partnership was obviously a manoeuvre to ensure that the title to the aeroplanes and equipment remained legally with parties sympathetic to the Nationalists, it was nonetheless genuine, as their subsequent resale and removal confirmed.

21
Epilogue

The people

How did those whom had been caught up in the case of the Chinese aircraft at Kai Tak fare after the saga had ended?

Claire Chennault continued to advise Chiang Kai-shek on aviation matters and drafted memos proposing fantasy schemes for Chiang's return to the mainland. Chennault was the public face of CAT for several years, although he was effectively a figurehead, until he fell ill with lung cancer in 1957. In his final days he was visited in hospital by Dwight Eisenhower, the wartime commander who had become President of the United States. After saying goodbye, Eisenhower called Chennault a 'true American hero'.

Chennault died believing that by their actions in the planes dispute he and Willauer had saved Taiwan from assault by 'the Reds', according to his widow Anna (Chen Xiangmei). She described their coup as a 'brilliant capture by purchase'. Anna lived to a ripe age at the Watergate Apartments in Washington DC, promoting the ChiNat cause, courting politicians, funnelling Taiwanese money to influential places and serving as vice-chairman of the Republican National Finance Committee.

Whiting Willauer left CAT in mid-1953 when the death of his son in an accident obliged him to return to the USA. Once Chennault informed him that an arrangement with the Nationalist government concerning the aeroplanes had finally been settled, Willauer wrote back expressing relief 'after all the sweat and tears we put into this quixotic gesture' and stating that 'despite the hell we went through . . . we probably saved Formosa, if not from a takeover by parachuters' then 'from a very nasty situation'. He felt that they had not been given full credit by the Nationalist government.[1]

Willauer's decade of clandestine efforts in China aviation for the USA was however rewarded by the administration. Through the influence of his long-term sponsor 'Tommy the Cork', Willauer was appointed US ambassador to

1. William M. Leary, 'Aircraft and Anti-Communists: CAT in Action, 1942–52', *China Quarterly* 52 (1972): 654, 668.

Honduras. It was thought that his experience would be useful in training guerrillas to parachute into neighbouring Guatemala to liberate it from socialist government.

Tommy Corcoran continued his career in Washington as congressional facilitator, political fixer, leg man and legal counsel. He formed a close relationship with Anna Chennault after her husband and his own wife had passed away. Corcoran died in 1981.

Willauer, Chennault and Corcoran's long-term secret service associate **Alfred T. Cox** remained vice-president of CAT until 1955. He wrote an account of the airline in 1967 as part of the CIA's clandestine services history.[2] It was publicly released in 2011. Wild **Bill Donovan** kept up a relentless pace, in 1953 becoming US ambassador to Thailand from where he could keep a wary eye out for communists in neighbouring Vietnam. However, even he could not overcome dementia, perhaps the result of the physical toll of his early years on the sports field and in combat, which set in as the 1950s progressed. He died in 1959, aged 76.

Alexander Grantham continued as Governor of Hong Kong until late 1957, which made him one of the longest-serving. He is also regarded as one of the most successful, having guided the colony through a difficult decade. Interviewed on American television in 1954 as 'Governor-General' of 'the island of Hong Kong' he gave a contented view of its present and an optimistic view of its future: life in the colony was 'tolerable' though 'very overcrowded' but 'people carry on', he said. Originally welcoming, they were disillusioned with the Communists whose true colours could now be seen, he thought. Hong Kong was definitely an asset to the free world, he asserted: the chances of war were not great, Hong Kong was a fortress, China was talking about increasing trade and Hong Kong was the best place to get information from behind the bamboo curtain. He did not mention the aeroplanes recently removed from Kai Tak that had caused so much trouble.

Grantham did mention the planes dispute in his autobiography of 1965 but only briefly, concluding that it was 'altogether a sorry business'. He thought that 'the British Government was more scared of what the US might do to Britain than what China might do to Hong Kong'. Grantham wrote nothing there about the disagreements between him and Whitehall, although he was more forthcoming in an interview for Rhodes House in Oxford some years later.[3] He lived until October 1978.

The captain who led the eleven defecting planes to Tientsin (Tianjin) on 9 November 1949, the former CNAC pilot **T. L. Chen** (Dali Chen), was

2. Alfred T. Cox, 'Civil Air Transport: A Proprietary Airline, 1946–1955', *Clandestine Services Historial Paper No. 87* (Washington DC: Central Intelligence Agency, 1969).
3. Alexander Grantham, *Via Ports: From Hong Kong to Hong Kong* (Hong Kong: Hong Kong University Press, 1965), 130–132, 163.

employed in Peking for CAAC, the successor airline to CNAC founded in the PRC. He and his fellow mutineers worked hard to make a success of Chinese aviation despite the loss of 71 aircraft. He attended CNAC reunions, looking sturdy and fit, until his death in 1990.

Chen suffered persecution during the 'Cultural Revolution', as did anyone in China who had the slightest overseas connections in their past. Chen's friend **C. H. Tang** (Tang Chong Huang) was jailed for seven and a half years. In 1988 Tang emigrated to Houston in the United States where he passed away at a great age in 2014. Similar punishment befell several other of the insurrectionists, including **Gordon Poon**, the pilot of the one plane that had reported to Peking.[4]

Chou En-lai relinquished his foreign ministry role in the late 1950s but remained Prime Minister of China until his death in 1975. **Chairman Mao** presided over a famine and then unleashed the terrible Cultural Revolution on the country in 1966 yet remained untouchable and was even revered by some up to and after his death in 1976. His great rival **Chiang Kai-shek** remained in charge of Taiwan until his own death in 1975 when he was succeeded by his son. Under American protection, Taiwan became an economic success and later a lively democracy.

For **Hartley Shawcross**, the Attorney General who had gotten the British government out of the difficulties created by the Hong Kong courts by the device of an Order-in-Council and who subsequently won the case in the Privy Council, an eventful life still had a long way to run even though he was then in his 50s. He had been a minister during the final months of the Labour government but the subsequent job of an opposition spokesman bored him. He felt increasingly out of step with his socialist colleagues—so much so that he was nicknamed 'Sir Shortly Floorcross'. He resigned from the House of Commons in 1958 and became a Life Peer, beginning a third career as a confirmed member of the Great and the Good. He became a serial chairman of countless private companies and public bodies. The most prominent of these were the Press Council, the Takeover Panel, Thames Television and the civil liberties organization Justice.

In old age Shawcross became rather impatient, earning another sobriquet, 'Sir Shortly Very Cross'. He lived up to the earlier nickname by joining the new Social Democratic Party in the 1980s. He outlived two wives and took a third when in his 90s: his family opposed the last marriage, claiming Shawcross had become mentally incompetent. He proved them wrong by eloping with his fiancée to Gibralter to marry. Shawcross explained that he took on so many offices so as to keep busy and interested in life. He claimed that he had seen

4. See cnac.org/tlchan01.htm and cnac.org/chtang01.html (accessed 9 September 2021). Another who travelled as a passenger on the defectors' flights, Ed Chin Man Wai, died in Hong Kong in 1988.

many of his friends retire completely, then promptly die. He himself managed to stave off the inevitable until 2003, when he was 101 years old.

One of the friends whom he must have had in mind was **Walter Monckton**, the KC who had come to Hong Kong in 1950 in a vain attempt to persuade Hong Kong's Full Court to overrule the Chief Justice. Monckton became Minister of Labour and National Service in the Conservative government elected in October 1951. Winston Churchill, returning as Prime Minister, wanted Monckton to use his emollient powers on the trade unions, which he did with some success. Monckton became Minister of Defence in 1955, a post he held during the Suez crisis the following year. He was opposed to British policy during the crisis, was transferred to a lesser office and later left the government. As Viscount Monckton of Brenchley he joined the board of the Midland Bank, soon becoming its chairman. The following year he added the chairmanship of the Iraq Petroleum Company. However, the roles of which he was proudest were the presidencies of two cricket clubs. He was also pleased to be the first chancellor of the University of Sussex in 1961. But, a hard worker and habitual worrier, his health was beginning to fail. Monckton died of arterio-sclerosis in 1965. He was succeeded as chancellor of Sussex by his old friend Hartley Shawcross.

John Simon, the aged and eminent lawyer-politician called to handle the case of the Kai Tak planes, returned to the House of Lords and to opening chess tournaments, the delicate task accomplished. Still vigorous, he continued to sit as a member of the Judicial Committee into his 80s until cut down by a stroke in January 1954. Among his colleagues on the committee for the planes case, Lord Reid went on to a judicial career that lasted until 1974 and drew wide admiration.

The two Chief Justices who tried the case fared less well. **Leslie Gibson** had returned to England in 1950, possibly because of ill-health, and been a legal adviser to the Colonial Office until his death, aged just 56 years, at Godalming, Surrey, in 1952. **Gerard Howe** was taken ill in Hong Kong during 1953 and retired to Dublin and London, passing away in 1955, also aged 56. **Ernest Williams** continued as a judge for some years, as did **Alwyn Scholes**. Williams eventually was appointed Chief Justice of the British Borneo Territories. Scholes became Hong Kong's senior puisne judge and acted as Chief Justice in 1970. **Trevor Gould** had served as senior puisne judge until 1957 when he moved to Kenya to become a Justice of Appeal on the East African Court of Appeals. There he may well have become re-acquainted with **John Griffin**, the Attorney General who had defied Wild Bill Donovan in January 1950 and that March had flown to London to advise Ernest Bevin on the legal position in Hong Kong. In the mid-1950s Griffin became Chief Justice of Uganda (where his career had begun and his sister Alice was prominent), then Acting Chief Justice of Northern Rhodesia. He returned to Uganda, as speaker of the National Assembly, before retiring to Malta, the ninth part of the British Empire in which he had lived.

Leading counsel who had appeared for American interests in all the Hong Kong phases of the dispute about the Kai Tak planes, **Leo D'Almada**, became a member of the Executive Council advising Governor Grantham. During the 1950s he took annual turns with **John McNeill** at chairing the Hong Kong Bar Association. Both retired from the law quite early. The radical career of **Percy Chen**, the red barrister, continued after the case. He stood unsuccessfully for election to the new Urban Council, became chairman of a leftist group, the Hong Kong Clerks Association, which pressed for more elections and was active in a number of communist organizations including the Chinese General Chamber of Commerce and the Hong Kong and Kowloon Federation of Trade Unions. He definitely was not on Governor Grantham's invitation list. Chen was present for the signing of the Sino-British Joint Declaration on the Question of Hong Kong in 1984.

A candidate who defeated Chen in the Urban Council election was his fellow junior counsel for the dissident airline employees, **Brook Bernacchi**. Bernacchi went on to a long career at the Bar, despite suffering a debilitating stroke in its latter part. He too pressed for democracy and a government more responsive to the needs of the ordinary citizen. He was well known for his investments on Lantau Island, including a bus company and a tea plantation. His proudest achievement was probably his founding of the Hong Kong Sea School.

Denis Blake, the solicitor for Chennault and Willauer and their firms, continued with his directorships, committees and influence until retiring from practice in the mid-1950s because of ill health. He passed away soon after, so did not live to see the houses at Shek O become homes for the super-rich and attain fabulous values in the property price inflation of the twenty-first century.

The British minister with the greatest involvement in the case of the Kai Tak planes was **Kenneth Younger**. He thought that the Privy Council's decision in the planes case was correct but predicted accurately that it would be used by the CPG as an excuse for stone-walling on the exchange of ambassadors by Peking. As Bevin's deputy at the Foreign Office, Younger would have been a sensible successor but party pecking orders dictated that such a senior post had to go to a more experienced minister, Herbert Morrison, who had little interest in foreign affairs. Shawcross would also have been a better choice. Like Shawcross, Younger found opposition politics tedious. In 1958 he resigned to become Director of the Institute of International Affairs at Chatham House. He kept notes throughout his years in politics and thereafter. They were published after his death.[5]

5. Geoffrey Warner, ed., *In the Midst of Events: The Foreign Office Diaries and Papers of Kenneth Younger, February 1950–October 1951* (London: Routledge, 2005).

Younger had hopes of a weighty ministerial position when Labour returned to power in 1964 but all that the new Prime Minister Harold Wilson offered him was a peerage and a junior ministerial post at the Foreign Office again, which he declined. He continued in public life as chairman or member of various bodies. Younger fared better than his predecessor as Minister of State, **Hector McNeill**, who had taken part in British government discussions in January 1950 about the differences then emerging with the Americans about how to deal with the Kai Tak aircraft. A heavy drinker, McNeill died suddenly aged 48 in 1955 whilst on a visit to New York.

Jim Griffiths, the Secretary of State for the Colonies who in the spring of 1950 had given Grantham instructions to keep the planes on the ground at all costs, proved to be the last holder of that position from the Labour Party. During the rest of that decade and the next, British governments of both parties followed policies of de-colonization, although Hong Kong's peculiar circumstances obliged it to be excepted. Griffiths became deputy leader of the Labour Party and, on its return to office in 1964, the first ever Secretary of State for Wales.

In America, the scourge of the State Department **William Knowland** continued as a senator for California until 1959 when he sought election to the governorship instead and was soundly defeated. He remained a fierce opponent of communism and supporter of the ChiNat cause. He chaired the policy committee of the Republican Party in 1953 and became Republican leader in the Senate in the middle 1950s. Despite his failure to become state governor, during the 1960s he led the party in California and went back into the family newspaper business. But he was secretly a heavy gambler and ran up large debts. He died of shotgun wounds, apparently self-inflicted, in 1974.

Dean Acheson remained US Secretary of State until the end of Harry Truman's term as President in 1953. Acheson withstood continuing attacks for what the administration's opponents called its 'liberal' or 'weak' foreign policy. He was able to do so because Truman relied upon and trusted him. Acheson's role in formulating the Truman Doctrine and in setting up the Marshall Plan and NATO led to his erudite but somewhat dull account of his career at the State Department being called 'Present at the Creation'. In the judgment of one of the department's veteran China specialists, Arthur Ringwalt, Acheson was 'able and pleasant', a contrast with his 'difficult and bigoted' successor John Foster Dulles.[6]

The US Consul-General in Hong Kong in late 1949 and the first half of 1950, **Karl Rankin**, who had provided staunch local support for efforts to extract the planes from communist clutches, soon moved on to Taipei. There he was the first US Minister and Chargé d'Affaires to Taiwan. Rankin wanted

6. Arthur Ringwalt, 'Oral History Interview with Arthur R. Ringwalt', interview by Richard D. McKinzie, 5 June 1974, trumanlibrary.gov/library/oral-histories/ringwalt.

to be designated Ambassador but with the US Ambassador to China, John Leighton Stuart, still nominally in office though ill in the USA, the State Department did not wish to suggest that it had accepted that Taiwan was a country separate from China by doing so.

The conservative Rankin firmly supported Chiang Kai-shek and the extension of US protection to Formosa. He sent fervent anti-communist dispatches back to Washington and was critical of optimistic predictions about the future of the PRC which he thought were misconceived and based upon wishful thinking. To Rankin, China had been in the throes of social revolution for more than a century and its root problems of over-population, shortage of food, poor education, absence of a common language and lack of efficient administrators were set to continue. He predicted continuing ferment.[7]

The foreign service diplomatists at the State Department and the Foreign Office who dealt with the problem of the planes at Kai Tak for the most part went on to the heights of their profession. **Walton Butterworth**, the large, gentlemanly southerner and former Rhodes Scholar, who in December 1949 as Assistant Secretary of State for Far East and Pacific Affairs had gone to see Ernest Bevin to register the US's discontent at not being awarded the planes and thereafter had withstood Knowland's attacks on the department, was to spend 40 years in the US foreign service. He had transferred to Japanese Affairs in late March 1950, handing Far East Affairs over to Dean Rusk. His career culminated in ambassadorships to, successively, Sweden, the European Economic Community and Canada in the 1960s.

Butterworth's deputy at Far East Affairs had been a fellow Princeton graduate, **Livingston Merchant**. They had both served in Nanking on George Marshall's doomed 1946–1947 mission to bring together the leaders of the opposing sides in the Chinese civil war. Merchant in Washington had been in the thick of efforts by the State Department to secure the planes by executive action and he, too, had faced down Knowland's attacks in the Senate sub-committee. Merchant was unusual amongst career foreign service officers in having a background in finance and commerce, joining the State Department only after the US had entered the Second World War. Described as 'the ideal of a foreign service officer', later in his career Merchant twice became US ambassador to Canada, on the second occasion being succeeded by his long-term colleague Butterworth. He became executive director of the International Bank for Reconstruction and Development in the mid-1960s. **Lew Douglas**, the American ambassador to Britain, left office reluctantly in 1950 and returned to Arizona politics and membership of various boards and commissions. His daughter had pursued an active social life in London and

7. Karl Lott Rankin, *China Assignment* (Seattle: University of Washington Press, 1964), 29, 34.

struck up a friendship with Princess Margaret who, with her husband Lord Snowdon, visited the Douglas family on their ranch in the early 1960s.

At the British Foreign Office, **Bill Pollock** (Sir William Montagu Pollock), author of two extended memoranda about Chinese aircraft at Hong Kong that in 1950 had explained the background and recent events for British ministers and diplomats around the world, continued enthusiastically to enjoy his eccentric lifestyle. This did not prevent him from holding ambassadorships in Syria, Peru, Switzerland and Denmark. Only in the last might he have been able to pursue his love of things Scandinavian. Pollock left the diplomatic arena in 1962, destined for more than 30 years in which to indulge his other loves, of music, cars, food and European culture. **J. J. Paskin** of the Colonial Office became Sir John and retired in 1953 as the British Empire embarked upon its final phase. **Eric Beckett** remained the senior legal adviser for several more years, sharing his knowledge and expertise through learned notes on current issues in various international law journals. His views on recognition of governments have gained ground with other countries in the last fifty years.

The principles

The PRC was not recognized by the USA until 1972 when President Nixon visited China and met Mao Tse-tung. Ironically, Nixon as a US senator in the 1950s had been one of supporters of Taiwan whose criticism of the Truman administration's China policy made US **recognition** of the PRC impossible.

The United Kingdom continued to approach acceptance of new regimes as a two-stage process of **de facto recognition** followed by **de jure recognition** until 1980 when Her Majesty's Government abandoned the practice of announcing formal recognition of new governments. HMG did so because such announcements were often misunderstood as implying approval despite assurances to the contrary, as had happened with its formal recognition of the CPG in January 1950. The replacement policy was to decide the nature of dealings with regimes which had come to power unconstitutionally 'in the light of our assessment of whether they are able to exercise effective control over the territory of the State concerned and seem likely to continue to do so'. This seemed not so different from the previous approach, except that there would be no announcement of formal recognition. Nevertheless, subsequently HMG was occasionally forced to make a public statement as to its attitude towards a particular insurgent regime. The Foreign Office continues where necessary to issue to British courts **executive certificates** as to the status of a regime from which HMG's attitude to a new government might be deduced. They are rarely so long or complicated as that issued in the dispute about the Chinese aeroplanes.[8]

The relationships

The impasse between Britain and China concerning the establishment of **diplomatic relations** continued until 1954 and after the ceasefire in the Korean War. Over dinner at a conference in Geneva to discuss Indochina, the British Foreign Secretary Sir Anthony Eden observed light-heartedly to Chou En-lai that the PRC did not even have a representative in London. Chou replied that China was willing to provide one, so it was agreed to exchange chargé d'affaires. Hence in September 1954 the British diplomatic team in Peking ceased to be formally on a mission to negotiate the establishment of relations and became full diplomatic representatives and Huan Xiang was appointed the PRC's Chargé in London, almost five years after recognition. An exchange of ambassadors did not occur, however, until 1972.[9] That was the year in which the USA formally recognized the PRC and likewise exchanged ambassadors. The President who oversaw this was Richard Nixon who as a congressman had been a fervent supporter of Taiwan and opponent of communism.

A change in the relationship between the USA and Hong Kong had already taken place. During the Cold War the Americans ceased to view Hong Kong as an insignificant, indefensible colonial left-over whose interests could be sacrificed and began to value it as an outpost of freedom and enterprise. A new US Consulate-General in its own dedicated building was constructed in the heart of the city and was progressively expanded to accommodate so many diplomatic, military and intelligence officers that Governor Grantham was moved to complain of its size. With China closed to outsiders, the colony became a valuable place for information gathering: the CIA and the US Information Service operated from the consulate and a 'listening post' for interception and analysis of signal intelligence was established at Little Sai Wan on the then-remote northeast shore of Hong Kong Island.[10] The US Navy soon came to appreciate the colony's deep harbour, high-quality docks and welcoming amenities for rest and recreation.

8. James Crawford, *Brownlie's Principles of Public International Law*, 8th ed. (Oxford: Oxford University Press, 2012), 153–154.
9. David Clive Wilson, 'Transcript of Interview: Lord Wilson of Tillyorn, 2003', British Diplomatic Oral History Programme, Churchill College, Cambridge, chu.cam.ac.uk/archives/collections/bdohp/.
10. Chi-kwan Mark, *Hong Kong and the Cold War: Anglo-American Relations, 1949–1957* (Oxford: Clarendon Press, 2004), 31–36. The station, established by the RAF in 1952, was staffed by British, Australian and American personnel. Its role diminished with the opening of China; it was decommissioned in 1982. The site, which included a sports field, tennis court and boat club, was then used by training centres and later as a refugee camp. In the 1990s Siu Sai Wan was developed into flats.

Although British business within China had virtually ceased by 1953 and the Soviet Union replaced the UK as China's main trading partner, PRC state enterprises were willing to do business with capitalist companies, especially those new to the China market rather than the traditional firms that had dominated before the communist revolution. State enterprises did more than nine-tenths of China's foreign trade by 1952 and almost all of it by 1955. After the end of the Korean War and the removal of sanctions, Sino-British trade expanded and in 1955 reached a new peak. Hong Kong's trade with the mainland similarly boomed.[11]

Once the planes had been removed from Kai Tak, the PRC had been firmly established and the Korean conflict had died down, **Hong Kong** benefited from the improved international and trade atmosphere. It recovered from the effect of sanctions and became a stable centre from which business could operate. It developed new export industries, particularly in clothing, which sustained its economy for several decades. Communist propaganda and agitation in the colony remained for the most part restrained and unsubversive.

The anomalous status of Formosa (Taiwan) was rectified in September 1951 when a treaty of peace between Japan and 48 other powers was signed. In the treaty Japan renounced all right, title and claim to Formosa and the Pescadores. In whose favour the renunciation operated was not stated because of the competing claims of the PRC and the Nationalist Republic of China, neither of whom was party to the treaty. Japan made a separate treaty with the Republic of China in April 1952 in which Japan confirmed its renunciation of title to Formosa.[12]

The airlines

CNAC was nationalized after 1949 and, with **CATC**, merged into the CPG's state aviation organization, the People's Aviation Company of China in 1952. They became part of CAAC airlines in June 1953.

CAT continued to be operated by the Central Intelligence Agency and performed invaluable service to American defence and foreign policy during the Korean War. It became the largest of the CIA's proprietary ventures, a lawful company whose business appeared to be private but in fact was owned by a state organization. In 1959 it became Air America but continued its clandestine functions.

11. James T. H. Tang, *Britain's Encounter with Revolutionary China, 1949–54* (New York: St. Martin's Press, 1992), 124, 159, 168; Wenguang Shao, *China, Britain and Businessmen: Political and Commercial Relations, 1949–57* (Basingstoke: Macmillan, 1991), 52.
12. James Crawford, *The Creation of States in International Law*, 2nd ed. (Oxford: Oxford University Press, 2006), 199–200. The USSR was party to neither treaty.

Despite the hopes of its directors, **Pan Am** never did re-establish itself in China. It became in effect the flag carrier of the USA, enjoying good business during the era of heavy restrictions upon the operation of airlines. But when de-regulation in the 1980s allowed greater competition 'legacy' airlines such as Pan Am lost profitability. It ceased business in 1991.

The aircraft carrier which evacuated the larger planes from Kai Tak in 1952, the USS ***Cape Esperance***, continued as an auxiliary carrier for US Sealift Command, ferrying planes across the Pacific, to western Europe and the Indian Ocean. She, like similar Casablanca class escorts, became uneconomic to operate and was decommissioned and sold in 1959. She was broken up in Japan in 1961.

The places

Bailey's Shipyard at Tokwawan, which CNAC had used as a workshop and store after its base had been removed from Kai Tak and which was the scene of communist defiance and agitation after the equipment had been repossessed in 1952, was assigned by CAT, Inc. to Zebra Corporation, another American company. Zebra obtained unopposed judgment for possession of the yard in April 1955. The court bailiff's attempts to gain entry on 9 May that year were resisted so the police had to assist in ejecting the remaining workers. The Chinese Civil Aviation Bureau demanded return of the yard and Peking Radio and the *People's Daily* said that Chinese people were indignant at the lawlessness and violence of the British authorities.[13] The yard became the site of a theatre in 1958. This in turn was redeveloped as blocks of residential flats in the mid-1970s.

Kowloon Walled City continued to be a bone of contention between Britain and China until the mid-1980s. During negotiations concerning the future of Hong Kong it was agreed that the urban slum would be demolished and replaced with a park. Kowloon City Park is today a pleasant recreational area.

Hong Kong's gracious Edwardian **Supreme Court Building**, fronting upon Statue Square in the centre of Hong Kong, had been the venue for the various hearings of the cases concerning the aeroplanes in 1949, 1950 and 1952. In the 1970s it was undermined by tunneling for the new Mass Transit Railway and had to be evacuated. Later it was renovated to become the home of the expanded Legislative Council, the court having moved to an unprepossessing new tower block at Admiralty. After the council decided it required less quaint accommodation, the old building was converted back to court use, this time by the Court of Final Appeal.

13. Report, *South China Morning Post*, 10 May 1955.

Despite its inadequacies, **Kai Tak airfield** continued as Hong Kong's civil and military airport for another 46 years after the Chinese aircraft had been taken away. A long runway on reclaimed land into Kowloon Bay was added for jet aircraft in the late 1950s and later extended. New terminal and other buildings were added. The RAF later cut back its presence and then withdrew. As Hong Kong prospered and international air travel became commonplace, the aerodrome was transformed into Hong Kong International Airport. Yet compared with modern airports it remained intimate and convenient, nestling between the mountain and the city, with stunning approaches over Kowloon City and the harbour, just one terminal and for many years an open car park on its apron. In the early 1980s reclamation work began for a replacement off the northern coast of Lantau but was abruptly stopped in 1985 because of government budget cuts in the face of recession. The project was soon revived as part of the boosting of confidence prior to the handover of the colony to the PRC. The last flights took off and landed at Kai Tak in the summer of 1998. The removal of the airport opened the way for high-rise redevelopment of the adjacent **Kowloon City**.

The redevelopment of the Kai Tak site itself took longer than 20 years, partly because of contamination by aircraft fuel. Aside from some former RAF buildings along Kwun Tong Road, the old buildings have all gone. Behind them, on the flat land that served as the original airport, stand housing estates, schools and governmental towers. A Mass Transit Rail line runs underneath, served by two stations. The young people of the cosmopolitan metropolis have little idea that it used to be an airfield, still less that it was at the centre of an international controversy about 71 Chinese aircraft all those years ago.

Timeline: Chronology of Principal Relevant Events

1949

January	• Communist armies victorious in battles at Hwai Valley
April	• Nationalist (KMT) government moves from Nanking to Canton • Chiang Kai-shek resigns as KMT President • *Amethyst* incident (until July) • CNAC and CATC establish offices and workshops in Hong Kong • CNAC and CATC airplanes start to be based at Kai Tak airfield
May	• Shanghai under Communist control • KMT blockade of China coast
June	• British and French governments favour early recognition of Communist government in China but USA urges caution • CATC headquarters in Canton • RAF reinforced in Hong Kong • Hong Kong authorities ask CNAC and CATC to vacate Kai Tak (refused)
July	• More than 80 CNAC/CATC planes and equipment at Kai Tak
August	• USA begins to close consulates in China
September	• CATC headquarters moved to Hong Kong • Hong Kong and Kowloon Aviation Workers Union founded • US and British foreign ministers Acheson and Bevin meet to discuss Far East policy • Chiang Kai Shek relocates to Formosa

		• Claire Chennault and Whiting Willauer's airline CAT busy evacuating KMT supporters from Communist advance
October	1	• Declaration at Peking of Central People's Government (CPG) as government of People's Republic of China (PRC) • Dismissal of Nationalist ministers by CPG • CPG in control of all but five provinces of China
	2	• Soviet Union recognizes CPG
	5	• UK consul in Peking sends note to Chou En-lai as foreign minister of CPG proposing relations
	12	• Nationalist government abandons Canton and moves to Chungking
	20	• Foreign Office (FO) legal adviser Beckett advises Bevin that British formal recognition of CPG legally justifiable
	21	• Emergency (Control of Ships and Aircraft) Regulations made by Governor of HK
	End	• Canton under Communist control • Britain consulting Commonwealth and other governments about CPG recognition • Discontent among CNAC and CATC staff in Hong Kong: some declare allegiance to CPG
November		• CPG Minister of Communications purports to appoint new directors of CNAC with Head Office in Shanghai • Chou En-lai instructs managing director Liu Ching Yi to take control of assets of CNAC • Chou declares CNAC property of CPG and expresses hope that all officers and workers will unite under Liu to protect assets • US embargo on export of strategic goods to China
	4	• Representation of Foreign Powers (Control) Ordinance enacted in HK
	9	• Chen Cheuk Lin and Liu, managing directors of CATC and CNAC, fly to Peking with 12 (two CATC and 10 CNAC) planes and report to CPG's Civil Aeronautical Administration, leaving emergency committee in control of other planes etc at Kai Tak • Majority of airlines' staff defect to CPG

10 • Willauer of CAT flies to Taipei to see KMT air force commanders and Chiang Kai-shek
• Chou En-lai declares planes 'sacred property' of PRC

11 • Chiang agrees with Willauer's proposal that CAT act as agent of Nationalists to secure remaining planes

12 • Chou En-lai (re)appoints Chen and Liu as general managers of CATC and CNAC respectively
• Chen dismissed by KMT
• Nationalist Minister of Communications comes to HK from Formosa
• Nationalist government moves to Chengdu

13 • Ango Tai appointed Acting President (governor) of CATC by Nationalists
• Nationalist Minister of Foreign Affairs, George Yeh, informs HK Governor that aircrafts' certificates of registration suspended and aircrew licences of no effect
• Yeh asks HK authorities to immobilize aircraft and suspend Kai Tak identity permits of CNAC and CATC employees; Governor suggests staff collect permits and return them (not done)
• Communist employees and sympathizers remain in control of aircraft

14 • CPG begins to pay airline staff
• Tai engages law firm Wilkinson & Grist which asks Attorney General of Hong Kong (Griffin) for help in protecting planes; AG suggests firm obtain court order

16 • Defecting employees dismissed by Tai who hires security guards for planes
• Willauer and accomplices deflate tyres of planes

17 • Governor Grantham announces aircraft will not be allowed to depart until Sino-British air agreement clarified
• Grantham orders removal of guards; employees loyal to CPG retake planes

24 • CATC begins legal action against 20 named employees/sympathizers
• Injunction granted to CATC prohibiting defendants from removing CATC assets and from entering CATC's property at Kai Tak (disregarded)

	25	• Defendants obtain injunction preventing removal of planes by airlines
	Late	• Willauer in USA approaches Tommy Corcoran for help in retrieving planes
December	1	• US State Department informs FO of US concern about the planes, asks if 'extraordinary measures' could be taken • Bill Donovan's firm appointed to represent Chennault and Willauer/CAT
	5	• Chennault and Willauer write to Nationalist Minister of Communications offering to buy airlines' assets
	8	• Nationalists abandon Chengdu for Formosa; virtually whole of mainland China under Communist control • State Dept instructs Rankin, US Consul-General HK, to assist CAT
	12	• Terms of sale of CATC accepted by Nationalist government • Registration certificates of aircraft cancelled
	13	• Terms of sale accepted by CNAC chairman
	15	• FO informed of sale during visit by US embassy officials and Donovan • UK Cabinet decides to recognize CPG on date to be fixed
	16	• CAT (Chennault) relocates operations from HK to Formosa • USA and France informed of UK decision to recognize CPG
	19	• Chennault and Willauer on-sell their interests to new Delaware corporation, CAT, Inc.
	20	• Pan Am sells its 20% stake in CNAC to CAT, Inc. • Aircraft registered in USA • State Dept informs London embassy of sale and registration, for communication to Grantham via UK government
	21	• Governor Grantham shown by Rankin, Chennault and Willauer certification by Nationalist PM of sale; Grantham said title depended on outcome of legal proceedings

	23	• Application by Chennault and Willauer to be joined as parties to actions rejected by HK Chief Justice Gibson but discharge of injunctions refused
	28	• US concern that ownership of planes etc will not be resolved prior to formal recognition of CPG by Britain • Daily visits to FO by US Embassy/State Dept officers • American allegations of sabotage and discrimination
	29	• Rankin, Willauer and Heppner (lawyer) inform Grantham that planes now US registered and urge that US markings be painted on them; workers replacing Nationalist emblems with Communist ones
	30	• Gibson CJ asks FO written questions about UK recognition of CPG • Meeting at FO between Strang (Permanent Secretary) and Holmes (US Chargé D'Affaires) who complains of lack of access to and sabotage of planes • Injunctions extended
	31	• Meeting of FO and Colonial Office principals to consider whole matter • Terms of sale ratified at CNAC Board Meeting in HK

1950

January	2	• UK ministers consider brief on situation • McNeill, deputy foreign minister, and Creech Jones, Secretary for Colonies, discuss position with Attlee, PM, and agree on points to put to USA
	3	• Oral reassurances by FO to State Dept • Memo 'Chinese Civil Aircraft in Hong Kong' prepared by FO
	4	• Donovan and Rankin see Grantham in attempt to persuade him to use executive powers to release planes to CAT, Inc., but Grantham insists title is sub judice; Donovan aggressive • Similar response from John Griffin, HK Attorney General; Donovan gives press conference
	5	• Donovan writes to Griffin urging him to intervene in litigation and suggesting British recognition of CPG be expressly non-retroactive

- In London, US representatives press FO for acceptance of validity of sale and complain that Grantham uncooperative
- Writs issued by CAT, Inc. against Chennault and Willauer for delivery of planes and damages for their wrongful detention
- Application for appointment of receiver of CNAC assets instituted

6
- Midnight 5/6: CPG recognized by UK as government of China de jure; recognition of Nationalist government withdrawn

9
- Williams J rejects application for appointment of receiver in earlier action
- Chou En-lai accepts temporary appointment of British Chargé d'Affaires Hutchison, suggests negotiations for establishment of diplomatic relations

10
- Continuing pressure by State Dept for release of planes to US interests: demand for executive assistance

11
- Strang complains at meeting with US Chargé d'Affaires Holmes about Donovan's conduct; Holmes raises further questions

12
- FO replies to US requests for executive assistance

13
- Donovan proposes to discontinue actions provided action taken to place CAT, Inc. in possession of assets

14
- FO written reply to US embassy re allegations of sabotage and discrimination against CAT, Inc. (made late Dec 1949) and other queries

20
- CAT, Inc. files further application for appointment of receivers
- Meeting between Holmes, with US embassy officers and lawyer for CAT, Inc., and Beckett, legal adviser to FO

21
- State Dept demands of FO that assets be protected as 'an American interest'
- Channault and Willauer obtain court's leave to serve Third Party Notice on defendants (communist employees of CNAC et al) in previous case

February	1	• Registration certificates for aircraft issued by CPG • Hearing for appointment of receivers begins (to 8 February)
	6	• Donovan suggests to Grantham that US might intervene in court case • Assistant Secretary of State Perkins calls at British embassy in Washington DC to emphasize seriousness of preventing planes falling into communist hands
	10	• US embassy in London 'extremely concerned' at developments • President Truman said to be personally interested in matter
	13	• Grantham replies to US allegations of sabotage, etc.
	14	• FO written reply to CJ's questions of 30 December 1949 about recognition • Long note of complaint to FO from US Embassy • Treaty of Friendship and Alliance, USSR-PRC
	15	• Assertive reply by FO to US complaints
	16	• State Dept concerned about one of FO's replies to CJ's questions
	17	• CJ formulates further question to FO re recognition
	22	• US embassy complains to FO that Grantham is without clear guidance and is leaning backwards to placate Communists • Warning to London by Grantham that likely case will be dismissed and injunctions will lapse
	23	• Gibson CJ dismisses applications for appointment of receivers on ground of sovereign immunity; injunctions removed • Governor instructed to accept no registration of aircraft pending decision on merits
	24	• Consternation in Washington DC at CJ's decision • Protests by Acheson to London and HK • State Dept apprehensive of effect of decision on US public opinion • UK Ambassador Oliver Franks warns of Congressional anger and threat to Marshall Plan and Military Assistance Programme, asks FO to issue statement as soon as possible

		• Rankin tells HK government recognition of registration by others would be confiscation of US property • Acheson informs press conference that US had 'vigorously protested' outcome
	27	• FO spokesman: British government will not interfere with workings of HK courts
	28	• Bevin in London sees Holmes and Butterworth of State Dept and assures them that all legal steps will be taken to prevent departure of aircraft until legal position reviewed, hopes registration formalities will provide delay • Certificates of registration in PRC presented to Governor
March	2	• Negotiations UK-PRC re establishment of diplomatic relations
	3	• Grantham expects CPG to ask for permission to allow planes to fly and asks London for guidance
	4	• Grantham instructed to refuse to permit flight on basis of Chicago Convention prohibiting double registration pending opinion from Law Officers
	5	• Grantham reply stresses importance to HK of neutrality in political issues
	7	• Colonial Office regards FO view as contrary to established UK government policy with alarming possibilities for trouble in HK
	8	• Notice of appeal lodged by CAT, Inc. but no injunction sought
	10	• Grantham protests the harm to British prestige in China if UK infringes rules of law
	11	• Shipment of equipment and spare parts for planes by sea from HK to northern China • FO minister Younger attends Cabinet discussion re planes then meets visiting US ambassador-at-large Jessup
	13	• FO written reply to Gibson CJ's questions of 17 February
	14	• Report by Commander of British Forces in HK that agents preparing to dispatch to China large quantities of aircraft parts, stores, etc out of HK to China

		• SE Asia Chiefs of Staff consider action to prevent shipment • SS *Empire Dirk* sails for northern China with shipment
	18	• Memo 'Chinese Aircraft at Hong Kong' finalized by FO, forming part of brief to English Law Officers for advice and basis of circular to British diplomats • Instructions from Colonial Office and FO to Law Officers finalized by departmental legal advisers
	21	• Circular 'Chinese Civil Aircraft at Hong Kong' prepared by FO giving answers to criticisms of UK policy • Grantham seeks clarification of his rights under Colonial Air Navigation Order
	23	• Minute by Sir Eric Beckett, FO, re powers under Colonial Air Navigation Order • US Senate sub-committee on appropriations hears complaints by Senator Knowland re planes, demands evidence from State Dept
	27	• Senate sub-committee hears and questions State Dept representatives; British attitude and policy criticized by Republicans; threat to oppose further military and economic assistance to UK • Acheson asks Franks, British ambassador in Washington DC, to ensure Grantham is aware of larger issues, including US-UK relations
	28	• Applications by CAT, Inc. for injunctions dismissed • Younger FO note: trouble flowed from Nationalist and US refusal to remove planes • Debate on foreign affairs in House of Commons
	29	• FO circular telegram to ambassadors and other diplomats outlining history and blaming Nationalists/Americans
	30	• More spare equipment dispatched from HK
April	2	• Time bombs set off by Nationalist agents damaging seven planes at Kai Tak
	3	• English Attorney-General Hartley Shawcross' first written opinion on legal position given to Colonial and Foreign Offices: advises use of Art 60 of Colonial Air Navigation Order to prevent planes from leaving • Memo 'Chinese Aircraft in Hong Kong' provided to British Cabinet

	4	• Chou En-lai blames British HK government for not protecting aircraft and impeding their departure, saying it will be responsible for any damage
	5	• Grantham resists use of Colonial Air Navigation Order
	6	• Cabinet meeting in London considers memo and opinion: Shawcross orally advises he now considers that use of Air Navigation Order inappropriate and change in law through Order-in-Council better • Shawcross to give second written opinion; Cabinet decision deferred • Colonial Secretary Griffiths tells Grantham to do everything possible to stop aircraft leaving without using Air Navigation Order • More spare equipment shipped to China
	8	• Grantham mentions powers under Emergency Regulations Ordinance and Importation and Exportation Ordinance to Colonial Office though opposes their use since that would destroy UK reputation for impartiality and AG Griffin may resign
	11	• Bevin in hospital (to 4 May); Acheson under continuing political attack in USA
	14	• Younger, FO minister, tells US ambassador Douglas that the planes cannot be held much longer
	17	• Second written opinion from Shawcross: using Emergency Regulations better than Air Navigation Order but matter is really one of political judgment and suggests Order-in-Council
	24	• Cabinet decides to issue Order-in-Council
May	8	• Talks between Bevin and Acheson: differences apparent
	10	• Supreme Court of Hong Kong (Jurisdiction) Order-in-Council, 1950, made and in effect
	13	• Reserved judgment of Full Court delivered: appeal dismissed • HK government takes custody of aircraft
	19	• CAT, Inc. begins fresh actions against CATC and CNAC for declarations that aircraft are CAT, Inc.'s property
	21	• CPG protests about 'most unfriendly attitude' of UK

	24	• Bevin, plainly ill, speaks on planes in House of Commons
June	22	• Younger: planes will not be allowed to leave until court decision on ownership
	24	• Outbreak of Korean War: N. Korea invades S. Korea • President Truman orders US forces to support S. Koreans and protect Formosa
	25	• UN resolution calling on N. Koreans to withdraw
	27	• UN resolution that members assist S. Korea
September		• S. Korean forces cross 38th Parallel
October	2	• Chou En-lai warns that China will intervene in Korea
	19	• UN forces occupy Pyongyang
	27	• Chinese troops in N. Korea; UN troops forced back

1951

January		• UN resolution that China has engaged in aggression
	21	• Communist advance in N. Korea halted
March	1	• FO minute: undesirable for aircraft to get into Chinese hands after their intervention in Korea
	27	• Trial/inquiry before Howe CJ re CATC planes
	28	• Grantham asks Colonial Office what to do if planes awarded to China
May	14	• UN embargo on export of strategic materials to China
	21	• Judgment by Howe CJ dismissing CAT, Inc.'s claim
	23	• Campaign in USA to save planes from Communists by Corcoran and Chennault
	28	• Consideration in London (to 18 July) as to action to detain/dispose of planes
July	20	• Appeal against Howe CJ's decision lodged
August	21	• Hearing of appeal by Full Court
October		• Change of government in UK
December	28	• Judgment of Full Court affirming decision of Howe CJ

1952

June	11	• Judicial Committee of Privy Council grants early hearing of further appeal
July	23	• Arguments heard in Privy Council
	28	• Result announced by Judicial Committee: appeal successful re 40 CATC aircraft
	29	• Order allowing appeal • Police seize aircraft and parts • Strong protest by CPG
August	15	• Two main British shipyards in Shanghai requisitioned
September	28	• US aircraft carrier *Cape Esperance* arrives in Hong Kong to take away aircraft from Kai Tak
October	8	• Judgment by Howe CJ concerning 31 CNAC aircraft
	13	• Reasons for PC decision given by Viscount Simon
November		• Three British-owned utility enterprises and shipping company in Shanghai requisitioned

1953

July	7	• Armistice in Korea

1955

May	9	• Communist employees evicted from Bailey's Shipyard

Acknowledgements

This account of the saga of the Chinese aircraft, or as it is sometimes known in Chinese 'the two airline incident', has been a long time in gestation. My interest in the saga was sparked by the Privy Council decision concerning ownership of the aircraft first read at the Bodleian Law Library at the University of Oxford in the summer of 1975: it was on the reading list for the course on public international law. The law report hinted at a deep political background which there was not then time to explore. I must, however, thank my tutor in the subject, a brilliant young post-graduate named Paul Craig, and the lecturer, Professor Daniel Patrick O'Connell, for their stimulating comments on the case.

A decade later, as a lecturer myself at the University of Hong Kong, I came across the case again in the pages of the Hong Kong Law Reports, except that it did not seem to be quite the same case. It was to do with a procedural application before the local courts and the parties and the winner were different from those in the Privy Council decision. From this it was evident that there was a complex legal background as well. A multiplicity of airlines seemed to be involved, all with acronyms which began with C. Later still, I came across another report about the disputed planes which seemed to be yet another case. With confusion thus worse confounded, the cases had to be set aside to concentrate on more pressing projects but I mentally promised to return to them one day, perhaps in retirement.

That day did not arrive until well into the new century during occasional discussions with colleagues in the Faculty of Law, especially Anthony Carty, on the international law aspects of the case. The colleague who really re-sparked interest in the saga was Dr Peter Wesley Smith who during a lecture about British considerations of the future of Hong Kong in the mid-twentieth century mentioned that he had come across materials concerning aircraft that had been held at Kai Tak after the Chinese civil war which he thought could form the basis of another lecture. When I explained that I too had looked into the topic, he suggested that we make a joint presentation about it, which we did in October 2017. Peter then disclaimed any intention to write about the saga and generously gave me the fruits of his research, including copies and notes of relevant Foreign Office memoranda which form the backbone of the story.

Retirement from teaching and practice destroyed all excuse for further procrastination. The enforced quiet life of pandemic restrictions provided the opportunity to make real progress with the project. The more one delved into the saga, the more complex it became and the more evident it was that some account of the geopolitical considerations of the era was required for an understanding as to why matters evolved as they did. It became a principal topic of conversation with friends whom I must thank for their polite interest and encouragement. I would particularly mention Dr Devin Lin, Alice S. B. Lee and Clarissa Wu.

Professor Jae Woon Lee of the Chinese University of Hong Kong was informative on certain aviation law aspects and generous in volunteering the services of Anfield Lam, his research assistant. Anfield directed me to a number of sources including the US Congressional Record.

John Budge of Wilkinson and Grist, solicitors, was generous in sharing information about the role in the case of his firm and its senior partner Mr Denis Blake and in providing a copy of the unpublished history of the firm by Carl T. Smith.

Two reviewers of the manuscript for Hong Kong University Press were positive, constructive and informative. The publisher, Peter Daniell, was entirely encouraging and supportive, as were his editors and assistants. Donald Chan took time from preparations for his International Baccalaureate examination to read and correct the manuscript in draft and demonstrated astonishing editorial ability for one so young. Finally, I must thank Brendan Clift for taking time away from his doctoral studies in Melbourne to add the finishing touches to the manuscript and saving me from several errors. Readers are invited to alert me to any errors that remain or further information about the saga via malcolmjmerry@gmail.com.